Y0-BRV-196

News by Radio

THE MACMILLAN COMPANY
NEW YORK · BOSTON · CHICAGO
DALLAS · ATLANTA · SAN FRANCISCO

MACMILLAN AND CO., LIMITED
LONDON · BOMBAY · CALCUTTA
MADRAS · MELBOURNE

THE MACMILLAN COMPANY
OF CANADA, LIMITED
TORONTO

News by Radio

Mitchell V. Charnley
UNIVERSITY OF MINNESOTA

1948　THE MACMILLAN COMPANY　NEW YORK

COPYRIGHT, 1948, BY THE MACMILLAN COMPANY

All rights reserved—no part of this book may be reproduced in any form without permission in writing from the publisher, except by a reviewer who wishes to quote brief passages in connection with a review written for inclusion in magazine or newspaper.

PRINTED IN THE UNITED STATES OF AMERICA

070.19
C.483n

Foreword

Radio news is no longer Johnny-come-lately. It is one of broadcasting's major program offerings, and perhaps broadcasting's major avenue to public service. It has developed hundreds of newsrooms, thousands of workers, and a good many millions of devoted adherents. It seems not incautious to say that it is here to stay.

Its practices and potentialities are, nevertheless, still in the category of new business. The men in its twenty-year-club would hardly outnumber the fingers of two hands. Its headlong development in the last decade has meant that most of what it has done has been empirical; it has rarely paused for self-analysis.

A first step in such analysis is description; a second, evaluation. *News by Radio* is an attempt at both.

News by Radio describes the special practices, principles, and characteristics developed in the brief life of radio news. It evaluates them in the light of their effectiveness or their failure. And, being a book for radio newsroom practitioners and for students of radio news, it suggests methods of achieving and expanding radio news effectiveness and of avoiding failures.

It is no accident that *News by Radio* relics heavily on comparison and contrast with newspaper practice. The newspaper, the first great medium of mass communication, solved some of radio's news problems before Marconi was born; it remains the largest field for actual news experience. Much of what radio news does it has learned or adapted from the press. To give the news man—practicing or embryonic—an understanding of the values of radio news, I can think of no more vivid or economical starting point than to lay press and radio side by side. On such a base can most soundly be built a knowledge of radio news's unique achievements, its latent capacities.

Finally, *News by Radio* rests on the conviction that the practice of

v

29461

radio news is a high calling; that news on the air presents vast opportunities to its workers and imposes on them vast responsibilities; that
if it faces limitations not borne by other news media, it also enjoys wide
ranges not open to them.

M. V. C.

Minneapolis, Minnesota

Table of Contents

1

News Takes the Air

On August 31, 1920, Michigan held primary elections. Nothing unusual about that.

That evening, in some hundreds of living rooms, bedrooms, basements, and garrets in the Detroit area, amateur wireless enthusiasts sat before their homemade receiving sets. Headphones pinched their ears. Their fingers fiddled with tuning coils as they picked up the Arlington time signal or the "eep! eep!" of Morse code whistling among "ham" senders or between lake ships and shore stations.

Suddenly into their headphones came a static-ridden human voice. It said something like this:

"This is Station 8MK. The *Detroit News* brings you early returns from today's Michigan voting. . . ."

That *was* unusual. Regular broadcasting of news was born that night.

— o —

The fact was that this station—first to put a regular daily schedule of programs on the air—had been broadcasting experimentally since August 20. But it was not until August 31 that the *News* carried the headline "NEWS RADIOPHONE TO GIVE VOTE RESULTS" and invited the public to listen in.

The "studio" was hardly pretentious. Up among the bound files in the *News* library, on a table crowded into a corner, rested a "de Forest Radiophone." It consisted of a rectangular panel about fourteen by sixteen inches in size, with several control switches and dials, a pair of voltmeters, and, at its top center, what looked like a telephone mouthpiece—its primitive microphone. There was no acoustically-treated chamber, no well-gadgeted control room, no chrome furniture. Into the mouthpiece a young man was talking—broadcasting election returns as they came up to him from the newsroom, a floor below.

From that day forward, without a break, Station 8MK put daily

1

programs on the air—recorded music, speakers, vocalists, cornet players, a "live" orchestra now and then. And news—local and regional news from the paper's staff, national and international news from the press services.

It was the inauguration of regular daily broadcasting, rather than the fact of broadcasting, that made those August dates notable. Dr. Lee de Forest had successfully broadcast the human voice some thirteen years earlier. On an evening in 1907 he had taken two young women to his cluttered experimental laboratory atop a building in midtown New York—a young Swedish concert soprano and a newspaper reporter. Faced by the confusion of wires, batteries, and other queer apparatus in the laboratory, the guests of the "father of radio broadcasting" were skeptical. At length Dr. de Forest persuaded the soprano, Eugenia Farrar, to sing two songs into the old-fashioned phonograph horn that served as a microphone—"I Love You Truly" and "Just A-wearyin' for You." But the reporter remained unconvinced. She was scooped.

For the next day, in the rival *New York Herald*, Dr. de Forest found a doubting little story to the effect that a Brooklyn Navy Yard wireless operator said he had heard "the voice of an angel" coming out of the air the night before.

The public was unimpressed, but de Forest continued his experiments. His excitement, and that communicated to David Sarnoff and other radio pioneers, were enough. In 1908 de Forest broadcast songs by Enrico Caruso; in 1910 he offered his handful of amateur followers Caruso, Madame Emmy Destinn, and others singing opera from the stage of the Metropolitan. On November 7, 1916, the *New York American* ran a wire to his experimental station at High Bridge, New York, and de Forest broadcast returns from the Wilson-Hughes election. They concluded with the statement that "Charles Evans Hughes will be the next president of the United States"!

But World War I threw the emphasis of wireless experimentation on message communication—point-to-point wireless—rather than on broadcasting. Private operations were forbidden for the duration. It was not until 1919 that the prohibition was lifted. In that year Dr. Frank Conrad, assistant chief engineer of the Westinghouse Electric and Manufacturing Company, who had begun broadcasting experiments in 1915, resumed his work and soon built up an astonishing audience for his twice-weekly recorded music broadcasts from 8XK in Pittsburgh. But it was only in 1920 that 8MK, later WWJ, made its appeal for a regular popular audience.

Those first regular broadcasts from Detroit, however, were quickly followed by a second series. Westinghouse, taking its cue from Conrad's success, set up a broadcasting station in Pittsburgh, and on November 2 opened it with news of that day's Harding-Cox presidential elections, obtained from the *Pittsburgh Post*. KDKA maintained a semiweekly schedule of broadcasts until December 1, when it went on a daily schedule.

— 0 —

Each of these broadcasting pioneers had chosen a news event, one sure of public interest, as the occasion for the station's initiation. But there is no reason to think that either, in 1920, envisioned radio as a medium capable of serious challenge to the newspaper as a purveyor of news, much less as an advertising vehicle. Rather, each saw it as a means of promotion of another enterprise. The backers of 8MK— pioneers in the use of the airplane and other devices in newspaper

---

WWJ and KDKA have long disputed the distinction of being the first commercial station on the air with regular daily programs. The facts: 8MK was licensed to the Radio News and Music Company, a de Forest sales organization. The broadcasts beginning August 20, 1920, went out from 8MK, but they went out from the *Detroit News* plant, under *News* operation and declared sponsorship, using a "radiophone" owned by the *News*. On October 12, 1921, the *News* was issued a full commercial rather than an experimental license, and its call letters became WBL; on March 3, 1922, they became WWJ. Regular daily programs were maintained throughout this period, and since.

KDKA was issued its full commercial license on October 27, 1920, and opened broadcasting operations six days later, on November 2. The claims of KDKA appear to be based on the facts that it always operated under the call letters KDKA, and that its commercial license predated that of WWJ.

On August 20, 1936, Dr. de Forest said during an anniversary broadcast from WWJ, "On the night of August 20, 1920, the first commercial radio broadcast station in all the world was opened. . . . Not until eleven weeks after its founding did WWJ share the channels of the air with a rival broadcasting station. The honor of being second . . . fell to KDKA."

promotion—thought of radio as a means of winning goodwill for the *News*. The men behind KDKA were the men of Westinghouse Electric, which had a receiving set almost ready for the market and which already saw ahead the radio wars with the newly-formed Radio Corporation of America. Westinghouse realized that if American families were to be persuaded to lay $125 on the line for the new machine, regular—and attractive—programs had to be provided.

Entertainment—that was the thing. And entertainment—of a sort—was the fare those two early stations offered.

Recognition of its promotional value was one of the two characteristics of the usual newspaper attitude toward radio as the early 1920's ran along. In the two years following the first broadcasts some hundred dailies set up their own stations, according to an estimate by the American Newspaper Publishers Association. Most of them followed the standard pattern: "Put on good shows, advertise the paper." One discordant, if prophetic, note came from the *Kansas City Star's* WDAF, established in 1921. The *Star's* advertising department offered a combination radio-time and newspaper-linage rate. The "commercialization of radio" was rearing its horned head. But few advertisers took advantage of the *Star's* offer, and few stations followed WDAF's lead.

The second characteristic was the marked friendliness of the press to radio. Marconi's wireless telegraphy, de Forest's audion, Alexanderson's alternator, Jack Binns' famous distress call from the sinking steamer *Republic* in 1909, communication by radio in World War I—all had been news. And the development of a great new industry was news. Newspapers published radio logs; they devoted many columns of general news space to the new entertainment medium. They even furnished driblets of news for broadcast. The *Philadelphia Public Ledger*, which didn't own a station, went to the length of recording news bulletins for a Philadelphia station.

Whatever the validity of KDKA's claim as first regular broadcasting station, there is no doubt that it has many radio news "firsts" to its credit. On March 4, 1921, it read on the air a copy of President Harding's inaugural address while the President was speaking in Washington. Through the spring it broadcast a number of notable speeches given in Pittsburgh; Herbert Hoover, Colonel Theodore Roosevelt, Jr.,

Secretary of War Weeks were among the speakers.

On April 11 it invented a new kind of broadcast: on-the-spot sports coverage. Johnny Ray and Johnny Dundee fought in Pittsburgh, and Florent Gibson, of the *Pittsburgh Post* sports staff, described the event before a microphone. On July 2 came the first of a long string of battles of the century—the fight between Jack Dempsey and Georges Carpentier at Boyle's Thirty Acres in Jersey City. Few heavyweight matches have had the ballyhoo that built up the meeting of Dempsey and the handsome Frenchman, and Westinghouse saw a chance to capitalize. It planned to open a new station, WJZ, in the New York area in a few months, and its engineers borrowed a transmitter from the bitterly competitive General Electric Company and set it up in railroad yards near the stadium. Major J. Andrew White, editor of an early radio magazine, put the fight on the air. Westinghouse estimated that some 200,000 listeners heard White's blow-by-blow account.

Soon after, KDKA began broadcasting big league baseball from Forbes Field in Pittsburgh. It had already begun to include Department of Agriculture market reports in its daily service, and this soon expanded into a regular farm service hour. When WJZ opened on September 30, it made World Series baseball bulletins its inaugural feature.

All of which is to say that the news broadcasting of those early days was largely built around special events, or aimed at specialized audiences. By a few stations routine news was put on the air—a news story read out of the newspaper could fill a gap between Victor records as well as anything else. But regular news programs to pull mass audiences were hardly dreamed of.

Nevertheless, the first timid blows in what was to become a knockdown conflict came as early as 1922. On February 20 the Associated Press asked its 1,200 member newspapers not to permit the broadcast of news that, according to its bylaws, was AP property. Apparently the impulse behind this request was not a desire to hamper the development of a competing agency for news dissemination, but rather an attempt to protect what was, in effect, commercially valuable merchandise. The AP was then, as now, a cooperative association of newspapers; its news property consisted not only of news gathered by its special correspondents, but also of all that the member newspapers gathered. The AP, because of its direct control by the newspapers themselves, has traditionally been close to the wishes of newspaper owners and editors. And these men did not propose that their property be used for gain by nonmembers.

The influence of the request was such that Westinghouse stations (there were now four) agreed to discontinue their "news flashes." But the action of the AP did nothing to prevent radio use of news from United Press, International News Service, or other sources. And the request, though it may have thrown a temporary roadblock before the expansion of newscasting, certainly did not prevent a good many stations from lifting news—telegraphic or local, AP or other—from the papers and putting it on the air.

The AP had, in fact, to backtrack in 1924. Its newspaperman directorate decided that broadcasting baseball scores was no violation of bylaws. It made an effort to keep returns of the 1924 national election a newspaper secret, and it fined one member newspaper, the *Portland Oregonian*, $100 on the paper's frank admission that AP reports had been used by radio. But no action was taken against other papers, many of which had unquestionably sinned (some, when the

---

NUMBER OF STANDARD BROADCASTING STATIONS IN THE UNITED STATES

(Federal Communications Commission statistics)

January 1, 1922	30	January 1, 1935	605	
March 1, 1923	556	January 1, 1936	632	
October 1, 1924	530	January 1, 1937	685	
June 30, 1925	571	January 1, 1938	721	
June 30, 1926	528	January 1, 1939	764	
February 23, 1927	733	January 1, 1940	814	
July 1, 1928	677	January 1, 1941	882	
November 9, 1929	618	January 1, 1942	923	
July 1, 1930	612	January 1, 1943	917	
July 1, 1931	612	January 1, 1944	912	
January 1, 1932	608	January 1, 1945	919*	(943)
January 1, 1933	610	January 1, 1946	940*	(1,004)
January 1, 1934	591	January 1, 1947	1,062*	(1,524)
		January 1, 1948	1,522*	(1,962)

* Stations licensed to broadcast. Figures in parentheses include also construction permits issued. Before 1945, the two figures were nearly the same.

question was raised, said they had permitted radio use only of returns from other than AP sources). It was estimated that ten million radio listeners had learned through the air of Calvin Coolidge's victory before their newspapers reached them.

The AP lowered the bars further in 1925 when it voted to permit broadcast of brief bulletins of news of "transcendent" importance.

Meantime, the newspapers were becoming aware of radio's growing competition for the advertising dollar. At its 1925 convention the American Newspaper Publishers Association, whose membership represented most leading dailies, gave to the radio industry the unsolicited (and unheeded) advice that it was likely to wring the neck of its golden goose by larding its offerings with direct advertising. Advertising, admonished the ANPA, might destroy the entertainment, educational, and goodwill values of broadcasting. It voted that its members refuse to give "free publicity" to programs involving direct advertising.

Radio's response was a program of gigantic expansion.

This was signalized in 1926 by organization of the National Broadcasting Company, and the next year by that of the Columbia Broadcasting System. Network development had no immediate significance as far as the broadcast of news was concerned. But it did provide a formidable competitor in entertainment and advertising. Networks could produce more costly and successful "shows" for their outlets than could the individual stations; they could sell advertising on a national basis. They could, and did.

In 1927 Congress recognized by adopting the Federal Radio Act that broadcasting was going into long pants. High time, said the industry. Regulation of radio had been under the antiquated Communications Act of 1912, designed to govern primitive commercial wireless traffic. Under this Act the assignment of wave lengths had been in the hands of the Department of Commerce. The system had fallen to pieces. It permitted stations to alter wave lengths almost at will; jamming by conflicting broadcasts had become more the rule than the exception, especially as the number of broadcasters mushroomed (more than 200 new stations had appeared in the eight months preceding the Act's passage). The new Act established the Federal

Radio Commission to assign frequencies and otherwise to administer broadcasting. And it first introduced to radio the phrase "in the public interest, convenience, and necessity"—a phrase common to most public utility legislation.

What, in radio terms, was "the public interest, convenience, and necessity"?

As interpreted by the FRC and translated (sometimes freely) by the broadcasting industry, it meant that radio schedules must include offerings of social value. They were certain to include advertising, for advertising, in the American system of broadcasting, paid the bills. They were certain to include entertainment, for entertainment insured that the advertising would be heard. But they had also to include public service features—features of educational value, features to edify and instruct, to serve the public welfare. Features such as lectures, "classical" music, programs designed to illuminate matters of public concern.

Features such as news.

In the late 1920's news was of small importance to the commercial purposes of broadcasting. Advertisers were little interested in news programs in terms of sponsorship, for the very good reason that other types of programs held greater audience appeal. From the broadcaster's point of view, however, news programs had two appreciable advantages: they helped to build up a station's, or a network's, hours of public service programming; and they were easy and inexpensive to put on the air. But the news problem was not yet one of radio's major concerns.

Newspapers, on the other hand, were becoming increasingly alarmed. News was the prime commodity they had to sell to the public; advertising was the breath of life. Radio was trespassing in both fields. The newspapers' fear of the trespasser led them into a false position—a position of meeting an irresistible force, not with an immovable object, but with illogic and halfway concessions. Railroads had tried to hamper the development of bus and truck transportation, and had failed because bus and truck transportation had been a useful advance in human intercourse. Newspapers, too, were to try to hamstring a useful social advance; they, too, were to fail.

In the fall of 1928, the three great press services—AP, UP, and INS—

yielded to the extent of furnishing returns of the bitter Smith-Hoover election to radio stations. Local newspapers in many cases cooperated similarly with local broadcasters. But if they hoped thus to establish a pattern of control of the amount of news that went into the nation's microphones, they were disappointed. For the radio news of that election served both to whet the appetite of many millions of listeners, and to increase radio's interest in making news a regular part of its daily menu. In December, for example, KFAB-Lincoln, Nebraska, inaugurated two "editions" of a radio "newspaper"—two daily broadcasts of news. It hired George Kline away from his city editorship of the *Lincoln Star* to direct them. Other stations developed similar programs.

And late in 1930 KMPC-Beverly Hills, California, not only opened a schedule of three fifteen-minute news shows daily, but organized its own news-gathering service to implement them. Its Radio News Service of America put ten reporters on the news runs regularly covered by the Los Angeles newspapers, developed a string of out-of-town correspondents, and went into what it described as "friendly competition" with all neighboring newspapers.

Such developments showed the direction of the wind. It was a wind that newspaper publishers could hardly ignore. In their plants, their staffs, and the news services that worked for them, they had investments of millions of dollars. Comparatively, radio investment was small. Yet the newspapers saw the newcomer using their chief commodity—often "pirating" it—at no expense, and putting it before an audience minutes or hours before the newsboys could hawk it.

More important than that: October, 1929, had come and gone. Newspaper "depression linage" in 1930 was 14 per cent below that of 1929. There was every reason to think the decline in newspapers' major income item would continue. In the face of that, radio advertising income was booming.

Newspapers now had no doubt that they faced serious competition. In 1929, the AP had again tried appeasement—a relaxation of prohibitions against members' broadcast of news to prevent members from getting news for broadcast from other sources. But this was only a halfway measure. It had effect only on radio stations with direct

connection with AP papers, a relatively small number. And the AP had
no effective policing method. The policy had little force.

So there was a rush by newspapers to get into the radio business.
Already about a hundred newspapers had radio connections. Others
began establishing stations, buying stations or setting up participating
or cooperative relationships with stations (the increase in number of
licensed stations from 1930 to 1938—612 to 721—was somewhat
smaller than the increase in number of newspaper-radio affiliations).

It is ironic that, when publishers became broadcasters, most of them
followed exactly the programming and advertising sales patterns
developed by radio. Some attempted to control sale of radio time so
as to favor their newspapers. Many thought of the broadcasting of
radio news as a means of promoting newspaper circulation—"for
further details, read your *Evening Bugle*"—and dependable observation suggests that they thought soundly. Newspaper sales have often
reached astonishing peaks just after radio has taken the cream off the
news (though radio got the break on the news of the Normandy invasion in 1944, newspaper sales for the day were reported at 20 to 50
per cent above normal. The same kind of thing was true on V-E Day,
at President Roosevelt's death, and on many other occasions). Total
daily newspaper circulations reached new highs annually during the

---

ADVERTISING EXPENDITURES IN RADIO AND NEWSPAPERS, 1927 TO 1946
(in millions of dollars)

	Radio	Newspapers		Radio	Newspapers
1927	5	775	1937	145	600
1928	20	760	1938	145	520
1929	40	800	1939	170	525
1930	60	700	1940	175	535
1931	80	620	1941	225	610
1932	80	490	1942	245	580
1933	65	450	1943	325	665
1934	90	500	1944	400	645
1935	105	530	1945	470	770
1936	120	580	1946	490	965

Statistics from *Printers' Ink* annual summaries.

1940's, when radio news broadcasting was also on a mounting curve. But in 1930 the only successful broadcasting pattern was that developed by broadcasters, and no newspaper going into radio invented anything new, or added anything to existing forms.

Moreover, the inroads of newspapers into the radio industry had direct relation only to a minority of radio stations, and to a smaller proportion of newspapers. The number of newspaper-radio station affiliations has never reached more than about a third of the number of all licensed stations, at the most liberal interpretation of newspaper-radio association (that is, including situations with newspapers in minority ownership). It has never reached above a sixth of all American dailies, and only to about 3 per cent of the weeklies.

Nevertheless, in 1931 the panic was on. In Portland, Oregon, the newspapers served notice on the radio stations that they would no longer publish radio logs unless stations paid for them at regular advertising rates (the stations refused; the newspapers withdrew the logs—and five days later put them back, unpaid, because reader demand for them was so great). In Kansas City the *Star*, an unusually powerful paper, succeeded in a like effort. In Minnesota the state Editorial Association passed a futile resolution. The Pennsylvania Newspaper Publishers Association approved a resolution with three resounding "whereases" and four "be it resolveds" speaking of the "jealous eye" of the broadcasting industry as it destroyed "the surprise value of the news," and not only threatening to "use their best efforts to outlaw any station or chain that seeks to usurp the newspaper function" but also calling on members and the news services to cease furnishing news to stations. California Newspaper Publishers Association took similar action in 1932. And the American Newspaper Publishers Association was told by its counsel, Elisha Hanson, that any "deal" with other organizations—such as the AP—to curtail radio's use of news would violate restraint-of-trade laws.

Another influence that doubtless added to newspaper jitters was the fact that a small Washington news service—the Consolidated Press, headed by David Lawrence of the *United States Daily*—offered news to stations. It procured four customers—not enough to alter circumstances substantially, but a foreshadowing of later developments.

Much of the burden of the fight, through 1932, fell on the unhappy shoulders of the AP. The UP and the INS, being private, profit-making enterprises in the business of selling news, were somewhat less subject to newspaper influence. But the AP's job was to "furnish" rather than sell news to its newspaper-owners, and it was in the middle. A questionnaire circulated among members showed heavy opposition to use of AP news for broadcast. The AP's concession on news of "transcendent" importance still held, however, and when the infant son of Colonel Charles A. Lindbergh was kidnaped in March of 1932, AP joined with other services in helping radio to do a notable job of spreading the story and appealing to the kidnapers to return the child. Radio reporters themselves worked on this story, alongside the newspaper and press service men; and such later notables as Boake Carter and Gabriel Heatter, among others, first began attracting sizable radio audiences by their Lindbergh-case broadcasts.

But the AP directorate decided against radio use of its 1932 election returns. The surprise of member publishers, then, was great when on election night they heard both CBS and NBC broadcasting AP bulletins on the election of Franklin D. Roosevelt. What had happened was this: Kent Cooper, AP's general manager, had learned at the last minute that UP had offered to sell election news to CBS for $1,000. To forestall such "subsidy of a competitor," Cooper decided to release the news free to the networks. Meantime, though Cooper didn't know it, UP had withdrawn its offer, after "consultation" with newspaper clients had convinced Karl Bickel, UP president, that the income received would not give UP papers "a very considerable reduction" in the cost of election returns. The result was that AP news went on the air. But so did UP and INS news; UP printers already installed in network headquarters were "mysteriously" turned on, and CBS had made a protective arrangement for coverage with the *New York Times* and the *New York Journal*, whose service included INS wire reports. Incidentally, two Hearst writers, Frederic William Wile and Edwin

---

Of 1,197 AP members in the winter of 1932–1933, 1,103 answered the questionnaire. Majorities, usually heavy, favored denial of AP news to radio chains, and even denial of the right of members to broadcast AP news. Only 223 did any news broadcasting.

C. Hill, announced the bulk of the returns for CBS; NBC had as its stars Arthur Brisbane, Walter Lippmann, and George B. Parker.

While the newspapers and the press services had thus been fumbling, radio went smoothly on its way. Baseball, football, and other sports broadcasts had long since become accepted radio features—in fact, as far back as 1926 and 1927, when the Tunney-Dempsey fights had gone on the air, the Scripps-Howard newspapers had sponsored the broadcasts. Commander Byrd had broadcast from the South Pole under *New York Times* auspices. The Republican and Democratic conventions of 1932 went on coast-to-coast hook-ups. On September 22, radio listeners heard William Beebe talking from his bathysphere as he was lowered 2,200 feet into the Atlantic off Bermuda. Microphones were set up in courtrooms—until judicial and public disapproval frowned them out—to pick up play-by-play accounts of sensational trials.

Most such broadcasts were in the nature of what came to be called "special events," rather than the simpler straight news programs to which the newspapers especially objected. But they all aided in establishing radio in the public mind as a purveyor of news. And they fortified the radio industry in its determination to do as it liked. If the public asked news of the broadcasters, news the public should have.

As 1933 came in, then, radio listeners heard full accounts of the attempt to assassinate Franklin Roosevelt at Miami. The new President's inaugural on March 4 went out on a record-breaking international hookup. Eight days later Roosevelt initiated the "fireside chat"— an event that was periodically to combine the President's striking "radio personality" and exceedingly skillful scripts with whatever news he chose to present, all in a manner to build bigger and bigger radio audiences among a people desperate for relief from the depression.

Moreover, the number of regular news programs was increasing. Though AP remained intransigent, UP and INS were selling news to stations willing to pay the tolls. A few newspapers owning radio stations—the *Milwaukee Journal*, the *Chicago Tribune*, the Hearst chain among them—were frankly insisting that radio news was a legitimate part of their business. And many stations with neither newspaper tie-ups nor regular news services were coolly lifting news—"pirating" it, the newspapers said—from the press and putting it into America's living rooms before the newspapers reached them.

A new factor in the struggle that was shaping up grew out of the energetic efforts of E. H. Harris, editor of the Indiana *Richmond Palladium* and chairman of the ANPA's radio committee. The ANPA for the most part represented the larger dailies; Harris wanted broader representation, especially to include the smaller papers that felt themselves the worst sufferers from radio competition. He formed a Publishers National Radio Committee, drew up a statement of the newspapers' grievances, and with it went to the AP and ANPA conventions in April.

ANPA at once responded by approving several "recommendations" offered by Harris—"recommendations" because the Association wished to avoid the danger of a charge of conspiracy in restraint of trade. Among them:

That the Association should protest against the selling or giving away of news in advance of newspaper publication, and should take legal action in cases of piracy.

"That all news bulletins broadcast, in fairness to newspapers, should be in the briefest possible form and prepared to whet the appetite of the listener for more news to be obtained through newspapers; and that credit for broadcasting all national and international news *be given to all newspapers of the United States.*"

That newspaper-owned stations be asked to limit local news broadcasts to brief bulletins, in order not to injure papers not affiliated with stations.

That free insertion of radio programs in newspapers be condemned.

Extreme as some of these proposals appear, they indicated the temper of the newspaper owners. When the AP convention met, it made another attempt to dam the flow of news to radio. It voted to bar

---

One day in the spring of 1933 Harry Fairley, editor of the Minnesota *Fairmont Sentinel*, went to a restaurant for lunch. From the restaurant's radio, tuned to a South Dakota station, he heard word for word the AP news report on which he had been working for the last hour. This station had not bought the news—its announcer was reading from an early edition of a local paper. Fairley's *Sentinel* would not reach its subscribers for another three hours. . . . Fairley's experience, and his rage, found counterparts all over the country.

AP news from network use, to limit AP members with radio affiliations to brief bulletins on matters of major importance, to set for such bulletins prescribed broadcast hours that would give newspapers a time advantage, and to make special assessments against members using AP news for broadcast. It was hoped that the mild concessions in this arrangement would obviate attempts by radio interests at news-gathering. It is dimly possible that the hope might have been justified had AP gone unsupported. But publishers put pressure on the other two big news services, and shortly UP and INS announced·not only similar regulations for their clients' use of news but also cessation of sale of news direct to radio stations.

That was the back-breaking straw. The battle was joined.

The "Press-Radio War"

The Columbia Broadcasting System responded vigorously. Under the energetic direction of Paul White, former UP man and CBS publicity director, it set up Columbia News Service, Inc. White established a main office in New York, with bureaus in Washington, Chicago, Los Angeles, and London. He gathered staffs of competent newspapermen for the bureaus, and supplemented them with some eight hundred string correspondents—men and women, mostly newspaper reporters, paid good rates for each bulletin they sent to a bureau. He made arrangements for procuring foreign news from the British Exchange Telegraph news agency, and financial news from the Dow-Jones service. By late September he had his pretentious organization ready for full-strength operation, and it provided news for two daily fifteen-minute newscasts by Boake Carter and H. V. Kaltenborn on the network.

NBC did not go to such lengths. Its "radio city room" in New York continued the scissors-and-paste brand of news-gathering it had been employing for some time; Abe Schechter, news director, made arrangements with the Consolidated Press for supplementary service. Its news, like that of CBS, was available for sponsorship.

Powerful as they were, the networks in 1934 served only a few more than a third of American broadcasting stations. But this did not confine newscasting to their affiliates. The "independent" stations continued their news broadcasts, evidently using early editions of newspapers just as they had before the press services' edict came out. *Editor & Publisher,* the newspaper trade journal, reported in May that New York City newscasts were "as voluminous and complete" as usual. News commentators such as Thomas and Carter, to whose use of up-to-the-minute news as basis for their "patter" the newspapers also objected, continued on their way.

In Sioux Falls, South Dakota, the AP brought suit against Station KSOO, charging piracy of news. A Federal court issued an injunction denying the station the right to use news gathered at others' "labor and expense" during the period in which the news retained commercial value. The injunction fixed this period at not less than twenty-four hours, thus differing from decisions in analogous cases, which usually set the commercial life of news at no longer than the period between publication of a morning and a succeeding evening paper. Today the period is usually considered to be about four to six hours.

Late in 1934 the AP instituted another suit against a radio station which, after long litigation that took it to the United States Supreme Court, resulted in a draw. In October the Washington *Bellingham Herald* obtained an injunction forbidding Station KVOS-Bellingham to use news from the *Herald* and two other AP papers, the *Seattle Times* and the *Seattle Post-Intelligencer.* On December 18 a Federal district court judge in Seattle dissolved the injunction on the ground that publication of the news in the papers threw it into the public domain. A year later the Ninth Circuit Court of Appeals in San Francisco reinstated the injunction, upholding the principle that a news-gatherer

NUMBER OF STATIONS AFFILIATED WITH MAJOR NETWORKS

	NBC Red *	NBC Blue *	CBS	Mutual †	Total
1927	23	18	13		54
1934	65	62	97	4	228
1944	142	195	142	223	702
1947	160	240	166	384	950

* NBC Red dropped the "Red" from its title in 1942, when NBC Blue became the independent Blue Network Company. Blue become the American Broadcasting Company in 1945.

† Mutual commenced operations in 1934.

(in this case, the AP) retains a protectable property right in news during its commercial life. But on December 14, 1936, the Supreme Court dodged the issue by a decision that the case was not within the jurisdiction of Federal courts, since the AP had failed to prove prospective damage of $3,000, the minimum sum necessary to establish it as a Federal case.

The KSOO case was almost the newspapers' only solace in 1933. Broadcast of news continued to expand. And the newspapers continued to exert pressure on radio to limit its news programs. One weapon was the threat of omission of radio logs—a threat that had little effect. Another was a hint that publishers would attempt to bring pressure on the Federal Radio Commission to prevent the renewal of licenses of stations that did not see the light. Moreover, the fact that NBC was greatly handicapped in newscasting since it had not developed an extensive news-gathering organization caused something of a split in radio's front. CBS was not eager to carry the torch alone. Late in 1933 publishers were able to announce that the two networks had appealed to the Harris committee for a meeting to discuss "the long-standing dispute between the broadcasters and the newspapers." Harris and the committee, at the same time, were ready to make some concessions.

On December 11 Harris convened his committee with representatives of radio and the press services—a meeting attended by enough notables so that it might lead to a showdown. Present were President William S. Paley of CBS and President M. H. Aylesworth of NBC; Roy Howard of Scripps-Howard Newspapers; Harry Bitner of Hearst Newspapers; J. H. Gortatowsky of INS, President Karl Bickel of UP, and Lloyd Stratton, executive assistant to General Manager Kent Cooper of AP; Alfred J. McCosker, president of NAB; General Manager L. B. Palmer of ANPA; and four ranking members of the Harris committee.

The group conferred for two days. When it adjourned, it had drawn up a "Press-Radio Plan" which it hoped would satisfy broadcasters and at the same time protect the press. It decreed that:

It would be administered by a seven-man committee—one each from ANPA, AP, INS, UP, NAB, CBS, NBC—under chairmanship of the ANPA representative and subject to review by the Harris committee.

Each of the three press associations would provide full daily reports, on which the Press-Radio Bureau could base two daily broadcasts of five minutes each, composed of bulletins of not more than thirty words on any one news event.

The five-minute broadcasts should be put on the air no earlier than 9:30 A.M. or 9 P.M.

The broadcasts should not be sold for commercial purposes.

CBS and NBC would undertake no news-gathering efforts on their own. The broadcasters would pay the costs of the Press-Radio service.

Occasional news bulletins of transcendent importance would be provided to broadcasters, to be used "in such manner as to stimulate public interest in the reading of newspapers."

Radio news commentators would be limited to "generalization and background of general news situations," eschewing spot news.

Here were concessions on both sides. The networks would agree to abide by the news schedule as outlined, would use only the news furnished by the Bureau, would use it without sponsorship, and would retire from the news-gathering business. The newspaper industry and the press services would not attempt to prevent newscasting—would, in fact, "cooperate" to the extent of making highlight coverage available to any broadcaster who wished to pay for it.

The plan was ratified, with slight modifications, by all parties in January, 1934. But it had four serious deficiencies:

It did not bind UP and INS to refrain from selling news to radio. In fact, both agencies repeated their reservation of the previous April, when they had withdrawn such service—that they would abandon their position should the necessities of competition demand it.

It did nothing to forestall the organization of new news services.

It did not represent the views of a majority of the radio stations—the independent, unaffiliated stations which had consistently, and not always silently, held to a belief in their rights to broadcast news as often as they wished, and under sponsorship if they wished; nor of a number of newspaper-owned stations which considered the plan an invasion of their private affairs (the Chicago Tribune, owning WGN, had already stated that "the people are entitled to the service for which the Tribune is equipped").

Most important of all, it flouted "the public interest, convenience, and necessity." The public had given abundant evidence that it wanted radio news. This all-powerful influence the newspapers proposed, and the radio signers of the plan agreed, to by-pass. This in spite of the fact that broadcasters had come to depend heavily on news programs, often unsponsored, as one of the means of demonstrating their public service.

All of which meant that the plan had two strikes on it before it came to bat. — o —

The Press-Radio Bureau made its appearance on March 1, 1934. Under the direction of James W. Barrett, city editor of the *New York World* at the time of its death in 1931, a New York headquarters and a Los Angeles branch were set up. The Bureau opened business with 125 subscribers to the New York service and 48 to the Los Angeles; these figures climbed to 160 and 65 within six months.

Press-Radio was not, however, greeted with unrestrained cheers. Senator Clarence C. Dill of Washington, co-author of the new communications bill then in Congress, called it "news suppression." Herbert Moore, the truculent and aggressive news editor of the disbanded Columbia News Service, said it was a conspiracy to restrict news. H. V. Kaltenborn, already known as an ace CBS commentator, declared that "the only saving grace of this agreement is that it will not work." And Harris, now chairman of the Press-Radio Committee, warned radio stations pompously that the Committee "would not vacillate" in its attitude toward stations refusing to cooperate.

The most striking immediate development, however—one apparently foreseen by no signers of the agreement—came even before March 1. WNAC-Boston, with the discontinuance of Columbia's news service, engaged a former State House reporter of the *Boston Transcript*, Richard Grant, to build a news-gathering organization to cover New England for the regional Yankee Network. Grant put on a battle in the capitol itself that resulted in a bill giving him space in the pressroom, in spite of newspaper dissent. He hired telephone reporters in forty-five New England centers, and within a year had spent $90,000 gathering news for the eight Yankee stations.

On the Pacific coast, Radio News Service of America—organized four years before by KMPC at Beverly Hills—announced a program of expansion. The American Newscasting Association and, a year later, the American Broadcasters News Association made their appearance. Individual stations here and there set up tentative news-gathering operations. And, most important, Herbert Moore's new "cooperative service" started on the night of February 28 to distribute news to twenty stations throughout the country.

Two impulses appear to have led Moore into the new venture. One was the obvious opportunity to build a successful business. The other was that he was outraged at what he considered the selfishness and shortsightedness of the newspaper interests. As early as December, 1933, when plans to disband Columbia News Service were announced, he started to plan a cooperative radio news organization. Working fast, he managed to open his service a few hours ahead of the beginning of Press-Radio operations.

The cooperative plan soon developed faults—something Moore said later he had expected. Western stations dominated its structure, and eastern stations protested the preponderance of western news. On March 21, therefore, Moore announced the formation of Transradio Press Service, Inc., a commercial news-gathering and news-selling organization. As key clients it had the Yankee Network in New England, WLS-Chicago (one of the stations which had set up its own news agency), KWK-St. Louis, KSTP-St. Paul, and KNX-Hollywood. Within a few months, Moore described Transradio as having bureaus in all the principal cities of the United States, special correspondents in several hundred cities and towns abroad, and a total organization of 7,000 workers. On April 23 he had arranged with the French news service, Havas, for 12,000 cablese words daily of foreign news (he shifted to Reuters on January 5, 1935).

By Moore's account, he quickly accumulated long-term contracts to assure a revenue of $100,000 a year—enough to pay operating costs. His original clientele of twenty stations grew to "nearly 100" in the summer, and 150 by December. Transradio's fees followed the "what-the-traffic-will-bear" pattern established by UP and INS; Moore reported that his subscribers were paying variously from $5.00 to $500 a week, according to their "rating."

The service furnished by Transradio ranged, according to the individual contract, from 5,000 to 30,000 words a day, with an average of 10,000—enough for four fifteen-minute broadcasts—plus flashes on important news breaks. It was couched in telegraphic form, to save wire tolls—a form that required rewriting in the radio station, or the most skillful kind of ad libbing by the announcer. This service was supplemented in August by the organization of Radio News Association, Inc., a subsidiary to transmit news to subscribers by short wave (a service less expensive than that using telegraph wires). A significant feature of the new service was that its news was written for radio, not for newspaper use (more about this in Chapter 5).

In short, though none of the other radio news services made much of a dent, Transradio appeared a thumping success. It immediately drew the cordial and united enmity of the newspapers and the press services. They ridiculed its service; they disputed Moore's claims about the extent of its organization, saying that many of its "bureaus" consisted of nothing more than reporters or radio announcers who turned to Transradio duties after their regular day's work was done; they accused it of being none too careful as to where it got its news. They railed at the fact that Transradio had no objection to news sponsorship. Their annoyance was increased when, in June, 1935, Moore added a newspaper to his clientele—the Georgia *Athens Times*. The *Times* was followed before the end of 1935 by the Pennsylvania *Harrisburg Telegraph*.

In May of 1935, Moore struck back. He filed a suit against all members of the Press-Radio Committee, including some 1,400 newspaper members of AP and ANPA, asking of a New York Federal court not only a judgment of $1,170,000 in damages but also a permanent injunction restraining them from interfering with his business. Here Transradio was to run up against bitter legal opposition, and the suit was to languish for years without decision. It was finally settled out of court.

Two other 1934 events, of importance in the history of American broadcasting, had relatively little immediate effect on newscasting. One was the organization, on July 11, of the Federal Communications Commission, succeeding the Federal Radio Commission, to administer the greatly broadened provisions of the Federal Communications Act of 1934. The other was the appearance on September 30 of a new "cooperative" network, the Mutual Broadcasting System, with four key stations headed by WGN of the *Chicago Tribune* and WOR of Bamberger's Department Store, Newark. Two years later Mutual expanded country-wide with the addition of the Don Lee Network in California, and other stations.

Press-Radio, meantime, was not doing so well. On March 1, 1935—
at the end of its first year of operation—the two branches of the Bureau
reported 245 subscribers. This meant that E. H. Harris's policy of non-
vacillation had failed to influence some 360 stations, most of which
presumably were broadcasting news gained from Transradio, from
one of the competing services, or from some "illegitimate" source. At
its April meeting, the Press-Radio Committee decided to continue
operations. But it acknowledged that news broadcasting competition
had become a reality; and it also approved the UP-INS reservation of
the right to sell news for broadcasting if competition should force them
to it. Further, it authorized its sixteen newspaper-owned subscribers
to use AP news to make up four fifteen-minute Press-Radio broadcasts
daily. At the ANPA meeting late in the month the revised plan, with
its concessions, was approved, and the newspaper industry sat back
with the hope that the problem was properly pigeon-holed for another
year.

Radio Gets the News

Within a month the pigeon-hole exploded. INS and UP announced
their decision to offer news for broadcasting to any newspaper client
owning or affiliated with a radio station, with no limitation on sponsorship. Shortly thereafter they extended this halfway measure to offer
their services to any radio station, without strings. By July, UP's leased
wire was serving eighteen points.

The UP-INS decision was the measure of Transradio's success. The
agency by this time reported 185 subscribers. Moreover, of 114 newspaper-affiliated stations, 27 were buying, experimenting with, or negotiating for, Transradio service. The UP and the INS could not look
with equanimity on a situation that forced into other hands contracts
they might as well have had.

To meet competition which its operations had been expected to circum-
vent, the Press-Radio Bureau issued in its first year the astonishing number
of 4,670 special bulletins—"flashes" on news of "transcendent" importance
—in addition to its two regular broadcasts each day. Twenty-three hundred
of these dealt with the Hauptmann trial; hundreds of the others with the
1934 elections, the World Series, and such "transcendent" events.

Other factors, of course, underlay the competitive situation. A prime reason for the attractiveness of Transradio news rather than that of Press-Radio was that it could be sold to advertisers. News sponsorship continued to be the whipping boy of the publishers; in its April, 1935, statement the ANPA's radio committee had expressed the fear that sponsorship would let advertisers censor and edit news not alone for their own advertising purposes but also in accord with their social prejudices. Thus, said the statement, the "news would degenerate into propaganda for the advertiser." There was also the newspapers' understandable opposition to permitting radio to take the cream off the news, especially if the news were to be furnished to radio by press services of which they, through membership or subscription, were the chief supports. Such a practice, as they pointed out, would mean that radio would in effect be getting news at their expense.

Underlying all the objections was the fact that radio advertising appropriations and radio's annual advertising income, after a brief recession at the pit of the depression in 1933, were steadily climbing. Newspaper advertising income, on the other hand, had declined steadily from 1929 to 1933, and the mild increase in 1934 was too small to be very encouraging.

If the newspaper position in the dispute was essentially actuated by self-interest rather than concern for the public, radio's was hardly different. The radio networks had, according to a writer in *Harper's*, "run up the white flag" in concurring in the Press-Radio plan. Though they paid lip service to the principle that news dissemination was as much radio's province as the newspapers', they did little to implement it. The stations that ignored Press-Radio did so for a very good reason: that the public wanted news, and that advertisers therefore wanted to sponsor it. But no overwhelming passion for the public was discernible in their attitude.

In brief, the controlling factors on both sides of the dispute were economic. Herbert Moore, commenting acidly on the defection of UP and INS, said that broadcasters were not interested in a free news service, no matter how good, unless they could sell it to advertisers. And he added, "The broadcasters who are actuated by a spirit of public service are about as rare as that kind of newspaper publisher."

The effect on Press-Radio was immediate. Haakon H. Hammer, former Pacific coast field representative of the Bureau, proposed an elaborate plan for extending the amount of news it furnished, making the service attractive enough to enlist all radio stations, and permitting sponsorship of news under certain conditions. The plan went by the board. On August 1, 1935, the Los Angeles branch of the Bureau gave up the ghost. The New York office, under Barrett, was continued annually by the ANPA through 1938 and until the spring meeting of 1939. Then, with no word of explanation or regret, it was allowed to vanish.

Meantime, the response to UP and INS offers was equally immediate. UP, taking a leaf from Transradio's book, announced that it would set up a special staff to edit news for the ear rather than the eye. By November 1, UP showed a list of some fifty radio clients, and INS's numbered nearly seventy. AP further relaxed its regulations so that newspaper members owning stations could use its news on the air, but maintained its restrictions against sponsorship. Transradio, having won a victory and, with it, dangerous competition, continued as the leading purveyor of news to the stations.

After 1935, the heat of battle subsided. The next three years were

---

Newspaper fears that sponsorship of news might lead to advertisers' censorship, editing, and distortion have not been borne out by experience. One deterrent is unquestionably the fact that news service contracts with radio clients contain clauses giving the services the right of cancellation if, in their judgment, their news is being broadcast in distorted form. No cases of this kind of action have been reported. Moreover, the FCC would look with narrowed eye on cases of distortion.

A third factor, especially in the latter years of newscasting, as radio newsrooms become manned by more and more competent editors, is that few radio stations are willing to put themselves in the position of yielding to advertiser requests for withholding or alteration of news. Unquestionably such requests have been made, and will be made. But the number of refusals is not far from the number of requests. Most broadcasters sell news on the basis of complete and inviolate control of the news content of broadcasts; most newsrooms themselves, indeed, operate on the principle of independence even of station management, as far as news content and emphasis are concerned. Innumerable cases could be quoted to support these generalizations.

marked only by the gradual increase in the number of radio stations buying news service, by improvement in the quality of service (on July 27, 1936, UP put into operation an eighteen-hour, forty-word-a-minute teleprinter system with news specially edited for radio), and more and more sale of news for sponsorship.

Not that newspaper circles gave up overnight their objections to radio dissemination of news. In 1935 the California Newspaper Publishers Association and the Inland Daily Press Association vainly invoked Federal aid, one to "return to the people the air channels now used by commercial interests," the other to "preserve the true news value by requiring all subject matter under the title of news to be broadcast only as unsponsored editorial service. . . ." In 1936, when its radio committee approved continuation of Press-Radio for another year, the ANPA asked careful government supervision of radio to guard against its monopolistic features. A year later it suggested that Congress enact a law requiring the FCC to designate "an appropriate time each day for radio stations to broadcast newspaper and press association news .

RADIO STATIONS SUBSCRIBING TO MAJOR NEWS SERVICES, 1936–1948

Year	Associated Press	International News Service	Transradio Press	United Press	Total
1936		72	188*	65	325
1937		92	230*	121	443
1938		117	212	212	541
1939		141	177	293	611
1940	65	172	175	331	743
1941	121	155	163	404	843
1942	238	178	79	461	956
1943	301	136	49	497	983
1944	344	134	42	504	1,024
1945	428	121	20	536	1,105
1946	488	99	15	544	1,146
1947	698	116	12	663	1,389
1948	842	128	7	796	1,783

* TP totals for 1935 and 1936 include 25 and 18 Radio News Association clients (RNA was a TP subsidiary).
The AP first made its news available for sponsored broadcasts in 1939. It inaugurated Press Association, as its radio-news branch, in March, 1941.
Figures (from *Broadcasting Yearbooks*, 1936 to 1948) are as of January 1 of each year, except the 1947 figures, which are as of February 15. (In April of 1948 AP reported that it served 966 radio stations, and UP that it served "more than 900.")

reports as furnished by the Press-Radio Bureau without exploitation by the advertisers." None of these resolutions and suggestions got much farther than the minute books.

For news broadcasting was firmly established, and neither the FCC nor any other government agency showed disposition to restrict it. Indeed, events were conspiring to increase rather than lessen public interest in radio news. On December 11, 1936, King Edward VIII made a world-wide broadcast of his famous "woman I love" abdication—a news event that drew what was described as the largest audience ever to listen to a speech. On October 1, 1937, Senator Hugo L. Black chose radio broadcast as the medium for replying to critics of his Ku Klux Klan affiliation: by use of radio, he said, he could prevent "editing or interpretation" of his remarks. Late in 1938, Fulton Lewis, Jr., opened a campaign for the admission of radio reporters to Senate and House press galleries. He won his fight in April, 1939, when Congress passed the necessary law—an event that was followed immediately by inclusion of radio men in White House press conferences. (But it was not until 1948 that radio newsmen won the right to active membership in Washington's famous National Press Club.)

Just before these last events had come Munich.

After Munich

The networks had been experimenting for some years with broadcasts from radio reporters abroad. In 1932, CBS had brought to its affiliates ninety-three programs from seventeen foreign sources—eleven of them from the Geneva Disarmament Conference. NBC celebrated its tenth anniversary, in 1936, by offering a conversation between Guglielmo Marconi, cruising on his yacht off Genoa, and three radio notables in this country. In the same year an NBC reporter brought America first news of the death of King George V. H. V. Kaltenborn, hidden in a haystack between Loyalist and Rebel lines in Spain, with a portable transmitter on his back, brought to CBS listeners a startling account of civil war in action, complete with live sound effects.

Both networks, though they had given up domestic news-gathering, had envisioned the possibilities of foreign news broadcasting. NBC's Abe Schechter and CBS's Paul White had been building up foreign staffs. NBC had foreign staff men in London, Paris, Geneva, Shanghai; CBS in London, Paris, Berlin, other centers. The public had responded favorably to the foreign broadcasts—actually rebroadcasts, for they came to network headquarters via short wave and were converted to standard wave lengths. But until September of 1938 they were essentially novelties: descriptions of colorful events, human interest shows. They had not established themselves as integral parts of the news picture.

Then came the Sudeten crisis in Czechoslovakia. Suddenly Europe was on the verge of war. America was distant, but it remembered 1917. The networks saw an opportunity, and what they did with their half-built foreign structures firmly established foreign news broadcasting among America's listeners.

During those days in September, when Chamberlain was commuting between London and southern Germany and Hitler was flaunting the specter of war, CBS and NBC put into American homes more than a thousand foreign broadcasts, from more than two hundred radio reporters. Edward Murrow from London, William L. Shirer from Prague, John T. Whitaker from Paris, Max Jordan from Munich—these men and many others gave radio listeners on-the-spot news of world-shaking events more rapidly and more colorfully than they had ever had it before. And in CBS's New York studio Kaltenborn sat before a microphone—virtually for twenty solid days—and analyzed, coordinated, interpreted. He went on the air many times a day. And he built up, during the Munich crisis, perhaps the largest radio news audience any man had ever boasted.

It appears that CBS and NBC undertook, and carried off, this noteworthy effort without precisely foreseeing its results. They were thinking, at least in part, promotionally—neither was willing for the other to get a commanding lead in the new field. They had employed top-ranking newsmen for the work, and the newsmen perhaps more than their employers realized that they were engaged in a gigantic public service enterprise.

But it quickly developed that the enterprise could be turned into dollars. The radio audience ate up the foreign broadcasts. It built up a new interest in radio news, one that showed 19 per cent of the listeners to evening network broadcasts during September tuned to news shows. This meant two things: That newscasting had to become more important than ever in radio programming; and that advertisers were going to be more eager than ever to make news the bait to draw listeners to their commercials.

After Munich the tempo of foreign news broadcasting slowed down. But the networks, not wishing to be caught short, and not too impressed by Chamberlain's "peace in our time," went immediately about the business of building up elaborate foreign organizations. At home, both the radio chains and the individual stations took steps to increase their news facilities.

And newspaper objections to radio news subsided from piercing shrieks to a grumble, then a mutter. Publishers were recognizing the validity of a statement by Mark Ethridge, general manager of the *Louisville Courier-Journal* and, for an interim period in 1938, president of NAB, that (in May, 1939) "the newspaper business has been fighting a rear-guard action for ten years—and a losing action, at that." At the April, 1939, ANPA radio committee meeting, which among other things signalized the demise of the Press-Radio Bureau, the publishers satisfied themselves with speaking mildly of "new and impressive records of cooperation between press and radio in public service enterprises" such as the Munich coverage, and describing the news-sponsorship problem only as a "questionable practice adverse to the prestige and larger interests of the medium indulging in it . . . a question yet to be answered."

Further acceptance of the inevitable came in May, when the AP lifted its ban on sponsorship of news furnished to members. Certain restrictions to protect newspapers without radio affiliations were set up.

An ANPA questionnaire showed that the number of papers that published radio listings as paid matter only had increased from 14 per cent of dailies in 1938 to 37 per cent in 1939; and that the number that published trade names of sponsors in such listings had decreased from 9 per cent in 1938 to 3 per cent in 1939. But an ANPA estimate of the number of dailies using radio logs as paid matter in 1948 put the figure at "probably less than 5 per cent"; a *Broadcasting Magazine* survey in mid-1948 put it at 19 per cent.

Direct sale of AP news to radio stations was not yet permitted—that was to come later.

Meantime, as this problem shook itself down and the networks built their foreign staffs, the next logical step was developing: the installation of newsrooms in scores of stations throughout the country. The networks had started operations of this kind in their key stations—New York, Washington, Chicago, Hollywood—before Munich. A number of the larger independent or chain-affiliated stations, and a few of the smaller ones in cities where keen newspaper-radio competition existed, had also done so. But after Munich, as the necessity for radio news became imperative, newsrooms began to spring up everywhere.

When German troops marched into Poland in September of 1939, all these preparations, domestic and foreign, justified themselves. There occurred the inevitable surge in the number of newscasts and in public interest in them, together with an immediate sprint among advertisers to sponsor the news. As in 1938, the upswing leveled off after the first shock of the news had cooled. But the new plateau of interest was higher than before.

The next six years were marked by a series of remarkable news broadcasts from abroad—not only the regularly-scheduled news shows but a number of striking "special events." On December 17, 1939, James Bowen of NBC thrilled the world when, from Montevideo, he described what he saw as the Germans scuttled the battered "Graf Spee" just outside the Buenos Aires harbor. When Hitler received the conquered French in the historic *wagon lit* in Compiègne Forest to accept their surrender, CBS's Shirer and William C. Kerker of NBC broadcast the sadly stirring tale—and gave the news to America more than two hours before Germany and France got it. Ed Murrow, Eric Sevareid, Vincent Sheean, and J. B. Priestley put on a gripping picture of London under the Nazi blitz on August 24, 1940.

Later, radio gave America its first news of the Japanese attack on Pearl Harbor; Cecil Brown made history with his stories of the fall of

In the first days of September, 1939, radio offered more news than some of its fans wanted. A university coed in one Midwestern city said heatedly, "I hope the war ends before Thursday. If it doesn't, they may cancel 'The Adventures of Lulubelle' again."

Singapore. Sevareid, turning a hand-crank to generate transmitter power, sent out (for rebroadcast) the story of his parachute hop from a falling plane into the Indo-Burmese jungle in August, 1943. Murrow put into American living rooms one of the most stirring of all broadcasts when, on December 3, he described the great Berlin air raid of the night before—a raid on which he had ridden as an observer. The two invasions of France brought scores of notable broadcasts—outstanding among them the play-by-play account given by Blue correspondent George Hicks from the deck of a warship off the Norman coast. Hicks did not actually broadcast the account, but rather made a recording of it at 12:10 A.M. on June 7, just as JU88 bombers plunged at the ship. The recording was sent to London and "processed for security"; then it went on short wave to all network headquarters in New York, there to be re-recorded. That night all four networks broadcast it.

Not only from radio's regular foreign correspondents but also from the men who made the news did America's radio audience keep abreast of the war's progress. Chamberlain's reply to Hitler and the British Empire's declaration of war went into microphones on September 3, 1939, hooked to world-wide radio circuits. On September 8, 1943, General Dwight D. Eisenhower used radio to announce the unconditional surrender of Italy. Roosevelt, Churchill, and many other leaders broadcast news to the world.

Meantime, radio news facilities at home continued to expand. And advertisers grew increasingly eager for a share in the profits to be derived from radio news sponsorship.

The AP at last concluded that it could no longer ignore the income that sale of radio news would bring. Its bylaws made no provision for radio station membership in the AP; consequently, in 1940, it set up a

---

Sevareid experienced heartbreaks on the first day of World War II. Great Britain had gone to war at 11 A.M. Sevareid had a broadcast from Paris scheduled at noon. Just before airtime he learned that France would officially be "in" at 5 P.M. Though other reporters had the story, censors had refused to clear it; Sevareid's script, however, was passed by a censor without comment. It would be a world-wide scoop. Just as the minute hand approached 12, the studio engineer stuck his head out of his booth and announced that New York had decided to cancel the broadcast.

subsidiary organization, Press Association, Inc. PA put into operation in March of the following year a teleprinter service carrying AP news rewritten for radio, and offered it for outright sale to radio stations. The prohibition on sponsorship was removed.

Many of the stalwarts of the Associated Press were unhappy about the departure. They pointed out that radio stations were buying PA and AP service at prices much lower than the cost of membership to newspapers in direct geographical competition. Nevertheless, the directors of AP were forced to the conclusion that, if income from the sale of news to radio could be used to decrease newspaper membership assessments, they must not turn it down. Moreover, they could not remain deaf to pleas from some newspaper members that owned stations; nor to the credits they heard daylong from their radios: "This news from the United Press" or "International News Service says . . ." Promotionally and competitively, AP had to get into the picture.

By the close of 1941, then, four full-time news services were available to radio newsrooms. Transradio, the veteran, had been in the field since 1934; UP and INS since 1935. Transradio provided a radio news service only; INS, a newspaper report only; UP and PA, both radio and newspaper wires. UP and PA delivered forty words a minute until July of

COMMERCIAL EVENING NETWORK TIME DEVOTED TO
"COMMENTATORS, NEWS AND TALKS"

Winter, 1938–1939	6.7%	Summer, 1939	7.5%
Winter, 1939–1940	10.0	Summer, 1940	11.9
Winter, 1940–1941	12.3	Summer, 1941	12.8
Winter, 1941–1942	10.9	Summer, 1942	15.5
Winter, 1942–1943	16.4	Summer, 1943	18 6
Winter, 1943–1944	18.0	Summer, 1944	17.5
Winter–Spring, 1945	17.9	Summer, 1945	19.3

Figures from *Broadcasting Yearbooks*, 1940-1946.

Radio news on the four major networks increased by more than 300 per cent during the war years. A study made in 1945 by the Duane Jones Company, a radio advertising agency, showed 1,251 hours of news on the nets in 1939, 5,522 hours in 1944. Sponsored news shows accounted for 40 per cent of the time (497) in 1939, for 48 per cent (2,651) in 1944.

1943, when both sped up their radio printers to sixty words a minute, the speed of their newspaper wires.

The growth of radio news to big-time operation brought forth more than once the suggestion that the radio industry should organize its own worldwide newsgathering service. Don M. Taylor, news editor of WLAC-Nashville, pointed out in 1945 that broadcasting already had, in its newsrooms and its widely-spread correspondents, the nucleus of such an organization; and many radio men agreed with him. But the proposal never arrived at the action stage, largely because thorough-going competition with the existing news services would be a gigantic, and a costly, undertaking. Moreover, it is said by many editors, the existing agencies are serving satisfactorily. Why seek a new responsibility?

During this period the number of newspaper-affiliated radio stations had increased only slightly (partly because construction and expansion in the number of radio stations was halted by wartime restrictions). But the FCC had looked with misgivings at what it considered the growing danger of monopolistic ownership of the two major channels of mass communication, and in March of 1941, under the leadership of soft-spoken but hard-driving Chairman James Lawrence Fly (Wendell Willkie once called him "the most dangerous man in the United States —to have on the other side"), the Commission ordered an investigation. Senator Dill, a sponsor of the Radio Act of 1927, had defined the problem, but had not argued it. It had appeared again in 1934, when the Communications Act passed Congress; Representative Otha D. Wearin of Iowa had introduced a bill in 1937 "to prohibit unified and monopolistic control of broadcasting facilities and printed publications" (the bill never reached a vote); in various actions between 1937 and 1941 the FCC had indicated that it believed the problem would

---

A thorough analysis of the relationship between press and radio from 1920 to 1941 is contained in a long manuscript prepared by Ralph D. Casey, director of the University of Minnesota School of Journalism, for the Newspaper-Radio Committee. It puts special emphasis on the attitudes of the ANPA, the news services, and the Press-Radio Bureau. It is available only in the files of the Newspaper-Radio Committee and in Dr. Casey's personal files.

some day demand a hearing. Fly became chairman in July, 1939, and evidence suggests that he considered the dangers in communications monopoly one of the major questions for FCC solution.

Hearings began in July of 1941 and continued spasmodically until January of 1942. Arrayed on the FCC side was a battery of attorneys, researchers, and expert witnesses; on the other the Newspaper-Radio Committee, organized by radio station-owning newspapers, under the chairmanship of Harold Hough of the *Fort Worth Star-Telegram* and stations WBAP and KGKO. The FCC argued that unified ownership of a newspaper and a radio station, especially in cities without newspaper or radio competition, concentrated control of the fare that was offered the public in a manner that was at best threatening to the public interest. Hough's witnesses—newspaper and radio men, constitutional lawyers, researchers in communications—presented the opinion that licenses should be granted to radio stations solely on the merits of their capacity to operate "in the public interest, convenience, and necessity," without reference to their ownership or affiliations; and that the experience of newspapers in serving news to the public meant that they would be better equipped to serve up radio news (in which the FCC was especially interested) than would stations without command of such background and experience.

For two years after the last public hearing, the case remained unsettled. Meantime the injunction set up by the FCC when the hearings opened, withholding new licenses for broadcasting stations from newspaper applicants pending the decision, remained in force. At length, in January, 1944, when it was sharply indicated that the FCC proposed to make the injunction permanent, the Commission suddenly announced that the investigation had been dropped, that no further action would be taken, and that licenses would be granted in the future strictly on the merits of individual applications.

FCC policy in the year and a half following the close of the war, when the number of standard (AM) licenses granted rose by nearly 60 per cent, seemed to favor non-newspaper applicants in contested situations. A storm arose over FCC hesitation to grant an FM license to the *New York Daily News*. The FCC based its hesitation on a questioning of *News* editorial

(*continued on next page*)

An FCC antimonopoly move of a different nature, however, was more effective. In 1941 the Commission ordered that no organization should own more than one network (the Supreme Court approved the order in 1943), and that no two major stations in the same area, or in overlapping areas, should be under one ownership. The first order was directed at NBC's great Red and Blue networks; it resulted in the sale of the Blue to Edward J. Noble in 1943 for $8,000,000 (it had opened on January 5, 1942, as the Blue Network Company, and changed in the summer of 1945 to the American Broadcasting Company), and in NBC's dropping the designation "Red" for its remaining network. The other caused the sale of a number of radio stations to new owners and among the new owners were a considerable percentage of newspapers. In 1944, for example, the *New York Times*, the *New York Post*, the *Washington Post*, and the *Chicago Sun* were among newspapers that became radio station owners. Many of the sales were made at prices fantastically high.

Radio newsmen found that one wartime headache did not require as much aspirin as they feared. The voluntary censorship code for wartime broadcasting banned weather reports, stories of military and

---

policy toward racial and religious minorities. After spectacular hearings during which the Commission was charged with left-wing zealotry and the attempt to censor, a preliminary decision to grant the license to the *News*— favoring this applicant over WLIB-*The New York Post* on the ground that to do so would promote radio competition between the two newspapers—was announced. But late in 1947 the FCC changed its mind and gave the frequency to a Methodist church applicant, saying that such a grant to a non-newspaper applicant would promote diversity in the ownership of media and competition in the dissemination of news and information.

In spite of the apparent policy, the Commission approved a great many newspaper applications in this period. In a Florida case it accepted a local newspaper's application over that of a competitor who owned another station. It granted an FM license to the *Providence Journal* (by a 4 to 3 decision) in spite of vigorous protests by state and municipal officials and official bodies. On October 1, 1946, 204 of the 540 FM licenses granted (37.8 per cent) had gone to newspapers. The 1948 *Broadcasting Yearbook* showed 445 standard and 288 FM stations affiliated with newspaper interests.

naval activity that were not properly released by authorities, some types of on-the-spot broadcasts, and a few other classifications of news. But it did not seriously interfere with most news broadcasting. Byron Price, director of the Office of Censorship, was an ardent devotee of the principle of giving both press and radio the maximum freedom consistent with national security, and successive versions of the code (first issued January 16, 1942; revised June 15, 1942, February 10, 1943, and December 10, 1943) became successively less restrictive. One week after the war in Europe ended—on May 15, 1945—a final revision eliminated entirely restrictions on weather news, types of programs and foreign language broadcasts, and lightened most other provisions. The Office of Censorship, high in its praise of American broadcasting for its voluntary cooperation, said that violations of the code had been few, unimportant, and mostly unintentional. All networks and most individual newsrooms adopted their own codes for safe wartime broadcasting; the NAB on December 19, 1941, had issued a detailed guide with whose suggestions broadcasters were in accord both in principle and practice.

The wartime manpower shortage hampered development of radio newsrooms in many stations. Aware of the increasing shortage, the NAB, the National Association of State Universities, and the American Association of Schools and Departments of Journalism in 1944 undertook to increase the flow of university-trained workers into radio newsrooms, and to heighten their competence. This move led to formation of the Council on Radio Journalism, a body of ten representatives chosen by the NAB and the AASDJ; among immediate Council actions were a statement of standards for education for radio newsroom workers and the erection of a system of "internships" in strong newsrooms for teachers of radio news work (see Appendix B). This, however, was a long-range program, not one to produce overnight results.

Meanwhile, radio news editors unable to employ men more and more frequently employed women. The fact that women in many cases turned out work equal in every way to that of men amazed some of their employers, and opened the door at least by a crack to their postwar employment. But not many of them remained on their jobs two years after V-J Day.

The firm and accepted status of radio news after the war was shown by a number of signposts. Among them:

More than 40 per cent of radio stations said, in response to a *Broadcasting Magazine* survey late in 1946, that they had added or planned to add more news shows to their schedules.

Radio listeners declared in a number of postwar surveys that their general preference among all types of radio programs was the news program. This was usually brought out by some such question as, "If you could have only one of all the types of programs now on the air, which one would you choose?" Without an important dissent, the largest percentages chose news.

The NAB Research Department reported late in 1946 that program listings were carried by newspapers for 96 per cent of all stations—81 per cent of them without charge to stations.

Newspapers throughout the country began to institute regular columns of comment and criticism on radio offerings. Prominent among such columns were those by John Crosby in the *New York Herald Tribune* and John T. McManus in *PM*. More than a hundred dailies and some weeklies carry such columns, among them the *Chicago Sun*, the *Detroit News*, the *Indianapolis Star*, the *San Francisco Chronicle*. . . . Perhaps stimulated by newspaper criticism was the weekly "CBS Views the Press" show inaugurated at WCBS-New York in the summer of 1947—a sharply critical program prepared and broadcast by Don Hollenbeck, CBS commentator, which immediately drew newspaper fire, but also newspaper praise.

The Associated Press in 1947 rewrote its bylaws to permit radio stations to become "associate members" of the AP—a type of membership that gives all the rights enjoyed by newspapers except voting privileges. (This move was in part an outgrowth of the Supreme Court decision enjoining the AP against "monopolistic" practices.) By the end of the year 456 stations had applied for, and been admitted to, associate membership. But E. R. Vadeboncoeur of WSYR-Syracuse and WINR-Binghamton, who was at the time chairman of the NAB News Committee, rejected such "unfair and one-sided" membership on the ground that, without voting privilege, it subjected the associate member to regulation in which he had no voice. A scattering of stations supported this view.

— o —

Technically, commercial radio was forced to a standstill during the war. Though experimental work in electronics made astonishing strides in the war years, much of it was "war-related," and almost none of it reached the commercial broadcasting stations. New construction was halted by priorities and FCC dicta.

In the postwar years, the industry worked full-tilt to recoup lost time. In four fields—facsimile broadcasting, news transmission, television, frequency modulation—of direct importance to news operations, developments began to appear.

Facsimile broadcasting—the process of using radio waves to actuate a receiving set that reproduces graphically, for the eye rather than the ear, printed matter, pictures, and the like—has been heralded as a direct competitor to the newspaper. On February 15, 1938, *Broadcasting Magazine* "published" the first "facsimile newspaper" at the NAB convention in Washington, as an experimental demonstration. A few stations were licensed by the FCC for experimentation. In its early stages facsimile reproduction did not worry newspapers much, for the "printing" it produced was hard to read, hard to handle, and extremely slow in contrast to oral broadcasting. Postwar developments, however, have met many of these deficiencies. In 1946 a group of Eastern radio station-owning newspapers banded together for experiment, and their laboratories succeeded in producing by FM broadcasting four typewriter-paper-sized sheets reproducing pages of a newspaper; the process took fifteen minutes, and the reading quality was "little impaired from the original." FM station WGHF-New York broadcast UP news to facsimile receiving sets in airliners, and one air line planned installation of receivers in all its big planes. In 1947 the *Miami Herald* announced plans for experimental facsimile reproduction of the paper. Early in 1948 WFIL-Philadelphia began regular facsimile news broadcasting.

Though these developments are all in the experimental stage, they suggest future possibilities. Meantime the Bankers Trust Company in New York is using facsimile for interbranch communication. Facsimile is certain to come into general use for specialized reporting such as market news and stock quotations; it may develop much wider importance.

Two new high-speed methods of news transmission appeared within two years after the war. Globe Wireless, Ltd., introduced equipment for sending 6,000 words an hour (in contrast to the usual teletype speed of 3,600 words) by radio. And RCA announced its amazing Ultrafax, which can, "by application of television principles to message transmission," reproduce a million words of copy a minute. Still in the laboratory, Ultrafax's use in news communication remains to be developed.

Television, after years of experiment, made its first public splash in April of 1939, when NBC and RCA put on the first "video" programs coincident with the opening of the New York World's Fair. The war soon put television behind scientists' doors. And television's immediate postwar years were beclouded by disputes over the development of color television, the FCC's allocations of frequencies, and other problems. But by mid-1948 the number of television receiving sets in use was approaching half a million—three-quarters of them in homes. About thirty stations were actually telecasting, and seventy more promised to be on the air by the end of the year.

Dispute in these postwar years as to whether television would become generally effective for newscasting gave way to broad optimism regarding its possibilities. It had already established itself as a prime tool in on-the-spot newscasts—football games, prize fights, parades, inaugurations, horse races (a London newspaper for some years before the war used a television image of important races as a source of racing news). Television carried the Republican and Democratic conventions of 1948, on video's first elaborate network, from Richmond to Boston along the Atlantic coast. Production costs and technical and production difficulties offered unsolved problems in its use in general reporting; but its enthusiastic prophets had no doubt that these would be met.

The news services and the networks both contributed, early in 1948, to meeting them. UP, linked with Acme Newspictures, offered two five-minute spot news-film shows daily, together with additional special features—a combination of newsreels and spot "stills." INS and International News Photos provided newsreel and other pictorial copy for the first daily ten-minute sponsored telenews show. (AP had dabbled briefly with a similar service, but early in 1948 gave it up.) The networks extended their own news-film activities, made contracts with television affiliates, and paid elaborate attention to special events.

The individual station located off the limited television network lines faced the most difficult problem, because of production problems and costs. Telenews offerings made up largely of "still" pictures with dubbed-in voice won few converts. But this was telenews in its infancy. Its development is certain to be rapid; exactly what form it may take not even the television men themselves know.

Frequency modulation—FM—offers vast possibilities for expansion of radio news broadcasting. FM provides better reception than does "standard" broadcasting; with its relatively low area coverage (an FM beam does not often range more than fifty miles) and its high selectivity, it opens the door for thousands of new stations (563 on the air on July 1, 1948, nearly as many more under FCC authorization); its installation and operation costs are usually lower than those of standard broadcasting. Where there are today some hundreds of radio newsrooms, depending heavily on wire services, there may tomorrow be thousands, each in direct "trade area" competition with newspapers. It is significant that the high proportion of newspaper applications for FM licenses in 1941 was one of the impulses behind the FCC investigation of newspaper-radio ownership.

FM operations will not attain full strength until litigation regarding FM patents and licenses to use them is settled, and until radio manufacturers make receiving sets plentiful and inexpensive. But some day, according to many radio men, FM broadcasting may take the lead from AM.

2

Who Listens? And How?

Forty million families maintain homes in the United States. Nearly thirty-eight million of them, about 94 per cent, have radios in their living rooms, and about half of the 94 per cent have "second sets" in bedrooms, rumpus rooms, or somewhere else. Nearly a tenth of the families own portable radios. Nearly a fifth of them have receiving sets in their automobiles.

In other words, there are more than sixty million radio receiving sets in the United States. With an average of two-plus listeners to each set, every man, woman, and child *might* be listening to the radio at one time.

How many of them *do* listen? What determines whether they listen? How do they listen? What do they want from their radios? And what are they given? What effect on listening have such factors as the bulk of the family pay envelope, the geographical areas in which they live, the season of the year, the hour of the day, the environment, their educational background, their sex?

And, especially, what are their attitudes toward radio news?

— o —

Paint yourself a mental picture of an "average" radio listening group. You are certain to put it in a living room. Perhaps you'll see in the picture a man—a grocer, a lawyer, a welder—his wife, and one or two others. It will be evening. Likely not all the "listeners" are listening only—one or more of them may be reading, or darning socks, or playing gin rummy. From time to time one of them may get up and twist the dial, or even shut off the current.

If that's your picture, you've hit it about right. Most radio listening is in the living room. Most of it occurs within the broad reaches of the "middle class" home. More radios are turned on in evenings than in daytime. The average radio audience is about two and a half persons.

Few radios remain tuned to one station for long periods.

The living room picture doesn't, of course, tell the whole story. Radios are also blaring, daylong and often nightlong, in restaurants, barber shops, pool rooms, club lounges, streamlined trains, university Unions. They are turned on in automobiles and even in football stadia where their owners are watching the very touchdown runs being described by announcers sitting a few rows above them. But broadcasting men have learned, from experience and statistics, to think of the living room audience as their prime group of listeners.

That means a number of things. It means, first of all, that the audience is a mass audience—the living rooms for a given program may be on Park Avenue, on a ranch in Arizona, and every place in between. The groups sitting in them include every kind of people. And the essential aim of the radio program, in most cases, must be

---

This discussion summarizes, rather than exhausts, the surveys that have told the radio industry what it knows, statistically and with considerable precision, about the radio audience. Reports of such surveys appear in books, in the trade press, in broadcasters' and advertisers' files, in university libraries, and elsewhere. Every worker with radio programming—including the radio news worker—will profit by acquainting himself with some of them. Among significant books:

Cantril, Hadley, *The Invasion From Mars*. Princeton, N. J., Princeton University Press, 1940.

———, and Allport, Gordon, *The Psychology of Radio*. New York, Harper and Brothers, 1935.

Chappell, M. N., and Hooper, C. E., *Radio Audience Measurement*, New York, Stephen Daye, 1944.

Lazarsfeld, Paul F., *Radio and the Printed Page*. New York, Duell, Sloan and Pearce, 1940.

———, and Stanton, Frank, *Radio Research, 1941*. New York, Duell, Sloan and Pearce, 1941.

———, and ———, *Radio Research, 1942–1943*. New York, Duell, Sloan and Pearce, 1944.

———, and Field, Harry, *The People Look at Radio*. Chapel Hill, N. C., University of North Carolina Press, 1946.

Lumley, F. H., *Measurement in Radio*. Columbus, O., Ohio State University, 1934.

NAB, *Radio Audience Measurement* (pamphlet). Washington, D. C., National Association of Broadcasters, 1946.

to achieve a common denominator—not necessarily the lowest—that will hold appeal for everybody.

And it means that the program must not only hold positive appeal but that, on the negative side, it must avoid offense. More of this, as it applies to news, in Chapter 3.

Not all those living room radios, of course, are turned on. In the evening hours, 6 to 10:30, from January, 1941, to December, 1946, the high monthly averages of sets in use, a little more than 30 per cent, came in December, January, and February; the lows, just under 20 per cent, in July and August. In daytime during the same years, the highs of about 17 per cent came in winter, the lows of about 13 per cent in summer.

The twin peaks of radio listening to given programs occurred on December 9, 1941, just after Pearl Harbor, and on February 23, 1942. On each occasion, each at 10 P.M. EWT, the program was a speech by President Roosevelt. The Hooper rating for each speech was nearly 80 (eight of every ten sets tuned to it). The daytime record is also held by FDR—a 65 rating for his appeal for declaration of war on Japan at noon of December 8, 1941. These percentages are far out of line with ordinary experience. Even Mr. Roosevelt, the most powerful attraction American radio has known, more commonly drew ratings in the 40's and 50's. President Truman's highest rating was 47.4 (April 17, 1945, at 8:30 P.M., just after Mr. Roosevelt's death); Winston Churchill's best was 45. The most successful sponsored network programs in the evenings, on the same basis, rarely surpass 40; fewer than a fifth of such programs average above 20.

Translating ratings into terms of total audience is a difficult business. It involves not only the percentage of respondents, but also the sizes of individual audiences. The Hooper organization figures that Mr. Roosevelt's two peak audiences were in the neighborhood of sixty million adults, with an undetermined number of younger listeners—

The Hooper rating is "the percentage of total calls in which the respondents report that they are listening to a given program being broadcast at that time." If 1,000 calls are made during a fifteen-minute period, and 150 respondents report themselves listening to a single program on the air in the period, the rating of the program is 15.

perhaps half the population of the nation.

These were national audiences, as are those of the network shows. Moreover, they were without competition—all networks were broadcasting them. An audience for a one-network program is almost certain to be smaller. That for a non-network, local program is relatively tiny.

Nevertheless, such a program rarely attracts an audience numbered in less than thousands. If it does, it is jerked in a hurry. An essential fact about radio broadcasting is that it is *broad*casting—that it is aimed at a mass audience.

The ratings point up two other facts: That radio audiences are larger in the evening than in the daytime; and that they are larger in winter than in summer.

Both facts relate to the hours at which the living room is likely to be best populated. In summers, the world gets out of doors. In winters, it stays home. Listeners are more likely to be at home in the evenings than in the daytime. Sunday evenings have the largest living room groups. Advertisers know this, and they also know which other evenings are "best." They buy radio time accordingly.

Many factors cause temporary variations in audience size. During the war gasoline rationing increased living room populations. But heavy employment on a round-the-clock basis, bulging incomes, growth of the armed forces, and obsolescence, disrepair, or unavailability of receiving sets decreased them.

Spectacular news events always build audiences. On the evening of December 7, 1941, between 7 and 10:30 o'clock the average of sets in use was 47.2; on D-Day, June 6, 1944, it was 40.7. On the evening of November 7, 1944—day of the Roosevelt-Dewey election—it was 50, with a peak between 9 and 10 o'clock of 56.6. Morning listening on August 10, 1945—V-J Day—was double that of a normal morning; evening of the same day was 65 per cent above normal.

At the end of 1943 the curves of sets in use and of "available audience," which had risen fairly steadily since Pearl Harbor, with seasonable variations, began to level off, and through 1944 radio audiences were somewhat smaller than in 1943. In 1945, thanks largely to such events as the death of Mr. Roosevelt, V-E Day, and V-J Day, they rose slightly. In 1946, the war over, another mild decline in sets in use appeared. (Hooper experts said that disruption in radio-listening habits growing out of return of daylight-saving time was in some degree responsible for the decline.)

The *manner* of living room listening is something for radio writers to think about. Often a program is tuned into a living room by one member of a family over the protest of other members. This means that some ears may be glued to the radio while others within its reach may be sealed against it, or at best listening casually. Many housewives keep radios going all day, as they work at household tasks, but actually *hear* little of what is broadcast. Some listening is purposeful and aware, but much is aimless.

Listening to radio news is likely to be purposeful and concentrated. Many thousands of listeners tune to news programs only, and listen carefully. That any listener *must* listen carefully if he is to *hear* a program is a matter to be discussed more fully later.

Several other factors are of importance in determining the size of the audience for any given program: What the audience measurement men call "economic level," what they call "cultural level," sex, age, and geographical situation.

On the whole, homes at the higher economic levels—those of high rental values, those whose pay envelopes are fattest—are least likely to listen to their radios (though they are the homes most likely to have second and third receiving sets). These are the homes whose occupants can most easily indulge in other forms of recreation. The listening pattern follows the economic pattern faithfully, but in inverse order— the lower the living standard, the higher the amount of radio listening. Studies indicate that this holds true down to the lowest income level, at which listening decreases slightly in contrast to the level just above— perhaps because homes at this level are most likely to be among the small percentage not equipped with radios.

The cultural level pattern follows the same outline. In general, men and women with college degrees listen less frequently, and for shorter periods, than those without them; those who have been through high school listen less than those who haven't; those with less than high school education are at the top of the listening scale. It is likely that these generalizations apply also to those who, without extensive formal education, have substituted "cultural" experience and personal learning for schooling; but no usable scale for identifying such individuals has been devised.

It has also been found—as would be expected—that the better educated (which is the minority) constitute the most likely audience for "serious" programs: Symphony music, sophisticated shows like "Information Please," discussion programs like "Town Meeting of the Air" and the "Chicago Round Table," erudite news commentators like Raymond Swing. But it does not follow that they constitute the largest portion of audiences for such shows. Their total number is smaller than that of those down the cultural ladder, and a higher percentage of listenership among them may amount to a smaller total than a lower percentage of a larger group.

The factor of *where* the listener lives is significant in two major directions: his section of the country, and his placement according to the urban-rural classification. Stations broadcasting for their own regions only attempt to suit programs to the particular tastes and needs of their listeners; nationally-broadcast shows must run the chance that some areas will be more receptive than others. Added to this is the element of time-differential. The program put on a national hook-up at 9 P.M. in New York goes into Pacific coast homes at 6 P.M.; that from Hollywood at 9 P.M. finds Atlantic seaboard listeners in bed at midnight. (Often programs facing this problem are not used by sections of a network where the time-differential is unfavorable, but are re-broadcast at more opportune times. One network, ABC, has an elaborate rebroadcast schedule to meet the difficulty.)

There is marked difference in the program preferences of urban and rural listeners. NBC's Farm and Home Hour, designed especially for farm families, is an obvious recognition of this variable; but the differences in taste affect response to many other types of programs. Moreover, rural audiences have been shown to run proportionately larger in the daytime than those in the cities, and proportionately smaller in the evening.

Sex produces another variable: women listen more than men, and to different programs. Age, too: those under 40, on the whole, listen more than those over 40.

What Do They Want?

What do listeners want to listen to?

A guide from which general conclusions can be drawn is the amount of sponsored evening network time devoted to various categories of programs. These are the shows offered when the radio audience is largest; they are the shows that advertisers are willing to gamble millions on. The advertisers' offerings undoubtedly lag somewhat behind audience tastes; they are subject to the whim of sponsors, and to sponsors' occasional inability to develop the types of offerings they might prefer. But on the whole they represent a considered judgment as to what the living room audiences will take—a judgment backed in many cases by highly intricate, expensive, and reliable audience measurement.

Evening network advertisers, as shown in the accompanying table, have put a good half of their money down on plays and variety shows: plays as presented by the Lux Radio Theatre (the most consistently successful of all such programs), the Screen Guild Players, Mercury Theatre (melodrama, comedy, serial drama, serious "unit-drama"); and variety shows such as Fibber McGee and Molly, Bergen and McCarthy, Jack Benny, Bob Hope.

TYPES OF PROGRAMS FOR WHICH SPONSORS PAY NETWORK RATES

These figures show the percentages of sponsored evening network time devoted to seven broad classifications of programs. Each column represents the period from October of one year through September of the next. The figures are approximations drawn from Cooperative Analysis of Broadcasting charts published in *Broadcasting Yearbooks*, 1939 to 1945.

Program Type	1937–1938	1938–1939	1939–1940	1940–1941	1941–1942	1942–1943	1943–1944
Dramatic shows	27.0	29.0	26.5	28.2	30 4	29.0	27.8
Variety shows	26.6	25.8	23.4	17.6	20.6	18.8	19.1
Audience participation	8.6	14.6	18.0	21.1	16.0	15.5	11.1
News, commentators, talks	12.0	7.0	11.0	12.6	13.2	17.5	17.8
Popular music	17.9	18.2	10.9	12.0	11.5	11.5	12.8
Familiar music	*	*	6.9	5.0	5.6	5.6	4 9
Serious music	7.9	5.4	3.3	3.5	2.7	2.1	3.2

* Familiar music included under popular music.

Third in the list for the seven-year period is the audience participation show—"Take It or Leave It," Kay Kyser, Dr. Quiz. Fourth comes the "news, commentator, talks" category—Winchell, Elmer Davis, Fulton Lewis, Heatter, Lowell Thomas. Lowest in the list are the music categories: popular music as represented by the Hit Parade, Kraft Music Hall, Fitch Bandwagon; familiar or oldtime music and classical and semiclassical music at the bottom.

Analysis of the table shows that the percentage of dramatic shows remains astonishingly constant over the years; that variety shows and all types of music show a gradual decline; that audience participation shows started low, climbed to a peak, and slipped badly; and that shows relating to news, with one departure from pattern, increased steadily until, in the final two years, they held a healthy third place. (Figures computed on a somewhat different basis showed substantially the same relationships for succeeding years.)

The rise of audience-interest during the war years is suggested by a system of indexing news-listening developed by C. E. Hooper. Hooper arrives at his index by multiplying the average rating of news programs by the number of sponsored broadcast hours. Taking the 1940 index as a base of 100 per cent, Hooper finds the indices rising to 433 in 1943, then falling to 412 in 144, 380 in 1945, 258 in 1946, and 261 in 1947. Though there are fallacies in this "rating"—it does not give weight, for example, to the fact that unsponsored news shows are not included—it indicates that opportunity for news-listening as well as the amount of news-listening are far higher after the war than before.

Another type of rating is that made by various surveys of listenership to individual shows. The CAB ratings, made annually for two decades, consistently showed variety programs as attracting the largest audiences. Jack Benny and the Fibber McGee and Molly show have ranked highest over the years, with Bob Hope, Charlie McCarthy, and Fred Allen near them. The remainder of the first ten among sponsored evening network shows, by this rating, is usually made up of dramatic and popular music programs. But in the summer of 1943, when the top variety shows were on vacation, an audience participation show ranked fourth, and Walter Winchell's news broadcast sneaked into tenth position; it held this place through the 1943–1944 winter months, and in the summers of 1944 and 1945 went to first place. Three other news shows made the summer lists of leaders in 1944 and 1945—Lowell Thomas, "March of Time," and Gabriel Heatter.

Differing forms of audience measurement show differing results. An early survey reported by Cantril and Allport showed familiar music to be most popular with the average audience, popular music second, and news third. And, as already reported in Chapter 1, a number of surveys during the war years or just after the war—conducted by the National Opinion Research Center at Denver, by the Department of Agriculture, by CBS, and by a number of other agencies which may be considered both disinterested and accurate—showed news programs as the type of fare most in demand among radio audiences.

What all these varying data appear to show is that entertainment—preferably light entertainment—remains the ranking attraction to the average radio listener. But there is no doubt that, as *Radio Audience Measurement* cautiously puts it, "the growth of the news program since the beginning of 1940 is one of the more remarkable phenomena in radio broadcasting." The rise of the news or news-related program in sponsored evening network time (and a like rise in the daily schedules of virtually every individual station in America) show radio- and advertiser-knowledge that news attracts mass audiences. Indeed, radio time salesmen have complained that prospective buyers clamor for more news shows than could possibly be put on the air.

This underlines an important factor: that there is a very definite ceiling on the number of news shows any one station, or network, can present. An entire evening might be devoted to variety shows, or musical shows, or drama, without danger of repetition in anything more than general pattern. Details would vary widely. But there is only so much news available; all newsrooms get it from the same sources; even in a time of fast-breaking war news the change from one hour to the next is usually minor. Though radio newsrooms are learning to vary presentation patterns, they cannot vary substance much if news shows follow closely one upon the other.

In 1937 NBC devoted 2.8 per cent of its total program hours to news. In 1944 the percentage was 26.4. In 1945 CBS devoted 26.9 per cent of its more than 28,000 network shows to news and sports.

In spite of this limitation, however, radio news presentation has become a big business. And this is a direct reflection of the vital interest of listeners in what's going on in the world. Whether the interest will always remain at wartime and postwar heights is a matter for speculation. That radio programming must consider news heavily in its plans is not speculative at all.

Who Are the Listeners?

Who listens to radio news?

An easy answer is "everybody." It's an answer that, in broad terms, is decently accurate. That storied trio, the butcher, the baker, and the candle-stick maker, all turn on the morning news on the way to put out the cat, listen to it casually as they gulp their noon pork and beans, hurry home in the late afternoon to catch it along with rhapsodies over vitamin tablets, and delay going to bed until the night newscast has come in. So, within the variations of their orbits, do the banker, the farmer, the professor, and the minister. So do their wives, sons, daughters, and maiden aunts. Some, it is true, skip this broadcast or that; some flee from Winchell but hang on Davis's every word (or vice versa). But just about everybody is likely to pick up some radio news every day.

Within the frame of this broad generalization, there are ascertainable differences. Many of them have been pinned down by reliable audience-measurement methods, others are being studied as fast as researchers can gather data and analyze them. In general, they follow the patterns suggested in this chapter.

Many studies of these questions have used a comparison of newspapers with radio as a source of news. Qualitatively, the radio newscast has often come out second best. The lower an individual's economic or cultural level, or the younger he is (and probably, therefore, the less informed), the more likely he is to depend on radio for his news. The evidence shows that those who have a sound orientation in current affairs—those who do more than the average amount of reading, who have more than high school education, whose occupations or environments throw them into physical or intellectual contact with the streams of major affairs—rely less on radio than do the less

29461

sophisticated. Seventh and eighth-grade students, just beginning an acquaintance with news, depend heavily on radio; by the time they become high school seniors, they have started to turn to other news media.

A corollary of this fact is that the upper and older levels on these scales are more likely to provide the audiences for the more "serious" news programs.

Quantitatively, the picture is not so clear. In 1939 a *Fortune* survey showed 63.8 per cent of the national population claiming newspapers as the source of most of its news, 25.4 per cent claiming radio. But a study by the National Opinion Research Center in 1945 (conducted for the NAB), showed 61 per cent getting most of its news by radio, 35 per cent getting most news from newspapers. A second NORC-NAB survey in 1947 showed a third set of figures: 48 per cent favoring the newspaper, 44 per cent the radio. No one can say precisely how these varying findings should be interpreted. It seems likely, however, that the peak of interest in radio as a news purveyor in 1945 may be attributed to broadcasting's dramatic development as a war news medium.

The surveys justify another inference. The *Fortune* survey shows those at the upper economic levels depending more heavily on newspapers than on radio news for their current information; the NORC surveys show a tendency among the better-educated to depend more on newspaper than on radio. That is to say, the more fortunate among radio listeners—those well-fortified with the world's goods, those who are relatively well-educated and well-informed—are likely to turn with *comparative* infrequency to radio news. On the other hand, radio is more likely to be preferred as a purveyor of news among those who for whatever reason—age, economic or cultural opportunity, home environment—have been less exposed to stimulative influences or to the labor of thinking.

The surveys present evidence on another score—evidence that has given the newspapers severe cervical pains. Respondents in each survey showed a marked lack of confidence in newspaper responsibility, in contrast to that of radio. Heavy majorities realized that radio has a time advantage in delivering news speedily to the consumer, and two-thirds to four-fifths that the newspaper gives the news more fully. But on the question of prejudice in the news, 17.1 per cent of the *Fortune* respondents and 16 per cent of the first NORC believe the newspaper "freer from prejudice" (*Fortune*) or "fairest, most unbiased" (NORC); 49.7 per cent of *Fortune* respondents and 57 per cent of NORC give the palm to radio news. Putting the question another way, the second NORC survey found 79 per cent calling radio "generally fair," 55 per cent applying the term to the press.

In what it called the "showdown," *Fortune* asked, "If you had heard conflicting versions of the same story from these sources, which would you be most likely to believe?" Radio drew a 40.3 per cent vote (radio press bulletin, 22.7; radio commentator, 17.6). Newspapers held the prime confidence of 26.9 per cent (editorial, 12.4; news story, 11.1; columnist, 3.4). "An authority you heard speak" was the choice of 13 per cent; 11.6 per cent said that it "depends on paper, writer, or speaker"; and 8.2 per cent offered no opinion. . . . The NORC survey offers no data on this point.

On these showings, and within the limitations suggested, radio news appears to have an amazingly strong hold on public confidence. Whether it deserves this confidence, in contrast to that placed in its chief rival in the news field, is a matter to be discussed in Chapter 3.

Methods of Audience Study

Radio broadcasting in the United States is only a little more than a quarter of a century old. But it has advanced more rapidly than most of the other major media of mass communication in seeking and find-ing information about the appeal of its offerings and the composition and attitudes of its audiences. This is partly due to the fact that radio is still young and aggressive, bound by few traditional practices or

---

The "news-environment"—the nature and importance of current news—has a marked impact on listener-attitudes toward radio news and news-paper news. Surveys by the Office of Radio Research in 1937 and 1938 showed that, in 1937—a time of "normal" news—fewer than half the popu-lation preferred radio to newspapers as news media. But in October, 1938—just after Munich—more than two-thirds expressed a preference for radio news.

fettering rules-of-thumb, as public opinion researchers and statisticians were developing techniques of sampling and other methods of gathering such data. It is partly due to the challenging novelty and importance of radio as a social influence—a factor that turned the special attention of social scientists to it. It grows partly from the violent competitive battle into which broadcasting was plunged, both within the industry and with other media—a battle which forced radio as a whole, as well as its component elements, to assemble batteries of fact as weapons for the fray.

The statistical and "scientific" knowledge about radio comes from three principal sources: the commercial agencies set up to provide data; the networks and smaller elements within the industry; and a number of disinterested agencies which have studied, or are studying, broadcasting as a social phenomenon.

The commercial agencies, whose function is to furnish to those who buy or sell time factual information to aid them in making their efforts more effective, use five principal methods of investigation:

1 The "coincidental method," in which telephone interviewers seek information about responses to particular programs while they are on the air. Limited by the fact that it reaches only telephone homes in cities, it is nevertheless widely relied on as a means of gathering many types of information. Chief agent in developing this method has been C. E. Hooper, Inc. (formerly Clark-Hooper, Inc.), whose "Hooperatings" are generally used by radio stations as well as by advertisers.

2 The personal interview survey, which sends interviewers to a selected sample of listeners. This method, usually employed by such agencies as Roper and Gallup as well as by many others, permits a thoroughly accurate sampling of audience by the cross-section method; it also makes it possible to ask more questions than can usually be asked by the telephone method. It is, however, more expensive and more difficult to conduct than the telephone method; and it usually entails "recall" questioning (questions about programs off the air by the time the survey is taken) rather than coincidental questioning.

3 The mail survey, which seeks information from an audience sample by the use of mail questionnaires. The mail survey is more difficult to "control" than the personal interview survey; often elaborate follow-up campaigns are necessary to insure that the sampling is accurately representative.

4 The mechanical recorder, which is a device attached to a radio receiver to make a permanent record of the hours and minutes during which

the receiver is turned on and the wave lengths to which it is tuned. Several firms, principal among them the A. C. Nielsen Company, have used such recorders placed in a large number of radio homes—a "fixed sample"—to gather information.

5 The "panel" or "listener diary" method, by which a fixed sample of radio listeners keeps formalized records of its radio listening and submits them at stated intervals to the agency employing it.

The telephone-recall method, employed for a number of years by the Cooperative Analysis of Broadcasting (an organization formed by the Association of National Advertisers and the American Association of Advertising Agencies), has been displaced by the coincidental and other methods.

A new device announced late in 1947 by CBS, however, may supersede all earlier methods: the "instantaneous audience measurement service," an application of radar which CBS says will "measure and report the audience to a broadcast instantaneously on a minute-to-minute basis at the very moment of listening." This electronic device will provide, for each radio home in a selected sample, information on when the set is in use, what program is being listened to, the income level of the listening home, and the city-town-or-farm location of the home.

Leader among the "disinterested agencies" is the Bureau of Applied Social Research (formerly the Office of Radio Research), under Paul F. Lazarsfeld at Columbia University. The Bureau has, in addition to using many of the methods described above and comparing their results with those of studies made for other purposes and by other methods—studies of reading at different levels, for instance—developed a "program analyzer" by which groups of listeners can record electrically their likes and dislikes in specific programs, second by second. The Bureau has contributed enormously valuable information to the knowledge of broadcasting.

— o —

Few radio stations, and even fewer radio newsrooms, are in position to undertake elaborate or costly audience research projects. Yet they have questions that must be answered if they are to render satisfactory service: How wide are their audiences? What types of news hold particular appeal for their particular listeners? Which of their news announcers are most effective? Should they extend, or reduce, their regional coverage? And so on. Fortunately, answers to most such problems can be gained by methods of audience investigation that are neither too expensive nor too difficult.

Most likely to yield dependable results is the personal interview study, using a carefully-built cross-section sample. This method demands skillful selection and training of interviewers, skillful questionnaire construction (as do all methods), and rather more time and more money than most of the other methods. Personal interviews of a random sample—at every third or fourth house, for instance—will yield "reliable results for most situations," according to audience research experts, and the method eliminates the need for building a cross-section sample.

Random or saturation mail surveys—usually the least expensive type—may also bring useful information, accurate enough to serve at least as general guides. It is possible, too, for most stations to set up listener panels—at higher cost, but with less effort after the panel is established, and with generally sound findings. Note that any survey may be broad in its purposes—it need not be limited to questions dealing with news programming, but may cover other matters as well.

Finally, day-to-day operations provide considerable information of value. "Questions often come up that the staff tries to answer," says one expert. "In answering them, the staff is doing an elementary job of research." Telephone calls and mail tell a newsroom a good deal about audience tastes and reactions. And the perceptive newsman will be able to turn most personal contacts, on duty and off, to his purposes. Laymen know all about how news should be handled, and sometimes what they know is stimulating or even accurate.

3

Is Radio News "Different"?

Consider Citizen N and Citizen R, two everyday Americans. Both profess an interest in the news—both want to know who's leading the American League, what the mayor's commission is doing about juvenile delinquency, what's happening in Paris, Moscow, and Timbuktu. Both have opinions, and both express them vociferously on occasion.

Citizen N is a confirmed follower of the press. At breakfast in the morning, in his living room in the evening, he sits and pages through his paper, skipping here and reading thoroughly there. The radio? "Waste of time," snorts Citizen N. "It's all in the paper. Anyway, I want my news when I want it—not when they decide to give it to me. . . ."

Next door Citizen R depends on the radio (as N, on summer evenings, all too well knows). Morning, noon, and night he tunes to news broadcasts—perhaps adds his favorite commentator most evenings. "Gives me all I need to know," he tells N. "Gives it to me boiled down, hotter than newspaper news. And I usually fix my kids' toys, or something, while I'm listening. . . ."

Both N and R have talking points. Each medium can do things the other can't. The advantages, or utilities, of one can best be considered alongside those of the other. What are the comparable and contrasting characteristics of the two?

The Radio	The Newspaper
Has much greater speed. Can put "hot" news into homes seconds after it becomes available.	Is slower—minutes slower, if a deadline is near; hours slower, if delivery time is long. But often has extra time for checking facts, developing "angles."
Presents most news in condensed style, and in relatively broad strokes.	Presents most news more fully, and with far more specific detail.

55

Can present some news as it happens—sports events, catastrophes, speeches, and so on. (This means fuller coverage, in some cases, than the press offers.)	Can do nothing of the kind. But has the function radio lacks of serving as contemporary historian, providing a permanent record of current affairs.
Offers limited selectivity of news—the listener takes what radio presents, when it presents it.	Offers the reader wide choice as to which news he shall read, how much news he shall read and when he shall read it.
Operates under "taboos" which cut down or eliminate certain types of news.	Offers a wider variety of news, including some types usually not broadcast.
Delivers its news to a family or small-group audience, usually in the living room.	Delivers its news to but one reader at a time.
Offers only about 2,000 words of news at a time. Offers only broad departmentalization within one news period. (Offers women's programs, sports programs, and so on at different periods.)	Offers ten to thirty times as many words, with wide departmentalization (including entertainment and opinion as well as news), in one issue, open to instant reader selection.
Can dramatize news, thereby adding to its effectiveness, both through production devices and use of the human voice.	Has only the relatively static device of printed words and pictures to achieve dramatic effect.

(Both radio and the newspaper can, and on occasion do, over-dramatize or "sensationalize" news. But radio, because of the emotional power of the human voice and of its dramatic devices, may be more stimulative—and so must be more careful—than the newspaper.)

Cannot be readily "checked back." Radio news is evanescent—it vanishes the instant it is broadcast.	Is available for reading, re-reading, and reference at any time.
Can be heard with little effort. Does not require the listener's undivided attention.	Requires concentration by the reader, and the mental effort of selection.
Is ordinarily directed at a mass audience. Radio news usually avoids specialized appeal or terminology.	Can be directed to special groups within the mass audience (women, businessmen, sports fans, etc.).
Is readily subject to misunderstanding or misinterpretation.	Is less readily subject to misunderstanding.

Citizen N, recognizing certain advantages of radio over the press, nevertheless thinks the press serves him better than radio can. He wants detail of the news. He's the kind of reader who, when a war is on, likes to keep a map, complete with colored flags, to show changes on the battle line. He thinks it important to study carefully the language of the Republicans' taxation plank—a twenty-five-word condensation isn't enough. And he reserves time to find out how Joe diMaggio is hitting, what his favorite movie critic thinks of Bette Davis's latest anguish, where General Motors stands on the market.

Citizen R, on the other hand, finds it satisfactory to get the news in broad strokes, in general sweep. Detail annoys and perhaps confuses him. There's a death-dealing flood on some Chinese river with a funny name—what difference how you spell it, when you can't even pronounce it? There's another Cabinet row on in Washington, between agriculture and commerce this time—or is it agriculture and labor? And so on.

In short, each news medium performs its peculiar service. Newspaper publishers have grown well beyond the fear that radio news will supplant their own. It is now clear that both, like airplanes and Pullman cars, are here to stay, each serving its own millions. Not mutually exclusive millions—they overlap and intermingle.

And if the cynical be inclined to argue that Citizen R, depending primarily on radio, cannot hope to be fully informed, that his radio simply is not adequate to keep him *au courant*, let it be pointed out that radio brings at least an overview of the news to thousands of thousands who might otherwise go quite uninformed; that all the evidence shows the tendency for the comparatively unsophisticated Citizen R to learn to supplement his radio-gained information by turning to his newspaper, *Time, Newsweek,* and other more detailed sources; and that the rise of newspaper circulations to new peaks has followed closely, if not causally, upon the rise of radio news as a national phenomenon.

The "Living Room Audience"

All of which is to say that Citizen R and his millions of kin constitute a special kind of audience. Radio news editors have learned to take into account a number of particular characteristics of this audience, and to edit news to accommodate them.

Of prime importance is the fact that the audience sits in its living room. This means, in the eyes of most radio news editors, that the newscast must bring into the living room only what its occupants would like to have there. Citizen R is no prude. He may exchange whispered stories with the boys at the office. But he doesn't repeat them in the family circle. And he's especially careful about his language, and the topics he and Mrs. R discuss, when Junior is in the room.

Consequently many radio newsrooms have put a severe limitation on news that involves sex acts or sex crimes. "Rape" and like words are often blacked out of the radio vocabulary; sometimes newspaper circumlocutions such as "statutory crime" are thought permissible. (Fortunately, the trend both in the press and on the air is in the direction of more honest, more exact, and less suggestive language—largely because the American public is becoming more sophisticated.)

This does not mean that sex news is omitted entirely, but rather that it is handled with restraint. For example: In 1943 the press devoted many columns to intimate detail of the trial of Charlie Chaplin on a charge of violation of the Mann Act. WCCO-Minneapolis and KMBC-Kansas City, both of which conduct extensive newsroom operations, handled the story under a policy that is fairly typical of the radio approach to this kind of news. Paraphrased, it says: "Put on the air a brief, unemotional story saying that such-and-such a sensational event has occurred; give it little or no attention during the course of investigation or trial unless there are strikingly important developments; use a brief story when the case is closed."

News of social maladjustment sometimes gets from radio what some critics consider unduly short shrift under the policies here described. Juvenile delinquency, divorce, news of violence are often "played down" by radio under such policies' guidance. There are critics—ranging from competent social psychologists to well-meaning if not always well-informed laymen—who praise both radio and the press for following this pattern, on the assumption that concealing such news will remove a stimulus to the weak-willed. On the opposite side are those who say that social cankers rarely receive therapy until the public becomes abundantly aware of them.

Growing from a similar notion—that it is not a matter for family-group consumption—is a limitation on radio news that might be considered offensive because of bloody detail. Gory specifications of accidents are usually barred. Indeed, the words "gore" and "blood" are sometimes on the proscribed list.

Radio editors also eliminate a good deal of news on a different ground—that it is not of general interest. The living room audience is, to repeat, a mass audience. The news selected for it must be that—within limitations such as those already suggested—of widest appeal. And that means that, on the whole, it must be news of considerable importance, or news of high intrinsic human interest.

Another factor of importance is the geographic distribution of the audience. Radio stations as a rule cover more area than do newspapers. The average smaller daily newspaper has a rather tightly-limited trade area—usually a few counties; its news selection is conditioned by this consideration. A radio station in the same city has a signal reaching perhaps half a state. The newspaper serves its area by devoting many columns to local or regional news; the radio station, because its area is larger and its news "space" smaller, cannot do as much with such news. It depends heavily, therefore, on national and international news from its wire service, and devotes relatively less attention to local and regional matters.

Not that radio newsmen ignore the local and regional. Chapter 8 describes the growing interest in news of this type, following World War II. It is an interest that will receive an immense stimulus as FM stations spread over the country, with coverage-areas much more nearly the dimensions of newspaper trade areas (in some cases they will be smaller). A fact which, it may be noted, will serve to increase newspaper-radio news competition.

The Office of Radio Research, in 1938, made a study comparing the coverage of different types of news by Cincinnati newspapers and radio stations. In only one field did radio, during a five-day period, offer more individual "items" than the newspapers: the field of foreign news and comments. Here the ratio was 54 newspaper stories to 100 radio stories. In government and political news, the ratio was 157 newspaper stories to 100 radio; in natural events and disasters, 220 to 100; in crime and corruption, 233 to 100; and on down the list through economic news (including stock markets), news of "social aspects," science and education news to those that received least attention from radio: religious news, art and education news, and "family" news. Newspapers offered more than three times as many stories as did radio in the five days. No comparison of the local and regional sources of stories was made.

Looking at these figures in another way, radio's coverage of foreign news and comments becomes even more significant. Radio presented almost six times as large a *proportion* of stories of this type as the newspapers—nearly 25 per cent of its total of 1,799 stories. It devoted a 40 per cent larger *proportion* of its space to natural events and disasters, and to crime and corruption, than did newspapers.

This study—exploratory rather than final—shows the trend of radio news emphasis before Munich. Had it been repeated or extended during the war, it seems certain that the percentage of radio news devoted to the foreign scene would have risen. And the percentage would probably rise if the figures were based on radio *time*—a more difficult statistic to pin down—in contrast to newspaper *space*.

But the trend would just as certainly have been in the other direction if the study had been made two years after the war. It seems unlikely, however, that the relationship would have been reversed.

Another characteristic of the radio audience that conditions selection of news for it is that it is an "ear-audience" rather than an "eye-audience." News that is inherently "heavy," news that involves sums of money, statistics, elaborate geographical detail, is difficult to present intelligibly for the ear. Some stories, even important ones, that depend on material of this kind are kept off the air for no other reason.

Allied to this is the fact that the ear is often an exceedingly inaccurate reporter. A radio station in an area with heavy Scandinavian-American population once proved this when it broadcast a story telling of the death of, let us say, a certain Elmer Peterson. Within minutes after the broadcast it received no less than fifteen telephone calls, wires, or personal visits from individuals shocked to learn of the death of "John Peterson," or "William Peterson," or "Elmer Johnson," or an "Elmer Peterson" who wasn't the right one—this in spite of the fact that the dead man had been thoroughly identified. Ears don't always hear the words the announcer says. For this reason, many radio stations during the war decided not to broadcast casualty lists.

That this ear-characteristic affects even more importantly the *manner* of radio news presentation is discussed in Chapter 5.

Finally, radio newsmen have learned to avoid the ever-present temptation to "hop up" their stories—to overemphasize the sensational angle, even to take advantage of the genuinely lurid that sometimes appears in the news. The reasons: Overemphasis, sensationalizing (as distinguished from calm, factual presentation) is dishonest reporting; the listener with his inaccurate ear is likely to add his own vivid imagination to sensational fact and come out with a vastly distorted view of the news; and overcolored news, by newspaper as well as radio, is almost certain to boomerang when the listener who knows the true facts compares them to the too-dramatic story he has just heard.

Facts Are Facts—or Are They?

It is important to remember, in considering the differences between newspaper and radio news, that at base it all comes from the same sources, by the same or similar channels. News itself is unequivocal. It is a precise and unalterable set of facts. When a fire occurs, it breaks out at one spot, from one (perhaps complex) cause; it starts at a given second, grows to a given magnitude, engulfs a definite number of combustibles, is "brought under control" at a given time by the measurable efforts of a certain number of identifiable fire companies. The same thing is true of a wedding, a wake, or a war. The facts themselves do not vary.

What may—almost always does—vary is the competence, the accuracy, the energy, the passion with which any set of facts is reported. This is a matter of human frailty. Let two men walk in conversation through a room in which ten observers are sitting, and ask the ten immediately afterward to write precise reports of the event. You will get ten reports that differ at the very least in minor detail, and more likely on major points. You may be told that both men were smoking, that neither was smoking, that one was smoking. You will get differing descriptions of their clothing, their remarks, their heights, the order in which they went through the doorway.

If one of your ten were a trained observer—say a newspaper or radio reporter, or a detective—the chances are good that his report would most nearly hit all the nails on the head, though even he may have struck some glancing blows. And if there were two reporters present, their accounts would likely most nearly resemble each other.

Yet you know that the facts were unchanging, that all observers had the same chance to observe.

The facts—the news—that newspapers and radio alike present to their audiences, subject to these human failings, are to large degree the same. As Chapter 1 shows, radio and newspapers receive most of their nonlocal news through the same channels—chiefly the UP, the AP, and INS. With few exceptions, all these channels offer accounts based on the same sets of facts: They operate on like principles, like backgrounds of experience, and like bases for news judgments; and all these combine to guide them to cover the same news events. When Congress convenes, a streamliner piles up, a tornado sweeps a township, or a movie star gets a divorce (oddly enough, this still comes under the head of news), reporters from all the press services gather information from the same sources and report it to both radio and newspapers.

To repeat: Newspapers and radio have the same grist for their respective mills. More than that: Radio stations often have identical grist.

The grist is not, of course, always ground up into the same sort of flour, nor does it often come out of the ovens in identical cakes. What the competent AP reporter sees at the opening of Congress, what he hears and what he thinks important are likely to differ at least mildly in form and emphasis from what his equally competent UP rival grinds out of his typewriter. One man's very skill with words may be enough

---

Until about 1945, it was common to hear radio newsmen speak of "processing" news for radio, and to call themselves "news processors." The NAB radio news committee decided that the term "process"—drawn from manufacturing and appropriated widely by the armed forces—was spurious in the newsroom, which had its own traditional terminology. On the committee's urging, radio learned quickly to return to "news editing," "news editors," and so on.

greater, or smaller, than another's to affect the comparative fidelity and authority of his reporting. And when the story gets to the newspaper, it is subjected to additional human variables: The judgment and craftsmanship of the paper's editors, the type and style selected for headlines, the position the piece is given in the paper.

For radio, the story is subject to two additional variables before it reaches its audience. Written originally by the reporter for newspaper use, it is then rewritten by a radio wire editor for radio purpose—and perhaps in the process subjected to subtle and unintentional mutations. When it is taken off the printer in the radio station, it is subjected to a process of selection, cutting, and emphasis analogous to the editing in a newspaper office. And then it is given over to the tender mercies of the announcer, whose voice, inflections, skill, and understanding have much to do with the form in which it finally goes on the air. (One of these steps is omitted in news transmitted by Transradio Press, which does not first prepare news for newspaper publication.)

All of these handlings, as well as the capacity of the individual reader or listener to grasp the news and fit it into major news patterns, affect the meaning of the news as it finally appears. Yet all of them taken together do not mean that radio and newspaper presentations are necessarily far apart. The news at the base is the same; and as the skill and competence of editors heighten, it will more nearly remain the same.

"Control" of the News

Another question inevitably arises: To what extent is radio news "controlled"? How much does radio ownership, the radio advertiser, or the economic philosophy and practice on which American broadcasting is based affect radio news offerings? What of "the public interest, convenience, and necessity"? What of freedom of the air?

In many ways the ownership, advertising, and general economic points of view of the broadcasting industry are similar to those of the press. The fact that newspapering has become big business is an accepted twentieth-century phenomenon. The day when a printer with a hatful of type and a three-figure bank account could found a newspaper is half a century past. The only great dailies started from scratch in a decade—PM in New York, the Sun in Chicago—demanded millions of dollars at the beginning, plus Marshall Field's willingness to lose money on them for a matter of years (and neither was a success!). Moreover, the number of newspapers has declined; ownership has tended to concentrate in fewer and fewer hands. This trend a good many critics have viewed with alarm. Their plaint is that newspapers tend to represent only the point of view of a tight little group—the point of view of corporate ownership. Usually such critics generalize too broadly, on too little evidence. It is obviously unsound to lump the *Christian Science Monitor*, the *New York Daily News*, the *Milwaukee Journal*, the *Detroit Times*, the Indiana *Goshen News-Democrat*, and the Virginia *Richmond News-Leader* under one set of descriptive adjectives; it is even more unsound to draw the adjectives from only one of the papers. So well-informed a student of the American press as William Allen White expressed the belief that "we . . . editors and owners, because of our large property investment, have taken the side of property unconsciously in many cases." White's implication seems a fair one. But he gives the newspaper owners credit for desire to operate their papers in the best interests of the communities they serve. He offers no suggestion of dishonesty in thinking or intent, of malice, or of unalloyed self-interest.

Radio can claim no special distinction on this score. Radio broadcasting has never been anything but big business. Its first backers were the big newspapers, the big department stores, and the great electrical industries. In its quarter century of history it has known no other type of internal control. When NBC sold the Blue network, its price was $8,000,000. A single station was sold in 1944 for $1,000,000; another in 1945 for $1,700,000. Broadcasting, with a few more than a thousand broadcasters, is a billion-dollar industry. The estimated cost of installing a 1,000-watt FM station and operating it for a year is more than $50,000—lower than comparable costs in AM broadcasting, but no shoestring.

Moreover, radio lacks one possibly stimulating influence: The centuries-old newspaper tradition of devotion to a cause, the traditional newspaper man's sense of social responsibility (which, though often misunderstood, abused, or aborted, and though sometimes honored more in lip service than in action, remains a vigorous influence). Radio has been told by legislative and administrative fiat that it must operate in "the public interest, convenience, and necessity"; the networks and many stations have their public service directors, their educational departments, and so on. Most of the men and women who activate these services are deeply genuine about their jobs. But it is questionable whether radio's impulse to "public service" would be more than the too-often dormant desire of decent citizens to play some part in social progress, were it not for Communications Act and FCC dicta and for increasingly articulate lay criticism. This impulse is something less than a vigorous, competently-implemented zeal growing out of recognition of broad social responsibility. (This is not to point an accusing finger at radio more than at any other arm of big or little business. The elaborate "service programs" of many corporations are all too often undertaken because they increase profits, or improve public relations, or may be charged against taxes.)

Only a few of broadcasting's ventures into public service have revealed a willingness to stick out the radio neck in the public welfare, at least in controversial areas. Radio has yet to produce a John Peter Zenger, a Horace Greeley, or a Joseph Pulitzer, who once said that he hoped the time would never come when there were no libel suits against his *New York World*—a colorful statement of his belief that courage, vigor, and daring in the public weal are part of the newspaper business. Radio programs have done a good deal to illuminate such social prob-

---

Radio's contribution to the war effort was, in the wartime term, all-out. An NAB tabulation shows, for example, that American broadcasting stations put on the air more than 1,100,000 war-related programs in the first three months of 1944—900,000 of them spot announcements, 100,000 fifteen-minute shows, the remainder varying from two minutes to daylong bond-sales drives. They devoted many hours—not infrequently at the cost of canceling revenue-producing programs—to important spot news shows. They gave time to hundreds of propaganda broadcasts, and in many cases paid all costs of production. Twice in the spring of 1945—at the time of President Roosevelt's death, and in celebration of V-E Day—they canceled scores of commercial shows in favor of patriotic efforts. During 1944 stations and networks contributed $74,000,000 in time on the air for war messages; advertisers contributed $64,000,000; performers gave $20,000,000 worth of talent.

lems as juvenile delinquency and such vastly important agricultural questions as soil erosion. But these are noncontroversial—everybody agrees that juveniles shouldn't be delinquent. There have been few offerings in more delicate areas—few programs, for example, like CBS's courageous "Open Letter to the American People" on the Negro-white problem, or WCCO's hard-hitting "Neither Free Nor Equal" series attacking prejudice and bigotry in the Northwest.

In fairness, it must be said that certain FCC policies have served as a deterrent to vigorous public service programming. Until 1944 the Commission asked re-application for station licenses every six months—a policy that kept stations continually in fear of offending (in 1944 the license period was changed to three years). The so-called "Mayflower decision" of the FCC (of which more in Chapter 11), underscoring the Commission's demand for impartiality among licensees, also worked in this direction.

These and other influences have led radio to make a god of lack of bias. Networks and individual stations whose air-waves have borne speeches on one side of a controversial matter make time available to responses from the other side; when they sell time to one political party, they open for purchase equal time to the others. In 1943, CBS went so far as to establish a rule that its commentators must inject no personal or editorial comment into their offerings—they must limit themselves to factual explanation and background. (This led to the resignation of Cecil Brown and H. V. Kaltenborn from the CBS staff, and to spirited disagreements by Drew Pearson, Walter Winchell, and other radio commentators and newsmen.) The middle ground—the ground of an objectivity that some call sterile and colorless—has been the ground on which radio has chosen to stand.

What effect all this has on news offerings—either of press or radio—is something of an imponderable. The charge that newspapers favor their own side is one of the favorite whipping boys of Upton Sinclair, Harold Ickes, George Seldes, and others among the noisier critics of the press. Most such critics, in their charges that newspapers omit (the favorite Seldes word is "suppress") news at the behest of their friends and supporters, are inclined to generalize far too broadly on far too little evidence.

Regardless of the extent of this kind of control of newspaper news, it appears to be an influence operating above and behind the radio newsroom, but at a greater distance. A like attitude of ownership, and like power, are there. But the radio newsroom is more widely separated from ownership than is the newspaper city room. News is the newspaper's prime commodity, and the wise publisher's first interest. It is merely one of a number of elements in what radio has to sell, and some of the other elements overshadow it. The newsroom is not one of the radio station's major subdivisions, and it does not often come under the intimate supervision—or even constitute a major interest— of the man in the office with the chromium furniture. Moreover, the requirement that the station operate in "the public interest, convenience, and necessity" is an influence against mishandling of news. It is not good, when a station is applying for renewal of license, to have it said that its management had suppressed such-and-such a story.

Radio has had some headaches of this kind. The charge has been made before the FCC that stations have altered, censored, or withheld broadcasts friendly to this or unfriendly to that element in society. In 1943, several Midwestern stations for a time refused, after once agreeing, to permit a farmers' cooperative association to broadcast its answer to a radio speech against it. In 1944 the United Automobile Workers told the FCC that WHKC-Columbus, Ohio, had yielded to the demand by the National Association of Manufacturers that it present a program designed to portray "industry as solely responsible for the nation's war production record," without giving labor an opportunity to respond. In reply, a representative of the station said that WHKC, "instead of throttling labor, is liberal in its policies and is one of the few stations in the country to sell time to labor unions"—a statement that, if accurate, is in itself revealing.

The fact that newspapers and radio both get so much of their news from the standard news services adds to the oneness of point of view. The AP is owned by the daily newspapers themselves; UP by the Scripps-Howard interests; INS by the Hearst interests. All are dedicated, in greater or less degree, to "objective," impartial, full coverage of the news. But the ownership attitude behind them is exactly that behind the newspapers, and closely akin to that behind the broadcasting industry.

The FCC was also asked to investigate, in 1948, charges that the ownership of KMPC-Hollywood had ordered three members of the newsroom's staff to "slant" news in accordance with the views of the station's president. The only case of this kind ever brought before the FCC, it had not been brought to a conclusion six months after the Commission agreed, in March, to investigate the charges.

But most of the charges of this type have been directed chiefly against programs emanating not from the newsrooms, but from other agencies in the stations. Such programs may be as much news as the material from the news printers. But this book is primarily devoted to the handling of news as news, and to go further in discussion of matters of this kind could easily become irrelevant.

— o —

What about the influence of advertisers on radio news presentation?

Back in the 1930's the newspapers, trying to deny news to radio, talked about the insidious power of sponsors on news programs as one of the chief arguments against news broadcasting. This was a smoke screen. Publishers knew then, as they do now, that individual advertisers have little potency against the firmly-entrenched newspaper with the courage to stand its ground. They have always been as quick to deny the Seldes-Sinclair charges of advertiser-influence as they were to forecast its menace to radio news. It is undeniable that on occasion newspapers have bowed before demands—or courteously acceded to wise suggestions, whichever way you want to put it—of advertisers; that newspaper policies have sometimes been shaped to favor the point of view of big space-buyers, or of national advertising associations. But most newspaper publishers—especially those whose financial feet are on solid ground—can more than match the critic with tales of advertisers whose importunities have been rejected. The fact is, as somebody has said, that it is advertising, not advertisers, that influences the press. It is a fundamental point of view, not the individual retail grocer, that may put an imprint on the news.

And the "may" in the last sentence should be emphasized. The newspaper record, from John Peter Zenger to the Joseph Pulitzers, is full of cases of the high integrity and courage of individual papers. Honest, hard-hitting publishers, reporters, editorial writers—men subject to no discernible extraneous influence—also make their impress on the newspaper scene.

The point has already been made that on this score the broadcasting industry differs little from the press. But, you say, there *is* a difference: The newspaper presents its news itself, but radio sells news to a sponsor who takes responsibility for it. Yes—if this were an accurate statement. Fortunately, it isn't. The radio station, or the network, does not sell to an advertiser a time-period in which he may present anything he desires *in the guise of news.* That isn't the way it works. Rather, radio sells a time-period in which the sponsor may present his own commercials (their length and even their form usually rigidly controlled by network or station rules); but the news itself is selected, edited, and often read into the microphone by the station's own news staff.

There are cases of direct advertiser-influence. Usually they are described in general rather than specific terms. A writer in the *Saturday Evening Post* in 1937 cited sponsor restrictions such as no mention of Hawaiian insularity, no derogatory remarks about California climate. He made the remark that "dollar considerations often ghost-write the sponsor's news program"; but he gave virtually no specific evidence to support his charge.

Since the advent of the professional radio newsroom, there have been fewer such complaints. Justifications for them nowadays are rare. In one station advertisers occasionally let the newsroom know that they thought it would be "nice" (they rarely put it more strongly than that) if such-and-such news were put into, or kept out of, their sponsored periods. In each case the news editor responded that he would consider the news on its merits (usually his decision was that it wasn't worth

---

The sponsor's influence may be more direct in the case of sponsored commentaries than in those of sponsored news shows. Usually a sponsor will not pay the heavy cost of broadcasting a commentator with whose views he does not agree. But Dixon Wecter, writing in the *Atlantic* for June, 1945, points out that three of the four networks offer rosters of commentators "with diverse personalities and points of view, from whom sponsors may choose"—men selected primarily for their competence rather than their views.

using); in the two cases in which advertisers attempted to wield a big stick via the front office, the news editor and not the advertiser was supported. One manager of an important radio station formally instructed his newsroom director: "I don't know anything about news. You're hired because you do. Your judgment is law. If I ever come in here with a request that you do this or that with the news—either on my own behalf or anybody else's—be so good as to kick me back upstairs, where I belong."

In a Chicago station with similar news policy, a case arose in which the advertising agency for an important news sponsor decided that it didn't like the manner—not the content or emphasis, but the manner—in which the newsroom edited the news. The station acceded to the request that an agency man be put into the newsroom to do the editing. After three days of listening to the shows that its man put together, the agency pulled him out and gladly returned the shows to newsroom editing.

In one situation, the amount of news offered by a station may be affected by the sponsorship system. An example: A Midwest station for years carried a 5:30 P.M. newscast. A sponsor offered the station for the 5:30 period a comic-dialog show, on a much more lucrative contract. The news show went out; and since the station had no place else to put it, the daily news offerings were cut by fifteen minutes. . . . But this situation in no way affected the quality of the news.

— o —

The personnel of the average newsroom is a factor in its performance. Radio is still a "young man's game." Most of radio's top executives are under fifty (the average age of the presidents of the four major net-

---

A number of radio stations—an increasing number—have a law that the man who edits a news show must also broadcast it. The principle is that the editor is a trained newsman, and that he alone can put his copy on the air with ultimate effectiveness—with proper emphasis, with entire understanding. This means that, in these stations, the news is not always read into the microphone by voices as golden as most professional announcers'. "But," says the director of a key network station in Washington, "voice isn't as important in newscasting as authority, understanding, an informed sense of proportion."

works on January 1, 1948, was forty-eight). The age level in the news-rooms runs closer to thirty, and hundreds of radio newsmen are just out of college.

This means that the newsrooms are in the hands of men (and a few women) of energy, ambition, and youthful point of view. There are few gray-haired old-timers in radio news, at least in point of experience —radio news hasn't lived long enough. And there are few gray-bearded rules-of-thumb. Radio news workers are subject to few of the restricting limitations of long practice.

Moreover, they are young enough not to have settled irrevocably in ruts, either of editing or of thinking. Though plenty of them have adopted some of the superficial exemplifications of "young intellectual" cynicism (young men and women often do, whatever their occupation, as a shield against greater experience and as protective coloration for their very youthfulness), not many have become truly hard-shelled. They still believe in themselves and in their jobs; they have not had time for disillusion or for the evaporation of their passion for a profession they think important.

They are, on the whole, an exceptionally able group. The fact that the rate of pay in radio is somewhat above that of newspapers gives radio news a considerable vantage in selection, and radio news directors have used it.

— o —

A final word. Radio news has to date not proved startlingly imaginative or inventive. In the foreign field, where it has developed a brilliant news corps (its members usually chosen from among the ablest of the younger newspaper correspondents), it has an outstanding record. But in the domestic newsroom, its one distinctive contribution is the development of an effective style for radio news writing. Little has been done with patterns for radio news programs. The development of local news-gathering and broadcasting, in spite of recent advances, is still in swaddling clothes. Few steps toward making radio news a vigorous champion of the public weal have been taken.

In channels like these lies the opportunity of radio as a disseminator of news. In their avoidance lie stagnation and futility.

4

The Radio Newsroom

On January 1, 1948, the FCC had licensed 1,522 AM stations to operate in the United States, and had granted construction permits to 440 more.

On the same date, exactly 1,500 AM stations were served by one or more press association news wires.

This does not mean that all except twenty-two licensed stations had press wires, for a number of wires were assigned to construction-permit stations not yet on the air. One hundred thirty-two commercial licensees and seventeen noncommercial—stations assigned to educational, religious, or municipal agencies—had no wire service. Eighty-three of the 132, however, had network affiliation presumably providing regular news programs. And a number of them were operating local news services of their own (some of them, as is shown in Chapter 8, vigorous and effective).

A good 95 per cent of American AM broadcasters, in other words, were providing service from newsrooms of greater or less pretension.

What is a radio newsroom?

In its simplest form, it is nothing more than a news printer set up in a closet off somebody's office, delivering its sixty words of news a minute. A few moments before each scheduled newscast an announcer rips off its long strip of copy paper, reads hurriedly through the stories—selecting, arranging, perhaps editing a little here or in-

RADIO STATIONS AND WIRE NEWS SERVICES

	One Service	Two Services	Three Services	Four Services	Five Services	Total
Jan. 1, 1944	685	134	21	3	1	844
Jan. 1, 1945	642	174	38	2	0	856
Jan. 1, 1946	632	182	42	6	0	862
Feb. 15, 1947	885	177	42	6	0	1,110
Jan. 1, 1948	1,262	198	36	3	1	1.500

Statistics from listings in *Broadcasting Yearbooks*.

serting a "transition" there—and dashes into a studio to put the news into a microphone.

In its most elaborate form, the radio newsroom is the pretentious establishment maintained by network key stations in Washington, New York, and Los Angeles. It boasts a whole battery of teleprinters— UP, AP, and INS newspaper wires, UP and AP radio wires, perhaps Reuters, Transradio, or other supplementary services, spare printers for emergencies. It occupies a big room, its wall acoustically treated, with desk space for its fifteen or twenty workers—editors, reporters, commentators, specialists, secretaries. On its oversized bulletin boards are maps and a score of notices and memoranda. Through soundproofed triple plate-glass windows in one wall is a broadcasting booth; in the booth, not only the microphone into which regular newscasts and spot flashes are read, but also the complicated system of switches, dials, warning lights, and other apparatus for picking up short-wave broadcasts from the other side of the world. Somewhere not far away is a monitoring service, where trained linguists listen to foreign radio stations.

The atmosphere of this newsroom is the ordered disorder of the newspaper city room—not the chaotic parody of a city room as Hollywood pictures it, but the tight, restrained haste of meeting deadlines and keeping constant vigil for the news-break. Neither the big network newsroom nor the printer-in-a-corner is typical, however—any more than the *New York Times* or the *South Side Shopper* is typical of newspapers.

Let's look in more detail at a newsroom somewhere in the middle— one, say, in an aggressive station in a medium-sized city. The room itself is perhaps twelve feet by twenty. Its walls and ceilings are paved with perforated acoustical board. It is lighted by the gray-blue of a battery of fluorescent tubes overhead.

Why should a radio newsroom, with teleprinters bringing it each day more news than it can possibly broadcast, pay out good money for its own editors, writers, reporters?

For a number of excellent reasons:

1 Competent news evaluation and judgment grow out of the background, experience, and training of men thoroughly versed in news handling.

(*continued on next page*)

Dominating the room is a big copydesk. At its head sits the director of newsroom operations . . . copy spread on the desktop beside him, a typewriter clattering under his fingers as he hammers out lead stories for a news show coming up. Around the rim of the desk sit one or two assistants, typing fast on other sections of the same show, or more leisurely turning out copy for later shows. Against a nearby wall are the printers—a newspaper and a radio wire are the usual minimum in such a newsroom, and there may be more. On a shelf on the wall is an A. T. & T. sports ticker under a glass dome, its staccato chatter rising intermittently above the steady pounding of the printers as it grinds out its narrow yellow tape.

Another wall is covered with a reference library. Here are files of all local papers, the *New York Times*, perhaps other dailies. There are an *Encyclopedia Britannica* and an unabridged dictionary. Shelves hold the *National* or *World Almanac*, a good biographical dictionary, *Who's Who in America*, state, national, and international legislative manuals and directories, city directories, the *United States Postal Guide*, the *New York Times Index*, pronunciation manuals, specialized guides in sports, agriculture, and other fields, local reference books. A pile of well-thumbed maps and an atlas overflow a table.

Walls near the copydesk have maps on them—maps of the world, the United States, the state, the city, the county. Perhaps, also, new maps

---

2   However skillfully written for broadcasting may be the copy brought in by news printers, the job of selecting stories and knitting them into effective newscasts is one for a news specialist.

3   Much news that comes, say, to an Iowa station by printer from Washington can be made more meaningful for the Iowa audience if it is rewritten and edited with a view to the special needs of the particular audience.

4   Frequently it is desirable that a given news program be written especially to suit the personality and "air-characteristics" of the man who is to broadcast it.

5   A station in a competitive situation, desiring that its shows "sound different" from those offered by other stations, must write its own copy to make sure that its news will not be broadcast word for word like that from rival stations' printers.

6   A station cannot get credit from the FCC for "local live" news shows if it merely broadcasts unedited printer copy (see Chapter 8).

of "hot spot" areas current in the news. Bulletin boards carry pieces of yellow and white copy paper from the printers: schedules of the day's routine, notices of changes in service, "confidential to editors" memoranda, occasional stories that for one reason or another aren't to be broadcast but that somebody thinks too good for his co-workers to miss. Here are the daily log of the station, typed instructions as to what to do when an important news flash justifies breaking into a non-news program, perhaps the week's schedule of staff assignments.

A corner is crowded with desks for "specialists"—sports newscasters, agricultural and other experts, commentators—and the office secretary. A big plate-glass window looks into a broadcasting booth which may double as the director's private office.

From time to time one of the editors rises from his typewriter to look at a printer, to rip off a strip of fresh copy. When five bells on one of the machines announce a "bulletin," somebody leaves his work to check on it. At the rarer ten bells heralding a "flash"—news of extraordinary importance—everybody jumps, and there is a quick consultation to decide whether to put it on the air at once. Copy continues to flow out of the typewriters.

The newsroom door swings continually. An announcer comes in to pick up his copy for a forthcoming newscast, settles himself at a desk in a corner to read carefully through it. From time to time he calls to an editor to check on a sentence, or takes a look at a pronunciation guide. A commentator comes in to verify a fact in a reference book, or to glance at the printers to make sure he has the latest word on the subject he plans to discuss. A girl from the outer office brings in the "commercials" for a sponsored newscast and throws them into a wire basket; she leaves latest editions of the local papers. An office boy changes a ribbon on a printer, puts a new roll of paper on another, files in a cabinet the copy for shows already broadcast. The attention of the director is demanded by a telephone call, or by the entrance of somebody who, having wormed his way past the reception desk out front, offers his reasons why news of his church sociable should go on every show that day.

A deadline nears, and tension heightens. Typewriters punch closing periods and stop. The announcer and an editor talk about a moot point in the copy. The announcer leaves for the broadcasting booth with a minute or two to spare. The workers stretch; somebody goes out for a cup of coffee; an editor remains on deck to check on late-breaking news. He sweeps used copy into waste baskets and "clears" the printers, taking off the new copy and separating it into neat piles.

Shortly work starts on the next newscast.

Newsroom Personnel

Such a newsroom staff consists of six or seven workers. One is the boss, one his assistant; they direct the newsroom operation, say, from 7 in the morning until 3 in the afternoon, and from 3 to 11. A third man has the "lobster trick," from 11 at night to 7 in the morning—he is insurance against the news break that comes in the middle of the night, and he's charged with getting up the early-morning newscasts. The other members of the staff work in staggered shifts through the day—perhaps only as writers and editors, perhaps doubling as local reporters, covering local stories in direct competition with the local newspapers.

Who are these workers? What is their equipment? How did they get into the newsroom?

When a Lincoln, Nebraska, station decided in 1928 to give America one of its first "newspapers of the air," it hired a newspaper man to direct the operation. CBS, in 1933, put a former UP man in charge of developing its news service. The pattern thus outlined has remained pretty well fixed. News, say the radio stations, is news; those best qualified to handle it are newsmen. A large percentage of radio newsroom personnel has been drawn from newspaper staffs, or from the ranks of those trained for journalistic work—graduates of the schools of journalism.

The logic of this is clear. If a man is to be charged with evaluating news for a mass audience, he must possess a sound understanding of what news is. Not merely what it is in the outmoded "man-bites-dog" sense, but what it is in origin, development, and social relationships. He must know how and where news is gathered; he must be able to assess the validity of news sources; he must be competent to pass on the comparative authority of two stories, perhaps conflicting, coming from two reporters on the other side of the world. He must be able to read between the lines of dispatches. He needs to understand the functions and operations of news channels, of national and international communication systems, of overt and implicit censorships. He must apply critical judgment to the work of individual reporters—he must know the Wallace Deuels, the Karl von Wiegands, the Bert Andrews', "Scotty" Restons, Hightowers, and all the rest. He must be equipped to judge quickly the values in a local story, and to gather quickly the facts for it—or to tell somebody else where and how to gather them.

All this he can do competently only if he knows news inside and out.

This is not to say that he can acquire this background only by being a newspaper man (Edward R. Murrow, one of the greatest of radio reporters, had little news experience before he became CBS European news director); nor that two years' experience as a police reporter, by itself, will give it to him. But it is more likely that a thorough grounding in news work will orient and inform him soundly than would experience as a doctor, a time salesman, an announcer, or a radio engineer.

No more will any wise man assert that journalistic experience alone is enough. The competent newsman—radio, newspaper, *Time*, or *Life* —must have also an orientation in society. He must have a thorough, finger-tip knowledge of history, government, geography; he must have some insight into psychology, some awareness of sociological conformations, and divergences; he must have a scientific skepticism, and a knowledge of the fundamentals of scientific thinking. He must be a man whose perspective is as broad as the sweep of the news itself. In short, he must be an educated man—whether by diploma or otherwise is immaterial.

Where do radio stations (or any other employers) find this paragon? They don't, of course, find him very often. But they look for him among the young and competent newspapermen more frequently than any place else. Most radio newsroom directors will tell you that newspaper experience, backed by sound education, is the prime requisite for membership on their staffs.

The statistics at the head of this chapter suggest the increasing dimensions of the newsroom personnel problem after World War II. The growing number of broadcasting stations and the expanding interest in local news coverage combined to create a heavy demand for qualified men. This demand of course existed throughout the radio industry—a fact doubtless contributory to the finding of a mid-1947 NAB survey that the average weekly wage of full-time broadcast station employes was $74, called by NAB "the highest average per employe in any American industry."

It also showed its special effect on newsroom personnel in the FCC's 1947 Employe and Compensation Report. The report showed that seven American networks and 924 AM stations employed, in February, 1947, 890 "news personnel" at an average weekly wage of $69.31— higher than the average for program personnel of all kinds, higher than that for announcers, singers, writers, and "other staff program employes"; lower than the average for sound effects and production men, musicians, and actors. "Nonstaff news personnel," however—including high-salaried commentators and the like—averaged $136.24 a week, higher than any other nonstaff personnel.

This meant that the qualified man could expect to enter a radio newsroom, at the beginning of 1948, at a wage perhaps slightly higher than the going rate in competitive fields (stations in less-than-metropolitan communities were paying competent school of journalism graduates $50 or $55 a week to start; those in big cities sometimes paid more, those in small towns often paid less).

Radio newsmen predict that demand for competent personnel will be active for several years. The anticipated development of FM broadcasting and the prospects of vigorous television news programming help to support such a prediction. None of this, however, suggests that radio news is an easy El Dorado. Definitions of adequate qualification are likely to grow more rigorous; one evidence of this is increasing emphasis on the desirability of having newsmen do their own broadcasting. Nobody knows just where the saturation level may lie, but it is an existing ceiling. And unfortunately for radio newsmen, the newsroom is perhaps more vulnerable to business recession than some of broadcasting's other departments. It is often easier to cut one news writer or reporter from the station staff than one engineer.

The radio industry's recognition of the need for development of a pool of properly prepared newsroom workers has been noted in Chapter 1. The formation of the Council on Radio Journalism by joint action of the NAB and the schools of journalism is one answer. The Council's statement of standards for university-level preparation of newsroom workers (see Appendix B) details the technical courses recommended for such preparation—training in news gathering, news writing, news editing, news evaluation and emphasis, plus fundamental work in microphone technique, station operation, and elementary electronics.

But it puts its major emphasis on general education, on background, on orientation in society. This, say both the industry and the universities, is the first requirement.

Newsroom Organization, Operation, and Cost

How does the newsroom fit into the station organization?

Practice has built up no universal pattern. Fairly common—and certainly most logical and desirable—is the news department independent of all station tie-ins except its responsibility to management. Not unusual, however, is the establishment of the news department as a subdivision of programming. In either case, the newsroom can operate effectively and self-respectingly only if its actual news functioning is autonomous—if its reporting, writing, editing, and news judgments are strictly and solely the responsibility of its director.

There is similarly no set pattern for the newsroom's internal organization, beyond the normal line of responsibility from reporter to writer-editor to director. "Informal" is the word for most radio news operations—few follow ironclad lines of organization or make the director, in practice, a dictator. The spread of responsibility among newsroom workers naturally relates directly to their degrees of competence. A rule in most newsrooms is that announcers bear responsibility only for reading the news—that they have no authority to edit or revise, except with newsroom approval.

This is generalization. Characteristic operative patterns may perhaps be described best by specific examples. Here are three—the first in detail, the others less detailed. The information they offer has come from their news directors or their station managers.

Station A is a 10,000-watt CBS affiliate in a small city in a Southern state. Its news operations, like those of the other two examples, are aggressive and thorough. Its organizational chart looks like this:

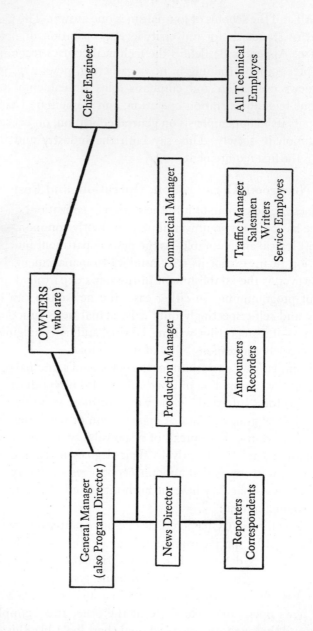

Overall Organization and Policy The news director is supreme in news, but is under the program department (headed by the general manager) in overall programming. The program department allocates newscasts to the station schedule, and the news department prepares the shows. The news director may substitute "flash" or other important news for any commercial programming on his own responsibility. He has entire authority for news selection, evaluation, and "play," subject only to the station's code of good taste. The station does no editorializing or commenting. It permits no sponsorship of local news shows.

Personnel and Salaries The news editor is paid $77.50 a week (top for the position is $90); four reporters (two of them women) are paid $54.60, $46.80, $46.40, and $40.56 (top for these positions, $60); college, high school, and other correspondents, about $40 a week at 50 cents a story. "Our outlying town news comes largely from mortuaries whose names are mentioned in funeral stories; in return they tip us to other news not involving death."

Daily Newscast and Staff Assignment Schedule One reporter goes on at 6 A.M., checks local stories, and with wire copy assembles a fifteen-minute newscast for 7:45 A.M. He then prepares a five-minute show for 8:55 A.M.

The news editor and a second reporter go on at 9 A.M., and the three concentrate on local news for a five-minute local show at 10:10 A.M. They then prepare a ten-minute show for 1:30 P.M.

The early man leaves at 3 P.M., and two night reporters go on. This four-man staff works toward the "big night edition" at 7:15 P.M. The two night men (the senior taking editorial responsibility) get up a five- to eight-minute show for 11:10 P.M. They stay on duty until sign-off at 12:05 A.M., watching for news-breaks and rewriting late news for use at 7:45 the next morning.

The staff also gets up a weekly half-hour "Feature Story" program, and a woman reporter prepares a fifteen-minute "society column" for Sunday use. All local newscasts "lean against" wire or network newscasts. The station uses several network shows in addition to locally-prepared programs.

One man in the news department broadcasts a fifteen-minute show daily, and one a five-minute. Most of the newscasts, however, are assigned to announcers. The station would like to have newsmen do all their own broadcasting, but "reporters with voices are rare animals. News sounds more authoritative if a genuine newsman puts it on the air; and the man who has to broadcast learns more about writing for the air."

Costs   The annual salary budget runs to about $16,000. Two news services, UP and INS, cost $3,400 a year. Other expenses, including telephone and telegraph tolls, recording costs, travel, and supplies, bring the total annual newsroom cost to about $25,000.

— o —

Station B is a 250-watt NBC affiliate in a small city in New York state. Its news staff consists of one man, a former local newspaper man who is paid $55 a week. He has sole responsibility for gathering and writing local news, for editing news shows, and for a five-day-a-week fifteen-minute local commentary (which he also broadcasts). The station schedules two five-minute and five fifteen-minute news shows daily, in addition to network shows, and includes local news on all seven. It uses tape-recorded news frequently. An arrangement with a local morning newspaper provides local news for use on the late evening show, after the news editor has gone off duty.

One announcer is assigned exclusively to news shows, and broadcasts all but the five-minute shows, which are put on by the program manager. The news announcer is paid $50 a week, only part of it charged to the news budget. All three of these men draw talent fees for sponsored shows, in addition to salary; this is not charged to the newsroom. The total newsroom salary item comes to $4,000 to $4,500 a year; the cost of AP wire service to $600 a year; travel, telephone tolls, and other expenses to about $1,500 a year. The total approaches $7,000 a year.

— o —

Station C is a 50,000-watt outlet in one of the nation's biggest cities, one carrying heavy network responsibilities. Its newsroom director, who has full authority over the news operation, is also director of news and special events for the network in his section of the country. It pays six news writers about $100 each a week, a wire-recorder specialist $150 a week, and three commentators about $150 each a week (but these are not charged against the newsroom, since the commentators are network performers). It offers eleven news shows daily, all fifteen-minute except one five-minute spot and a ten-minute recorded show. It also carries several network news shows.

The station's annual salary budget, exclusive of director and commentators, runs to about $35,000 or more. Its cost for AP, UP, and INS trunk newspaper wires, the AP state wire, and AP and UP radio wires is about $38,500 a year. Other costs run its annual expense well above $80,000. But it gets most of this back in the $75,000 a year paid by local news clients as a service fee for news-gathering, writing, and editing. Annual time charges for the newsroom's shows amount to about $250,000 a year.

5

How Is It Written?

In every radio newsroom an invisible precept hangs over the typewriters:

Write for the ear!

The radio audience is an aural audience. The man speaking into the microphone can reach his listener through no other sense. He cannot thump his lectern, wave his fist, or pace the stage. If he indulges in the dramatic pause so effective on the lecture platform, his radio audience thinks a tube has burned out. He has neither the listener's eye nor the psychological effect of mass response to aid him in putting over what he has to say. He must rely on words alone, plus whatever adornment inflection and tone may give them.

This "ear-characteristic" means that the radio news writer must give his copy the maximum of ear-appeal. And radio newsmen agree that the effective manner by which to make copy easy to listen to is to make it sound like the kind of verbalism to which ears are most accustomed:

Conversation.

The "conversational style" is the goal at which the radio news editor aims. He seeks to adapt the informality, the simplicity, the easy flow of ordinary conversation to his need to present a great many facts, some of them complex, in very brief time. This does not mean that he thinks of himself as a dialog writer, one attempting to reproduce realistically, with all its elisions, vulgarisms, slang, and grammatical idiosyncrasies, an actual conversational manner. But it does mean that his finished newscast must have the *flavor* of a man's unaffected talk.

How does he achieve this flavor?

The Conversational Style

It is not difficult to name the salient characteristics of everyday conversation. First of all, conversation is informal, without pomp or affectation. It is simple—it uses common, readily-understood words, it is colloquial, it says what it has to say in broad strokes rather than finely-etched detail. Its rhetoric is straight-forward; it employs short sentences, sometimes half-sentences.

All of these characteristics are to be found in good radio news writing.

There are, of course, other characteristics of the conversational manner: loose diction, vulgarisms, solecisms, faulty grammar, and the like. Inaccuracy, too—the ease with which the human tongue wonders from fact is proverbial. Radio news avoids these characteristics; it does not need them in order to attain the flavor it seeks. The effect can be achieved by suggestion rather than realism.

Soon after the United Press offered to its radio clients news written for broadcast, it issued a set of mimeographed instructions on handling radio news. The first sentence in the several revisions of this informal manual—as well as the theme of the first chapter of the book which the manual finally became, *United Press Radio News Style Book* by Phil Newsom (1943)—was, "Writing news for radio really is telling a story orally."

"Telling a story orally"—what does it mean?

Suppose an automobile skids and ends up against a telephone pole at a corner as you are walking by. The driver is seriously injured, a passenger is cut by a broken windshield. You describe the event to your family at dinner:

"A sweet accident at the corner this afternoon—right down at Maple and Fourth. The driver was smashed up—took him to the hospital. Yeah—I was just walking past. This car skidded, and first thing I knew there it was, sliding right into the telephone pole. Fellow driving was jammed against the steering wheel—guess it crushed his chest. His face was cut, too—blood all over the place. The man with him? He got cut up some too, but not so badly. . . . No—the car didn't seem to be hurt so much, except the radi-

---

Wells Church, CBS director of news broadcasts, is quoted by an *Editor & Publisher* interviewer as saying that "in the newspaper it's *readability* that the editors strive for; on the air, it's *listenability*. . . . The newscast writer must consider the mental image he is creating; how to keep it clear for the listeners; and how to keep down those 'phone calls which used to plague every radio newsroom when long-winded sentences written for reading and not hearing were read on the air."

ator grill and the windshield. I stayed until the City Hospital ambulance came and took 'em away. . . ."

You pick up your evening paper. In it you find something like this to report the event:

Two men were injured, one seriously, when an automobile skidded and crashed into a telephone pole at Maple avenue and Fourth street at 2:15 P.M. this afternoon.

One, Arthur Williams, 45, 2719 Hawthorne road, the car's driver, is in City Hospital with multiple contusions and possible chest injuries. The other, John Payson, 51, Metropole hotel, was sent home from the hospital after his wounds were dressed.

The car skidded as it approached the corner, and hit the telephone pole, witnesses said, at about thirty miles an hour. Williams' chest was crushed against the steering wheel. The car damage was slight.

Try reading the newspaper version aloud; compare it to the conversational version. You note at once that the newspaper story makes "bad listening"—though its condensation of essential facts is skillful printed chronicling of the event—because of its very compactness, because of the large number of details compressed into small space, because its manner is not that to which the ear is accustomed.

Now listen to your favorite newscast as it presents the story:

Another Midland auto accident this afternoon . . . and a driver badly injured. He is 45-year-old Arthur Williams, who lives at 2719 Hawthorne Road. His companion, John Payson of the Metropole Hotel, got off with minor cuts.

Williams' car skidded at the corner of Maple avenue and Fourth street, and smashed into a telephone pole. The steering wheel crushed Williams' chest. He is in City Hospital.

There are differences between this story and the conversational version. But the differences between it and the newspaper story are more marked. Like the dinner-table version, the radio story opens with a general statement rather than the detail-packed lead of the newspaper story. It offers many fewer details than the newspaper story; and it is told in relatively simple, straightforward sentences. It has no "credit lines" such as the "witnesses said" of the newspaper story.

The news services providing both newspaper and radio versions of the same stories make like distinctions. Note the differences among stories taken verbatim from news printers operating in a radio newsroom:

From the United Press newspaper wire:

BULLETIN

Washington, Aug. 16—(UP)—Gen. Dwight D. Eisenhower said today he would order a full-scale investigation of alleged "intolerable" conditions reported in the Army's Mediterranean command by Robert C. Ruark, Scripps-Howard columnist.

The Army chief of staff told newsmen at National Airport here that a top War Department official, probably Army Inspector General Maj. Gen. William Wyche, would leave for Italy early next week to conduct a first-hand investigation.

Eisenhower said the Army's investigation would take "from ten days to two weeks." He said the investigator would make a formal report to him.

In a series of columns from Italy, Ruark has accused Lt. Gen. John C. Lee, U. S. Mediterranean commander, of making life "intolerable" for enlisted men but correspondingly easy for officers.

Eisenhower said Lee has asked the War Department to investigate the charges. The investigation will be made, Eisenhower said.

Eisenhower landed at the airport shortly before 6 P.M. EDT., returning from a two-week tour of Army installations in Alaska. He told reporters he knew "little" of the charges against Lee. But, he added, when he was in Italy last year he found morale "surprisingly good."

"Conditions may have changed since then," Eisenhower said.

The chief of staff reported that Army forces in Alaska are "doing a good job and their morale is high." But he said that additional facilities, particularly living quarters, are needed. He added that the Army will have to begin "to get construction going up there."

From the United Press radio wire:

Our commander in the Mediterranean theater, Lieutenant General John Lee, has invited all American correspondents in Italy to visit any Army installations and make any investigations they want to. The general's invitation was accompanied by mimeographed copies of articles in Scripps-Howard newspapers criticizing his administration.

In Washington meanwhile, General Dwight Eisenhower says he will order a full-scale investigation into allegations of intolerable conditions in the Mediterranean command. A top War Department official will leave for Italy early next week to conduct a first-hand inquiry into the charges made by Scripps-Howard columnist Robert Ruark.

From the Associated Press newspaper wire:

Washington, Aug. 16—(AP)—Gen. Dwight D. Eisenhower, Army chief of staff, said today an investigator—probably the inspector-general himself —will go to Italy to check on the administration of Gen. John C. H. Lee, commander of the Mediterranean theater.

Eisenhower, who arrived at the Washington National Airport at 4:50 P.M. (EST) from a tour of Alaskan defense bases, told reporters that Lee himself had wired the War Department asking that an investigation be made.

"Lee has asked the inspector-general to look into conditions and that's exactly what we'd do anyway," the chief of staff said.

"We'd do it if for nothing else than to defend the officer himself."

Eisenhower said that Maj. Gen. Ira T. Wyche, the inspector-general, probably will make the trip. He said that Wyche likely will leave Washington Monday and it will take "approximately ten days or two weeks" to complete the inquiry.

Eisenhower said he did not "know much about" published reports concerning Lee's administration and the morale of American troops and that "about all I know is what I saw in the papers."

A series of articles in the past week by Robert C. Ruark, an American correspondent, alleged low morale among troops in Italy.

The chief of staff said that when he was in Italy in October of last year he found the 88th Division in "surprisingly high morale." However, he said he did not go down into the southern part of Italy where General Lee has his headquarters.

The investigation in Italy, Eisenhower said, will be "almost like a grand jury hearing." After the investigation the inspector-general will return to Washington to make a report to the War Department.

"As far as the 88th Division is concerned," Eisenhower continued, "as long ago as ten months ago, I found no conditions such as have been reported. What has happened since, I wouldn't know, but I wouldn't imagine there has been much change."

Eisenhower said Gen. Omar Bradley, Veterans Administration chief, probably will visit Italy during his tour of American bases in Europe, but that Bradley has not been asked to investigate the reports involving General Lee.

Sun-tanned and appearing in excellent spirits, Eisenhower and his party arrived here in his DC-4, the Sunflower II. He flew non-stop from Denver, where he had spent last night.

Asked whether he plans to retire as chief of staff to begin his duties as the President of Columbia University in New York, Eisenhower replied that the date still is "indefinite—it depends on when the President says I can go."

He said he found the troops in Alaska have high morale and are "doing the best they can with what they have to work with." He added that many facilities are in "poor" condition and "we've got to get some construction in that region."

From the Associated Press radio wire:

Washington—Army Chief of Staff General Eisenhower says an on-the-spot investigation will be made of the administration of General John C. H. Lee, the Mediterranean theater commander.

A series of articles by American correspondent Robert Ruark (of Scripps-Howard) have been published in the past week, claiming the morale of troops under Lee's command is low.

The chief of staff made this statement—"Lee has asked the inspector-general to look into conditions and that's exactly what we'd do anyway. We'd do it for nothing else than to defend the officer himself."

Eisenhower made his announcement upon arrival at Washington airport from a tour of Alaskan defense bases. He said he did not know much about the published reports concerning Lee's administration and the morale of American troops. In Eisenhower's own words—"About all I know is what I saw in the papers."

The chief of staff said that the inspector-general—Major General Ira Wyche—likely will leave Washington Monday. He said the investigation in Italy will be almost like a grand jury hearing.

Eisenhower said General Omar Bradley probably will visit Italy during his tour of American bases in Europe. But Bradley has not been asked to investigate the report involving General Lee.

— o —

From the United Press newspaper wire:

Batavia, Java, Aug. 16—(UP)—U. S. Consul General Walter A. Foote tonight asked the Indonesian Republican government to say flatly whether it would or would not renew peace negotiations with the Dutch.

Foote visited Indonesian Vice Premier A. K. Gani in Batavia upon instructions from the State Department in Washington, according to a reliable informant. He told Gani that war, or something very like it, still went on, despite the cease-fire orders issued by the United Nations Security Council and the American offer of good offices.

Therefore, Gani was told, the United States wants to know if the Indonesian Republic is not willing to accept the American offer, which presumes a renewal of negotiations with the Dutch. If Indonesia does not, Foote told Gani, the United States wants to report it to the Dutch and the Security Council.

Foote also expressed his government's disappointment at the Republic's failure to answer the American offer directly. The Indonesian reply suggested that the United States use its influence to get the Security Council to send an international commission to investigate the dispute.

Foote told Gani that if the Republic was willing to renew negotiations with the Dutch, the United States would do its best to bring both sides together.

From the United Press radio wire:

American Consul-General Walter Foote has put a direct question to the Indonesian Republican government.

He asked the Republicans tonight to say flatly whether they will renew peace negotiations with the Dutch.

Foote is understood to have visited the Indonesian vice-premier in Batavia upon instructions from the State Department in Washington. And he reportedly told him that war, or something very like it, still went on despite the cease-fire orders issued by the U-N Security Council.

The United States wants to know whether the Indonesian Republic is willing to accept the American offer to mediate the dispute. Our offer presumes that the Republicans would negotiate with the Dutch.

— o —

From the Associated Press newspaper wire:

Jackson, N. C., Aug. 18—(AP)—Sheriff J. C. Stephenson of Northampton County today re-arrested seven white men on charges growing out of an attempted lynching of a young Negro here last May 23.

The sheriff served a bench warrant issued by Superior Court Judge J. Paul Frizzelle charging each of the seven with conspiring to break and enter a jail and with breaking and entering a jail with intent to kill and injure a prisoner.

The defendants, each of whom was immediately released on $2,500 bond, are: Robert Vann, pickle factory worker; Russell Bryant, filling station operator; Linwood and Gilbert Bryant, brothers, carpenters; Glenn Collier, barber; Joe Cunningham, assistant theater manager; and W. C. Cooper, lunch stand operator, all of Rich Square.

The same seven men originally were arrested on the same two charges plus a charge of kidnaping. They were released Aug. 5 when a grand jury failed to indict them.

The grand jury also failed to indict the Negro, Godwin "Buddy" Bush, who had been charged with attempted assault with intent to rape a young white woman.

The defendants have been ordered to appear before Judge Frizzelle Sept. 2 when he will sit as a committing magistrate in the case.

The new legal move was ordered by Gov. R. Gregg Cherry who termed the action of the grand jury "a miscarriage of justice."

A group of white men took Bush from the county jail in what Sheriff Stephenson said was an obvious attempt at lynching. But Bush escaped and hid in the woods for two days before surrendering to the protective custody of the FBI and Solicitor Ernest Tyler.

From the Associated Press radio wire:

Jackson, North Carolina—The Northampton County sheriff has re-arrested seven white men in connection with an attempted lynching of a young Negro last May 23rd.

Sheriff J. C. Stephenson served a bench warrant issued by Superior Court Judge J. Paul Frizzelle. It charges each of the seven with conspiring to break and enter a jail—and with breaking and entering a jail with intent to kill and injure a prisoner.

The same seven men originally were arrested on the same two charges plus a kidnaping charge. They were released August fifth when a grand jury failed to indict them.

At that time, Governor R. Gregg Cherry called the grand jury action a miscarriage of justice. The governor ordered the new legal move which led to the re-arrest of the seven men.

— o —

From the United Press newspaper wire:

Detroit, Aug. 16—(UP)—Chrysler Corporation, the world's third largest auto producer, hiked its entire line of car prices today as the auto industry was attacked by the CIO Auto Workers union for "pure and simple profit eering."

As Chrysler announced boosts of $75 to $130, leaving Ford Motor Company the only major producer still holding the price line, R. J. Thomas, UAW vice president, demanded a federal investigation of "profiteering" and high prices.

Chrysler, announcing it was forced to join the trend toward higher prices because of "increased material and labor costs," said the new prices would be effective Monday and applied to Plymouth, Dodge, DeSoto and Chrysler cars and some Dodge trucks.

Chrysler was the sixth producer in five weeks to announce new postwar boosts, the virtually industry-wide hikes affecting about 75 per cent of all car production.

Thomas charged that six major producers (General Motors, Chrysler, Hudson, Mack, Nash and Studebaker) had earned a total of $374,000,000 before income taxes in the first six months of 1947.

Asserting that the auto industry should be "giving price cuts to the American people, not raising prices," Thomas asked Attorney Gen. Tom Clark to investigate the auto monopoly, steel distribution and auto prices.

From the United Press radio wire:

Vice President R. J. Thomas of the C-I-O Auto Workers Union has demanded a federal probe of what he calls the auto industry's profiteering and high prices.

His demand came as Chrysler corporation boosted its prices on its passenger cars and trucks. General Motors, Nash, Packard, Hudson and Kaiser-Frazer also have hiked price tags in the last two weeks.

The union chief charged that six major auto companies have earned a total of 374-million dollars in the first six months of this year before income taxes. Thomas listed them as General Motors—which reported earnings of 147-million—Chrysler, Hudson, Mack, Nash, and Studebaker.

Thomas said that instead of price increases the auto industry should be giving price cuts to the American people. He asked Attorney General Tom Clark to investigate what he called the "auto monopoly," steel distribution, and auto prices.

He said the earnings amounted to a profit of 222 dollars per car and that G-M's unit profit was 300 dollars. He said that before the war 50 dollars was considered a good return.

— o —

From the Associated Press newspaper wire:

Rochester, N. Y., Aug. 16—(AP)—Mary Jane di Rosa rode to the altar in a wheelchair today, determined that an ankle fracture sustained in a fall while preparing her trousseau should not delay her wedding.

She draped her white satin gown and bridal veil over the wheelchair and, right leg in a cast, rode down the aisle of St. Anthony's Catholic church to become the bride of Ralph Gentile.

"No postponing the wedding for me," she said. "I just didn't want to put it off."

From the Associated Press radio wire:

FEATURE

Rochester, New York—This was going to be shoes and rice day for Mary Jane di Rosa, and nothing was going to hold up the wedding—not even an ankle fracture.

Mary Jane suffered the injury in a fall while preparing for her wedding.

But the guests who came to the ceremony at Rochester's St. Anthony's Catholic church were not disappointed.

They saw Mary Jane ride to the altar in a wheelchair to become the bride of Ralph Gentile.

As the bride explained: "No postponing the wedding for me. I just didn't want to put it off."

— o —

Simplicity

These contrasting stories point up a cardinal principle in radio news writing: simplicity. Simplicity in diction, simplicity in sentence structure, simplicity in manner.

The ear is a fuzzy observer. It does not always hear truly the words that are spoken—it may carry to the brain something quite different from the meaning of the words themselves. Moreover, it cannot go back and rehear, as the eye can reread. All of which means that the radio news writer must fashion his copy so that it will have the percentages with it—so that it will offer the highest probability of accurate reception. And that, in turn, means that everything about it must be as simple as he can make it.

The first rule in simplicity—which, in this context, is synonymous with clarity—is, "Use simple words." Words that are in common use.

In the second week of August, 1945, when the world was waiting tensely for news of Japanese capitulation, a station in Washington broadcast a statement that "Charles G. Ross, secretary to the President, will go on the air about 11 tonight." Shortly after 11 the station was bombarded by telephone callers who demanded that the speech by President Truman be presented as promised. They had heard only that ". . . the President will go on the air."

In a Midwestern city during a polio epidemic, a local station reported, "In the last three days, sixty-three new cases have been identified." In one home in the city, a mother started frantically to make plans to get her three small children out of town. What she had heard was that "sixty-three new polio cases have been identified." She knew that this was several times the daily rate of the preceding week; had she heard the entire sentence, her fright would have been averted. Incidentally, the script writer would have been surer she would hear it properly if he had not written an inverted sentence—if he had put the phrase "in the last three days" at the end rather than the beginning of the sentence.

Words that are widely meaningful, that are generally accepted and understood. When Elmer Davis was broadcasting his masterful five-minute news summary each evening before World War II, he won a huge popular audience; Raymond Swing was on the air each day with a commentary that attracted few but highly literate and highly educated listeners. A word-analysis of the two men's scripts showed that Davis almost never used words beyond the first 2,500 in point of general usage (according to the Thorndyke analysis); Swing used a high percentage of words as far along the scale as the third and fourth 2,500, and sprinkled in a few beyond the eighth.

More concretely: It is bad radio to say that King George was "ensconced on the regal dais" at formal reception. It is effective, and accurate, to say that he was "seated on the throne." "Freedom from slavery" is better than "liberation from servitude." Millions of radio listeners wouldn't know what a holocaust is, but they'd recognize at once a disastrous fire. "Danger" is better than "peril," and "boy" or "young man" than "youth." The newscast that tells you the British police in Haifa have "cordoned off" a section of the city achieves not only a solecism but also an obscurity.

Words that have specialized or technical meanings are, under this same principle, to be avoided. Some thousands of readers of *Broadcasting, Billboard, Variety,* and the rest of the entertainment and radio press know the meaning of "video," but for the millions who don't you have to say "television." Say "record," not "platter." It's a good deal clearer to call him the "weather man" than the "United States meteorological observer."

But remember that the American language is fluid. It is constantly changing, constantly enriching. H. L. Mencken and a lot of others

---

Max Wylie, in his book *Radio Writing,* repeatedly makes the point that good writing is good writing, whether for radio or for any other medium. True, up to a point. "Ensconced on the regal dais" is not only bad radio (though it appeared in a newscast) but also writing to which a prison sentence should be attached. But not all good (that is, effective) writing is good radio writing. Few critics would say that the writing of Keats, or Shakespeare, or President Conant of Harvard, or Dr. Morris Fishbein— each for its own use and audience—isn't good writing. But little of it would be effective radio.

have shown that words technical or esoteric yesterday—"jive," "bazooka," "gland," "polio," "nuclear fission"—are colorful and meaningful today. Watch for words that are coming into general use.

Another caution on words or groups of words: Avoid expressions with ideas that are hard to grasp quickly. Statistics, for instance—they're almost always difficult. Your radio listener won't get it, most of the time, if you write:

The city lost 9 thousand 875 dollars on its electric light plant last year.

But he will understand this:

The city lost nearly 10 thousands dollars on . . . .

Though there are cases in which exact figures must be cited, round numbers are usually to be preferred. It may be necessary once in a while to write:

Mayor John D. Winship has 11 thousand, 909 votes and his opponent, Elmer Clark, has 6 thousand 927, with 89 out of 97 precincts reported.

But in most cases this is better:

Mayor Winship has nearly 12 thousand votes and his opponent, Elmer Clark, just under 7 thousand, with almost all precincts reported.

Note that the mayor's first name and initial are omitted, since they're not needed for identification.

Occasionally, a name may best be omitted entirely. If it's a name that is little known, and one that in itself adds nothing to the meaning of the news, it may be most effective to use title or identification without the name:

The director of social welfare in the county says that 200 families have been driven from their home by the flood.

Often, when statistics are part of the news, they can be made meaningful by apt illustration:

The Japanese report that 125 thousand residents of Hiroshima were killed by the atomic bomb. That's as many people as there are in Spokane, Washington.

OR:

The two cities are 240 miles apart—about the distance of New York from Boston.

This illustration, good for a broadcast in the New York or New England area, should be altered if it were to cover the state of Minnesota:

The two cities are 240 miles apart—about the distance of Minneapolis from Fargo.

What about bromidic words and phrases? "Avoid them like poison," say all the manuals on English composition and news writing. Avoid them because, however good they may have been when first used, they have lost their color (a bromide becomes a bromide usually for no other reason than that it is a sharp, or easy, or colorful means of expressing a fact or an idea. But by the time it has attained bromidic status it has lost its pristine and often imaginative flavor and usually become a lazy and dull substitute for effective diction). Avoid speaking of Sinatra as "The Voice" and Bacall as "The Look"; avoid "high-powered motor cars," "blunt instruments," and "gala occasions."

But there is this to be said: Now and then a bromidic word or phrase, however much overused, may be the quickest and most readily understandable means of saying what the writer wants to say. Perhaps the best rule is something like this: If what is gained in easy understanding and in time is greater than what is lost in imaginativeness and color, use the stereotype. The writer's judgment is the best guide to usage.

A final word on diction: Hyperbole is a dangerous tool.

Webster says that hyperbole is "exaggeration for effect"; and exaggeration in radio copy may produce a disastrously wrong effect. The ear being as inaccurate a recorder as it is, overstatement is likely to mean overemphasis; or the exaggeration is likely to be taken as sober fact. Don't say that "the downpour has flooded every basement in town" or that "Midland is being overrun by a plague of Japanese beetles" unless you mean exactly what you say.

— o —

Rule two in radio news-style simplicity concerns the sentence. Just as words and phrases must be chosen for their broad understandability, sentences must be constructed for the same purpose. A first precept: The simple declarative sentence is the prime sentence tool of the radio news writer. It is, of course, the prime tool of any writer of effective prose. Its importance is greater for the writer-for-the-ear than for most other writers.

The reasons for this are obvious. First, the simple sentence is logical; its subject-verb-predicate order is the order most readily grasped. Second, it is the most common sentence in ordinary conversation. Third, it is likely to be a decently short sentence—one that the hearer can take in at a gulp. Fourth, chances are that it will be easiest for the announcer to voice effectively.

Some illustrations of the point:

BAD: The new bridge across the Hudson, which will shorten the automobile route from central New York to New England points by 50 miles, will be opened today at a ceremony participated in by governors of seven states.

BETTER: The new Hudson River bridge will be opened today. The bridge will cut 50 miles from the automobile route between central New York and New England. Governors of seven states are to take part in the opening ceremony.

BAD: Seven ocean liners brought into New York Harbor today the largest influx of returning European visitors since the late summer of 1939, and tomorrow another seven, including the Queen Elizabeth, will bring an equally large number.

BETTER: The largest number of travelers returning from Europe on any one day since 1939 arrived in New York Harbor today. Seven ocean liners brought them.

Tomorrow seven more liners, led by the Queen Elizabeth, arrive.

One of the more heinous sins of the radio news writer is to indulge in the newspaper practice of putting danglers on sentences:

Fourth of July celebrations in Midland will be carried out by 29 civic organizations, it was announced today by John T. Hillary, chairman of the Civic and Commerce association holiday committee.

The dangler is both long-winded and puzzling. In radio copy, it's a millstone. Much better would be:

Twenty-nine of Midland's civic organizations will take part in this year's Fourth of July celebrations. This announcement was made today by the chairman of the city's holiday committee—John T. Hillary.

For radio purposes, it would probably be best to leave out the second sentence altogether. Newspaper practice is to present every fact in detail. Radio news must often be telescoped—cut down to the essential facts. (Note that among the examples of AP and UP copy earlier in this chapter, radio stories are shorter than newspaper in all except the final example. In this example, a feature story, the radio copy is a few words longer.)

Akin to the problem of danglers is that of credit lines with quotations. In most cases they should precede the quotations:

BAD: "We shouldn't assume that sulfa and other wartime drugs will cure all the world's ills," Dr. Emmons said.

BETTER: Dr. Emmons said, "Sulfa and other wartime drugs won't necessarily cure all the world's ills."

There are—as to almost every other suggestion in this book—exceptions. In some cases context will establish adequately for the listener the identity of the speaker, or the fact that a quotation is being presented. But usually both of these facts must be made clear ahead of the quotation.

Usually a form of the simple verb "say" is most effective in radio copy. "Dr. Emmons said" (or "says") is commonly to be preferred to such labored substitutes as "stated" or "asserted" or any of the scores of variants some teachers like to insert in "themes." But now and then, especially when a quotation is running to several sentences, phrases such as "Dr. Emmons went on to say," or "he explained," are effective. Radio news writers don't often permit direct quotations to run to more than three or four consecutive sentences unless they are presenting complete statements—President Truman's brief V-J Day proclamation, for example. That went on the air hundreds of times,

---

Use of a direct quotation to open a radio news story, without preceding identification of the speaker, is especially perilous to ready understanding. Experienced radio news writers avoid this usage except in the rare cases in which the quotation is short and pointed, in which it establishes the subject of the story clearly and sharply, in which it at least suggests the authority behind it, and in which it can be followed quickly by a credit line. In which, in short, it might just as well have been used without the quotation marks. One such rare case:

"The Munich agreement means peace in our time."

That was the statement of Prime Minister Neville Chamberlain. . . .

usually with only an introductory remark such as: "Here is the President's proclamation."

Inverted credit lines—in the so-called *Time*-style—are anathema to radio newsmen. "Said Dr. Emmons" is about as artificial and unconversational as anybody could make a phrase.

Such phrases as "and I quote" and "end quote" are likewise shunned by skillful writers. The need for them can be avoided in most cases by careful use of the more conversational devices.

How long should a radio news sentence be?

A good deal of nonsense has been spread on the books in answer to this question. Frequently an "average length" of fifteen words has been set up as a desirable norm. Actually, there is no pat answer. Good sentences—readable, understandable sentences—may be of any length from a few words up to twenty-five or thirty. The shorter sentence is most common; if you look at a page of professional radio news copy, you will find few that run to more than a line and a half of typewriting. There will be a few longer, and a few shorter. The longer sentences will be relatively simple, rarely of more than two clauses. The shorter will be direct and often especially forceful because of their brevity. Sometimes, indeed, they'll be no sentences at all, in the grammar-book sense; they'll be instead mere phrases. For example:

State University won another football game this afternoon. Its ninth in a row—a real record. . . .

OR:

Another veto at the United Nations session today—again a Russian veto. . . .

OR:

Even a New Yorker would hardly have recognized the Yankee Stadium today. Not a soul in the stands . . . not a player on the field . . . not a sign of life anywhere.

The reason? Well, you'd never guess. It was. . . .

Such verbless phrases often add vigor and life to a newscast where carefully-complete sentences would deaden it. They're direct, they're brief, they're colorful. Most of all, they're conversational.

Don't overdo them!

More important for the radio news writer than thoughts of sentence length is an appreciation of rhythm. This is a subtle thing. Poets have a skill with rhythm, as have competent prose writers. An intangible quality, it has to do with sound and pacing rather than grammar. A piece of radio prose of sentences all of the same length, or the same unvarying structure, is bumpy—as monotonous as the click of Pullman wheels on a railroad track. A piece with too painfully varied sentences is likely to sound artificial. Rhythm in radio writing—whether it's a talent or a laboriously-acquired craft—is achieved through an awareness of the auditory effect of successions of words. A beginner may have to read his own product aloud endlessly in order to arrive at this awareness. But he must arrive at it if he is to write successfully for the microphone, if he is to write in speakable phrases and clauses, word-groups that let the announcer talk in normal cadences.

Vitality

Let us say, once and for all, that the vitality with which a radio news program reaches its listeners depends heavily on the microphone-personality of the man reading it.

Then let us add quickly that a program's life, color, and vigor will be greater, on the lips of either a "good" or a "bad" announcer, if the copy he reads is lively, colorful, and vigorous.

How are these qualities attained?

In high degree, by practice of the principles already offered in this chapter. Copy that is smoothly conversational, that is simple and direct, that has readable rhythm is decently easy to present in lively manner.

But the skillful radio news writer knows that he can add to the life of his copy by judicious use of verbal tricks that are as old as the earliest class in English composition. He knows that what are called "color words" are important; that well-selected verbs and nouns are strong, meaningful words, that specific words are more vigorous than general words. He knows that the active verb has more drive than the passive. He knows that colloquialisms, even slang, are often valuable. He uses conversational contractions—"he'll," "can't," "they're"—to replace some of their stiffer equivalents.

Since he's skillful, however, he avoids overuse of any of these devices. Too much reaching for colorful words, too frequent use of adjectives and adverbs, is likely to lead to bombast or absurdity. William Saroyan points out, in the preface to his *Daring Young Man on the Flying Trapeze*, that "some writers will go so far as to help an innocent word with as many as four and five other words" and kill it "by charity." To say in radio copy that a fire "utterly destroyed" a building is not likely to be as effective as merely to say "destroyed." "Destroyed" is a strong word, carrying the whole meaning.

On the other hand, to say that "a large crowd" attended the football game is not nearly so vivid as to call it "a hilarious throng"; and to say that it "filled the stadium" doesn't do as effective a job as to report that it "packed every seat in the bowl."

Another forceful device is use of the second person. The news writer can frequently gain interest by this direct appeal to his listener. Examples:

You'll be interested in this story from Washington. It reports that a reduction in taxes. . . .

President Truman is going to take another trip this week. Only last month, you'll recall, he went to Missouri for a long weekend. . . .

A debilitating stylistic habit of some writers is probably the result of grammar school insistence that word repetition is a literary sin. An example of bungling avoidance of repetition:

President Truman says we ought to have a larger army. The Chief Executive told a press and radio conference today that national security demands it. The nation's commander-in-chief went on to say. . . .

Colorful writing needs to be kept in tune with its subject-matter. Here is a lead provided by one of the news services on a winter weather story:

"Old Man Winter still is kicking his heels like a new-born colt throughout most of the nation. The Atlantic coast is being put to bed under a blanket of snow—a blanket that is expected to turn into a comforter of some 10 to 12 inches in depth."

There's color here, and a light touch. But—that same cold spell had caused a dozen deaths, and widespread suffering. The color was out of key with the somber nature of the total story.

All of which is not to deny that repetition may become clumsy. The point is that it is much to be preferred to cumbersome, labored attempts to sidestep it.

Not only that: In many situations repetition—not of words, but of facts or statements—may be the heart of effective radio news writing. If the fact or statement is hard to understand, or if it demands emphasis, repeating it may be the best method of underlining it:

There'll be no school today in Midland, Blankton and Millville. Heavy snows have closed all the roads. Let me repeat that—no school today in Midland, Blankton and Millville.

Again

Here's something of personal importance to nearly 10 thousand residents of Midland—today is the last day to register for voting in November. Election officials say that almost 10 thousand eligible voters in Midland haven't yet got their names on the books. If you're in that 10 thousand, and want to vote, get down to the county court house today—before 9 o'clock this evening.

— o —

One of the most thrilling broadcasts of World War II was that made by Edward R. Murrow of CBS from London on December 3, 1943. Murrow had just returned from a heavy RAF bombardment of Berlin; his radio description of his experience in the plane "D for Dog" is a model of restrained but powerfully revealing radio news copy. Two paragraphs* from the broadcast will illustrate its effectiveness:

Jock was wearing woolen gloves with the fingers cut off. I could see his fingernails turn white as he gripped the wheel. And then I was on my knees, flat on the deck, for he had whipped the "Dog" back into a climbing turn. The knees should have been strong enough to support me, but they weren't. And the stomach seemed in some danger of letting me down, too. I picked myself up and looked out again. It seemed that one big searchlight, instead of being 20 thousand feet below, was mounted right on our wing tip. "D-Dog" was cork-screwing. As we rolled down on the other side, I began to see what was happening to Berlin.

* From an uncopyrighted pamphlet, "orchestrated hell . . ." published by the Columbia Broadcasting System, 1944.

The clouds were gone, and the sticks of incendiaries from the preceding waves made the place look like a badly laid out city with the street lights on. The small incendiaries were going down like a fistful of white rice thrown on a piece of black velvet. As Jock hauled the "Dog" up again, I was thrown to the other side of the cockpit and there below were more incendiaries, glowing white and then turning red. The cookies—the four thousand pound high explosives—were bursting below like great sunflowers gone mad. And then, as we started down again, still held in the lights, I remembered that the "Dog" still had one of those cookies and a whole basket of incendiaries in his belly . . . and the lights still held us. And I was very frightened.

Analysis of this passage may be gratuitous. But its merits should not be overlooked: The dependence on nouns and verbs rather than on descriptive modifiers; the simplicity both in word-choice and structure; the attention to highly specific detail; the use of colorful similes, and of colloquial language; the use of "and" to introduce four sentences— a strictly oral mannerism.

The Murrow show was not, of course, a straight news program—it was a "special event," and a highly personal narrative. But the script holds suggestions for any radio news writer.

Do . . . Don't

Radio news—because of its advantage in speed over the newspaper— has come to place heavy emphasis on use of the present tense. Most newspaper news is in either past or future tense. To speak in strict accuracy, radio news is most of the time in exactly the same boat; but because the newscast so often is able to report an event within minutes of its occurrence—indeed, often while it is still occurring—radio editors have developed the use of the present or the present progressive ("Lawyers of the state *are meeting* in Indianapolis . . .") to give flavor to the sense of timeliness. Obviously this is a usage that may be abused; the scrupulous editor won't employ it unless accuracy justifies it. Here are some examples:

The leader of the striking electricians in Tulsa says his men won't go back to work unless. . . .
President Roosevelt is dead.
Thousands of baseball fans are pouring into New York for the World Series opener. . . .

A corollary of this usage is that the word "today" should be used in moderation. Often the verb-tense obviates the necessity for a specific time-word.

— o —

Pronouns may get a radio writer into a lot of trouble. When they appear in a printed news story, their antecedent relationship is usually clear. But in news for the ear, pronouns should not be used unless their reference is lucidity itself. This usually means that they should be separated from their antecedents by no more than two or three words. For instance:

BAD: Governor Albright is to appoint a new secretary of state. He will make the appointment after. . . .

BETTER: Governor Albright is to appoint a new secretary of state. The governor will make. . . .

PERMISSIBLE: Henry Moody is the new secretary of state. He took office. . . .

BETTER: Henry Moody is the new secretary of state. Moody took office. . . .

Related to this chance of misunderstanding is the careless use of the internal qualifying phrase. Suppose a listener were to tune in to a broadcast in the middle of this sentence:

Alice B. Toklas, for many years secretary to Gertrude Stein, has published a book written in straightforward English. . . .

The listener, if he came in on the words "Gertrude Stein," would be puzzled no end.

— o —

The letter "S" no longer whistles every time it goes on the air. Nevertheless, careful writers guard against processions of sibilants (such as "processions of sibilants") in their copy. A row of S-sounds is difficult for the announcer, and it grates on listening ears. It can usually be avoided by rephrasing.

Alliterations of any kind, as a matter of good sense, should be examined twice. "Tennessee tempests are turning tables on tropical temperatures today" is not only a tongue twister, but also an ear offender.

Like alliteration and its danger, juxtaposition of similar sounds should be avoided. "Swedish ships" is hard to say; "Chinese zeal" hard to say and to understand.

— o —

One of the means of attaining simplicity, directness, and concision in radio news copy is the omission of unnecessary facts. Certain classifications of facts are habitually excluded:

Given names of well-known public figures. You may effectively write General Eisenhower, Premier Stalin, Governor or Senator So-and-so. But Generalissimo Chiang Kai-shek is better than General Chiang, since not many listeners would readily identify the shorter title.

Ages. Ages are inconsequential unless they make the news—in an eighteen-and-eighty-five marriage, for instance, or a Carnegie Hall performance by a nine-year-old violinist.

Street addresses. If they're not vital to understanding the news ("A million-dollar fire has been brought under control in the heart of Chicago—at the corner of State and Madison"), they're commonly omitted, except in local news shows aimed directly at concentrated local audiences.

Texts of formal announcements, communiqués, and the like. Usually summaries in stories are enough.

— o —

In any writing it's wise to avoid leaning on words that are already overworked. Journalese is rarely effective usage. Criminals may better be "arrested" than "taken into custody"; when three are "apprehended" in the same week, it's not necessarily a "crime wave." "Solons" may "probe" a "crisis" in headlines. Not, if you please, on the air. Don't keep calling it a "full-dress peace conference" (as did one of the news services, ad nauseam, in June, 1946) unless "full-dress" is literally what you mean. Don't write "claims" unless you mean "claims," nor "bandit" unless you mean "bandit."

This chapter has already warned against overwriting. And Chapter 3 has described taboos on certain types of words and news-situations.

Putting the Story Together

How do all these precepts add up to produce the effective radio news story?

First, the lead.

The term "lead" comes from newspaper news writing. But early in the development of a specialized style for radio news—soon after Transradio Press began, in 1934, to offer its service to any buyer for radio use —it became clear that newspaper style wouldn't do for the ear. The newspaper lead, characterized by inclusion of a string of major facts in a sometimes cumbersome, long-winded sentence, especially wouldn't do.

Before long, radio news editors were talking about the "soft" lead for radio stories, as opposed to the "hard" newspaper variety. These terms aren't in use today; but the principle of the "soft" lead remains.

The principle is that the radio news lead should ease the listener gently into the story—tell him in general terms enough about the story so that he may more readily understand the details when they are presented. It sets the framework for the story; sometimes it merely tells

---

When the Chicago stockyards burned in May, 1934, two radio news services were operating: The Press-Radio Bureau and Transradio Press. The Bureau furnished to its clients a special 43-word bulletin on the fire:

"A disastrous fire was raging in Chicago's stockyards tonight. All available apparatus was summoned by a general alarm. Three firemen are reported killed. Two bank buildings, the Drovers National Bank and the Live Stock National, with large funds in their vaults, are destroyed."

Transradio's story:

"Lurid tongues of flame visible for hundreds of miles stabbed the night here as a raging inferno sweeps southwestward through Chicago's stockyards, greatest in the world.

"Thousands of persons are streaming from the old tenement houses of Chicago's South Side carrying their belongings with them in a frantic exodus from the fire area as a southwest wind sweeps the flames on through miles of the stockyards toward the center of Chicago.

"Thousands of firemen from every section of the city, reinforced by other companies from Chicago's suburbs and nearby Illinois towns, are fighting desperately to check the blaze that threatens the entire city.

"The odor of burning meat permeates the atmosphere. Smoke hangs like a black fog over the city."

The Press-Radio story is brief, factual, told in short sentences—and colorless. The Transradio story, striving for color, is overwritten, told in overlong sentences, and apparently a newswriter's attempt to compensate with verbiage for lack of specific facts.

him that he is about to be told a story. It rarely offers all the major facts. Some examples will illustrate:

Newspaper	Radio
DANBURY, Wis.—A woman, thought to be about 20 years old, was shot to death in a lonely rural farmhouse 16 miles from here late Friday night and the house became her funeral pyre as the slayers set fire to the dwelling before leaving.	A young woman was shot to death late last evening in a lonely Wisconsin farm house. OR: The body of a young woman, shot to death and burned beyond recognition, was found in a lonely Wisconsin farm house last night.
Last minute efforts to prevent a strike of St. Paul milk drivers failed at a conference this morning but a concession will be presented to the workers at a meeting tonight for final decision as to whether all milk deliveries will be halted at midnight.	We still don't know whether St. Paul milk deliveries will stop at midnight tonight. OR: St. Paul families won't know until a milk drivers' meeting this evening whether they'll have milk tomorrow. OR: Here's the latest on the milk situation.
PORTLAND, Ind.—Five servicemen were killed today and thirteen others were injured, when a C-47 Army transport plane from Wright Field, Dayton, Ohio, crashed on a river bank near Pennville, Ind.	An Army transport plane crashed on an Indiana river bank today, and five servicemen were killed. OR: Five servicemen were killed today when an Army transport plane crashed in Indiana.

This is simplification. The radio lead must not lose its listener, kill his interest, in a welter of detail. It must, on the other hand, orient him toward the facts which are to follow.

And it must do the job interestingly. Radio—as has been said before in this book—faces stiff competition. The radio news lead that does not capture its listener at once may lose him to his bridge game, his novel, or his stamp collection. The opening words of the lead, ideally, should promise him something worth his attention. Analysis of the radio leads above will show some more successful on this score than others.

Radio news writers, because of this need for initial attention, have learned to avoid opening stories with unfamiliar names, with over-ordinary word-combinations, with long-winded explanatory phrases. Examples:

Weak	Better
Arthur Brownstein of Midland is to talk before	Mayor Brownstein of Midland is to talk before . . . .
The President says	President Truman says . . . .
Congressmen seeking re-election may have to kiss all the babies in Sangamon County if	Kissing babies—all the babies in Sangamon County—may be a chore facing Congressmen seeking re-election.
Arthur Jones, director of the regional subdivision of the state War Manpower Commission, is to	A War Manpower Commission official is to . . . He is Arthur Jones . . . .
At a meeting of the Izaak Walton Society in Midland Community House tomorrow night, local fishermen will	Midland fishermen will get together tomorrow evening. They'll meet at the Midland Community House to . . . .

But some words gain "lead-strength" by their very familiarity or intrinsic interest: "The weather today . . . ," "the World Series . . . ," "Hollywood . . . ," "Christmas . . ."

In summary: The lead should be brief, simple, interesting, "easy"; it should introduce the listener smoothly to the details he is next to be given.

— o —

Everything that has been said in this chapter—both about leads and about radio style in general—applies to the organization and manner of the rest of the story. Its job is to give the listener the detail into which the lead has led him, and to do it as compactly, directly, and simply as may be. Since a radio news story rarely runs to more than 400 words—most contain fewer than 200 words—it must be selective. With due regard for the maintenance of balance and accurate over-all impression, it eliminates the petty detail considered a part of the usual newspaper story—much of the less significant detail making up the latter half of a newspaper story organized in the standard "order of decreasing importance" will find no place in a radio story. Its purpose, rather than to give the listener *all* the facts, is to give him the *meaningful* facts—those that paint in broad strokes the event from which the story grows, those that may be readily grasped and remembered.

There exists no arbitrary pattern for organization of the radio news story. It usually follows a plan similar to that of the newspaper story: lead first, then development of the principal facts. But chronological order of facts is more frequently used by the radio news writer than by the newspaper man, for two reasons. It is easy to understand, and it is closer to the conversational pattern.

The examples of radio copy earlier in this chapter illustrate these suggestions. For full measure, however, look at five more radio news stories—all taken from AP and UP radio wires on August 16, 1947 (the radio wires must repeat stories, rewritten, so as to make them available for successive newscasts).

From the Associated Press radio wire:

Top political leaders discussed the pros and cons of the accomplishments of the Eightieth Congress today. G-O-P National Chairman Carroll Reece defended his party's efforts, and took occasion to criticize a C-I-O review and voting guide as "a piece of impudence." The Democratic view was given by Senator Alben Barkley of Kentucky. Barkley said the Republicans ignored the people while they piled up ammunition for the 1948 election campaign.

— o —

Washington—Republican National Chairman Carroll Reece has taken notice of the C-I-O's 1947 voting guide—and he evidently doesn't like it.

The voting guide is a listing of the voting records of Congressmen published last week-end by the C-I-O News as a guide to union members. Beside each legislator's name the labor organization placed the symbol "R" or "W" to denote a right or wrong vote on selected measures from what the C-I-O calls its progressive point of view.

Reece says the voting guide is a new attempt at dictatorship which will meet with the same degree of success attained by the 1946 model. The G-O-P leader claims it is part of a campaign to misrepresent the record of the Republican Congress.

Senate Democratic Leader Alben Barkley has had something to say about that Republican record. He says that in domestic affairs the Republican-controlled Congress painted a sorry picture of partisanship and subservience to special interests, ignoring the needs of the mass of the people.

From the United Press radio wire:

Republican National Chairman Carroll Reece says the C-I-O and the Democrats are spreading confusion among workers as to what he terms "the true intent and meaning of the Taft-Hartley labor law." The G-O-P chairman says the confusion has been created by some union leaders, who hope to continue their dictatorial control of workers.

— o —

A Republican leader charges the C-I-O and the Democratic party with spreading propaganda to confuse the real meaning and purpose of the Taft-Hartley labor law.

Republican National Chairman Carroll Reece says that union leaders have deliberately created confusion in their efforts to continue their control over the workers. And Reece charges that the same campaign is being carried on by what he terms "the politically-motivated antagonism of the Democratic administration, from the President on down." The Reece statement was issued tonight by the G-O-P National Committee in his absence. He is traveling in South America.

— o —

Republican National Chairman Carroll Reece spoke up tonight in defense of the Taft-Hartley labor law. He asserted in a statement that the C-I-O and the Democrats are spreading confusion among workers as to the true intent and meaning of the law.

He said some labor leaders are propagandizing workers in the hope of continuing what he described as their "unbridled dictatorial control of workers." Confusion among workers also is being caused, Reece said, by the Democratic administration's "antagonism" toward the labor law.

Reece said a recent poll conducted by Opinion Research Corporation showed that although a majority of workers were opposed to the act as a whole, they overwhelmingly approved of specific provisions of the law.

The Radio Feature Story

Radio news programs carry "feature" stories—that is, human interest stories, stories dealing in pathos, humor, adventure, and the like—as do the newspapers, in about the same proportions and for the same purpose. The feature story is the frosting on the cake, the leavening of the serious news.

In the construction of this kind of story the two media come more nearly together than in their handling of straight news. Both are likely to lead such stories with "suspended interest" openings:

Newspaper	*Radio*
John Jones, laborer at the Midland Iron works, didn't want his pay check.	This is the story of a man who didn't want his pay check.
John Jones, 1917 Hunt street, at least gets credit for trying.	Well, here's a Midland man who certainly gets credit for trying.
His 8-year-old sister told Bobby Parker, 5, never to go near the brook. . . .	Little Bobby Parker—he was only 5—was told many times not to go near the brook.
Ever wonder what a polar bear does in 100-degree weather?	Ever wonder what a polar bear does in hundred-degree weather?

There are other similarities. The chronological arrangement of facts is likely to furnish the pattern for many such feature stories. There is greater latitude for imaginative writing and for the use of color. Most such stories are short.

The contrast between newspaper and radio treatment of a common type of longer feature is well shown here:

From the United Press newspaper wire:
New York—(UP)—The wartime pinup girl soon will be as outdated as the flapper of the roaring twenties unless she washes off the excess makeup, puts on a good girdle and dons some chic clothes, Miss Brownie of the Fox-Brownie fashion house said Saturday.

Miss Brownie, one of New York's top designers, naturally is in favor of women with clothes. But she sincerely believes that men like the Hollywood type of siren only for display on barracks walls and warship lockers. They don't intend to come home and marry them.

"The pinup girl is a caricature of a woman," Miss Brownie said. "She exaggerates her features and her figure and leaves nothing to the imagination. The only type of beauty which will last is that of the feminine, stylish woman."

She illustrated her point by describing a fashion show she gave recently for wounded veterans. The show featured girls clad in scanty night-club costumes and models wearing clothes Miss Brownie had designed.

"The boys whooped and hollered when the chorus girls appeared, but they reserved their long low whistles for a girl who wore a demure black velvet dress with a high white lace collar and white cuffs," she said. "The chorus girls were startling and glamorous, but the well-dressed girl was the one they would like to come home to."

To convert "pinup glamor" into much-to-be-desired chic, Miss Brownie prescribed these steps: A stiff dose of soap and water to scrub off all mascara, eye shadow and rouge, a good girdle, an upswept hairdo, a wardrobe of dressmaker suits, evening clothes and platform shoes.

From the United Press radio wire:
New York—Here's a word of warning to the nation's wartime pin-up girls. And it comes from one of New York's top fashion designers.

Miss Brownie—of the Fox-Brownie fashion house—predicts that unless the pin-up girl reconverts she will soon find herself as outdated as the flapper of the roaring twenties.

Miss Brownie sincerely believes that the only type of beauty that will last is that of the feminine, stylish woman. The men—she says—like the Hollywood siren type only for display on barracks walls and warship lockers. They don't—she adds—intend to come home and marry them. Miss Brownie's definition of a pin-up girl is—in her words—"a caricature of a woman."

And to illustrate her point the top-flight designer describes a fashion show she gave recently for wounded veterans. The show featured pin-up girls clad in scanty night-club costumes and models wearing clothes that Miss Brownie had designed.

The veterans—she reports—whooped and yelled when the chorus girls appeared. But they reserved their long, low whistles for the girl who wore a demure, black velvet dress with a high white lace collar and white cuffs.

Miss Brownie prescribes three steps to convert pin-up glamour into feminine charm. First, a stiff dose of soap and water to scrub off all excess make-up. Then a good girdle to tone down the curves . . . combined with an upswept hairdo for high style. And finally—with a plug for her profession—Miss Brownie prescribes a wardrobe of dressmaker suits, evening clothes and platform shoes.

And before this new stylish American woman goes out for the evening, Miss Brownie warns her not to leave her dressing table unless her make-up is subtle and her clothes discreet. Then—says Miss Brownie—she will be feminine, poised, natural, and—terrific.

The term "feature"—again as in newspaper usage—is also applied to longer, more exhaustive "time-copy" articles. These are not news stories, but background explanations or human interest treatments of timely or seasonable (in contrast to spot-news) subjects. Each of the two radio news services offers a number of these features, in the form of five-, ten-, or fifteen-minute daily or weekly broadcasts; since they are intended for sponsorship, however, the copy is written for three-and-one-quarter-, seven-and-one-half-, or eleven-and-one-half-minute periods (at a rate of about ten words a minute). AP offers, for example, "Washington Today," a daily commentary on the national capital's activities; UP matches it with "Under the Capitol Dome." AP has its "Farm Fair," background and commentary on current agricultural developments; UP has "On the Farm Front." Both services offer sports features, women's features, and others of the same general nature—about a dozen each.

These features are characterized by currency and authority of information, informality of manner, and breadth of appeal.

The Mechanics of Radio News Copy

Rule 1 in the preparation of radio news copy is: *Make it legible.*

Copy that is not instantly and unmistakably legible—perhaps by an announcer who has had little chance to go over it in advance—is obviously loaded with booby traps. The announcer must never be led into error; he must never be hung up by having to puzzle out something he can't read at a glance. This does not mean that the editor who types the copy must make it letter-perfect—there probably never lived the newsman who could type that well. It does mean that errors must be clearly and unmistakably corrected.

Copy from the news service printers comes typed in capital letters, double-spaced (some AP copy is triple-spaced). A few announcers, taking their cue from this copy, prefer their locally-written copy in caps. But most copy turned out in radio newsrooms is in capital and small letters, double- or triple-spaced according to local practice or a particular announcer's desire. A few simple rules aid the writer to avoid errors or illegibilities that might mislead the announcer:

If a typing error occurs, never strike over. Instead, xxxxx out the offense and rewrite the word. (Later, black out the error with a soft black copy pencil—carefully, so that the editing does not create a new chance for mistake). This rule is especially important in the cases of initials, capital letters, figures, and other symbols that do not have spelling context to aid the eye in identifying them.

If you edit typewritten copy in pencil, do it neatly. Use as few inter-lineations—typewritten or penciled—as are consistent with speed in getting the copy to the announcer. If time permits, retype paragraphs or pages in which editing might cause confusion.

Include phonetic spellings of words that might puzzle the announcer —usually, though not always, foreign words. *Be sure*—don't phoneticize Joliet, as did one press service editor, "HO-LEE-AYE." The accepted form:

General MacArthur ordered the break-up of the Zaibatsu (ZY-BOT'-SOO) in order to . . . .

Don't phoneticize unnecessarily. And don't, as did one of the national book clubs in a script for which it hoped radio stations would give it free time, put an asterisk after the word in question and the phoneticization as a footnote at the bottom of the page!

Be generous with punctuation—commas, periods, and dashes especially. Newspaper and magazine style calls for as few commas as clarity permits; radio style just the opposite. Commas should be put into copy wherever they are needed to suggest slight voice pauses. Dashes in radio copy surround parenthetical expressions (some radio editors and some announcers prefer rows of periods or "suspension points" instead of dashes) or indicate longer or more pronounced pauses. For example:

Then—says Miss Brownie—she will be feminine, poised, natural, and—terrific.

Thomas listed them as General Motors—which reported earnings of 147-million—Chrysler, Hudson, Mack, Nash, and Studebaker.

The two cities are 240 miles apart—about the distance of Minneapolis from Fargo.

Tomorrow seven more liners, headed by the Queen Elizabeth, will arrive.

State University won another football game this afternoon. Its ninth in a row—a real record.   •

OR:

State University won another football game this afternoon—its ninth in a row . . . a real record.

Use plenty of capital letters. In radio copy, meaning is often immediately suggested by capital initials on titles and other words which, in ordinary newspaper "down style," would be written with small letters. It is better to write "the General moves today" than "the general moves today."

Make paragraph indentations deep—at least ten spaces.

Make paragraphs short—usually no more than five or six lines.

Underline (by typewriter or pencil) words that demand special announcer-emphasis. But don't overdo it. Announcers don't like to be told their business.

Put end-marks at the close of all stories—either on the typewriter or in heavy black pencil. An effective typewritten end-mark is a row of the # symbol (########). Some writers use the conventional newspaper symbol, –30–. Some use their own initials—usually modestly written in small letters rather than caps.

Number all pages, consecutively.

Indicate clearly in the script the spots where you think commercials may best be inserted. The announcer may not follow your suggestions if timing doesn't work out right, but they often help him.

Hyphenate as few words as possible at the ends of lines. Some writers make no end-of-line hyphenation an absolute rule—a pretty good one.

NEVER let a sentence begin on one page and continue to the next. A period, end-mark, or continuation line should be the last typewritten symbol on every page.

Try to avoid continuing a paragraph from one page to the next.

If a story continues from one page to the next, mark MORE, in typewriter or pencil, clearly at the bottom of the first page.

Use abbreviations sparingly, or not at all. The abbreviation "Adj."—and many others—may prove puzzling. Many newsrooms insist that even such words as "Mister" and "Doctor" be spelled out.

Write figures unmistakably as you want them to read: "one thousand" rather than "1,000," "25 hundred" rather than "2,500." A widely-followed rule commands that figures smaller than 1,000 be expressed in figures, others spelled out: "2 million 500 thousand," "8 thousand 500," "750 thousand," "37 billion." The UP *Radio News Style Book* proscribes "a million" because of the chance that it might be heard "8 million." Some radio newsmen insist on hyphens in figures: "37-billion," "2-million 500-thousand."

Make all pages uniform in size—8½ by 11 inches. A smaller page inserted in a script may confuse the announcer; a larger page is difficult to handle.

Put on the script only what you want the announcer to read (except for necessary editing marks). A script cluttered with nonessential pencilings and other marks may trouble him.

Do not use newspaper copyreading symbols on radio copy. They may be confusing to one not familiar with them.

Finally . . . break as many of these rules as the announcer who is to read your copy desires. Tailor copy to fit his particular taste.

Accuracy

Whatever his failings, the prime aim of every responsible worker with news is accuracy. Whatever the loose popular wisecrack about it, the degree of accuracy attained by those who gather and write news is enormously high.

Many of the radio news problems in maintaining a high standard of accuracy are precisely those of any other medium. The heart of accuracy is fact. Earlier in this book (Chapter 3) is discussed the difficulty of determining just what the facts are; within this limitation, however, the ardent hope of every news writer is that he may work with unequivocal and unquestionable names, dates, places, quotations, and other facts the sum of which truly and truthfully describes an event.

Assuming that the news writer has such unequivocal material at his disposal, he needs to exercise everlasting vigilance to make sure that he gets it down on paper without error. He must check facts that he has not personally verified; he must make sure that he writes "250" when he means "250" and not, in haste, "260" or "350." He must write with simplicity and clarity that surpasseth all misunderstanding. He must edit his copy with an eye to every comma.

All of this applies to every news writer, whether his work is for newspaper, news magazine, news letter, or newscast. But the worker in radio news faces special problems.

He must produce copy that will be audibly as well as visually accurate.

This means that he has to keep constantly before him the precept with which this chapter opened, and its corollary as well: that the ear is a fuzzy recording instrument. If he fails for an instant to remember either precept or corollary, he may find himself writing copy that, though factually accurate, carries a false impression to the listener.

That is to say, he may write copy that will leave with a hearer an impression contrary to its true meaning.

Observance of the suggestions in this chapter will steer him away from most such pitfalls. But he must remember that radio copy is heard once and once only—unless he sees to it that significant or easy-to-mistake facts are made indelible. For example:

A report from Moscow—by way of Madrid—says that Premier Stalin will give no Russian food to Germany this winter. It's an unconfirmed report . . . and it's in direct contradiction to what Stalin promised last week. According to this story, Stalin is angry because Germans haven't raised enough of their own food.

The report may or may not be true. Remember, it's unconfirmed—and it comes to us through an often unreliable channel.

The fact that the news in this story is probably untrustworthy could hardly be missed. But without the qualifications that appear in every sentence, it might be mistaken for indubitable fact. If, for instance, the story appeared like this:

Until 1947, little published material on handling radio news was available. About the only volume—beyond two mimeographed handbooks published before the war and now out of date—was:

Phil Newsom, *United Press Radio News Style Book* (United Press Associations, 1943). A brief simplified manual offering fundamental precepts for radio news style.

The postwar development of radio news and of university instruction in radio news writing and editing led to the publication of a number of books and manuals, intended both for classroom and radio newsroom use. Among the books:

William F. Brooks, *Radio News Writing* (McGraw-Hill, 1948). A brief manual, with emphasis on NBC practice and a good chapter on news for women.
Carl N. Warren, *Radio News Writing and Editing* (Harper, 1947). A primary textbook in radio news practice.
Paul White, *News on the Air* (Harcourt, Brace, 1947). A vastly readable book, excellent on network news procedures and on news dramatization.

(*continued on next page*)

Premier Stalin is quoted as saying that Russia will give no food to Germany this winter. Stalin is angry because Germans haven't raised enough of their own food. This position contradicts Stalin's promise of last week.

Repetition, as has been said before, is a priceless tool of the radio news writer, even when it uses up precious seconds.

And emphasis on the source of news, when it concerns a matter of which there may be the slightest doubt, is mandatory.

Among the manuals of radio news practice:

B. L. Hotaling, *A Manual of Radio News Writing* (Milwaukee Journal, 1947).

Baskett Mosse, *Radio News Handbook* (Medill School of Journalism, Northwestern University, 1947).

INS Radio News Manual (International News Service, 1948).

6

How Does It Go Together?

The Format of the News Program

News broadcasting is not old enough for ossification to have set in; no pattern or format for the news show so fixed as that of the newspaper story has grown up. Radio's very flexibility demands daily adjustment to such factors as the nature of the news that makes up a show, the personality of the man who is to broadcast it, the competition it faces, its purpose, its audience. These factors and others—some fairly constant, others changing from day to day—operate to control the form of a news broadcast.

Nevertheless, radio news editors have developed a widely flexible guide for organization of the news show—departmentalization. It is no more than a loose guide, subject to daily alteration or outright jettison. But its outlines are clear in most news shows you hear.

The pattern is characterized by division of news into a few main categories—five or fewer, as a rule. In any news show there is pretty sure to be an international department, a national, a state or regional, a local—in effect, a geographical pattern. Some editors think it effective to add a human interest category; most don't.

The departmental format has a good deal to recommend it, for both editor and listener. Its simplicity and orderliness make it easy to arrange and fit together, whether it is being written from scratch in the newsroom or merely clipped from the teleprinter. The same simplicity and orderliness help the listener to understand the often involved interrelationships of news—they give him a clarity of news picture that he wouldn't get if he were told, in jumbled succession, of a strike in Detroit, a Latin-American counter-revolution, the latest United Nations impasse, a two-alarm fire on East Twelfth Street, and a second strike in Los Angeles.

Usually the show opens with a punch. Its editor selects the story he thinks holds greatest interest or importance for his audience, and moves

119

directly into it. If the story is one from the international scene, he follows it with other news under the same head. Then he draws a breath
and starts off on a second category.

During World War II this format was pretty firmly formalized—war
news led ninety-nine in a hundred shows. Often half the news-time
went to stories from the fighting fronts. Then followed international
diplomatic and political news, war-related national news, other national
news; finally, regional and local news. It was a rare day, from 1941 to
1945, when something other than war led the news program. After V-J
Day, as the news from Europe and the Pacific grew less dramatic, the
stereotype of leading with international news was quickly discarded.
But the departmentalized format remains.

Within the main categories, as in the show as a whole, this pattern
customarily follows what the reporting textbooks call the "order of decreasing importance." The strongest story comes first; the next strongest second; and so on.

(Some radio newsmen hold that newscasts should open not with the
day's "best" story, but rather that a short and "softer" story should precede. They argue that the show as a whole should open "easy," lead
the listener in, just as the first sentence of the individual story does.
Those who follow this principle are in a minority.)

Radio news editors are inclined to frown on human interest categories—that is, on saying to their listeners, "We will now make you
laugh or cry for two minutes." They prefer, rather, to use human interest stories spotted through the show where they are appropriate. Some
editors insist that a show close with a light touch, a humorous story (as
do many announcers, who think such material gives them opportunity
to close with a virtuosic fillip). But most who have tried this convention have found that on many days the humorous stories are very sad
indeed. The most satisfactory rule for use of the human interest story

---

The departmentalized pattern was dominant in the war years partly
because the radio wire services followed it. On both UP and AP radio wires,
copy for five- and fifteen-minute newscasts was served up in this form.
This meant that radio stations without rewrite staffs had little choice but
to accept it. Doubtless the fact that the pattern was presented to them so
frequently influenced radio newsmen doing rewrite jobs to make it habitual.

seems to be that of a Pacific coast editor: "Use 'em when they're good, when they're short, when they're in good taste, and when they fit smoothly into the show."

The departmentalized pattern, though it is the common one, is by no means sacrosanct. It may effectively be varied, for instance, by opening with an outstanding story of regional interest—a story about an unseasonal blizzard, perhaps—then picking up the international and national news and returning at the end to more regional stories. The order of the main categories may be—and should be—altered according to the nature of the news. A summary of the major news, in one-sentence bulletin form, may be used either to open or close the show, regularly or on special occasion.

Many departures from the basic pattern suggest themselves; and the wise editor will experiment with all he can invent, both to gain variety in his broadcasts—though he must always remember that regular listeners like familiar patterns—and in the hope of developing successful new patterns. For example: WCBM-Baltimore designed a fifteen-minute daily news show in three parts: first, the "How-Time-Flies" department, reviewing Baltimore news of one, five, and fifteen years ago; second, a "Club Calendar," a list of outstanding current club and civic events; finally, an interview with an authority on a current topic. ABC's "Three Views of the News," a summer replacement for the Winchell show, is similar in form—Ben Grauer on current events, Ed Thorgersen on sports, and a visiting fireman (such as Schiaparelli, the dress designer) on a special topic. WIND Chicago, running fifty newscasts a day, devoted the 7-to-8-A.M. period to six ten-minute news periods, each on a different category of news. Late in 1947, NBC began broadcasting a "second edition" of its 7:15 P.M. "News of the World" roundup—the later "edition" at 11:15. NBC says that the second show is "not a re-

---

KVOA-Tucson opens a fifteen-minute afternoon newscast with a quick spot summary covering the last half of the show, and closes with a spot summary covering the first half. "Thus," says KVOA, "both the listener who tunes in late and the one who tunes out early get at least the gist of the whole show." KVOA adds that this format might be even better adapted to a breakfast-time show, aimed at the listener who may have to run to catch a street car.

peat broadcast. Maintaining the format of the first program with
Morgan Beatty presiding at the news desk in Washington and calling
in NBC correspondents throughout the world, the second edition will
be completely revised up to air time to incorporate reports of latest developments."

The five-minute news show is a condensation of the longer program.
It is usually firmly departmentalized; its bulletin-like stories are arranged according to a standard routine, with little variation. It rarely
offers straight human interest material. Its crowded space—only three
to three and one-half minutes if it's a sponsored show—permits no more
than forty or fifty words to any but a vastly important story, and no time
at all for entertainment.
                                     — o —

A variation in effect, though usually not in basic organization, is
achieved in what is called the headline show. It borrows a technique
directly from the newspaper—the use of a brief summary, sharp and as
dramatic as may be, at the head of each story. The technique is simple:

AMERICAN DIPLOMAT LOST IN AIR CRASH
A dispatch from Hawaii this morning tells us of . . . .

This pattern has its virtues. The headline has punch and emphasis;
properly used, it sharpens listener-attention toward the news to follow.
It breaks the even flow—the monotonous flow, if the announcer is un-
skilled—of the straight-copy show, and may thereby gain dramatic
effect. It keys each story in advance, tells the listener what to expect;
sometimes it may be devised to tell him only enough to arouse his
interest (as, for instance, in a question-headline: WHAT ABOUT
ATOMIC BOMB SECRETS?).

But it has a number of shortcomings:

It is artificial, just as the newspaper headline is artificial. Its attempt
to summarize may result in misleading oversimplification. It breaks
the "conversational" flow of the broadcast; it may seem to be throwing

---

Some newscasts make regular features of what they call "last-minute
bulletins"—brief shots of striking news thrown into a minute's time just
before sign-off. This device has its danger: It's likely to be artificial, for its
implication that three or four bulletins have just come into the newsroom is
not always truthful, and now and again the listener is going to know it.

equal emphasis on each story, or undue emphasis on minor stories; it sometimes calls unfortunate attention to the mechanics of putting the show together.

It is more effective in a two-voice than in a one-voice show—one voice for the headlines, another for the stories. This adds mildly to the production problem, and considerably to the cost.

Unless deftly handled, it may separate unduly stories that ought to be tied together. It may turn a listener away—if the headline doesn't interest him—rather than attract him.

The repeated breaks in the flow of news—especially as stories in the show become shorter and of less significance—may become annoying to the listener. This tendency can be reduced by grouping a number of related stories under one headline; but this departure from pattern may in itself puzzle the listener.

It is a little harder to write than the straight-copy show. And news service copy, designed for other use, requires more editing to fit into the pattern.

For these reasons, the headline show is not widely used. It may nevertheless have its place in the over-all schedule of the station with so many news shows daily that variety in pattern is desirable.

— o —

Most departures from usual format find their justification in this need for variety; in the necessity of offering a show different from the one a competitor is putting on the air at the same time; in the desire to fit a show to a special situation; or in the personality or special capacities of a particular broadcaster.

An example of the show fitted to the man was that broadcast every morning in a Midwest city by a former foreign correspondent. During the war, he dealt almost exclusively with war news; often he devoted his

A news editor who makes a regular practice of breaking the rule that radio news stories must be short is Dick Crombie of KJR-Seattle. On one of his regular news shows timed so as to compete with those on other stations, Crombie uses only one to three stories in a fifteen-minute period. He believes that he not only gains diversity, offers the listener a different kind of radio news diet, but that he also offers major stories developed with background, so that their meaning as well as their barebone facts are presented.

entire time to exhaustive development of the day's two or three most important war stories. To use his background and experience, he usually wove comment on the news in with its factual presentation. The war over, he turned to a more conventional pattern.

In another case, a man of breezy personality, skillful at humorous ad libbing, appears to organize his shows by throwing all the stories into the air and presenting them strictly in the order in which they come down. This makes a pretty bad show for the thoughtful listener; but this newscaster gains a considerable audience, thanks to the effectiveness of his manner.

A news broadcaster on a 5,000-watt station in the Northwest comes on the air just after a network international round-up. He devotes only a closing minute of his time to national and international news; most of his show goes to local and regional news, with a three- or four-minute commentary on a local news situation at its midpoint.

The format of the network international round-ups, familiar to all radio listeners, grows out of their nature. Usually they operate from New York or Washington; they take their listeners in turn to distant corners of the earth to bring in foreign correspondents, with news of the national scene opening or closing the period.

Occasionally news shows deal with one event only. Scores of broadcasts went out from San Francisco in the spring of 1945 with news of nothing but the United Nations conference. A natural disaster such as a Mississippi flood, an accident such as the crash of an army airplane into the Empire State Building, a local parade welcoming a visiting dignitary to the city—any such event may call for broadcasts devoted to nothing else. Shows of this kind—usually considered in the "special events" classification—depend partly on prepared script, partly on ad lib color and description, often partly on interviews. They are to be discussed in more detail in Chapter 9.

Where Does the News Come From?

The bulk of the news on which American newscasts are built—to repeat what has already been said more fully in Chapters 1 and 3—comes from the news services. These services offer two types of service to radio newsroom: News written especially for broadcast comes from AP, UP, and Transradio; news written for newspaper publication, from AP, UP, and INS (about a dozen stations, in 1947, bought this kind of service from the British Reuters service, and four from the Canadian Press News).

What do the radio wires provide?

Let the UP wire serve as example (but remember that such examples are "dated" almost the day they're written, for specific practices on all services change frequently).

It clicks off its sixty words a minute, twenty-four hours a day, printing its stories on yellow paper off a big roll long enough to last for more than a full day's service. The heart of its service is its series of "round-ups"—nine departmentalized summaries a day, each providing enough copy for about ten minutes of broadcast time. These round-ups are "cleared" from a main UP bureau—say New York or Chicago—at periods when they are most likely to serve broadcasters' needs for fifteen-minute newscasts. The first one moves before six in the morning to furnish copy for early shows, others at irregular intervals through the day until the ninth in late evening. They follow a general rather than a set pattern. There are always sections to cover international and national news, and—a postwar innovation—regional sections summarizing the latest regional news. The order in which these sections are presented varies according to the nature of the news, except that the regional section always comes last. On occasion there may be additional sections: one devoted to news of labor-management problems when such news is extensive, one on a special occurrence such as a national election, one on a great natural disaster or a weather phenomenon of broad proportions, one on "sidelights"—brief disconnected stories of general interest. They are scheduled to move through the printer without interruption, at stated times, but they are sometimes broken for bulletins or the less-frequent flashes.

Each round-up is followed by "The World News in a Nutshell"— half a dozen ten- to fifteen-word paragraphs summarizing the major news highlights.

Second, the UP wire provides a dozen five-minute broadcasts entitled "News of the World in Brief." These follow a more definite pattern than the longer round-ups—fifty-word summaries of half a dozen stories of widest (usually international) news first, then as many of national news, then a few paragraphs of regional news.

To supplement these summaries, which carry no "date lines" (on the radio wire, the term "date line," though generally used, is a mis-nomer, for it gives only the place of origin of the news, without the date), dozens of individual stories occupy some of the time between them—most of them short, but some running to 300 words or more. These stories carry date lines:

WASHINGTON—CONGRESS IS IN AN UPROAR TODAY . . .

Often they cover more fully events summarized in the round-ups or "World in Brief" shows; more frequently they are stories on events of limited or regional importance or interest. Most of them are straight news, but a score of them a day are headed SPORTS, and another score—human interest stories—FEATURE.

About a dozen times a day (the number varies from bureau to bureau) the printer interrupts the flow of news on the trunk wire—the wire whose copy originates, say, in New York or Chicago—for regional "splits." A "split" is a period during which the regional UP bureaus send to their clients stories originating in their own geographical areas. Often a split follows immediately on a round-up, or a five-minute show, to provide the regional section. Splits of this kind are usually brief—three to ten minutes on the wire. But some run to fifteen minutes or longer.

Weather receives particular attention. In the early morning and the late afternoon the printer grinds out the latest weather forecasts—a long string of them, covering all the areas served by a regional wire. Special forecasts supplement these regular features from time to time. When an event such as the season's first cold wave comes along, stories headed UNDATED WEATHER move several times a day on the wire.

Markets also get regular space. Stocks and bonds, grain, produce and livestock markets—both listings of opening and closing prices and summarized stories about trends on all such markets—are routinely reported; the news editor knows that at stated times each day he will receive this kind of news from both national and regional sources.

The editor also knows that he must watch for special warnings on individual stories. A story may be headed EDITORS: NOTE THE NATURE OF THIS STORY. This usually means that the story deals with crime, sex, or other subjects against which some stations have prohibitions. Or it may be headed FOR AUTOMATIC RELEASE AT 7:30 P. M., or HOLD FOR RELEASE—EXPECTED ABOUT 6 P. M. In the one case he may schedule it for use at 7:30, without further instruction; in the other, he must watch the printer for the release.

He learns to watch, too, for corrections of matter already moved on the wire, and for "repeats"—repetitions of stories or sections of stories requested by individual newsrooms whose printers have for one reason or another gone temporarily off the beam. Occasionally he is told, IMPORTANT NEWS EXPECTED FROM THE WHITE HOUSE ABOUT NOON; occasionally he finds the flow of news interrupted by interbureau messages, usually in code.

Some stories are headed ATTENTION EDITORS. Usually these stories deal with news of peculiar interest to the radio industry, with new service plans of the UP, or like matters. They are put on the wire for the information of the editor rather than for broadcast—though he is free to use them if he wishes.

Finally, there are a large number of daily and weekly features—most of them five-minute broadcasts for one voice; some longer and more elaborate. Most of the daily features move on the wire between midnight and 4 A.M., when the wire service day begins—the four-hour period when broadcasts are fewest and news activity at its lowest. A few—news commentaries and the like—move at regularly scheduled periods during the daytime. The list changes from time to time, as

---

A sample of the kind of story to which special attention is drawn:

ATTENTION EDITORS:

Dallas, Texas—News Commentator Cedric Foster (of Mutual Broadcasting System) has been named defendant in a 100-thousand dollar slander suit.

The suit was filed . . . .

news trends change ("Today's American Hero" was dropped soon after the end of the war); but the list in early 1947 is typical:

For women: "Women in the News," "In the Women's World," "In Your Neighborhood," "Good Eating." *For farm audiences:* "On the Farm Front," "Farm Market Survey." *Sports:* "Speaking of Sports," "Great Moments in Sports," "Sports Lineup," "Sizing Up Sports." *Business:* "Tomorrow's Business," "Weekly Business Review." *Commentary:* "Today's UP Commentary," "United Press Reporting," "Under the Capitol Dome." *General:* "Time Out," "World of Tomorrow," "In Movieland," "Your New Home," "Names in the News," "Highlights."

In the same period, the UP radio wire provided a number of extra features:

Seven series of scripts: eighteen broadcasts called "Along the Baseball Trail" and sixteen on "Sizing Up the Majors"; twenty-four on gardening, twelve on income tax, and six each on the Moscow Big Four meeting, fashions, and retail shopping. And five single broadcasts on Washington's birthday, Thomas A. Edison, Alexander Graham Bell, Adolf Hitler, and infantile paralysis.

The AP radio wire corresponds closely, in many ways, to the UP. It offers five fifteen-minute summaries a day, the first clearing in time for a 7 A.M. broadcast and the fifth at 10:45 P.M.; it supplements these with periodic suggestions that editors may combine a number of specifically designated stories and summaries to make up other fifteen minute shows. In general pattern the AP fifteen-minute summaries are similar to the UP round-ups.

"Bulletins" and "flashes" are regular features of all news wires. Bulletins are terse summaries—one or two sentences—of "hot" news events; they are heralded by five bells on the printer, and they take precedence over other news, often interrupting stories on the wire as they break. The AP radio wire triple-spaces them for attention; the UP heads them "A Bulletin from the United Press" (a bid for getting the words "United Press" on the air). Radio news editors become blasé about bulletins—they know that bulletins are customarily followed by enlarged stories marked SUB. Unless an editor is close to a deadline, or a show is actually on the air, he's likely to wait for the SUB.

Flashes are something else. Signalized by eight to ten bells on the printer,

(*continued on next page*)

AP presents twelve five-minute newscasts—the first clearing shortly after midnight (the AP day runs from midnight to midnight) and the last at 11:30 P.M. These, too, are similar to their UP counterparts.

And in most other ways the two services are alike. AP has, to correspond to "The World in a Nutshell," a series of "Spot Summaries" that move hourly around the clock. It carries its special sports, human interest, market, and weather news. It keeps its newsrooms up to date by providing frequent SUBS for earlier or developing stories. It carries six regional splits in twenty-four hours, some of them serving (as on the UP wire) as the regional sections of fifteen-minute shows. Similar

---

they appear only when sensational news occurs: the death of a President, the end of a war, the cessation of a strike of national proportions. They are couched in telegraphic terms:

FLASH   WASHINGTON

PRESIDENT DIED THIS AFTERNOON

Like the bulletins, they are followed by enlarged stories, but more quickly, and often in "takes" or separate paragraphs headed MORE PRESIDENT'S DEATH or ADD ROOSEVELT. Development of the stories they announce may take all the wire's space for many succeeding hours (there was little but invasion news on the wires for twenty-four hours following the flash of June 6, 1944, on the Allied landing in Normandy).

Bulletins and flashes on the radio wires usually come a few seconds later than those on the newspaper wires, thanks to the necessity for rewriting for radio.

Radio listeners know that any program on the air may be interrupted for news of this character—more frequently for flashes than for bulletins. Radio news editors have learned that sometimes too great haste does not pay. In April of 1945 the AP flashed a premature declaration of immediately forthcoming German surrender; radio put it on the air, only to find that UP was not carrying the story and that Senator Connally had talked not wisely but too well at San Francisco. The next month INS was first with a flash on President Roosevelt's death; most radio newsmen, though they put it on the air immediately, said carefully that "International News Service [or "a news service"] has announced" the tragedy, or that the news was unconfirmed. In August, a false flash mysteriously found its way onto the UP radio wire, declaring that JAPAN ACCEPTS SURRENDER TERMS. Though it was followed in a matter of seconds by a "kill" order, many radio stations had already broadcast it.

corrections, special notices to editors, interbureau messages, and so on appear.

AP's special features (AP calls them "telescripts")—many of which correspond directly to those of the UP—in early 1947 were:

For women: "Women Today," "Listen, Ladies," "To Market, To Market." *For farm audiences:* "Farm Fair." *Sports:* "The Sportsman," "Sport Special." *Commentary:* "Between the Lines," "Behind the World News," "Washington Today." *General:* "Jigsaw News," "Side Street America," "Flashes of Life," "Stars on the Horizon," "Sideshow," "Today in History," "It Happened During the Week," "Leaders of Tomorrow," "Preview of Tomorrow."

Transradio Press, which offers radio newsrooms the third wire written and edited for broadcast, follows a pattern similar to those of the AP and UP radio wires. It is limited by two factors: Its service runs only eighteen hours a day, from 6 A.M. to midnight; and it does not have the vastly extended news-gathering organization built up by AP and UP, a fact that holds its service largely to national and international news (it offers no regional splits). Features of TP service:

An hourly bulletin-like "headline" summary of major news, "Transradio Headlines."

Fewer summarized, "ready-made" broadcasts for either five- or fifteen-

---

What, you ask, if AP and UP services are so much alike, is the basis for a choice between them? The most voluble speakers on this subject are the sales representatives of the services.

A good many radio editors say that for most practical purposes one service is about as satisfactory as the other (there are, it is true, violent partisans of each). Without question a radio newsroom can, with decently intelligent editing, do a good job of newscasting with either service. In the early competitive days of the two services—say in 1941—there were many radio newsmen who thought UP service sometimes overwritten, striving too hard to achieve vigor, color, brightness; and as many who thought AP, in the conservative AP newspaper-writing tradition, underwritten, lifeless. Since that time both services have settled into a sound and generally satisfactory radio news style; in this matter, too, they now closely approach one another.

On what basis, then, make a choice? Among the factors that influence station decisions are: price of service; a belief that one service—or the other —provides generally sounder news coverage (national and international, or regional, or both); the matter of competition—the fact that a competitor is using one service may lead a station to select the other.

minute periods. Use of the periodic suggestions for combining selected stories to form such newscasts (like the AP wire's suggestions for the same purpose).

Heavy emphasis on sports news.

As many as twelve, or more, brief daily "commentiques" of 200 to 300 words each, rather than five- or fifteen-minute commentaries.

Emphasis in "Radio Intelligence for Executives" on news of the broadcasting industry, much of it not intended for broadcast.

Emphasis on Washington news.

Inclusion of a number of the special features like those carried on AP and UP wires (but fewer of them, in part because TP is not operating in the early morning hours when such features are often moved).

— o —

The newspaper wires whose printers operate in many newsrooms are primarily useful to stations with news-writing or editing staffs. Their stories are intended for readers, not for listeners, and since they offer no material tailored for radio use they cannot ordinarily be used effectively for broadcast without rewriting. An increasing number of stations, however, are depending entirely on rewritten news; for such stations the newspaper wire is usually thought to be more satisfactory than the radio wire. It operates at the same speed as the radio wire—sixty words a minute—and it can produce no more copy in a day. But it gives more detail on almost every individual story (note again the contrasted examples in Chapter 5); it offers every story that the radio wire carries, and some the radio wire doesn't (both get their news from the same reporters), since some types of stories are considered

---

The question arises: Why, if the newspaper wire gives individual stories in greater detail than the radio wire, and since it operates at the same speed, can it offer more stories? Why isn't the radio wire, with its shorter stories, more inclusive? The answer: The newspaper wire repeats itself comparatively little. Once a story has been fully told, it is unnecessary—for newspaper purpose—to retell it. The newspaper copy desk can use the early morning story as well at noon, if there are no new developments on it, as it could use one hot off the wire. But the radio wire must retell a story half a dozen times in the same period. AP, for instance, would put the story on its radio wire in two fifteen-minute scripts, three or four five-minute scripts and perhaps a "separate" during a six-hour period. Its newspaper wire would carry the story only once.

unsuitable for broadcasting. In general details of operation, it resembles the radio wire closely.

Into the newspaper wire picture comes INS, a third entry. INS officials hold that its copy, intended primarily for newspapers, is so expertly and interestingly written that much of it can be broadcast effectively "with only the minimum of editing that any copy ought to have before going on the air." Most radio newsrooms, however, seem not to go along with this opinion. Three-fourths of the INS printers in radio stations in early 1948 were in newsrooms receiving at least one other service—presumably a radio wire service in most cases. Only thirty-two stations (according to *Broadcasting Yearbook*) were operating newsrooms with INS service only.

The three major news services are in agreement on the meaning of advance release notices. In 1948 they announced that stories released for morning papers would become available to radio at 7 P.M., Eastern time; those released for afternoon papers at 7 A.M., Eastern time.

— o —

What are the sources of news other than the wire services?

Not until after World War II was any other source of great importance to more than a few pioneering stations. Those few were the stations which had developed their own local and regional news coverage. This is the most important *undeveloped* source of news for radio; it is discussed at length in Chapter 8. It is enough here to say that it should be considered vital to most stations.

Certain other sources, however, exist. One is the A.T. & T. sports ticker which some newsrooms boast—the fastest sports news service, since it reports events like baseball games inning by inning (the press services usually report them only every three innings). There are always "handouts" coming into every newsroom—prepared "free publicity" from all kinds of organizations that would like mention of their affairs on the air. Some of these are worth air time; most aren't. They come to the newsroom in mailbags, by telephone, by personal bearer.

NBC and CBS furnish special Washington news services to their affiliates—recorded programs of special interest to an affiliate's locality, such as an interview with a Congressman, and the like. A service called Radio Washington offered regional Washington news to individual radio stations in 1946, and built up a list of some dozen clients, but apparently found this list insufficient to make the operation successful.

Putting the Rewrite Show Together

The first task of the man who is to write copy for a newscast is to organize his material.

He starts by "clearing the printers"—taking from them all the copy that has moved since the last previous show. Let us say he has two newspaper wires at his disposal. He reads through all the copy—rapidly, for he has learned a "skimming" technique—and cuts or tears off each story as he goes. He balances one service's story against the other's, deciding whether he'll need only one, or both, to write his story. He disposes of each story as he goes along. He may put it into one of several piles on his work table—national, international, regional; or more specialized, such as labor, sports, diplomatic, United Nations. He may throw it into a waste basket, if he's sure it's of no use to him or other editors. He may file it for future reference. Or he may lay it aside for the farm editor, or the sports man, or some other specialist on the station's staff.

If his newsroom also provides radio wire service, he may follow the same process with a second set of copy. Though he may use the radio wire little, it's helpful to him to know what news the wire is playing, and how it's being treated. Many radio news writers prefer to depend heavily on newspaper wires, however, since they offer more news than

---

Actually, the competent news man—radio or newspaper—begins work long before he gets near his office. He keeps constantly abreast of the current news and its implications, by reading newspapers, listening to newscasts, reading *Time* and *Newsweek* and other such publications. And he reserves some of his spare time for books like those of John Gunther, and other means of building up his background knowledge. He cannot waste precious minutes, once he sits before his typewriter, looking for such material—a necessary part of his working equipment.

radio wires and since merely reading radio copy may influence style or approach.

Now his job becomes the organization of specific departments of his show, and of specific stories within each department. Probably he has already decided—while he was sorting the copy—with which story to lead his show, and at least in a general way how he is going to follow it. He picks out the copy on his main story, and anything that should be related to it, and makes a separate pile of it. Perhaps he goes to the newsroom's reference shelves for background information; perhaps he examines a map on the wall. If he is very methodical, he may organize all the copy he expects to use in the same manner, and arrange it all in order. More likely, having got ready for his first story, he goes to work on it.

If you're watching him, you're likely to be astonished at the speed with which he writes. He seems to be working "from memory." In effect, that's what he's doing. Rather than pick each sentence or fact laboriously from examination and re-examination of the copy, he writes the story from the knowledge he has gained of it in the earlier reading. Occasionally he refers to the wire copy to pick out a title, a date, a specific statistic. The experienced radio news writer believes that this method makes it easier to write his copy in smooth, broad strokes rather than in fine detail.

He starts his typewriter going two to two and a half hours before the show is scheduled. Few radio news editors can turn out a complete show in less than two hours—about ten minutes for each triple-spaced page of copy.

His first words may or may not be a conventional opening—"good morning" or something of the kind. The preference of the man who is to read the copy governs this.

In any case, he is sure to work hard over the first sentence—work to make it a short, sharp, striking sentence that will be easy for the reader to "punch" and sure to catch the listener's interest. Such a sentence, perhaps, as:

Justice is catching up with the top-ranking Nazis this morning.

OR:

Half a million more men are out of work today.

OR:

The Midwest is fighting its way out of the season's worst snow storm.

OR, PERHAPS:

We told you this morning that the Governor would have an important announcement on the proposed session of the Legislature. Now we can give it to you. There'll be no session . . .

Then he goes on to develop the story, probably telling it in greater detail than he would grant most stories. Since it's his lead story, he may let it run to 300 or 400 words, a length pretty sure to make it his longest single piece of news. Midway through it, he may get up for another trip to a reference source, or make a telephone call to check on a fact or get additional information. Finished with it, he stuffs the copy on which it is based into a waste basket, or lays it aside for possible use in a later show.

Now comes his second story, and a new problem—that of "transition," moving smoothly and conversationally from one story to the next. Discussion of the transition problem appears later in this chapter.

Thus he moves rapidly through the show, checking his copy, discarding printer material as it's used, perhaps rearranging order of stories as he goes. Every half hour or so he checks the printers again—checks bulletins to see whether they affect stories he's using, rips off new material he wants. Bulletins or fresh stories may force penciled revision or complete rewriting of some of the work he has done. If the show is one that carries a mid-commercial, he suggests the place for it at about the midpoint of his copy—probably at the end of a major news department. After this suggestion, he again follows the wish of the announcer as to whether to write in a second opening device: "Now back to the news," or something of the kind.

He tries to complete the show fifteen or twenty minutes before air time. He has now written about a page more copy than the announcer customarily uses—enough for a margin of safety. The last page or so is made up of short stories; perhaps the writer pencils heavily in the margin of those he thinks may best be omitted the word OPTIONAL or some other symbol. If the show customarily closes with a human interest story, or if the writer thinks a particular story a peculiarly effective closing, he marks it clearly as the "kicker."

Now comes the job of editing—careful checking of every word of the copy for possible errors, for infelicitous phrasing, for illegibility. Overtyping or "x-ing out" must be clarified or blacked out in pencil Interlineations must be sharply defined.

The copy now goes to the announcer, if he is other than the writer. The announcer reads it through carefully, questioning the writer from time to time about phrasings, meanings, pronunciations. He may do some editing himself—underlining words or phrases he decides to hit hard, or words that demand special care; perhaps marking pauses or breathing spaces; perhaps altering phraseology here and there.

Meantime the writer is back at the printer, making a last-minute check on late news. He may find something that demands rewriting of some of the copy. If it's a late afternoon show in summer, he may turn to getting the late baseball scores. Perhaps these or a not-off-the-printer story he won't have ready by the time the show takes the air. In such case, the writer bangs out the copy as rapidly as possible and tiptoes into the broadcasting booth to give it to the announcer. Then back to the printers, to watch for possible news-breaks up to the end of the broadcast.

Exactly what goes into such a newscast is shown in the exhibit

---

How to figure the length of a show?

Baskett Mosse, former NBC news man now directing radio news courses at Medill School of Journalism, presents in the *Newscaster* a chart of three methods for quick estimate of the time-length of a news script. The simplest of the three is based on the number of typewritten lines. For an average 15-minute show (12 minutes 30 seconds of news), 188 lines are needed; for a 10-minute show (8 minutes of news), 120 lines; for a 5-minute show (3 minutes 30 seconds of news), 53 lines. (The average line, written on a pica typewriter from margin to margin, includes ten words.)

The word basis: A 15-minute show requires 1,880 words or 9½ pages of copy; the 10-minute, 1,200 words or 6 pages; the 5-minute, 530 words or 2½ to 3 pages. (A page is pica-typewritten, with margins of about an inch at the sides and 1½ inches at top and bottom.)

The inch basis: A 15-minute show, 62½ inches of copy; a 10-minute, 40 inches; a 5-minute, 17½ inches.

given—an exhibit presenting both original teleprinter copy (and some other suggestions of source material) and the finished newscast copy. This show was written from stem to stern by two newswriters in a Minneapolis radio newsroom for broadcast at 12:30 P.M. on December 1, 1945. It drew its material primarily from the Associated Press newspaper "A" wire (serial numbers slugged A), the United Press newspaper Midwest Trunk wire (slugged IIX or PR), the AP radio wire (slugged APR), and the UP radio wire (slugged MS). The opening weather story was based largely on telephone calls to the United States Weather Bureau and other local sources. Occasionally the writers drew on their own knowledge of the current news.

Careful examination of the wire copy and the rewrite underlines one of radio news's hazards—departure from original fact. In several cases the rewritten copy does not say exactly what the original says—note the story from Italy and the Higgins story as particular examples.

The newscast's typewritten copy, triple-spaced and in caps and lower case on yellow copy paper, with deep paragraph indentations and very small margins, ran to 207 lines. Of these, the announcer used only 165. He discarded five short stories (one of them a repeat of an earlier story), totaling 34 lines, before going on the air; he edited out three short paragraphs, totaling eight lines, during the broadcast.

The copy for the newscast appears here in large type; the original wire copy, comments, and explanatory material in small type. Passages in the wire copy used directly in the final copy are in italics. Care has been taken to present both wire copy and final copy exactly as it appeared, with typing or other errors included.

The Newscast

Northwest residents woke up this morning to find streets and highways covered with a glassy sheet of ice. It didn't take them long, either, to discover that driving was very difficult and that most busses weren't running. In the Twin Cities and Duluth, motorists trying to get to work were soon caught in traffic jams at the bottom of hills. A number of accidents have been reported as cars skidded into one another or crashed into stationary objects such as telegraph poles.

The worst part of today's storm and ice is that it may continue through Sunday. The weather bureau tells us that the rain is due to continue all day and that it probably will turn into snow tonight or tomorrow. Weather bureau forecasters say that because of the low cloud cover there isn't going to be any increase in temperature, either. That means the present icy conditions are here to stay for at least the next 24 hours.

Highway department officials are extremely pessimistic about road conditions. They warn motorists not to travel unless it is absolutely necessary—and then they are urged to drive with extreme caution. Conditions are particularly bad in northern Minnesota and north-eastern Wisconsin. The temperature in these areas is around the 28 degree mark, which means it isn't cold enough for snow and not warm enough to melt the ice.

There was no bus service either in or out of the Twin Cities until mid-morning. The Northland Greyhound canceled all trips out of the Twin Cities until about 10:30 a. m. when two busses were sent out, one to Willmar and another to Bemidji. The Deephaven busses also started running about the middle of the morning. Anoka, Stillwater, Mercury and Medicine Lake busses also are in operation, but they are running very late.

According to the weather bureau, temperatures are warmer in southern Minnesota and South Dakota, and the ice has turned to slush. Driving is still hazardous, however, and drivers in those areas should proceed with caution. It's quite possible that temperatures will drop before nightfall, thus restoring the icy conditions which were prevalent this morning.

At Grand Forks, a light rain is falling right now, but as yet there is no ice. But since the weather bureau predicts a drop in temperatures, you Grand Forks residents had better be prepared for difficult driving conditions there.

This present storm is very widespread. It is centered in central Kansas with icing conditions extending from Missouri north into Canada, and from central North Dakota to eastern Wisconsin. The weather bureau expects no relief until sometime tonight or tomorrow, when snow is expected, thus taking at least some of the glaze from the icy streets and roads.

The weather situation remains bad over much of the Northwest, and the ice that is forming in Minnesota will continue to pile up. And tomorrow it will hit Wisconsin, to make driving hazardous there.

The Dakotas will have cloudy skies today and tomorrow, with lower temperatures tonight, and a little light rain in eastern South Dakota today.

(To this point the newscast is built from material gained by telephone. Now wire copy is used:)

HX74

Chicago, Dec. 1—(UP)—Weather forecast:

Wisconsin—Rains south and central and *freezing rain or drizzle* extreme north portion *tonight. Slightly warmer.* Sunday cloudy with rain snow northwest portion.

Iowa—*Rain tonight changing to snow flurries* extreme west portion late tonight. Warmer east and colder extreme portions, *Sunday* mostly cloudy and *colder.*

Minnesota—*Rains south and light freezing rain or drizzle north portions this afternoon and tonight, with rain changing to snow north and snow flurries southwest portions late tonight or early Sunday.* Snow north and snow flurries south portion Sunday. *Colder Sunday afternoon.*

RW1122A

Minnesota will continue to have its freezing drizzle during the day, which will turn into snow tonight or early tomorrow. The mercury will drop tomorrow afternoon.

Wisconsin will get its freezing drizzle tomorrow, and the temperature will climb slightly.

And in Iowa, rain tonight will change to snow. Tomorrow will be colder.

The present Twin Cities temperature is right on the freezing mark, and will stay there, meaning that ice will get thicker and slipperier during the rest of the day. So watch your driving and your footwork.

(Material for the following paragraph comes from an earlier newscast.)

Weather is the main topic of conversation in several other parts of the country today. New Englanders still are talking about their two-day snow storm which moved out over the Atlantic last night. It left behind 45 persons dead, and a heavy deposit of ice and snow. Com-

munications were disrupted, and coastal areas suffered considerable
damage from high winds and lashing tides.

A76WX
    TRUMAN
By Ernest B. Vaccaro
    Washington, Dec. 1—(AP)—*President Truman and nearly 200 guests,
including five disabled soldiers,* caught the football fever today as they
bundled up in their warmest clothes for a holidayp in Philadelphia.
    Distinguished friends were in Cabinet and Congress were invited to
accompany the Chief Executive to the Army-Navy classic aboard a special
White House train scheduled to leave at 8:45 a.m. (EST).
    The soldiers, all amputation cases, were Isadore Turnasky, Fernand R.
LeClaire, John L. Eisenmann, Albert Berlanger and Walter Leszcynsky.
They are patients at Walter Reid Army Hospital here.
    Aides said the President was disappointed that more enlisted men at
the Hospital couldn't go along but that he gave his last tickets to these
five.
    SU741AES NM

A94WX
    BULLETIN
FIRST LEAD TRUMAN
By Ernest B. Vaccaro
    Washington, Dec. 1—(AP)—President Truman, taking along five dis-
abled soldiers, left the capital today to join 102,000 other fans at the
Army-Navy football game in Philadelphia.
    SU904AES

A95WX
    BULLETIN MATTER
    Washington—First add first lead Truman x x x Philadelphia.
    The President's special train, carrying nearly 200 guests including Con-
gressmen and Cabinet officers, pulled out at 8:45 a.m. (EST).
    Although an old Army man himself, Mr. Truman went to the game as
a neutral observer. *He arranged to sit on the Army side during the first
half and on the Navy side during the last half.*

A96WX
    The five soldiers accompanying Mr. Truman, all amputation cases, were
Albert Belanger (CQ), Fitchburg, Mass.; John L. Eisenman (CQ), Wey-
mouth, Mass.; Fernand LeClaire, Willimantic, Conn.; Walter Lesczczysn-

sky (CQ), Wilmington, Del.; and Isadore Turansky (CQ), Erie, Pa. All were from Walter Reid Army Hospital here.

The soldiers, among the first to go aboard the train, got the last of the President's tickets. Aides said he was sorry that more men from the Hospital couldn't go along.
    (NO PICKUP)
    SU907AES

Three other special trains, loaded with Congressmen, Army and Navy officers and their friends, made the trip from Washington to the Philadelphia classic. Space on the specials was sold out weeks ago.
    CC934AES NM

A107PX
    PX OUT   .
        Army-Navy Weather
    Philadelphia Dec. 1—(AP)—The sun poked out for the first time in three days today and it'll stay out for the Army-Navy game, the weatherman reported.

    But "it'll be a little stiff," he added, because the wind will be blowing briskly through the open north end of Municipal Stadium—and the temperature "won't get much ofer 40."
    NQ948AES   NM

A121PX
    PX OUT
        WITH ARMY-NAVY (100)
    Philadelphia, Dec. 1—(AP)—*Football mad fans put in a hard night before the Army-Navy game.*

    Edmund Baer, manager of the Benjamin Franklin Hotel, reported:

    1. *As many as eight men slept in a room, and cheerfully too.*

    2. *Sample rooms, function rooms, ballrooms and cots set up on an impromptu basis were used for sleeping.*

    3. *Officers of the Army and Navy slept side by side with enlisted men and civilians in lobbies and lounges.*

    Night clubs reported a rush trade, much of it from carefree visitors who had no knowledge of where to lay their heads.

    And many a fan got his sleep in an all-night motion picture house.
    CZ1042AES

        (Note that AP stories on the "A" wire are timed in Eastern standard time, the others in Central standard. The symbol "CQ" in A96WX means "correct"—spelling corrected from that in A76WX.)

HX62
    WITH FRALEY
    Philadelphia, Dec. 1.—(UP)—*Its fair and cold* with a temperature of 36 degrees predicted by the weatherman for the Army-Navy grid classic today.
    The sun was shining on a dry cold day. The field was in excellent condition and everything was in readiness for the starting whistle.
    RW1003A.

A129PX
    BULLETIN
PRECEDE WASHINGTON
    Philadelphia, Dec. 1—(AP)—*A special train carrying President Truman, five disabled soldiers and nearly 200 guests to the Army-Navy football game arrived in Philadelphia at 11:18 a. m. (EST) today.*
    CZ1143AES NM

    Mr. Truman told reporters there were 200 blankets at the Municipal Stadium to protect the Presidential party against the wintery weather.
    Happiest of the group which came over on the special train were the disabled veterans from the Army's Walter Reed Hospital at Washington.
    They got their tickets and top level transportation by writing the President a direct appeal for seats to the big game.
    NQ1152AES

    As the special train sped towards Philadelphia, the President made a surprise visit to car six where he shook hands with the soldiers, all sergeants.
    "I'm glad you could come," he told them. "I hope you have a good time. There are blankets for you if you get cold."
    It was Mr. Truman's first Presidential visit to Philadelphia.
    In a happy frame of mind, he went from car to car on the White House train, shaking hands with members of the party, calling most of them by their first names.
    He said today would be his fifth trip to an Army-Navy game.
    It was his first on-the-record trip out of town since he cancelled scheduled visits to North Carolina, Georgia, Missouri, Oklahoma and Texas. He made a secret flight to Grandview, Mo., last Sunday to visit his mother, Mrs. Martha Truman, on her 93rd birthday.
    NQ1201PESNM

    Governor Edward Martin and Mayor Bernard Samuel went aboard the special which arrived 15 minutes ahead of schedule.
    After an official greeting from these two officials and other welcomers, the President left at 11:55 a. m. for the Municipal Stadium.
    CZ1208PESNM

The President and his guests reached the Stadium at 12:03 and went directly to his private box on the 50-yard line on the Army's side for the, first half.

Mr. Truman was greeted by officials of both the military and naval academies. The President entered the Stadium in a limousine accompanied by a police escort.

JJ1225PES

HX75

Philadelphia, Dec. 1.—(UP)—President Truman, his official family and more than 100,000 other spectators poured into Philadelphia's huge Municipal Stadium today for the 46th renewal of the Army-Navy football classic.

A *bright, dry, cold day* greeted the thousands of game-bound fans who filled the Stadium to capacity an hour and a half before game time waiting expectantly for the annual pre-game parade of midshipmen and cadets.

The President arrived by special train from Washington with Mrs. Truman and his daughter Margaret.

The city was jam-packed for the occasion with five-star generals and admirals, Congressmen, Cabinet members, GI's from army and navy hospitals and those of the general public lucky enough to grab ducats for the game.

Included among the greatest collection of gold braid ever assembled outside of a Presidential inauguration were Adms. William F. (Bull) Halsey, Jonas Ingram and Royal Ingersoll; Cice Adms. H. C. Leary; Rear Adms. Milo F. Draemel and John H. Brown. Secretary of the Navy James V. Forrestal will head the Navy delegation.

Gen. Douglas MacArthur was unable to make the game due to pressure of business in far away Tokyo. A reservation had been held for MacArthur until game time.

RW1126A.

The weather is clear and cold in Philadelphia today where President Truman and his party of nearly 200 guests are watching the Army Navy football game. The contest started about 12:30—at the same time we went on the air a few moments ago.

President Truman and his guests reached the stadium about 11 o'clock central time, and went directly to a private box on the 50-yard line on the army's side of the field. During the half, the President will move over to the Navy side as custom demands.

A special train carrying the President and his guests arrived shortly after 10 o'clock this morning. Aboard were five disabled soldiers from the army's Walter Reed hospital in Washington. They got their tickets and transportation to the game by writing directly to President Truman.

As the train was speeding toward Philadelphia, the President himself made a surprise visit to the car occupied by the soldiers.

"I'm glad you could all come," Mister Truman said as he shook hands all around. "I hope you have a good time. There are blankets for you if you get cold." The President was in a happy frame of mind this morning. He went from car to car on the train shaking hands with other members of his party, calling most of them by their first names. He told newsmen that this is the fifth time he has seen an army-navy football game.

The civil aeronautics authority in Philadelphia canceled all flights in and out of Southwest airport and within a ten-mile radius of the stadium where the game is now going on. The order was issued as a protective measure for President Truman.

Philadelphia hotel men say that football fans put in a hard night as they waited for game time to come around. One hotel manager reported that as many as eight men slept in a room—and they did so without complaining. Cots had to be set up in sample rooms and ball rooms. Officers and enlisted men slept side by side in hotel lobbies and lounges.

HX44

By John L. Cutter

United Press Staff Correspondent

Washington, Dec. 1.—(UP)—*The Pearl Harbor investigating committee* is determined to nail down the reason for the delay in decoding and translating Japanese messages intercepted before the Dec. 7, 1941, attack.

The committee took a week-end recess today but expects to plunge back into the question when hearings resume Monday. Maj. Gen. Sherman Miles, who was head of Army Intelligence at the time, will return to the witness chair.

Evidence before the committee shows that . . . (the story continues for 51 lines more, detailing evidence given by General Miles before the committee).

D812A

HX56

Washington, Dec. 1.—(UP)—*The Senate appropriations committee today prepared to take up $122,275,000 (M) worth of flood control and rivers and harbors projects approved by the House.*

House approval was given overwhelmingly despite objections of its appropriations committee members who asked delay of consideration until next year.

The projects for which the House voted funds included:
       Rivers and Harbors
    New Work

Great Lake to Hudson River Waterway	2,000,000
Mississippi River Between the Missouri River and Minneapolis	8,439,500
Flood Control	
Garrison Reservoir, N. Dak.	2,000,000

(The story continues with eighteen other similar items, none in the WCCO area.)
    RW946A.

While all the excitement was going on in Philadelphia, Washington was quieter than usual this morning. The Pearl Harbor probers are taking the day off. The House and Senate are in recess for the week end. Members of the Senate appropriations committee are preparing to take up the 122-million dollar flood control and rivers and harbors bill passed by the house yesterday.

If the measure is passed it will mean 2-million dollars in federal funds for the Great Lakes waterway, 8 and a half million for improvement of the Mississippi river between Minneapolis and the point where it empties into the Missouri, and 2 million more for the proposed dam at Garrison, North Dakota.

HX47

       By James E. Roper
          United Press Staff Correspondent

Washington, Dec. 1.—(UP)—Congressional pressure today virtually assured a public airing of charges that State Department representatives have been acting contrary to U. S. policy, particularly in China.

Chairman Tom Connally, D., Tex., of the Senate foreign relations committee revealed he would ask the committee to admit the public and the press on Wednesday when it hears the story of Patrick J. Hurley, who resigned as ambassador to China. Hurley charged procommunist and pro-

*imperialist foreign service representatives undermined his diplomatic work
in China.*

*The foreign relations committee will vote Monday on whether to follow
Connally's lead and thus order the first open meeting of the committee
at this session of Congress.*

Hurley also was invited to testify . . . (the story continues for 23 lines
more, presenting a number of Congressional statements on the subject).
    D831A

The Senate foreign relations committee will vote Monday whether
it will open the Patrick Hurley investigation on state department policy
in China to the public. The hearing is scheduled for Wednesday.

HX45
        By Ruth Gmeiner
                United Press Staff Correspondent
    Washington, Dec. 1.—(UP)—*The government today handed farmers
a blueprint for 1946 production* outlining cutbacks from high wartime
levels for most food crops, livestock and livestock products.
    *Secretary of Agriculture Clinton P. Anderson, in announcing national
farm production goals for next year, urged farmers to plant 356,244,000
acres in crops.*
    This would be 5,500,000 acres more than were cultivated this year, but
boosts in corn and cotton production make up most of the increase.
    The goals for poultry, milk and eggs . . . (the story continues for 33
lines more, with other details of the proposals).
    D821A

Secretary of Agriculture Clinton Anderson today outlined his 1946
food production program for the nation's farmers. He urged farmers to
plant 356-million acres in crops, which is 5 million acres more than were
planted this year.

HX70
    London, Dec. 1.—(UP)—*United Nations delegates listened to hours
of American travelogues and speeches today* and looked at Movies and
brochures *designed to persuade the UNO to establish its permanent headquarters in certain parts of the United States*
    *Atlantic City, the Black Hills, Boston and Chicago presented their cases
to the preparatory commission's sub-committee this morning,* and others
were scheduled for this afternoon.
    Contesting claims ranged from a no-strike pledge by Boston labor against

the UNO to a Black Hills contention that no one ever would waste an atomic bomb on that sparsely settled area.

Paul Bellamy, Black Hills representative, offered 100 square miles in the states of Nebraska, South Dakota and Wyoming.

Bellamy outlined the resources and physical aspects of the Black Hills. He suggested that trade could be stimulated by setting up shops at headquarters, "because American tourists like to buy things." He promised there would be no import duties, but gave no hint that he had checked the point with U. S. government officials.

JR1625A

PR4

Pierre, S. D., Dec. 1.—(UP)—*Arguments for selection of the Black Hills as the United Nations Organization capital were to be presented today to a UNO preparatory commission sub-committee in London by Paul E. Bellamy, Rapid City businessman.*

Bellamy, who had informed Governor M. Q Sharpe of the appointment, declared that "competiionis tough" because of the lack of housing, printing, educational and communication facilities and of the great distance of the Hills from Europe.

Sharpe, however, in a "best wishes" message reiterated the argument that the absence of a large city in the Black Hills "is to our advantage for many reasons."

CD1046A

In London, United Nations delegates listened for hours while Americans from Atlantic City, the Black Hills of South Dakota, Boston, and Chicago urged the organization to locate the world capital in their respective areas. Speaking for South Dakota is Paul E. Bellamy, a businessman from Rapid City.

HX14

BULLETIN

1ST LEAD TRIAL (OECHSNER)

Nuernberg, Dec. 1—(UP)—*Rudolf Hess flew to Britain to lure King George VI back to Germany for a peace conference with Adolf Hitler, the United Press learned today as the war crimes tribunal ruled that Hess was mentally capable of standing trial.*

MORE ET457A

HX16

ADD 1ST LEAD TRIAL (OECHSNER) X X X TRIAL.

In a statement describing his flight, Hess revealed that Hitler knew nothing of his scheme. Hess wrote a letter to Hitler before leaving Germany in which he described his plans, it was learned.

Hess parachuted onto the Duke of Hamilton's estate in Scotland on May 10, 1941, only a few weeks before Hitler attacked Russia.

BJ516A

HX19

ADD 1ST LEAD TRIAL NUERNBERG (OECHSNER) X X X RUSSIA.

Lord Justice Sir Geoffrey Lawrence, British presiding justice, announced when court opened today that the tribunal considered Hess sane after his melodramatic statement yesterday confessing that he had faked his loss of memory.

Hess asked that he be permitted to continue in the trial, and the tribunal agreed to his request.

(PICK UP 3RD PGH EARLY: HESS ROSE X X X).

BJ531A

HX21

BULLETIN

WITH TRIAL (OECHSNER)

By Ann Stringer

United Press Staff Correspondent

Nuernberg, Dec. 1.—(UP)—*Rudolf Hess parachuted into Britain in 1941 to bring King George VI back to Germany for a peace conference* before Adolf Hitler opened his attack on Russia, the United Press learned exclusively today.

MORE BJ535A

HX28

ADD HESS NUERNBERG (STRINGER) XXX TODAY.

Hitler knew nothing of his deputy fuehrer's scheme . . . (the story continues for 38 lines, mostly concerned with retelling Hess's 1941 exploit).

BJ615A

A25

BULLETIN

FIRST LEAD WAR CRIMES

Nuernberg, Dec 1—(AP)—*The international military tribunal ruled today that Rudolf Hess, who confessed he had been faking amnesia, must continue to stand trial with 19 other Nazi leaders accused of war crimes.*

MK421AES

A27

BULLETIN MATTER

FIRST ADD HESS-WAR CRIMES X X X WAR CRIMES.

Lord Justice Sir Geoffrey Lawrence, . . . (the story continues for 97 lines, devoted to trial proceedings of the day before. It does not mention Hess's purpose, played up in the UP story).

WE-KA802AES

A100 (200)

WITH WAR CRIMES

Nuernberg, Dec. 1—(AP)—Gaunt-faced Rudolf Hess, childishly self satisfied at getting the spotlight in the international war crimes trial, laid aside his novel today and amused his fellow Nazi defendants with his tale of faking amnesia before the world.

Hess had Grand Admiral Karl Doenitz and Erich Raeder shaking with laughter before the court session opened when he told them how he pretended loss of memory and partial insanity. All other defendants were absent yesterday when Hess made his sensational confession and most of them were convulsed with laughter when they learned of it for the first time today.

Freed of further need of maintaining the absent-minded pose of a man who remembered nothing of the war years and his ruthless power as Hitler's deputy, Hess followed the court proceedings closely. Missing for the first time was the novel which he read during the opening days of the hearing.

Hess boasted of his skilled navigation on his mysterious flight to Britain four years ago when questioned briefly in his cell before the trial by Maj. Douglas Kelley, U. S. army psychiatrist.

He confirmed reports that he had left a note to Hitler telling him he was going *to appeal for peace* in the hope of what he called saving civilization from bolshevism. He told Kelley *he wanted to make a direct appeal to Britain's king.*

KA925AES

Rudolf Hess told the international war crimes tribunal this morning that he went to Britain in 1941 in an effort to arrange a peaceful settlement of the European war. He said he planned to talk King George of England into coming to Germany for a conference with Adolf Hitler.

The court ruled that Hess will have to stand trial along with the 19 other Nazi war criminals.

A104
   (240)
FIRST LEAD MAGNATES
By Charles Chamberlain
   Iserlohn, Germany, Dec 1—(AP)—*Seventy-six steel magnates repre-senting Ruhr industries worth billions of dollars were arrested at their homes last night in a series of raids by hundreds of British security police and troops.*

   The raids began at 11 p. m. and were so thorough that only eight of the original list of 84 marked were not apprehended. Picking them up was only a question of time.

   The industrialists were caught in circumstances ranging from drinking champagne to taking stomach pills before going to bed.

   A director of the August Thyssen steel works was embarrassed when the British said they found him in a bedroom with the blond 24 year old daughter of a baron.

   Fritz Baum, manager of the Ruhr gas utility in Essen, was drinking champagne with his wife and two friends. Rat poison pills were taken from Walter Eichorst, another director of the Thyssen works.

   Dr. Karl Lipp, head of the purchasing department of the Hoesch steel combine of Dortmund, was given permission to play a bedtime lullaby on the violin to his son before being taken away.

   Most of the industrialists were in bed and all came quietly, police said. The arresting parties operated on information partly supplied by an American intelligence detachment at Duesseldorf.

   Senior British intelligence officers said the magnates would be transferred to an internment camp in the British zone where they will be interrogated and masses of documents relating to the Ruhr industries will be studied with the possibility of charging some of the men in custody with war crimes.

   Those arrested x x x picking up second graf.
   MT939AES

A45
   95
   Aversa, Italy, Dec 1—(AP)—*German General Anton Dostler was shot to death by a firing squad today for ordering the execution of 15 American soldiers captured behind the German lines in Italy in March, 1944.*

   Dostler, the first German general to die for war crime participation in western Europe, was convicted in October by an U. S. court martial, which disregarded his defense plea that in ordering the executions he was carrying out the commands of higher officers.

   Holding himself stiffly erect in the prisoner stockade, the German general died without flinching before *a firing squad of U. S. soldiers.*

The 15 American soldiers were captured and executed without trial after they had landed behind German lines near La Spezia in a daring raid to blow up a railroad tunnel.

DN552AES

Also in Germany, British troops arrested 76 German steel company executives last night in a series of raids in the industrial Ruhr area. And General Anton Dostler of the German army was executed this morning by a firing squad of 15 American soldiers. The execution took place in Italy, where a year and a half ago Dostler ordered the execution of 15 Americans found behind German lines.

A5

   –95–

   AMS IN

   Tehran, Iran, Nov. 30.—(Delayed)—(AP)—*The Russians began carrying out a surprise evacuation of Tehran last night.*

   The railway station, communications centers and private billets including the military headquarters were completely evacuated.

   The governor of Azerbaijan, appointed recently by the central Iranian government, arrived in the provincial capital of Tabriz today from Tehran in a plane put at his disposal by Soviet authorities.

   JR229AES

A39

   (150)

   TEHRAN, IRAN—FIRST ADD RUSSIAN EVACUATION X X X SOVIET AUTHORITIES.

   Meanwhile, the Iranian foreign ministry said the Russian note refusing passage of Iranian troops into trouble spots of northwestern Iran asserted that "fighting and bloodshed would break out" if Iranian troops entered the territory and that the Soviet government would be forced to bring in additional soldiers.

   The note denied that Russia was intervening in the political or economic affairs of Iran and termed untrue allegations that the Soviet government had given help to Kurds of that region.

   —DASH—

   A Tass dispatch broadcast by the Soviet radio and recorded in London confirmed the Iranian text and commented that the Russian note declared the Tripartite Treaty of 1942 "was not always observed by the Iranian side in its part concerning the maintenance of internal order on Iranian territory."

"Behavior of some representatives of military and gendarmerie detachments by far not always contributed to the establishment of peace and order in the districts to which they went, and last year appropriate representations were made to the Iranian government on this matter," the broadcast said.

JR518AES

A83 (200)
By Vern Haugland
Bekassi, Java, Dec. 1—(AP)—*Naked bodies, believed to be those of 18 Indian soldiers and four Englishmen, were found in a shallow grave in this village 12 miles west of Batavia today.*

The Dutch news agency Aneta said the bodies were those of the crew and passengers of a transport plane which crashed in Batavia's outskirts last Friday.

An Indonesian woman, who had been held prisoner in the barracks where the men were confined, led *a British unit* to the burial spot, about 50 yards from the prison. She said four white men and 18 Indians were brought here naked in trucks last Saturday evening. They were beaten that night, she said, and Sunday they were led to the nearby river bank, one by one, with their hands tied behind them. *There they were individually assaulted by yelling men with "anything that would cut,"* the woman said.

The woman, who had been imprisoned because she was married to an Amboinese, said she overhead a telephone conversation which indicated that an Indonesian general was informed about the prisoners and had ordered them killed.

British native troops, acting on reports that the missing airmen had been in Bekassi, sent a patrol to this village yesterday. They found it deserted, with only a Dutch youth and three Amboinese women in jail. This morning a battalion with tanks, mortars, artillery and air support set out again from Batavia. They reached here without difficulty in mid-morning.

KA820AES

The Russians staged a surprise move in Iran during the night, and began withdrawing their forces out of Tehran, capital of that country. British troops in Java have discovered the bodies of 22 persons near Batavia. They are believed to be those of four Englishmen and 18 Indian soldiers murdered by Indonesians when their plane was grounded.

A54FX

"95"

CHINESE

By Spencer Moosa

Chungking, Dec. 1—(AP)—*Russia has agreed to delay withdrawal of Soviet forces from Manchuria until Jan. 3, the Chinese government announced today.*

The agreement will enable Chinese government personnel to take over the administration of Manchuria and will permit Chinese government troops to move in before the Soviet withdrawal is completed, the announcement stated.

It was for this purpose, the Government said, that the date was changed. *The Russians had been scheduled to withdraw Dec. 3,* but Generalissimo Chiang Kai-shek feared that Chinese Communists—thick in Manchuria—would assume control if Soviet forces were evacuated that soon. Central government troops have not yet been able to penetrate the territory in controlling strength.

Chinese government troops now are driving toward Mukden. Dispatches reported the Nationalists advancing along the Peiping-Mukden railroad have reached a point 20 miles from Tahushan, 65 miles west of Mukden. They have not yet contacted Chinese Communist forces reported to have dug in near Tahushan.

A55FX

The dispatches reported alleged representatives of several Communist puppet forces approached Nationalist headquarters at Shinhsien with offers of surrender.

A semi-official Nationalist dispatch charged that some 200,000 Communist troops are preparing a four-pronged drive aimed at placing the strategic maritime province of Shantung entirely under Chinese Red control. The dispatch said Communist forces destroyed a sizeable stretch of the Tientsin-Pukow railroad north of the junction city of Hsuchow as a preparatory move in the drive.

DS324APS   NM 95

It was announced officially in Chungking today that Russia has agreed to postpone for one month her withdrawal of troops from Manchuria.

(The paragraph above was deleted from the newscast before it was broadcast.)

A77CX (KX FX)
    STRIKES AT A GLANCE
BY THE ASSOCIATED PRESS
    (CX) Five big strikes account for about four-fifths of 550,000 workers idle in nation's 145 labor dispubes.

Major developments:

Automobiles—Await CIO Auto Workers' reaction to General Motors plan to make parts for rivals while 70 GM plants are strikebound.

Meat packing—CIO Packinghouse Workers back up wage hike demand, vote 20 to 1 for strike.

Railroad equipment—End walkout which delayed equipment for new Pullman cars, Simmons Co. employes return at Kenosha, Wis.
    –DASH–

A78CX
    UNDATED STRIKES (610)
BY THE ASSOCIATED PRESS
    (CX) General Motors President C. E. Wilson has surprised the auto industry with his plan for GM to produce parts and accessories for its competitors while GM itself is not making cars because of the CIO Auto Workers' strike.

    Wilson, in a letter last night to President R. J. Thomas of the striking CIO United Auto Workers, outlined his proposal. He said GM is willing . . . (the strike roundup story continues for 53 lines, dealing with the GM strike and other strikes).
    AB759AES

HX38
BY UNITED PRESS
    General Motors Corp. officials today waited for the United Automobile Workers (CIO) to make the next move in the coast-to-coast walkout which has shut down 93 plants and kept 225,000 GM workers from their jobs.

    Following the first renewal of negotiations in the 11-day-old strike, *the company last night proposed a partial resumption of operations for the benefit of other automobile manufacturers.* A Union reply was expected momentarily.

    The proposal, as outlined in a letter to UAW President R. J. Thomas from C. E. Wilson, head of the giant General Motors firm, provided for the reopening of GM parts and accessories divisions to work exclusively on material for other auto manufacturers.

    Wilson's statement that the GM tie-up . . . (the story continues for 59 lines, with details of this and other strike situations).
    BJ705A

HX4

By Allen V. Dowling
United Press Staff Correspondent

Detroit, Dec. 1.—(UP)—*Partial resumption of General Motors operations to provide parts for other car makers was up to the United Automobile Workers Union (CIO) today.*

The management proposed such a work resumption and expressed hope that negotiations with the UAW might lead to an end of the GM strike now in its 11th day.

In a letter to R. J. Thomas, head of the powerful union, Corporation President C. E. Wilson offered to reopen GM parts and accessories divisions to work exclusively on material for other auto manufacturers. A union reply today was indicated by a spokesman for Thomas.

At the same time, Harry W. Anderson, . . . (the story continues for 45 lines, devoted to details of the GM strike situation).

ET423A

The auto industry still is awaiting a reply from the United Auto workers regarding the sensational offer made yesterday by General Motors. The company, you remember, said it will keep making parts for its competitors even though it can't use them itself.

HX11

Chicago, Dec. 1.—(UP)—*A weeklong "demonstration" walkout against Montgomery Ward and Co. will end on schedule at the close of business today, union sources said.*

Samuel Wolchok, president of the United Retail, Wholesale and Department Store Employes (CIO), said in New York last night that he was well satisfied with the success of the nationwide strike, first of a series planned against Ward's "tyrannical labor policies."

The union leader cited a company offer to increase wages of some 7,000 Chicago employes as proof of the effectiveness of the work stoppage and said the URWDE would continue efforts to obtain increases for all Wards' employes.

Ward spokesmen however, consistently have contended that the mail order firm's business was little affected by the walkout. The company issued a statement yesterday that more than 70 per cent of its employes remained on the job throughout the strike, called a week ago to protest Ward's refusal to arbitrate.

Local 20 of the striking union met today to hear details of the company's wage offer, which includes an increase in the minimum rate from 45 to 60 cents an hour and a general five-cent-an-hour boost for workers in Ward's Chicago properties.

Company and union officials will meet Monday to discuss the offer.

ET449A

The demonstration walkout of Montgomery Ward employes in half a dozen cities is scheduled to end today. It was called, you know, in protest against the company's policy against collective bargaining by the store employes union. Remember, the Saint Paul store of Montgomery Ward is not affected by the strike, and will be open as usual all day today.

(Middle commercial)

MS4

BY UNITED PRESS

Undated—*North Dakota merchants today are praying for the miracle of a real Santa Claus—one with an extra large sleigh.*

For it looked today as though that's about the only way they'll get holiday merchandise delivered in time for Christmas shoppers.

A survey of nine major North Dakota cities by the United Press *revealed the 14-day over-the-road truck driver strike has placed merchants behind the proverbial "eight-ball" insofar as holiday stocks were concerned.*

The survey included Fargo, Grand Forks, Williston, Minot, Valley City, Devils Lake, Jamestown, Mandan and Bismarck.

MORE D8—754A

MS5

ADD UNDATED N. D. STRIKE XXX BISMARCK.

Christmas shoppers were already jamming . . . (the story continues for 30 lines, with details of shopping conditions in several of the nine cities).

D909A

MS13

St. Paul, Minn., Dec. 1—(UP)—*Less than carload freight shipments were moving in and out of the Twin Cities again today with lifting of an embargo placed on such shipments Nov. 24.*

The car service division of the American Railroads Association cancelled its ban on in-coming freight loads of less than carload size, effective at 12:01 a. m.

Simultaneously, the Interstate Commerce Commission suspended its embargo on outgoing freight of this class.

The ban was imposed because the Midwest truck drivers strike caused freight to pile up in the Twin Cities.

D923A

APR7

Washington—*Fourteen senators have asked AFL teamsters and Midwest truck operators to meet them in Washington Sunday for an airing of issues in the truck drivers' strike in seven Midwest states.*

The group telegraphed both the president of the teamsters and of the Midwest Truck Operators Association.

Among those signing the telegrams were Minnesota Senators Ball and Shipstead.

J

The outlook for Christmas shoppers in North Dakota continues to be a bleak one as a result of the strike of over-the-road truckers. It is beginning to look as though deliveries of many items of holiday merchandise is going to come too late to do much good.

A survey of nine major cities in the state presented a universally gloomy picture. Merchandise in some spots may be exhausted long before Christmas. And railroads have indicated that they are not able to cope with added traffic.

The shipping situation was eased somewhat in the Twin Cities area, with the lifting of the embargo against less-than-carload lots of merchandise. The embargo was imposed in order to help clear the pile-up of goods in railroad warehouses due to the truck drivers' strike.

And in the truck strike, the latest development is the request of fourteen senators that the union and operators meet with them in Washington. The meeting would call for an airing of all the differences between the two parties.

HX43

First Creek, Wash., Dec. 1.—(UP)—*Salvage of a school bus and its cargo of 14, including 13 children, was believed near today, with the discovery of the vehicle's motor hood 170 feet down in the cold waters of Lake Chelan.*

Lt. L. P. Ross, working in relays with five other divers, found the hood late yesterday, leading anxious relatives of the victims to believe the big school bus had been located.

The bus careened into the deep glacial lake from a narrow mountain road last Monday during the height of a snow storm, carrying 15 children and the bus driver to their deaths.

An examination paper signed by Louis Acklund, 11, one of the tragedy's victims, was found at a 150 foot depth by Diver J. C. Hannah. Walter

Arthur McGray, commercial diver from Seattle, submerged 260 feet in the deepest plunge of the day.

The divers will follow buoys marking the path of the bus along a steep underwater cliff today, hoping to find it within 300 feet, the maximum depth to which they can safely go. If it is beyond that point, grappling hooks could be used.

D759A

The last chapter in the tragic story of the school bus which plunged into the waters of Lake Chelan in Washington may be written soon. It is believed that the bus with its fourteen bodies may be recovered in the near future.

Divers, working in shifts, found the hood of the vehicle in one-hundred-and-seventy feet of water. The divers have marked the path of the bus along the underwater cliff, and hope to find it before they reach the three hundred foot depth. Beyond that point, they will not be able to operate, and grappling hooks may have to be used.

A102KX
(100)

Kansas City, Dec. 1—(AP)—*Kansas City civic leaders are considering plans for the construction of two-car garages as the possible answer to the city's critical housing shortage.*

The garages, as outlined in the proposal submitted *to labor and construction representatives* by Mayor John P. Gage yesterday, would be used as human dwellings until permanent homes could be built.

Approved by the representatives, the plan calls for the organization of two non-profit corporations to buy materials and build the garages.

Such structures, according to Mayor Gage, could be mass produced cheaply and would be useful when the emergency has passed.

GG830ACS NM

Two-car garages may be resorted to as a means of relieving the housing shortage in Kansas City. Civic leaders there are planning the construction of a number of the garages, and would use them as dwellings until permanent homes can be built.

Labor and construction representatives have approved the plan, which calls for the formation of two non-profit organizations to buy the materials and erect the garages.

###

HX48

Washington, Dec. 1.—(UP)—*Shirley Temple said last night that juvenile delinquency is not the fault of teen-agers but that the blame rests with communities where they grow up.*

"Young men and women do not want to be bad—if they are, it is because the community somehow failed them," she told the National Youth Conference and board meeting of the General Federation of Women's Clubs, which continues today.

The 17-year-old movie actress, now the wife . . . (the story continues for 21 lines with other details of Miss Temple's talk and those by other speakers).

D837A

Actress Shirley Temple has joined the ranks of movie stars who are becoming social conscious. Last night the 17-year-old star told the National Youth conference and Board meeting of the General Federation of Women's Clubs in Washington that juvenile delinquency is not the fault of the teen-agers, but that the blame should fall on the communities which produced them.

"Young men and women do not want to be bad," Miss Temple told her audience, "and if they are it is because the community has somehow failed them."

(The paragraph above was deleted from the newscast before it was broadcast. The paragraph that follows came from a telephone call from police headquarters.)

Minneapolis police have asked us to aid in locating Vivian Weir, the daughter of John Weir who formerly lived at 2533 Colfax avenue south in Minneapolis. Mr. Weir died this morning at General hospital. The name again—Vivian Weir.

APR21

SUBS APR 14

(DULUTH)

St. Paul—*A former commander of the Minnesota American Legion, Earl V. Cliff, has taken issue with the location of a proposed two hundred bed veterans hospital at Duluth.*

Addressing the concluding session of the Legion's annual convention in St. Paul today, Cliff charged that this would be a violation of the Veterans Administration's announced policy of establishing such institutions near medical centers.

Cliff stated he believed that base hospitals in this state should be built near the University of Minnesota, or the Mayo Clinic. This would permit taking advantage of the services of medical experts at those institutions.

The former commander went on to say that if the Duluth hospital is to be only a feeder institution, then he believed the veterans administration should first get busy on construction of base hospitals . . . and let the feeders come later.

JM1145ACS 1

The proposed location of a veterans hospital at Duluth has been attacked by a former commander of the Minnesota American Legion, Earl V. Cliff. Cliff told the concluding session of the annual Legion convention in St. Paul that base hospitals in Minnesota should be established near the University or the Mayo Clinic in Rochester.

Cliff said that the Duluth location would be a violation of the Veterans' Administration policy of locating such hospitals near medical centers.

APR20

Minneapolis—*A representative of the New Orleans ship builder, Andrew J. Higgins, is said to be enroute to Minneapolis today in connection with a possible expansion of the firm.*

The representative is being sent as a result of invitations extended by the Minneapolis Civic and Commerce Association, and the Minnesota distributor of Higgins products, the McGovern-Stewart Company.

JM1143ACS 1

Andrew Higgins, the New Orleans shipbuilder, is reported to be on his way to Minneapolis in connection with the choice of a new location for his boat-building firm.

The Minneapolis Civic and Commerce association extended an invitation to Higgins to locate here when it was rumored that he was liquidating his New Orleans plants as a result of labor troubles.

APR22

SUBS

Litchfield, Minn.—*The jury in the second degree murder trial of Mrs. Alice Broderius and Walter Reinke at Litchfield, still has not reached a verdict.*

The jury began its deliberations shortly after five p. m. Friday and con-

tinued until 11 o'clock. At nine o'clock this morning, a fresh start was made, but to noon there had been no indication that a verdict had been reached.

The defendants are charged with killing Rudolph Broderius, husband of Mrs. Broderiusbn when he and three friends visited the Broderius turkey ranch near Cosmos, Minn.

JM1148ACS 1

The jury in the Litchfield murder trial of Mrs. Alice Broderius and her hired hand, Walter Reinke, still has not reached a verdict. The jury started its deliberations at five o'clock yesterday afternoon, and recessed around midnight. It resumed its consideration of the case at nine this morning.

The jury has the choice of acquitting the pair, or convicting them of second or third degree murder or manslaughter. The pair are charged with shooting and killing Rudolph Broderius and wounding three of his companions.

(The paragraph above was deleted from the newscast before it was broadcast. The five stories that follow, for which wire copy is not here included, were also deleted.)

A young Minneapolis couple who eloped early in the week are back home again,—and happy about being there.

Eighteen-year-old William Heegel Jr. of 3829 Thirty-fifth avenue south and his sixteen-year-old bride returned to the home of the bride's parents.

The first problem confronting the young couple is the question of family disapproval. And after that they are going to battle with the housing shortage—which is far from a pleasant prospect for newlyweds, young or old.

Deer hunters in North Dakota have had good luck during the five-day season which ended last night. Chief Game Warden E. M. Lee estimated that six thousand deer were shot during the period.

Some two thousand hunters were disappointed, because eight thousand licenses were issued.

South Dakota may soon learn whether its bid for the world capital of the United Nations Organization will be accepted. The representa-

tives of 22 communities in the United States and two in Canada are
arguing the relative merits of their localities before the committee
which will decide the location.

Ralph Bellamy of Rapid City is appearing in behalf of the Black
Hills site.

A Minneapolis man who disappeared last September and was believed drowned in Mille Lacs Lake has turned up in New York City.
Robert H. Lee, a newspaper reporter, disappeared at the same time that
his boat was found floating upside down on the lake.

When discovered in New York, he was suffering from malaria and
pneumonia. His family believe that his disappearance was caused by
war neurosis.

Three opinions handed down by Minnesota attorney general Burnquist indicate that circumstances may have a lot to do with
the question of whether or not a returning veteran may have his job
back.

All of the opinions concerned school employes. Burnquist ruled in
one case that a man who gave up his job to join the Navy should have
his job back. In another case, an Ely teacher who had coached basketball before joining the services had refused to take a new assignment as
swimming coach. It was ruled that he must teach swimming if he wants
to keep his job.

And in the third case, a school bus driver went into service without
notifying the school board. His contract later expired, and Burnquist
ruled that his rights as a veteran expired with the contract.

Putting the Radio Wire Show Together

Building a newscast from radio wire copy is simpler and faster than
writing one from the newspaper wire, but many of its problems are
similar.

To see what happens in the process, let's watch the growth of a 12:15
P.M. show for KUOM-Minneapolis on August 27, 1947.

KUOM is the University of Minnesota station. Its shows, since it is
an educational station, are without sponsorship; this means that, in

the 12:15–12:30 period, it has fourteen minutes and thirty seconds for news. Experience has shown that the announcer who reads this show needs about 230 lines of copy, plus a closing headline summary, for the period. The newsroom has the Associated Press radio wire.

The editor arrives in the newsroom a few minutes before 10:00 (there have been no earlier news shows on KUOM this morning). His first job is to prepare a two-minute headline-summary show for use at 10:57. From the printer he takes the sixth five-minute news summary, which had cleared at 9:30; he reads it through rapidly, then edits it down to about half its original length and dispatches it to the station. Now he's ready for the 12:15 show.

He finds on his desk a note saying that the show is to be broadcast from the KUOM remote booth at the State Fair grounds instead of from the studio upstairs. This means that he must make gestures in the direction of State Fair news in editing the show, and that copy must be ready at 11:30 instead of 12:00, in order to give a courier time to take it the four miles to the grounds.

The printer had last been cleared at midnight. The editor takes off it the hundred-foot strip of copy that has moved since that time: two fifteen-minute summaries, five five-minute summaries (in addition to the one he has used), six or eight feature scripts, a batch of spot summaries, two regional splits, and some forty or fifty individual stories. He methodically clips the file of copy, and arranges material in separate piles—international, national, special features, regional, and so on. A good deal of the copy he discards—the five-minute and the first fifteen-minute summaries, the features his station has no need for (some that may become useful as background material he files in a cabinet in the corner), the sports copy (his station pays little attention to professional sports), and so on.

Ordinarily he would now skim through all the major copy to decide which of the day's stories to emphasize, and how to organize his show. But since today's newscast is to emanate from the State Fair, he decides to open with a Fair story. He goes to the latest regional split, and finds a story on record-breaking attendance flowing through the gates, together with a brief round-up of the day's program. He takes this copy and a Northwest weather forecast to the typewriter and turns out a one-page story that becomes the first page of the broadcast (the script is reproduced on this and following pages). He heads the page KUOM-12:15-8-27-47, and numbers it prominently in the upper left-hand corner. He counts the lines and notes the number in the lower righthand corner.

1)

KUOM — 12:15 — 8-27-47

OUT

~~Here~~ at the Minnesota State Fair,, ~~we're broadcasting from the KUOM booth in the grand stand~~ attendance is heavy again today. The weather is fine --- sunny . . . a light haze in the air . . . not too warm. And crowds are pouring through the gates in what seem to be record numbers.

Already, you know, attendance at the Fair is well ahead of the previous record. Yesterday nearly 80 thousand people came --- and that brought the four-day total to more than 300 thousand. That's 70 thousand more than the best previous attendance for the first four days, in 1941.

Today is the big day for 4-H youngsters at the Fair. Topping their program will be the selection of the healthiest 4-H boy and girl in the state, and the crowning of the 4-H style queen.

Judging of the health king and queen began yesterday --- and the winners will be announced tonight. For the first time health improvement and leadership in community health projects will be considered in choosing the champions. In former years the boys' and girls' individual health only was considered.

Former service men on the grounds will meet in the new agriculture building today --- as part of ceremonies honoring war veterans. On the entertainment program of the day, there'll be more harness racing --- this is Dan Patch day, in memory of the famous old pacing champion. Special recognition also is planned for the Arrowhead region of Minnesota, and the city of Duluth.

The weatherman says that temperatures here --- and through all the ~~Northwest~~ Northwest --- will remain moderate . . . about 75 to 80. But There may be a few showers in some sections.

2D

Now he turns to the latest fifteen-minute summary—if he's lucky, it will provide the basis for a good deal of the rest of the show. He discards the headline summary with which it opens, since the pattern of this show calls for a summary at the close rather than the beginning. The first story is one about two State Department men going to a Paris con-

Now let's look at the foreign news.

TROUBLED GREECE STILL IS LABORING ~~TODAY~~ TO WEATHER HER LATEST CABINET CRISIS. PREMIER-DESIGNATE CONSTANTIN TSALDARIS HAS HELD NEW CONFERENCES WITH AMERICAN AMBASSADOR LINCOLN MACVEAGH. AND TSALDARIS HAS ANNOUNCED THAT HE INTENDS TO PROCEED AT ONCE WITH THE JOB OF FORMING A ~~NEW~~ CABINET OF HIS OWN.

IT IS EXPECTED THAT THE NAMES OF THE NEW MINISTERS WILL BE DISCLOSED WITHIN A SHORT TIME. GREECE HAS BEEN WITHOUT A CABINET SINCE THE GOVERNMENT FELL LAST SATURDAY IN A DISPUTE OVER OPERATIONS AGAINST GUERRILLA FORCES.

TSALDARIS IS RELYING UPON THE SUPPORT OF THE CHIEF OF THE NATIONALIST PARTY--GENERAL STYLIANOS ZERVAS--IN HIS CABINET-FORMING TASK. PARTY REPRESENTATION IN HIS PROJECTED RIGHTIST CABINET EVIDENTLY WILL BE NARROWER THAN THAT OF THE PREVIOUS GOVERNMENT. IT IS SAID, HOWEVER, THAT TSALDARIS WILL BY NO MEANS BE ASSURED OF A MAJORITY WHEN THE GREEK PARLIAMENT CONSIDERS A VOTE OF CONFIDENCE ON MONDAY.

THE GOVERNMENT OF FRANCE TODAY ANNOUNCED FURTHER REDUCTIONS IN DAILY BREAD RATIONS TO THE FRENCH PEOPLE. THE ACTION WAS ATTRIBUTED TO "THE DEPLORABLE STATE" OF FRANCE'S GRAIN HARVEST THIS YEAR. A COMMUNIQUE ISSUED BY THE FRENCH CABINET SAID THE DAILY BREAD RATION WILL BE REDUCED APPROXIMATELY SIX OUNCES.

17

ference; this is the latest news in the summary, but he doesn't like it
to open the international department because he thinks its chief virtue
is recency rather than interest or importance. He chooses in its place a
story on the Greek cabinet crisis. Reading the story carefully, and
checking it against other earlier stories on the same subject (a practice

3/

ACROSS THE ENGLISH CHANNEL IN LONDON, THE HIGH COURT OF JUSTICE
HAS POSTPONED UNTIL FRIDAY A HEARING ON AN APPLICATION FOR A
WRIT OF HABEAS CORPUS. THE APPLICATION HAS BEEN BROUGHT BY THE JEWISH
AGENCY AND IT SEEKS TO PREVENT THE DISEMBARKATION OF 4,400 JEWISH
REFUGEES IN GERMANY.
     MEANWHILE, INFORMED SOURCES IN PARIS SAY THE FRENCH GOVERNMENT HAS
GIVEN A FAVORABLE REPLY TO A BRITISH REQUEST TO MOVE THE REFUGEES TO
FRANCE BY TRAIN AFTER THEY REACH GERMANY NEXT WEEK.

     BRITISH AUTHORITIES AT HAMBURG, GERMANY, ARE MAKING EXTENSIVE
PREPARATIONS TO RECEIVE THE 4,400 (CORRECT) JEWISH REFUGEES, BEING
SENT TO THAT PORT FOR DEBARKATION. ONE BRITISH OFFICIAL SAID IT IS
BELIEVED ABOUT 1,000 OF THE REFUGEES MAY NEED MEDICAL ATTENTION.
THE JEWS HAVE BEEN ABOARD SHIP FOR 46 DAYS SINCE THEY LEFT A
SOUTHERN FRENCH PORT LAST MONTH IN A FUTILE ATTEMPT TO SLIP THROUGH
THE BRITISH BLOCKADE OF PALESTINE.

                         #

     TWO TOP-DRAWER AMERICAN DIPLOMATIC POLICY MAKERS ARE ON THEIR WAY
TO PARIS. THEY WILL REPRESENT THE FIRST AMERICAN PARTICIPATION IN
LAYING THE GROUND WORK FOR WAR-RAVAGED EUROPE'S RECOVERY UNDER THE
MARSHALL PLAN.
     THE TWO-OFFICIALS--GEORGE KENNAN, DIRECTOR OF THE STATE
DEPARTMENT'S POLICY PLANNING BOARD, AND CHARLES BONESTEEL, SPECIAL
ASSISTANT TO UNDER-SECRETARY OF STATE ROBERT LOVETT--LEFT TODAY BY
PLANE. A BRIEF STATE DEPARTMENT ANNOUNCEMENT SAID MERELY THAT THE
TWO OFFICIALS ARE GOING TO PARIS FOR CONSULTATIONS WITH AMERICAN
OFFICIALS ON, QUOTE, "STATE DEPARTMENT MATTERS, INCLUDING THE PROBLEM
OF EUROPEAN RECOVERY."

                         #

                                                              21

he follows with each succeeding story), he decides that it does the job. He edits out two words; he types at the head of a sheet of copy paper "Now let's look at the foreign news"; he pastes the Greek story below this transition, and puts an end-mark just below it.

The next story is easy—a brief piece about food shortage in France.

3A)

THE TRIAL OF 24 DIRECTORS OF THE BILLION-DOLLAR GERMAN I.G. FARBEN
CHEMICAL TRUST OPENED TODAY IN NUERNBERG, GERMANY, WITH THE DEFENDANTS
SITTING IN THE SAME DOCK WHERE HERMANN GOERING AND HIS NAZI
HENCHMEN SAT.

THE FOUR-MAN UNITED STATES COURT HEARD THE PROSECUTION CHARGE THAT
THE FARBEN *TRUST* DIRECTORS DELIBERATELY FOSTERED ADOLF HITLER'S WARS OF
AGGRESSION FOR THEIR OWN PROFIT.

THE UNITED STATES CHIEF OF COUNSEL FOR WAR CRIMES--BRIGADIER GENERAL
TELFORD TAYLOR--DECLARED THAT THE MEN WERE NOT BEING TRIED AS
NAZIS. SAID HE:

"THE INDICTMENT ACCUSES THESE MEN OF MAJOR RESPONSIBILITY FOR
VISITING UPON MANKIND THE MOST CATASTROPHIC WAR IN HUMAN HISTORY.
IT ACCUSES THEM OF WHOLESALE ENSLAVEMENT, PLUNDER AND MURDER."

TWENTY-TWO OF THE 24 INDICTED GERMANS WERE IN THE DOCK TODAY,
TWO OF THEM RECOVERING FROM ILLNESSES AND UNABLE TO BE PRESENT.
TWENTY-ONE OF THE 24 HAVE PLEADED INNOCENT TO THE VARIOUS WAR CRIMES
CHARGES CONTAINED IN THE BLISTERING, TWENTY-THOUSAND-WORD INDICTMENT. 14

#

ACROSS THE WORLD IN CHINA, PILOTS OF THE CHINESE AIR TRANSPORT
SERVICE ARE SEARCHING TODAY FOR BALES OF MONEY--DUMPED FROM A PLANE.

PILOT ROBERT ROUSSELOT OF NOEL, MISSOURI WAS FORCED TO JETTISON A
HUGE CARGO OF CHINESE CURRENCY MONDAY WHEN HIS CHINESE NATIONAL
RELIEF AND REHABILITATION ADMINISTRATION PLANE DEVELOPED ENGINE TROUBLE
IN WESTERN CHINA.

THE SHANGHAI OFFICE OF THE AIR SERVICE SAYS THAT IT DOES NOT KNOW
HOW MUCH MONEY WAS INVOLVED, BUT OTHER SOURCES SAY SUCH SHIPMENTS
USUALLY ARE VALUED AT ONE-MILLION DOLLARS IN UNITED STATES MONEY.

#

22

Since "France" is the fourth word in the story, he decides that no transition is called for. He pastes this story on page 2, without change.

For the third story, he combines paragraphs from two stories on the subject. Some editing is necessary here, for simplicity and to avoid repetition.

4/

```
     THE LONDON CONFERENCE AIMED AT WORKING OUT PLANS FOR THE
RESTORATION OF GERMAN INDUSTRY APPARENTLY HAS MET WITH CONSIDERABLE
SUCCESS. AN OFFICIAL SPOKESMAN SAYS THAT MOST DIFFICULTIES WERE
IRONED OUT AT YESTERDAY'S SESSION BETWEEN AMERICAN-BRITISH-AND-
FRENCH DELEGATES. AND A COMMUNIQUE GIVING THE BROAD RESULTS OF THE
THREE-POWER TALKS IS EXPECTED LATE TODAY. THE PARLEY IS BELIEVED
TO BE NEARING AN END.
```

\#

```
     A DUTCH ARMY COMMUNIQUE NOW ACCUSES THE INDONESIAN REPUBLICAN
ARMY OF 500 SEPARATE VIOLATIONS OF THE UNITED NATIONS CEASE FIRE ORDER
SINCE IT BECAME EFFECTIVE AUGUST 4TH. MEANWHILE, THE NETHERLANDS
GOVERNMENT HAS TAKEN THE FIRST STEP TOWARD THE ESTABLISHMENT OF A
PROJECTED UNITED STATES OF INDONESIA. THIS WAS THE ANNOUNCEMENT THAT
THE DUTCH HAVE ESTABLISHED THE SELF-GOVERNING TERRITORY OF EAST BORNEO,
AN AREA WHICH TAKES IN THE RICH OIL REGIONS OF BALIKPAPAN AND TARAKAN.
```

\#

BEFORE

```
     IN A STATEMENT READ TO THE INTERNATIONAL TRIBUNAL IN TOKYO,
FORMER PREMIER HIDEKI TOJO (TOH'-JOH) HAS DEFENDED THE MOVEMENT OF
JAPANESE TROOPS INTO SOUTHERN INDOCHINA IN JULY, 1941. THE BE-
SPECTACLED, BALD-HEADED FORMER JAPANESE OFFICIAL SAID THE TROOP ACTION
WAS WHAT HE TERMED "AN APPROPRIATE MEASURE OF NATIONAL DEFENSE."
```

\#

```
     ALSO IN TOKYO, SIMPLE BUT IMPRESSIVE SERVICES HAVE BEEN HELD IN
MEMORY OF THE LATE AMBASSADOR GEORGE ATCHESON, JUNIOR, AND NINE OTHER
PERSONS KILLED IN AN AIR CRASH AUGUST 17TH. GENERAL AND MRS.
MAC ARTHUR WERE AMONG THE SEVERAL HUNDRED SPECTATORS WHO GATHERED
IN A FLOWER-FILLED CHAPEL TO HEAR THE NON-SECTARIAN SERVICE.
```

\#

23

Now he goes through other stories, completing pages 3, 4, 5, and 6 with international news or national news of international import. Most of this copy he takes from the fifteen-minute summary; one story, however, is a date-lined "separate"—the story at the top of page 6. He uses this story, blacking out the date line, because of the heavy Scandinavian

5)

TWO AMERICAN TRAVELLERS DESCRIBE AN ACT OF VIOLENCE IN INDIA IN WHICH THEY WERE INVOLVED. THE TRAVELLERS ARE LIEUTENANT COLONEL CHARLES CAPLE OF LITTLE ROCK, ARKANSAS, AIR ATTACHE TO THE AMERICAN EMBASSY IN NEW DELHI, AND MISS JANE LORANGER OF SACRAMENTO, CALIFORNIA, WHO IS WITH THE UNITED STATES INFORMATION SERVICE IN NEW DELHI. THE AMERICANS WERE RETURNING FROM A VACATION TRIP WHEN THEIR TRAIN WAS STOPPED NEAR A VILLAGE ~~CENTER~~ BY A ~~SIKH~~ MOB. THE RIOTERS KILLED 15 MOHAMMEDAN PASSENGERS AND TWICE UNSUCCESSFULLY TRIED TO BREAK INTO THE AMERICANS' COMPARTMENT.

#

FORMER PRESIDENT HERBERT HOOVER SAYS THE WORLD FOOD SITUATION —IN HIS WORDS—"DOESN'T LOOK VERY GOOD." HOOVER EXPLAINED THAT THE AMERICAN FOOD SURPLUS THIS YEAR IS NOT AS GREAT AS LAST YEAR. AND THE WORLD NEED AT PRESENT, HE SAID, IS PROBABLY GREATER THAN IN 1946. *HOOVER*
~~THE 73-YEAR-OLD EX-PRESIDENT~~ GAVE HIS VIEWS IN CHICAGO ENROUTE TO NEW YORK, WHERE HE WILL ASSUME THE CHAIRMANSHIP OF THE NEW CONGRESSIONAL COMMISSION FOR REORGANIZATION OF GOVERNMENT BUREAUS. HOOVER EMPHASIZED THAT HE HAS NO OPINIONS—FOR PUBLIC EXPRESSION AT LEAST—CONCERNING A POSSIBLE REPUBLICAN CANDIDATE FOR PRESIDENT IN 1948. THE FORMER PRESIDENT DECLARED EMPHATICALLY THAT HE WOULD NOT ACCEPT THE NOMINATION EVEN IF IT WERE OFFERED TO HIM. *HE SAID,* ~~73-YEAR-OLD HOOVER:~~ "NO MAN ~~AT MY AGE~~ *73 YEARS OLD* SHOULD TAKE THE NOMINATION."

#

30

population in KUOM's listening area. Most of the copy requires little
editing. From one story (page 4) he removes what he thinks is a dull
opening phrase, and substitutes a preposition; from another (page 5)
he takes a repetition of the phrase "73-year- old."

National news he finds slim. There's a long story on the forthcoming

6)

COPENHAGEN, DENMARK--A FOUR-POWER SCANDINAVIAN MEETING OPENED
TODAY IN COPENHAGEN WITH THE FOREIGN MINISTERS OF SWEDEN, NORWAY,
ICELAND AND DENMARK TAKING PART. A DANISH FOREIGN OFFICE SPOKESMAN
SAID THE MINISTERS WOULD DISCUSS THE MARSHALL AID-TO-EUROPE PROPOSAL
AND THE QUESTION OF A EUROPEAN CUSTOMS UNION.

    IN ADDITION, THE MINISTERS WILL TRY TO ARRIVE AT A JOINT NORDIC
STAND ON SUCH ISSUES AS THE PALESTINE AND FRANCO SPAIN PROBLEMS.
THESE PROBLEMS GO BEFORE A UNITED NATIONS PLENARY SESSION NEXT
MONTH.

    AT LAKE SUCCESS, NEW YORK, A SPECIAL RECEPTION COMMITTEE HAS BEEN
SET UP TO GREET TWO EGYPTIAN DEMONSTRATORS WHO TWICE HAVE BEEN THROWN
OUT OF THE UNITED NATIONS SECURITY COUNCIL CHAMBER. U-N SECRETARY-
GENERAL TRYGVE LIE SAYS THE TWO EGYPTIANS WILL BE BARRED FROM THE U-N
HEADQUARTERS AREA. AND LIE SAYS THAT IF THE TWO DEMONSTRATORS SHOULD
SLIP IN THEY WILL BE HANDED OVER TO THE POLICE.

    A CONGRESSIONAL COMMITTEE ALSO HEADED FOR EUROPE TODAY.
COMPOSED OF 16 LEGISLATORS, THE GROUP WILL VISIT 15 COUNTRIES TO STUDY
THE VARIOUS ASPECTS OF THE AMERICAN AID PROGRAM. THE ACTING CHAIRMAN
OF THE SPECIAL COMMITTEE, REPRESENTATIVE CHRISTIAN HERTER OF
MASSCAHUSETTS, SAID THE CONGRESSMEN WILL CONCENTRATE ON A STUDY OF
MEANS OF CARRYING OUT THE MARSHALL PLAN.

20

American Legion convention; he uses this intact with a little editing and the insertion of the word "Well" to open it. The other, on increasing automobile prices (page 8), he decides needs a new lead. This he writes on the typewriter; then he attaches all but the first paragraph of the original story.

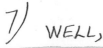

WELL,

THOUSANDS OF AMERICAN LEGIONNAIRES HAVE BEGUN TO TIGHTEN THEIR GRIP ON NEW YORK CITY, WHERE THEIR 29TH CONVENTION OPENS TOMORROW. THERE'S CONSIDERABLE BEHIND-THE-SCENES LEGION ACTIVITY, SUCH AS DISCUSSIONS OF *WHOM* TO BACK FOR NATIONAL COMMANDER THIS YEAR. BUT MUCH OF THE ACTION IS PUBLIC AND CARRIED OUT IN A SPIRIT OF GAYETY AND FUN. *A HEAVY*

BEFORE THE RAIN DRENCHED THE CITY YESTERDAY AFTERNOON, ONE GROUP OF LEGIONNAIRES BEGAN A WATERING PROCESS ALL THEIR OWN--WITH WATER PISTOLS. THEIR VICTIMS WERE MOSTLY WOMEN. AND WHEN CROWDS WERE SLOW IN MOVING, SOME LEGIONNAIRES SPURRED THEM INTO SPIRITED ACTION WITH ELECTRICALLY-CHARGED CANES.

THE BIG 40 AND 8 PARADE IS TOMORROW NIGHT. AND THE MAIN LEGION PARADE WILL *COME* SATURDAY.

FATHER KNICKERBOCKER UNDERSTANDS THE NEED FOR RELAXATION AND POLICEMEN WILL NOT INTERFERE WITH THE FUNMAKERS UNLESS THEY ARE CAUSING SERIOUS INCONVENIENCE TO THE PUBLIC.

EIGHT CANDIDATES FOR THE POST OF NATIONAL COMMANDER HAVE SET UP HEADQUARTERS IN SUITES IN THE PENNSYLVANIA HOTEL. PRELIMINARY SURVEYS ARE SAID TO INDICATE THAT POLICE CHIEF JAMES F.O'NEIL OF MANCHESTER, NEW HAMPSHIRE, HOLDS A SLIGHT LEAD IN THE EARLY STAGES OF THE ELECTIONEERING. MIDDLETON, OHIO'S MARTIN V.SOFFEY AND S.PERRY BROWN OF BEAUMONT, TEXAS, ARE CLOSE COMPETITORS FOR THE TOP LEGION POST. SELECTION OF A NEW NATIONAL COMMANDER MAY WIND UP IN A THREE-WAY CONTEST ON THE CONVENTION FLOOR.

#

22

Now he turns to regional news. The latest regional split is now moving on the printer; on it he finds a late State Fair story. He uses this story with a new lead which gives him an opportunity to mention again that the broadcast is coming from the Fair grounds. He follows it with three other stories taken from the splits.

8/

Going to buy a new automobile this year?

If you are, you can figure the cost right now. The auto industry expects that --- now that Ford and Studebaker have joined the other big companies in price increases --- the prices will hold through 1947. But next year the story may change.

AUTOMOTIVE INDUSTRY OBSERVERS POINT OUT THAT EXTENSIVE RE-TOOLING IS PLANNED FOR THE 1948 NEW CAR MODELS. AND THEY SAY THIS PROBABLY WILL RUN INTO MILLIONS OF DOLLARS. AS A RESULT, THEY BROADLY HINT THAT RETAIL PRICES MIGHT BE ADVANCED EVER MORE NEXT YEAR. THE OBSERVERS EXPLAIN THAT THE CURRENT PRICE BOOSTS HAVE HAD NOTHING TO DO WITH THE RE-TOOLING, BUT RESULTED, INSTEAD, FROM A PAYROLL BOOST OF ABOUT 150-MILLION DOLLARS FOR THE AUTOMOTIVE INDUSTRY. THE RISES ALSO ARE ATTRIBUTED TO HIGHER COSTS OF MATERIALS, TOOLS, DIES AND OTHER EQUIPMENT. Vicious circle isn't it. wonder what Widding THE FORD MOTOR COMPANY ANNOUNCED PRICE INCREASES YESTERDAY AND SUNDAY. AND LAST NIGHT THE STUDEBAKER CORPORATION COMPLETED THE CYCLE BY MARKING UP ITS PASSENGER AND TRUCK PRICES FROM $50 TO $115. THE BOOSTS FOR THE INDUSTRY AS A WHOLE HAVE BEEN FROM $45 TO MORE THAN $225.

\#

16

Time to count lines. The ten pages, he finds, give him 199 lines; he needs 230. He checks the University news sent over by the University news bureau, and estimates that he'll get about ten lines from it. So he looks through all of the unused copy, and checks the printer, for additional stories. Regional and national copy furnishes nothing more. He

9)

Here's some more State Fair news ~~— remember, we're broadcasting direct from the Minnesota Fair Grounds today.~~ This news is about completion of three more types of cattle judging.

(MINNESOTA,)

THE FRANLO FARMS HERD FROM HOPKINS CARRIED OFF MOST OF THE PRIZES FOR HOLSTEINS. WINNING 14 OF THE 17 BLUE RIBBONS OFFERED.

R. E. PUTNAM OF HARVARD, ILLINOIS, TOPPED THE JERSEY ENTRIES, WITH OTHER AWARDS GOING TO MACK MANOR FARM AT ORLAND, INDIANA...GEORGE W. COLLINS OF MONTICELLO, MINNESOTA, AND PAUL SUNDBERG OF SOUTH HAVEN, MINNESOTA.

TOPPING THE MILKING SHORTHORNS WERE THE ENTRIES OF CARL AND EDWARD LARSON OF KASSON *(MINNESOTA)*...THE McMARTIN HERD OF MADELIA *(MINNESOTA)*...J.T.ADKINS OF PRENTICE, ILLINOIS, AND THE WEIDNER PRAIRIE FARMS OF DALTON CITY, ILLINOIS.

THREE MEMBERS OF THE MOSES FAMILY FROM KASOTA *(MINNESOTA)* WALKED OFF WITH THE LION'S SHARE OF THE PRIZES FOR SHROPSHIRE SHEEP. C.V.MOSES TOOK THE GRAND CHAMPIONSHIP AWARD WITH HIS AGED RAM. THE OTHER WINNERS WERE HIS FATHER CLAYTON MOSES, AND HIS SON, DUANE.

IN FOUR-H COMPETITION, 14 YEAR OLD ROLD LARSON OF BIG LAKE *—ALSO IN MINNESOTA—* WON THE GRAND CHAMPIONSHIP WITH HIS FIVE WHITE ROCK CHICKENS.

‡

HERE'S GOOD NEWS FOR MOTORISTS IN THE TWIN CITIES AREA. THE SECRETARY OF THE RAMSEY COUNTY PETROLEUM RETAILERS ASSOCIATION, HARRY FRANKLIN, SAYS THERE WILL BE PLENTY OF GASOLINE FOR AUTOISTS OVER THE LABOR DAY WEEK-END.

THERE HAD BEEN SOME FEARS THAT THE SUPPLY WOULD BE INSUFFICIENT TO MEET THE EXPECTED HEAVY DEMAND. FRANKLIN SAID THAT HERE AND THERE A STATION MAY RUN OUT OF GASOLINE, BUT THAT WILL BE THE EXCEPTION RATHER THAN THE RULE.

#

22

takes a short Chinese story from the remains of the fifteen-minute summary, and a long new story on the trial of German industrialists in Hamburg; from the latter he eliminates the word "Farben" because he thinks it may puzzle a good many listeners. These two stories total twenty-two lines, and become page 3-A. He now has 221 lines.

~~#~~10)

~~MINNEAPOLIS~~--THE SECOND PUBLIC HEARING ON THE CONTROVERSIAL QUESTION
OF RENT CONTROL AND EVICTION IN MINNEAPOLIS WAS HELD LAST NIGHT.
AND AT THE END OF SEVERAL HOURS OF PRO AND CON DISCUSSION IT WAS
EVIDENT THAT THE CITY COUNCIL COMMITTEE CONDUCTING THE HEARINGS WILL
MOVE SLOWLY IN THE MATTER.

AFTER LISTENING TO THE ARGUMENTS, THE COMMITTEE VOTED TO TAKE THE
PROPOSED ORDINANCE UNDER ADVISEMENT AND GO OVER IT LINE BY LINE WITH
THE CITY ATTORNEY.

SUCH PROCEDURE WOULD MAKE IT ALMOST IMPOSSIBLE TO HAVE A
RECOMMENDATION READY IN TIME FOR THE COUNCIL'S MEETING FRIDAY. AND THE
COUNCIL IS NOT SCHEDULED TO MEET AGAIN UNTIL SEPTEMBER 12TH.

SOME SEVEN HUNDRED PERSONS JAMMED THE COUNCIL CHAMBERS FOR THE
SESSION, AT WHICH SOME LABOR REPRESENTATIVES CLAIMED THE NEW ORDINANCE
DOES NOT GO FAR ENOUGH....BUT WITH REPRESENTATIVES OF THE LANDLORDS
STATING THAT THE NEW REGULATIONS WOULD NOT MAKE ANY MORE ROOMS
AVAILABLE.

THE PROPOSED ORDINANCE WOULD EXTEND EVICTION
STAYS FROM THIRTY TO NINETY DAYS.

~~ST. PAUL~~--TWO-WAY RADIO TELEPHONE COMMUNICATION HAS BEEN PUT
INTO SERVICE BY A ST.PAUL TAXICAB COMPANY ⟨*THE*⟩ ⟨BROWN AND WHITE⟩.

THE RADIO PHONES WILL PERMIT THE COMPANY DISPATCHER TO KEEP IN
CONSTANT TOUCH WITH CAB DRIVERS, AND THUS ROUTE THEM MORE QUICKLY TO
TAKE CARE OF CALLS FOR SERVICE.

18

Going to the typewriter, he turns out thirteen lines of University news.

Then he glances at the latest spot summary from the wire. Not what he wants. He goes again to the typewriter and hammers out his own closing summary.

//

        On the campus of the University of Minnesota tonight --- there'll be
a piano recital open to the public. The artist is John Wannamaker, an
instructor in music at Drake University. Mr. Wannamaker, a summer student
at the University, will give his concert in Scott Hall at 8:30.
                        #########

        The dispute on the campus over wages of non-teaching, civil service
employes is at a standstill today. The latest news --- since Governor
Youngdahl has appointed a fact-finding committee --- is the letter just
made public by President Morrill.

        In the letter, President Morrill says that the present University
wage scale is higher than that outlined in an agreement between the union
and the University last January. It's over this agreement, calling for
retroactive pay, that the dispute centers. President Morrill says that
the 1947 Legislature granted the University funds which have been used
to raise wages above the scale the agreement called for.
                        #########

                                                                    13

The clock says 11:25 as he completes it, and the announcer appears—
with word that the broadcast is going out from the regular studio,
rather than from the Fair grounds. This calls for some quick editing on
pages 1 and 9.

The broadcast is ready—234 lines and summary.

12)

Now, the summary of the major news:

      Minnesotans are crowding to the State Fair in St. Paul. Attendance
is already far ahead of the previous record. And the weather today is good
again.

        #######

      In Greece, the new premier --- Constantin Tsaldaris --- is having a
tough time to get a cabinet together.

        #####

      The London conference on plans for restoration of Germany is meeting
with considerable success.

        ######

      In New York City, thousands of American Legionnaires are preparing for
the opening of their convention tomorrow.

        #######

      Automobile prices are expected to remain at their present levels for
the rest of this year. All the big manufacturers have raised their prices in
the last few days.

        ######

      A St. Paul petroleum industry official says there'll be plenty
of gasoline for motorists over the Labor Day week-end.

        #####

Now the announcer reads it carefully—in more leisurely manner than usual, since he has plenty of time. As he goes through it, he underlines words he wants to emphasize, and circles words whose pronunciation he must watch carefully (for example, "Greece," "France," and "further reductions" on page 2; "Balikpapan" and "Tarakan" on page 4). Into the auto price story on page 8 he inserts an aside.

At 12:15 he goes on the air—the editor meanwhile watching the printer to make sure there are no news-breaks that demand inclusion in the show. After the broadcast, the announcer reports that the copy came out "on the nose"—just the right length.

Moving from Story to Story

A newspaper story, under its own headline, stands on its own feet. Except in the few cases in which several stories drop out of a multi-column headline, or one story is tied to related news by some other typographical device, interrelationships are not so commonly shown.

Relationships among stories in a newscast are of first importance. One of the prime tasks of the news editor is to achieve the effect of relationship, of continuity, of easy flow. Three principal reasons:

1. Listener-understanding is aided when like stories are properly tied together, when news events of allied nature are described sequentially. The departmentalized format of most newscasts grows out of this fact. It is obviously more effective, from the point of view of the listener, to link all the labor news in a news show together than to offer it scattered throughout the broadcast.

Clip-and-paste, or "tack-up," newscasts like that just described are usually put together on ordinary copy paper—8½ by 11½ inch soft-finish paper, yellow or white. Such paper is easy to handle, takes mucilage readily, doesn't rustle as the announcer handles it close to the mike. Some editors use wire staplers to attach the copy to the paper backing; most use glue or mucilage in the familiar small bottle with rubber applicator. In using glue, care must be taken that none escapes from under the edges of the copy. If it does, it may cause pages to stick together.

Some announcers prefer only one story to a page. Others are willing to have the editor put on a page as many stories as he can place there, as long as he is careful with his end-marks or his MORE symbols when a story continues from one page to another.

2. The "conversational tone" of the news show is enhanced by showing relationships. It is easier for the listener to keep up with a newscast that flows easily from one subject to another than with one that bumps each time a new story is introduced. And such a newscast sounds more like conversation.

3. Skillful use of transitional devices is economical of time.

All of which is not to say that a newscast, to be effective, ought to be a mass of transitions with stories connecting them. Overuse of the linking devices becomes artificial, hence annoying to the listener. Some stories simply can't logically be tied to anything else (though this in itself might suggest a transitional device). Moreover, the occasional sharp break—usually signalized by a slight announcer-pause—serves to accent a story, and to avoid monotony. No conversationalist would be likely to talk for twelve to fifteen minutes straight without occasionally changing the subject. No newscaster should be asked to.

What are the devices?

First, the simple conjunctions.

The radio writer takes a cue from the conversational habit of prefacing many sentences with "and." The word—often thrown in conversationally where it might better be left out—is a smoothing device, a device for maintaining continuity. It can be, and is, used widely in radio news copy to introduce sentences—sometimes within paragraphs, sometimes to open new paragraphs or even new stories. There's danger in its overuse—it shouldn't appear as often as in casual conversation. There are news editors who eschew it. But the bulk of practice favors it, and with good reason.

Often its best use is not merely as a lone conjunction, but rather in connection with a phrase or clause that continues the transitional idea. It should normally be followed by a genuine addition—something that logically builds on or adds to what precedes. For example:

And there's more news of stormy weather from Tampa.

A number of examples of its use—most of them effective—occur in the KUOM script in this chapter, and in other scripts and excerpts of scripts in this book.

Another of the simple conjunctions of wide usefulness is "but."

"But" introduces a contrast; for contrasting stories or ideas it is often an excellent introduction. Suppose a story in a newscast tells of fine local weather. The next story, introduced in the example above by "and," might then open:

But down in Tampa they're expecting a hurricane.

Like "and," "but" should not be overused.

The other simple coordinating conjunctions ("or," "for," "nor") are not so generally useful.

A widely-used one-word device is the interjection "well." It's another that some writers avoid as they would poison. But their dislike of it usually grows from careless overdependence on it. If often serves smoothly to introduce stories of certain types—usually stories of less than serious nature:

Well, here's a queer story about a dog.

OR:

Well, Slugger Ted Williams has done it again.

See also page 7 of the KUOM script.

A second class of conjunctional devices is the group of conjunctive adverbs: accordingly, also, besides, hence, however, moreover, nevertheless, so, still, then, therefore, thus. Often they can be employed to advantage. Careful writers, however, avoid vulgar or clumsy misusages. "Also" should introduce only something having kinship with the preceding story—not merely another story (it should be used sparingly in any case, for it's a clumsy sentence-opener). "Thus" should be used to mean "in this manner," not "therefore." And so on.

A number of phrases have come into general radio news use—time phrases, place phrases, other connective phrases. Representative time phrases:

At the same time	More recently
This morning	Meantime
Word has just come	Just before the speech
We haven't yet heard	

Among the most abused time-connectives in newscasting are "meantime," "meanwhile," and "in the meantime." Used jealously, they may accomplish excellent transitions. But they should appear only when they show a close relationship. That is to say, it is hardly permissible to use "meanwhile" to show only that one story occurs while another of no similarity or relationship is taking place; it should be used to mean that the second event not only has a time kinship but also a kinship in general nature.

Place phrases serve not only as connectives, in the sense here described, but also to move the listener easily to a new geographical area of news activity. They are often of vital necessity to clarity of understanding. If one story deals with an event in Los Angeles, for example, and the next with one in Chicago, the listener must be told at once of the change in locale. The simple "in Chicago" is the most common and the most useful such phrase; it is also the easiest to overwork.

If a newscast uses date lines, the place phrase is unnecessary. But most don't; and in such shows, every change of locale must be made clear. If a story doesn't actually open with a place phrase, the location should appear (when it's important) somewhere in the first or second sentence. Examples of this appear in almost all the international stories in the KUOM script: "Troubled Greece," "the government of France," "across the English channel in London," "two top-drawer American diplomatic policy makers are on their way to Paris," and so on.

Among commonplace phrases are:

In the Far East	Nearby, in New Jersey
Down in Texas	From far-off India
Across the Atlantic	On the Manchurian front

Subject-matter transitional devices are also common. Useful and effective if they don't appear too often are such phrases as:

Speaking of railroads, here's . . . . .
On the political scene
More news about the American Legion.

During World War II the most overworked of all transitional devices was probably that employing the word "front." One heard from every radio that news was coming "from the European front," or the Asiatic, or the Pacific, or the home—or the women's, on occasion! Many news writers came to avoid it for this reason. A very good reason.

Another effective transitional device is the reminder phrase—"you'll recall that," "you remember we told you that" and the like. Such phrases not only introduce stories smoothly but also flatter the listener.

To tie two or more stories together, news writers often employ an opening phrase covering them all. Place or subject phrases such as many of those cited above accomplish this purpose. Another method:

Two stories come from Chicago this morning.
One says that . . . .
The second Chicago story has to do with . . . .

OR:

Here are a couple of stories that will amuse you.

Typical Radio Station News-Days
KABR-Aberdeen, S. D.

7:15 A.M.   15-minute program, using news and "Farm Fair" (AP feature)

9:15 A.M.   15-minute straight newscast, using 5-minute summary, South Dakota news on the regional split, and other late news

10:45 A.M.   5-minute news-feature program, using "Behind the World News" (AP feature)

12:00 NOON   15-minute straight newscast, based on 5- and 15-minute summaries and other late news (no regional)

10:00 P.M.   15-minute straight newscast, based on 5- and 15-minute summaries, the South Dakota split, and other late news

All shows come straight from the AP radio wire, without rewriting, editing, or paste-up. KABR is a 5,000-watt Mutual affiliate.

WHO-Des Moines, Iowa

7.30 A.M.   15-minute straight newscast, its news selected to take advantage of the fact that the WHO signal gets outside of Iowa at the early morning hour

8:45 A.M.   10-minute two-voice program: a man for 5 minutes with a round-up of world news; a woman for 5 minutes, with news of special interest to women

12:30 P.M.   15-minute straight newscast, using world-wide news and a heavy proportion of Iowa news (since the signal at this hour does not carry as far as in the early morning)

5:00 P.M.   10-minute straight newscast—same pattern as the 12:30 program

6:30 P.M.   10-minute straight newscast—same pattern as the 7:30 program

10:15 P.M.   15-minute straight newscast, a general news round-up. Often followed by a second 15-minute program with "public-service" news

11:30 P.M.   15-minute combination of news round-up and background of the news

All shows except the 5 P.M. are written entirely in the WHO newsroom. The 5 P.M. leans heavily on AP and UP radio wire copy. WHO is a 50,000-watt NBC affiliate.

KOIN-Portland, Ore.

7:15 A.M.   15-minute straight newscast, a general news round-up

12:00 NOON   15-minute straight newscast, a general news round-up

2:00 P.M.   10-minute feature newscast, opening with brief "headline summary"

3:00 P.M.   15-minute straight newscast, a general news round-up

10:00 P.M.   15-minute straight newscast, a general newscast

All shows combine copy from AP and UP radio wires. The 10 P.M. "Five Star Final," is the day's chief show, and is about half rewritten from the wire copy. KOIN is a 5,000-watt CBS affiliate.

WRC-Washington, D. C.

5:30 A.M.   1-minute straight newscast (WRC origin)

6:00 A.M.   5-minute straight newscast (WRC origin)

7:00 A.M.   15-minute straight newscast (WRC origin)

7:30 A.M.   5-minute straight newscast (WRC origin)

8:00 A.M.   15-minute network round-up (2 minutes from WRC)

8:30 A.M.   5-minute straight newscast (WRC origin)

9:30 A.M.   5-minute straight newscast (WRC origin)

12:00 NOON	15-minute straight newscast (WRC origin)
1:45 P.M.	15-minute Washington news round-up (network show of WRC origin)
6:00 P.M.	5-minute straight newscast (WRC origin)
6:05 P.M.	10-minute news commentary (WRC origin)
6:45 P.M.	15-minute network round-up
7:15 P.M.	15-minute news round-up (network show of WRC origin)
7:45 P.M.	15-minute network commentary
11:00 P.M.	5-minute straight newscast (WRC origin)
11:15 P.M.	15-minute news round-up (network show of WRC origin)
12 MIDNIGHT	5-minute straight newscast (WRC origin)
12:55 A.M.	5-minute network round-up

All the shows of WRC origin except four of the 5-minute straight newscasts are written entirely in the WRC newsroom, using AP 24-hour newspaper A wire, UP night and day newspaper trunk wires, INS day and night wires, day and night Washington City News Service, and special NBC correspondents' service. The four 5-minute "tack-ups" are taken from the UP radio wire.

WRC is a 5,000-watt NBC-owned station, the network's point of origin for all Washington shows. The daily schedule shown here is heavier than those for KABR, WHO, and KOIN because it includes network as well as local-origin news shows (the other three, like all network affiliates, supplement their own schedules by adding network news shows).

7

Multivoice News Shows

The single-voice news show dominates radio's news programming. Most stations presenting newscasts with more than one voice schedule them as weekly rather than daily offerings.

This is not because of doubt of their effectiveness. Skillful use of two or more voices on any program adds to its interest. It is not "natural" that one voice indulge in a twelve-minute monolog; the average man is not accustomed to hearing any voice, even his own, continue for more than a few seconds without interruption. Moreover, the use of more than one voice provides variety, color, sometimes drama and conflict; it may speed up an otherwise lagging show. The radio listener is interested in people—within limits, the more people the more interest. Variety of intonation and accent, variety of personality as revealed by voice, change of pace, the rise and fall of question and answer—all these are desirable qualities in radio broadcasting.

Why, then, are not more news shows cast in the multivoice mold? Why, when sponsors are so vitally aware that drama and entertainment are qualities that draw listeners and sell products, do they not ask for them, in news shows, in the larger measure that departure from the one-voice pattern would insure?

The reason is not simply that the listener, through habit, has developed a high degree of acceptance of news presented by one announcer.

Nor is it that news in itself has high intrinsic interest—that the twentieth-century human, being a literate animal with an increasing sense of the interdependence of his own welfare on the thousand cross-currents of contemporary events, is eager enough to get the news so that he will take it in any form.

The reasons (they have been suggested earlier in this book):

Time　It takes longer to get a multivoice show ready for the air than a one-voice show. To write it is a little more time-consuming. To prepare it for broadcasting takes more time. It has to be "cast"—that is, the voices have to be selected (though this may not have to be done anew for every broadcast). And it uses up precious time on the air. You usually can't get as much news into the multivoice show as could be packed into the simpler form.

Production It may have to be rehearsed. Two news announcers accustomed to working together on a two-voice show perhaps won't require rehearsal. But if the program involves use of radio's other principal tools—sound and music—or if a number of voices appear in the script, the production-rehearsal problem grows.

Cost This factor is closely related to the time and production elements. Two announcers get twice as much salary as one; a cast of actors requires a sizable talent fee. Rehearsals cost money. The multivoice show is more expensive for the station, more expensive for the sponsor.

Nevertheless, there are multivoice shows on the air. As competition for audiences grows keener in a news world in which the ready-made stimulus of war is lacking, as a half-dozen or more FM stations in one county start their battle for the county's listeners, broadcasters' interest in the more involved news-forms may grow stronger. There is every likelihood that the coming years may see more rather than fewer of them.

There have been developed three basic types of news-show using two or more voices:

1. The simple multivoice show
2. The radio news interview
3. The news dramatization

The Simple Multivoice Show

Essentially, this type of show—most common of the plural-voice news programs—employs more than one voice for variety and emphasis,

---

Such multivoice programs as the networks' international news round-ups, or the three-part show designed by WCBM-Baltimore (described in Chapter 6), are not considered here. They are, in effect, combinations of a number of one-voice presentations, each complete in itself, without the interweaving that makes them closely-knit units.

sometimes for clarification, but not to create any illusion of reality. It is not an attempt to reproduce dialog. Rather, it is closer to the pattern of the printed newspaper story, with its headline and subheads. It is as though a newsroom director said, "I have several voices to work with. In what simple manner can I use them effectively?"

The simplest pattern for such a show is that using one voice to present "headlines," the second to give the news under the headline. This kind of newscast often describes itself under such a title as "Headlines in the News" or "Today's Headlines."

Its writing and problems, discussed in Chapter 6, are not difficult. The individual stories in it are handled much as are those in a straight newscast, with such modifications and simplifications in their openings as may be called for to take advantage of the fact that the subject or key of the story has already been given. There need be no attention to the usual transitional devices, since the headlines serve the purpose.

Such a show is usually introduced—as should be all shows departing from the standard straight newscast pattern—by an announcement calling attention to its special nature and perhaps introducing the owners of the voices. This means that a third voice, that of the announcer (who commonly reads the commercials), comes into the picture—a fact that provides added opportunity for variety—and also increases cost and the chance of miscuing and fluffs.

As a variation on this basic pattern, the headline voice may give sentence introductions—"in Times Square a hundred thousand New Yorkers are welcoming the New Year" or "a disastrous airplane crash is just reported from Cleveland." Other variations will suggest themselves.

A multivoice show at its simplest may readily be built from the KUOM newscast in Chapter 6:

ANNOUNCER: Again Station KWWW presents "Headlines in the News." Here are Gil Gray and Glen Smith, with latest headline stories:

GRAY: STATE FAIR ATTENDANCE BREAKS RECORDS

SMITH: The crowds are thronging to the Minnesota State Fair again today. The weather is fine . . . . etc.

GRAY: GREECE LABORS TO SOLVE CABINET CRISIS

SMITH: ConstantinTsaldaris—just named premier of Greece—is trying to form a new cabinet . . . . etc.

GRAY: BREAD RATIONED IN FRANCE

SMITH: France's grain harvest is in "deplorable state" this year. And
the French government has just announced . . . . etc.

To convert this pattern into the variation mentioned above:

GRAY: Bigger crowds than ever before are going to the Minnesota
State Fair this year.

SMITH: Fine weather is bringing record crowds to the Fair grounds
again today . . . . etc.

A number of other departures from the basic pattern have developed
—some of them successful, others not so good. Here are examples of two
patterns used during World War II:

ANNOUNCER: Good evening, ladies and gentlemen.
Today, the Allied troops hurled back all Axis attacks in North
Tunisia.
The RAF hit back again over Germany last night—giving Ber-
lin severe air blows on the birthday of Hitler's Luftwaffe.
In the Southwest Pacific, General MacArthur's airmen are
still waiting to attack a Jap convoy.
And in Washington, Secretary of the Navy Knox said, "We'll
utterly destroy the Jap fleet before the war is ended."
Here are Gil Gray and Glen Smith with the details:

GRAY: Allied troops have pushed back all of General Jurgen von
Arnim's attacks in Northern Tunisia. . . .
        (Gray then continues with detail of the Tunisia story,
        the RAF story and the MacArthur story. After establish-
        ing the Knox story, he says:)
Knox asserted:

SMITH: We will utterly destroy the Japanese fleet before this war is
ended. We probably will . . . . etc.
        (At the end of the Knox quotation, Gray resumes; Smith
        comes in only when he is giving verbatim quotations in-
        troduced by Gray.)

— o —

ANNOUNCER: Headline news in the world today . . . brought to you by Gil Gray, Glen Smith, and Kenn Barry.

(MUSIC: FANFARE)

ANNOUNCER: First, from the North African theater.

GRAY: British hurl back wide Nazi tank attacks near Hedjez-El-Bab in Tunisia. (PAUSE) Montgomery and the Eighth army wheel into position south of Mareth line.

ANNOUNCER: On the Russian front.

SMITH: Red troops smash westward from Kharkov. (PAUSE) Nazis resist stubbornly in muddy Donets sector.

ANNOUNCER: The air war over Europe.

BARRY: American heavy bombers smash at Brest in France. (PAUSE) RAF medium bombers attack Dunkerque in third day of sustained air activity on the Continent.

ANNOUNCER: And here are the summaries.

> (Gray then follows with the stories he has introduced; Smith with his stories; Barry with his. This will consume about a third of a fifteen-minute show. The pattern is then repeated, with minor variation.)

Both of these patterns, making more than orthodox use of the announcer, are more complicated than the basic pattern. They illustrate excellently the principle that confusion increases in direct ratio to complication. Both would be harder to follow than a simpler form.

The first also illustrates, however, a legitimate and effective use of the added voice—to present a quotation. This device makes it possible to give quotations understandably and uncluttered by credit lines, and longer than the one-voice show can offer.

Alternation of two voices from story to story is often entirely satisfactory. But to alternate voices within a story, for no apparent reason except to use two voices, is bad:

GRAY: Out at the Minnesota State Fair, attendance is heavy again today.

SMITH: The weather is fine—sunny . . . a light haze in the air . . . not too warm. And crowds are pouring through the gates in what seem to be record numbers.

GRAY: Already, you know, attendance at the Fair is well ahead of the previous record. Yesterday nearly 80 thousand people came— and that brought the four-day total to more than 300 thousand.

SMITH: That's 70 thousand more than the best previous attendance for the first four days, in 1941 . . . . etc.

Another practice best avoided is illustrated in the following passage (actually written for broadcast, but fortunately stopped before it got on the air):

ANNOUNCER: The weekly round-up of Washington news, presented every Saturday at this time by Gil Gray, Glen Smith, and Kenn Barry. Here's Gil:

GRAY: Thanks, Larry, and good evening, radio friends. There are many things happening in Washington right now. So many debates going on among senators, representatives, and war administrators that—well, we don't know quite where to start.

SMITH: Probably the best topic of conversation right now, Gil, is the farm-labor bill. Stimson and McNutt are two of the men on the administration's top ladder who've found in the past few days that they can't come to agreement.

GRAY: That's right, Glen. McNutt strongly opposed—

BARRY: I'd like to interrupt, Gil.

GRAY: Go ahead, Kenn.

BARRY: Just to mention something about . . . etc.

The fallacy of this ardent attempt at informality and conversational tone is evident. In the first place, it isn't good copy—its writing is artificial. In the second, and more important, the attempt to present news as though in a casual conversation deprives it of prime qualities: objectivity and authority. These aren't newscasters presenting facts, but rather three men discussing—better, perhaps, gossiping about—facts. The listener is pretty sure to find what they offer less convincing and authentic than it ought to be.

A woman's voice is used on some multivoice shows, usually to present news of feminine interest or quotations from women. One such show is "Colorado Speaks," a weekly half-hour program presented successfully for some years by KLZ-Denver to summarize the opinions of Colorado newspapers on current affairs. After a standard opening, Voice A presents a brief summary of the topics the press has been discussing. Voice B—used for this purpose only—then comes in: "Appraising the Japanese situation, Hubert A. Smith of the Denver *Catholic Register* says that:"—This is followed by Voice C's quotation from a *Register* editorial. At its end, Voice B introduces another quotation, and Voice A gives it. This pattern, continued through the show, presents excerpts from twenty-five or more newspaper comments. The fourth voice, a woman's, is used for quotations from women editors. The show, carefully backgrounded with music, involves production problems not usually tackled in such programs.

A Los Angeles station has used a multivoice technique in a daily show to present a mélange of news, feature material, excerpts from books and magazines, and the like.

In summary, it may be said that the multivoice pattern, in its many variations, serves a useful purpose; that it may be very effective if it isn't labored or tortured into illogical, artificial forms; but that it is certainly secondary to the straight newscast form because of its time, cost, and production problems.

The Radio News Interview

Properly used, the interview is a simple and effective method of introducing meaning, authority, and color into radio news or news commentary.

Poorly used—as too frequently it is—it is likely to be stilted, or stumbling, or artificial, or all these. Worst of all, it may "sound like an interview" rather than an interested and interesting conversation. More of this later.

By definition, the radio news interview is the broadcast in which an authority is brought before the microphone to present, in response to the "leads" of an interviewer, facts or competent opinion on a subject of news interest. Usually the interviewer is a member of the station staff—an announcer, a newscaster, a staff specialist in sports or agriculture. The "authority" is a person selected because, by experience, background, or position, he is able to offer facts and comments which a listening audience will accept as competent. Suppose the subject is a rowdy post-football game celebration by high school students; the authority might be a high school principal, a student participant, a policeman, or the motorist whose car was overturned by the youngsters. If it's a problem of international politics, the interviewee might be a university political scientist, a national officer of the Foreign Policy Association, or a foreign correspondent. Occasionally both participants may be guests—the high school principal interviewing the police chief, or a professor interviewing a distinguished visiting authority. Occasionally there may be more than one interviewee—the broadcast may become a three- or four-way conversation.

In any case, the program is one in which, in simplest terms, there are a questioner and a respondent. Thus it differs from the multivoice programs described earlier in this chapter. It is a multivoice show, but not one in which all voices are used strictly for expositional purposes.

Obviously the interview is a means of adding vitality to news presentation. Not only does it introduce the dramatic effect of dialog rather than monolog (the *substance* of any news interview could be written into a straight newscast). It also brings to the audience a personality of interest and authority.

But a more significant value in its use lies in the opportunity it offers for showing the background, the meaning of the news. A newscast over a station in an agricultural area can present all the *facts* about the drouth that threatens to hamstring farm production; but to give listeners the *meaning* of the facts the word of an agronomist, or a dirt farmer, or an agricultural economist is needed. And the interview is a most effective method of offering the expert word. This is of course directly analogous to the newspaper's use of the news interview.

Scores of such radio interviews—perhaps the majority of them—are ad-lib. This is often satisfactory when the interviewee is sure the mike isn't going to bite him, and when the interviewer is skillful enough to

Interviews are used in many shows other than news. Most of the things said here about news interviews may also be said about other types of interview programs—personality interviews, special feature interviews, and so on.

direct the broadcast with pace, judgment, and smoothness. Often, however, one or another of these conditions may not hold. The likely result is a broadcast that falters or stutters, one that is repetitious, one that sends listeners in droves to the opposition station. Though the interview from script offers its own pitfalls, it is less likely to miss fire than the ad-lib variety. Many stations require that scripts for all such broadcasts be submitted twenty-four hours or more ahead of mike-time for checking and possible improvement.

Whether script or ad-lib, most interviews require a good deal of pre-broadcast preparation. At the least, the participants need to confer on areas to be covered, some of the leading questions to be asked and answered, the order of topics, and so on. Experienced radio men often conduct such a conference in the broadcasting booth, the mike on the table between interviewer and interviewee, to accustom the neophyte to talking with the mike in front of him.

At most, preparation for the radio interview may call for a good deal of study of the subject by the man who is to write the script (it's most desirable for the writer also to act as interviewer), for a long discussion of it by the participants, for writing the script and submitting it to the interviewee, for revision, and possibly for a rehearsal or two. It isn't often that all these steps are carried out. But several of them must precede every interview.

At least a rudimentary script is necessary even for the ad-lib interview. It consists sometimes of nothing more than scrawled notes on the topics the interview is to cover, or perhaps a list of questions the "straight man" is to ask. An outline's virtue is not only that it provides to the questioner material for his part of the performance, but also that—if it's carefully made—it sets an orderly pattern for the program. Without it, there would be probability of omissions or confused and confusing presentation.

What are the qualities desirable in a "good" radio interview script?

Let it be remembered that the radio interview is neither a casual conversation between two individuals nor a catechism of one individual by another. It is something between the two. It is not the first, except in rare cases, because it is presumed that the man featured in the interview knows a great deal more about his subject than does the questioner, or the listener whom the questioner represents. That's the reason he's on the program. The two are not presumed to be conducting a wholly informal conversation, one characterized by the realism of dramatic dialog. On the other hand, a degree of informality, of the conversational manner, is necessary for precisely the same reason that it's necessary in straight news presentation; and nothing is less effective aurally than the mechanical question-and-answer device.

The best result is likely to be attained when the script writer keeps in mind the point just made: that the questioner represents the listener. The listener is at ease in his living room; he is presumably interested in the subject, and he is glad to have the authority brought into a chair on the other side of the fire place to expound it. All of which means that the questioner's approach should be, in effect, the one the listener would adopt if the situation were real instead of imaginary.

The effective script, then, is one in which the questioner is somewhat in the position of the student who has read the text, but doesn't think he knows all the answers. He wants to know more, and he's well enough informed so that he can converse on the subject, can ask intelligent questions. He guides the course of the interview to the points he and the listener want to reach. And he does it in a manner suiting the circumstance—usually a circumstance in which the authority of the interviewee entitles him to be treated courteously, not with the familiarity of a barroom buddy.

Take this last point first. Recall the radio interviews you have heard in which the synthetic familiarity, the first-name chumminess, has been artificial, unconvincing, often annoying. Then let your first rule be, "Don't make the speakers pals unless they *are* pals."

An example of what not to do:

ANNOUNCER: . . . . and here is the eminent pediatrician, Dr. Albert Morgan. He will be interviewed by Gil Gray.

GRAY: Good to have you here this evening, Doc.

MORGAN: Thanks, Gil. I'm glad to be here.

GRAY: Suppose you start, Doc, by telling us how you got into this work . . .

The point is obvious. Dr. Morgan and Gray likely never clapped eyes on each other before they met to arrange the interview. The listener knows this, and he isn't fooled by the artificial familiarity. He would be more at ease, and more impressed by the speaker's authority, if the script went something like this:

GRAY: Good evening, Dr. Morgan.

MORGAN: Good evening.

GRAY: First, Doctor, I'd like to know how you got into this work . . . .

In some interviews, of course, first names or nicknames are appropriate. If a newspaper sports editor, for example, is interviewing a football coach he has known for years, it would be ludicrous to use formal titles. But the too-common assumption in radio that facing each other across a microphone justifies verbal back-slapping is best forgotten.

The examples above, good and bad, illustrate another important device in interview-writing: that of presenting early in the script whatever information is necessary to establish the expert's right to speak. In some cases the formal introduction of the broadcast will do this. In most it is desirable to let the interviewee himself tell the listener something of his background or experience. Usually this can be managed in one brief speech—forty or fifty words. Then the interviewer can turn the conversation directly onto the subject.

Another tip on the use of names: Don't use them too often. They should appear frequently enough in the opening speeches so that the listener will have plenty of opportunity to set in his mind the identification of the voices; after that they should appear much less often.

How much should the interviewer talk? How long should speeches be? How frequently should questions be inserted?

The answers to problems like these grow out of the need to keep the program moving, to keep it conversational in manner. Few men in conversation talk in long speeches—unless a speaker is telling an anecdote or presenting a well-integrated exposition, he rarely talks without interruption for more than three or four sentences. In a fifteen-minute interview, the authority may be given half a dozen speeches of 150 words or so—perhaps even longer, on occasion. But he is not giving a formal talk—he is conversing. He should not be forced to orate too long in one place.

Therefore, on a page of interview copy, you'll ordinarily expect to find four or more speeches—two or three by the questioner, responses by the interviewee.

Again, it should be remembered that it's a rare conversation in which one man ends every speech with a question mark. Some of the interviewer's remarks must be questions. A good many of them should be declarative sentences, or half sentences—often devices for rhetorical effect, devices to break up what might become overlong monologs. Speeches like these:

I see what you mean.
Not much chance of success in that kind of thing.
I certainly didn't know that there are water buffalo in Patagonia.
I wish you'd enlarge on that.
Well, we've had the same kind of thing happen here in Midland.

Most conversations are well larded with such words as "well," "yes," and other short helpers. They are useful in interview scripts.

A caution: Men and women chosen to appear in radio interviews are not often radio actors. They are not skilled at timing speeches, at simulating laughter. Consequently speeches that call for split-second interruptions, chuckles, and the like are to be avoided. "Straight copy" is always better than anything demanding specialized microphone skill.

Similarly, it's dangerous to write humor into interview scripts. Vast is the number of untrained speakers who can put humorous lines into a mike and make them come out funereal.

The following interview*—broadcast over ABC on January 7, 1946— is skillfully written. As you examine it, remember that it is special pleading—an exposition of the position taken by the steel industry toward the strike impending when the interview went on the air. It employs a distinguished newspaper specialist as the questioner, and a leader in the steel industry as interviewee. The questioner's first speech lays the scene (it's the longest single speech in the script). After that,

---

* From an uncopyrighted pamphlet, "Management's Job," published by American Iron and Steel Institute, 1946.

the questioner moves to the background, and the interviewee—with the adroit help of the straight man—carries the show.

ANNOUNCER: Good evening, ladies and gentlemen. Under the sponsorship of the American Iron and Steel Institute, this program brings you an interview with Ernest T. Weir, chairman of National Steel Corporation and a director of the Institute. Mr. Weir will be questioned by John G. Forrest, financial editor of the New York Times, on the general situation in the steel industry as it looks today. Mr. Forrest.

FORREST: Thank you. As I understand it, Mr. Weir, the highlights of the situation in the steel industry tonight are these:
One—Last spring, most steel companies signed renewal contracts with the CIO's United Steel Workers Union. Those contracts were to run until the autumn of 1946, and they contained clauses prohibiting both strikes and lock-outs.
Two—Several months ago, the union demanded an increase of $2 per day in straight-time pay.
Three—The steel companies replied that they could not pay a wage increase because they were now losing money on most of their steel products—that substantial price increases would be necessary to allow most steel companies to break even, let alone pay wage increases.
Four—Last November, the OPA refused to allow a price increase. However, the President has directed OPA to re-study the matter and make a new report no later than February 1.
Five—The union held a strike vote in November; the majority of steelworkers voted for the strike, and the union leaders have set January 14—one week from today—for the start of an industry-wide strike.
Six—Last week, the President appointed a fact-finding board which is to report on the steel wage issue as it affects the union and the United States Steel Corporation. Is that a fair summary, Mr. Weir?

WEIR: Yes, Mr. Forrest, you are a good reporter.

FORREST: Mr. Weir, I suppose you noticed in the Times today that the steel board has requested the union and the United States Steel Corporation to return to collective bargaining. Would any agreement arrived at by collective bargaining, or any facts found by this board with respect to the United States Steel Corporation, apply to the steel industry as a whole?

WEIR: Mr. Forrest, the steel industry is composed of from 150 to 200 corporations of all kinds—big and little. I think it's quite obvious that a situation that might apply to one company would not necessarily apply to all the rest.

FORREST: By the way, Mr. Weir, does your company have a contract with the United Steelworkers?

WEIR: Some of our subsidiary companies do. Others have contracts with independent unions—the United Mine Workers and the Weirton Independent Union.

FORREST: The United Mine Workers, I assume, will not be a party to the steel strike. How about the Weirton Union?

WEIR: The Weirton Independent Union, which is the bargaining agency for the production and maintenance employees of the Weirton Steel Company, has not indicated any intention to strike.

FORREST: Has it made any wage demands, Mr. Weir?

WEIR: It has—and is continuing negotiations with the Weirton management in accordance with the terms of its contract.

FORREST: Now to get back to the general situation. As I see it, you have three separate factors that influence the present situation—management, the union and government.

WEIR: Yes, that's true, and, unfortunately, unions and government now attempt to exercise functions that are properly the sole responsibility of management.

FORREST: Responsibility of management? How is that, Mr. Weir?

WEIR: It is management's job to balance the different groups that make up each company, to coordinate their functions, and to direct their activities. In whatever it does, management must consider *all* of these groups. You know you can get a pretty fair idea of a company's operations by watching an orchestra at work.

FORREST: You may be right, but an orchestra and a steel company seem pretty far apart to me.

WEIR: Not so very far. Anyone watching an orchestra sees management and production being carried on right before his eyes. An orchestra may have over 100 musicians. Each individual may be a skilled artist with his particular instrument, but in the orchestra, the musician does not play as an individual but as a member of a particular section of the orchestra and as a member of the entire orchestra. To produce orchestral music, each musician and each section of instruments must do the right thing at the right time. They can't do that without management—in the person of the conductor. The conductor is doing a management job and the orchestra a production job from the first note to the last.

FORREST: And I suppose, Mr. Weir, the orchestra audience compares with the buying public?

WEIR: Right—the buying public calls the industrial tune. An orchestra may have the best musicians and instruments in the world, but without the conductor, it would never produce music. It would just produce noise. Without management, industry's production would be the equivalent of noise.

FORREST: Do you imply that industry today does not have the cooperation that is necessary to efficient production?

WEIR: I imply more than that and to illustrate, I would like to refer to the orchestra once more. Then I will leave it and stick to industry. Suppose there was a fellow sitting in one section of the orchestra who could cancel the conductor's directions and give other directions of his own. Then suppose that there was another fellow—one who did not know much about music—sitting beside the conductor who tugged at his elbow now and again to give suggestions, advice and orders. Under these conditions, you can well imagine what kind of performance an orchestra would give. And the management of any business today is up against conditions very much like that.

FORREST: All right, Mr. Weir. Let's apply that comparison to industry. Who are the fellows responsible for the "sour notes"?

WEIR: Well, the fellow who could overrule the conductor is a certain type of union leader. The fellow tugging at the conductor's elbow could be one of many bureaucrats in Washington, D. C.

FORREST: Will you tell us specifically how these things prevent management from discharging its responsibility?

WEIR: Gladly, but perhaps we should first *name* some of management's responsibilities. Management's basic, long-range, overall responsibility is to the public as a whole—to produce more goods and better quality at lower cost. Industry also has a responsibility to be efficient, and to provide a fair return on the investment of its stockholders. In the past, American management, workers and investors, together, have discharged these responsibilities well enough to give the average American the highest standard of living ever known in any country or at any time in history.

FORREST: A few moments ago, you intimated that steel companies could not pay the wage increase demanded by the union without violating the responsibility of management. Will you please explain that?

WEIR: Well, since steel companies are now making most of their products at a loss, they are not getting enough money from customers to pay the wage increase. So they would have to get it from other sources. The first step, of course, would be to wipe out dividends to stockholders because dividends are paid out of profits and there wouldn't be any profits. The next step would be to rob the business of funds vital to its very existence.

FORREST: You mean funds such as surplus, reserves and depreciation set aside to replace machinery and materials, and funds for the building of new plants?

WEIR: Yes. And there would not be enough money from all sources together to pay the wage increase. Most steel companies would operate in the red. The result for stronger companies would be increased debt and for the weaker companies—bankruptcy. Under today's conditions, management cannot pay the huge wage increase demanded by the union and at the same time meet its responsibilities to the public and to the owners.

FORREST: What do you mean, "under today's conditions"? Are things so much different now?

WEIR: Yes. The *unions* now attempt to make management's decisions on prices, on profits, on production schedules, on depreciation reserves, and on many other phases of industrial operation. Management cannot be a divided thing. Whoever has the responsibility for management must have the *right* to manage.

FORREST: And I suppose you also mean that whoever has the right must accept the responsibility.

WEIR: Exactly. If the unions and government are now permitted to make management decisions, then the public must realize

that the United States is being placed under an entirely new
economic system. We know what the present system has accomplished in the way of goods, jobs and wages, and in creating the highest standard of living in the world. Do we want
to change that system?

FORREST: Well, Mr. Weir, on the basis of a good many years' experience
as a financial editor, I think I can say that American management has given us the world's best job of management, and
on its record it is a safe assumption that it will continue to do
that kind of job.

WEIR: I'd like to say, Mr. Forrest, that your newspaper and many
others have been doing a good job of explaining the functions of management. Some thoughts along this line were well
expressed by a fellow newspaperman of yours—Edward T.
Leech, president and editor of the Pittsburgh Press—in an
editorial which pointed out that American business has:

"1   Given the world's highest quality
"2   At the world's lowest prices
"3   While paying the world's best wages."

He pointed out that tinkering with the works by amateurs will
not make the works run better, but may stop them from running at all.

FORREST: What do you think should be done, Mr. Weir?

WEIR: Mr. Forrest, I think that Congress should pass legislation that
would take away the position of marked favoritism that labor
unions now hold under the one-sided Wagner Act. Such new
legislation should take labor relations out of politics and take
politics out of labor relations. It should compel unions—as
well as management—to accept responsibility equal to their
power.

FORREST: Then do you think that the right to strike should be pro-
hibited?

WEIR: Absolutely not. After all, the right to strike is merely an extension of the individual's right to take a job or leave it. The
only way strikes should be restricted is in the manner of conducting them. The right to strike should not be construed as a
license to use violence and hoodlumism—as has been true in
so many cases.

FORREST: Well, do you believe then that the Steelworkers Union has the right to strike next week?

WEIR: No!

FORREST: Why not?

WEIR: Because the union is breaking its word. In the contracts, signed only last spring, the union pledged itself not to strike for the duration of the contracts.

FORREST: I noticed an ad in the paper this morning signed by the United Steelworkers, CIO, where they deny they are violating the contract—

WEIR: I saw the ad and it is characteristic of the CIO's tactics. Suppose we let the no-strike clause speak for itself. Here is one from a typical contract: "During the term of this Agreement, neither the Union nor any Employee, individually or collectively, shall cause or take part in any strike, or other interruption or any impeding of production at any plant of the Company covered by this Agreement. Any Employee or Employees who violate the provisions of this Section may be discharged from the employ of the Company."

FORREST: Mr. Weir, you have said, I believe, that you, and steel management in general, are in favor of high wages, but that you object to the present union demand for higher wages. Isn't that a contradiction?

WEIR: I am in favor of high wages—the highest that can possibly be paid—and I'll stand on my record as an employer as well as on my words. Steel management in general feels the same way. But there is a difference between *money* wages and *real* wages. I am in favor of higher wages that are based on the production of more goods and services. They are *real* wages. Everyone benefits from them. By producing more we can all have more.

FORREST: Yes, but the steel union bases part of its case for a wage advance on the increased productivity of the industry.

WEIR: Yes, but it talks about the future. It is asking an increase in *anticipation* of something that may or may not happen. For this reason, the wage demand is unsound. But I have confidence in this country. I believe that eventually, on a perfectly sound basis, steelworkers will receive higher wages than the union now demands. Those wages will come only if management in the steel industry is permitted to use its brains and its know-how in turning out more steel and better steel at lower cost.

FORREST: Fine. How soon will that day come, Mr. Weir?

WEIR: Your guess is as good as mine, Mr. Forrest. But we will make a start toward it, just as soon as we get reconversion really moving. There is the biggest demand in history for goods of all kinds. Our warehouses and storerooms are empty. The way to solve our problems is to get rolling—get producing the things that people need and want. Increased production is the real source of higher real wages. And those higher real wages will come if, with its responsibility, management also is allowed to have the *right* to manage.

ANNOUNCER: Thank you, Mr. Weir and Mr. Forrest. You have been listening to Mr. John G. Forrest, financial editor of the New York Times, interview Mr. Ernest T. Weir, chairman of National Steel Corporation and a director of American Iron and Steel Institute. This program is one of a series sponsored by American Iron and Steel Institute. If you would like a copy of tonight's broadcast, write to the American Iron and Steel Institute, Empire State Building, New York 1, New York.

Dramatizing the News

Radio's most effective means of telling a story is through dramatization. This is as true of the presentation of news as it is of fiction, drama, history, biography, anything else. Dramatization is the tool which makes "documentaries" so effective. Skillfully employed, it will do more to throw a body of news-facts, or a set of news-opinions, into their proper focus than any other method, for it more nearly approaches reality. It has tremendous effectiveness for the presentation of background, for filling in the gaps in the listener's knowledge—gaps that make it impossible for him to understand a news situation fully. It may be either selective or exhaustive; it may cover a day or a century. It offers opportunity to use a variety of techniques—full-fledged drama, interview, speech, straight news. And it has the potentiality of building bigger audiences than most straight news shows can hope for.

But—

You can count on one hand the dramatized news shows you know of. The familiar trilogy—time, cost, and production problems—provides the reasons.

The essence of radio news is speed, and dramatizations cannot be thrown together. Writing the news drama is time-consuming. It demands not only skillful script writers and fundamental news materials, but also many hours of research—often by a staff of specialists —and sometimes a dozen rewrites of portions of the script. And it calls for casting, rehearsals, music, sound-effects—all the trappings that go into any other kind of radio drama and that add to its cost as well as to the time it needs. It is significant that most such shows appear on the air but once a week, and that few stations have undertaken them—programs of this kind are usually on the networks, underwritten by big advertisers or the networks themselves.

In spite of all these disadvantages, radio has had one internationally famous news dramatization, the "March of Time," and a number of lesser shows, both on the nets and on individual stations. Both AP and UP provided transcribed fifteen-minute shows of this kind during the war, dramatizing news experiences of their war correspondents. And the newsroom or its first cousin, the special events department, is usually called on to write the script. Now and again—if not for a regular program, then for a centennial celebration or a Community Fund drive show—the man in the newsroom may find himself suddenly asked to turn dramatist. For a talent fee, if he's lucky.

What kind of material does he choose?

First of all, newsy material—subjects that can readily be hung on current news pegs. Though there may be exceptions to this rule, they should be rare (else the show won't be a *news* dramatization). The news peg may be no more than a peg—a bit of dramatization may spend 95 per cent of its time telling the history of the beginning of logging in the Pacific Northwest, but its place in the script should be justified by the fact, for example, that the oldest sawmill on Puget Sound has just given up the ghost.

Second, human interest material. Dramatization means, among other things, the revelation of human values. A topic that yields incidents of adventure, of humor, of pathos—incidents involving people—is likely to be easiest to mold into dramatic form. The topic need not, however, always be one that shrieks of human interest on its surface. Most radio listeners would think a bank statement sadly deficient in human qualities. Yet a skilled news dramatist might build from a bank-statement peg a sharply effective show that reveals in understandable terms the meaning of a statement's dull statistics, or the human-interest story that lies behind a bank's growth, or the relation between the statement's showing of drastic reduction in savings deposits and the recent economic facts of life of the bank's clientele.

Third, material that demands interpretation. Dramatization, as has been said, may be radio's most effective tool for throwing into clear light the confusions of a new tax plan that leaves most laymen fumbling and mumbling. A series of brief lay-language vignettes, each showing how some provision of the plan affects the individual tax payer, may do the best possible job of helping the listener to understand how his own pocketbook will be attacked.

The local or regional station undertaking news dramatization is wise to shape such shows largely or even entirely around local or regional subjects. Such subjects lie in the area of its principal service; they are usually subjects on which it can most easily procure adequate information. Moreover, they avoid competition with the few similar broadcasts on the networks—broadcasts presumably done by agencies with more money, facilities, and talent available. The local station can't often compete with "March of Time" in a dramatization of the problem of displaced persons in the Upper Ukraine; it can do a job nobody can touch on the accomplishments of Lake County 4-H clubs in livestock feeding, or the need for local support of a Red Cross campaign.

It is not within the scope of this book to provide all the instructions for doing such a job. All the instructions, sad to relate, don't appear in any book; only by trial and error will most radio writers learn the high art. But there are books largely devoted to dramatization: Max Wylie's *Radio Writing* (Rinehart, 1949) and Erik Barnouw's *Hand Book of Radio Writing* (D. C. Heath, 1947) are the most useful. By all odds the best dissertation on news dramatization is the chapter in Paul White's *News on the Air* (Harcourt, Brace, 1947); but even Mr. White doesn't give all the answers. By studying such guides, by endless practice, and by application of his knowledge of the fundamental principles of radio news selection, judgment, and presentation the newsroom man may develop acceptable skill.

As a start, look at a typical "March of Time" script.* "March of Time" has been on the air since March 6, 1931. Since that date it has become one of America's best-known radio shows. The *Time* people will tell you that producing a show takes the better part of a week: A story and planning conference, for example, on Monday morning; research and script writing Monday, Tuesday, and Wednesday; rehearsals Thursday and Friday, final production Friday evening. They'll also inform you that there are 220 "cues" in the average show—a third to musicians, a third to actors, the remainder to Westbrook Van Voorhis as the "Voice of Time," and the sound effects men.

Before you read the script, a few notes on it: It includes five sections, the last three of which are mentioned as teasers in the opening announcement. The first two and the fourth are thoroughgoing dramatizations; the third is a straight speech; the fifth is a combination of dramatization with what this book calls the multivoice technique. There is one frank commercial, between second and third numbers (*before* the listener has heard any of the numbers announced in the opening, after his appetite has been whetted by the two brief unannounced numbers); there are also mentions of *Time's* colleagues, *Life* and *Fortune*, in connection with two of the numbers. The original script, intended to fill thirty minutes, was written in 589 lines; in rehearsal this was cut to 544. The first, second, and fourth numbers run three to four script pages; the third and fifth, to six pages. Van Voorhis, the "Voice of Time," is VAN.

Now the script, complete (the lines cut out in rehearsal are placed within brackets):

(MUSIC: HIT THEME)

VAN: THE MARCH OF TIME!

(MUSIC: THEME UP AND DOWN)

ANNOUNCER: TIME, the weekly news magazine, takes you to the news fronts of the world: Can Fascist Spain survive in a democratic Europe? The heroic and tragic story of an American

* By written permission of *Time Inc.*, October 7, 1947.

guerrilla chief in the Philippines. And a personal meeting with the first U.S. Marine to return from Iwo Jima. Stand by for the MARCH OF TIME!

(MUSIC: THEME UP TO CURTAIN)

VAN: Good evening, ladies and gentlemen. This is Westbrook Van Voorhis speaking for the editors of TIME Magazine.

It is now the Allied Watch on the Rhine.

U. S. civilians at home, remembering how we dealt with Italian civilians, and well aware of the doughboys' soft heart, may well ask: How are we treating German civilians? Are we coddling them? A new answer and a firm one came this week in a cabled report from officers of the American Military Government of Neuss, first Rhine city to come under American control. In the Rathaus, or city council house, the U. S. captain in charge marches into the office of the Buergermeister, or Mayor of Neuss.

(SOUND: MILITARY BOOTS TO HALT)

MAYOR: Ach, good morning, Herr Captain! I am at your service.

CAPTAIN: (TOUGH) O. K. You can continue as mayor of this town, but I'm the boss. Get that straight.

MAYOR: Ja wohl. I shall cooperate.

CAPTAIN: As long as you do, and as long as your people behave, okay. Otherwise, out you go. In the first place, all civilians will be confined to their homes until further notice.

MAYOR: But Herr Captain, how can they? Where can 30 thousand people go? Half the homes in Neuss are in complete ruin!

CAPTAIN: [I don't care where German civilians live.] They've got to stay off the streets so as not to get in the way of our military operations. My order will be obeyed.

[(MUSIC: STING)

[(SOUND: SOME OFFICE BUSTLE IN B. G.)

[MAYOR: (CAUTIOUSLY) Herr Captain . . .

[CAPTAIN: Well, out with it, Buergermeister! Are your town cops helping my military police clear the streets as I told you?

[MAYOR: Alas, Herr Captain, my police are prisoners of war, your prisoners. Apparently your soldiers rounded them up thinking they were German soldiers. Their uniforms are green gray . . .

[CAPTAIN: If we've made a mistake, we'll release them, put them in civilian dress, and give them arm bands. But if a German has a uniform, it's better to throw him in a prisoner of war pen and investigate later.]

(MUSIC: STING)

(SOUND: SAME)

DOCTOR: (VERY CAUTIOUS) If you please, Herr Captain, I am the sanitation official . . . Water and sanitation facilities have broken down completely, of course . . .

CAPTAIN: Well, round up whatever German doctors there are, and let them take care of any civilians who get sick . . .

DOCTOR: But your own medical corps . . . your own wonderful sanitary equipment . . .

CAPTAIN: Not a chance, doc! I'll see that notices are posted where water is available; that it must be boiled before drinking. That's all we can do at present.

(MUSIC: STING)

(SOUND: SAME)

MAN: But, Herr Captain! You do not understand. Meine frau—she will have the baby any minute! Now your army doctors . . . I have read how they . . .

CAPTAIN: Not in Germany. Go get a midwife or one of your German doctors and consider yourself lucky if you find one. It's your affair, not mine.

(MUSIC: STING)

(SOUND: SAME)

CAPTAIN: What's the trouble now, Buergermeister?

MAYOR: It is my people, Herr Captain. They stay off the streets, as you command. But they are hungry. I beg, I implore you to release emergency army rations to them!

CAPTAIN: Look, Mayor. We got better use for our army rations. Collect whatever food there is in the shops that hasn't been destroyed. Then, gather the food your civilians have hoarded in their homes . . .

MAYOR: Hoarding? Oh, nein . . .

CAPTAIN: And *sell* it to these hungry people of yours. The money will
            go into a food fund that won't cost us a cent. Because we
            aren't putting out any.

MAYOR: But you are already housing and feeding some civilians.

CAPTAIN: Sure, we're feeding three thousand. They're Russians, Poles,
            French, Dutch, Belgians and a few Algerians we found here
            in Neuss. And we're going to keep on feeding 'em, until we
            can get 'em back to their homes. They're entitled to it. You're
            not!

(MUSIC: IN . . . .)

VAN: That's the way American Military Governors handle German
            civilians. If you've been worrying about it, forget it. Worry
            about something better or worse.

(MUSIC: CURTAIN)

(MUSIC: HIT ORCHESTRA AND VOICES—RODGER YOUNG
            —ENOUGH TO ESTABLISH—FADE)

VAN: This week a new war song is marching into American hearts:
            The Ballad of Rodger Young, written to honor all infantrymen
            in the name of one. Its author, Private First Class Frank
            Loesser, writer of "Praise the Lord and Pass the Ammunition"
            and many another topflight hit. The story of Private Rodger
            Young that led Composer Loesser to write what may well be
            the war's top song is told in LIFE magazine.

VOICE: Rodger Young of Clyde, Ohio, was one of the smallest men
            in Company B of the 148th Regiment in the 37th Infantry
            Division. But he was a good soldier. How good was revealed
            in an incident that occurred just before the 37th Division
            went into combat, for the first time, on New Georgia Island
            in the southwest Pacific. Sergeant Young approached his
            company commander.

YOUNG: Sir, I have a request to make.

OFFICER: Yes, Sergeant?

YOUNG: I've been slightly deaf, sir, ever since I was in high school.
            When we were in training at Camp Shelby, sir, my ear trouble
            got worse.

OFFICER: Having trouble now Sergeant?

YOUNG: Yes, sir, worse than ever.

OFFICER: And you want a medical discharge?

YOUNG: Oh, no, sir. I'm just afraid my poor hearing will interfere with my job as a squad leader. I may miss some important message, or some sound in the jungle. That'll be dangerous for the men under me.

OFFICER: Then what *is* your request, Sergeant?

YOUNG: Sir. I want to be demoted to the rank of private.

(MUSIC: BRIDGE)

VAN: Soon thereafter the 37th Division landed on New Georgia, fought bitterly resisting Japs back through the jungle. Late one afternoon the platoon in which Rodger Young was fighting was ordered to withdraw a little for the night. The platoon suddenly was pinned down by intense fire from a Japanese machine gun concealed on higher ground only seventy-five yards away.

(SOUND: MACHINE GUN FIRE OFF—IN AND OUT AS CUED —BATTLE SOUNDS)

SERGEANT: Hold it, you guys! Hold it! Anybody hit?

YOUNG: I am.

SERGEANT: Rodge. Hit bad?

YOUNG: No.

SERGEANT: Okay, you guys. Pull back. Keep low.

YOUNG: Hey, Sergeant! I got that machine gun spotted. I'm going after it.

SERGEANT: Come back here, Young!

YOUNG: (OFF) I'll get 'em! Stay where you are!

(SOUND: MACHINE GUN FIRE. THEN SEVERAL GRENADES)

SERGEANT: They hit him again!

MAN: He's still throwin' grenades, though!

(SOUND: GRENADES—MG FIRE—THEN A BIG GRENADE BLAST AND QUIET)

MAN: He knocked the gun out!

RIGBY: Yeah—but they got *him!*

(MUSIC: BRIDGE)

[VAN: The Commander of the 148th Infantry, Colonel Lawrence K. White, wrote to Private Rodger Young's mother:

[WHITE: Private Young fought and gave his life in order that you and his other relatives and friends might continue to enjoy our American way of life. We are indeed proud to be members of Private Young's Regiment.]

VAN: President Roosevelt gave Private Young posthumously the nation's highest award for heroism, the Medal of Honor. That is the story that led Composer Loesser to write the Ballad of Private Rodger Young, and, in honoring one hero, to honor all infantrymen. Here is the Ballad of Rodger Young.

(MUSIC: VOICES AND ORCHESTRA)

VAN: This week on the Rhine and across the vast arc of the Pacific, American commanders are making many bold decisions based on many different facts. All day long and all night long these facts pour in—reports from the battle lines, reports on supply and transportation conditions behind the fronts, intelligence reports about the enemy ahead. And back here on the home front, editors are having to do much the same kind of thinking . . . to help Americans understand the complicated, everchanging current of the week's news. All this week, for example, the editors of TIME, The Weekly Newsmagazine, have been receiving reports from their correspondents on every battlefront of this war. For instance, there are five TIME and LIFE men on the Western Front—men like Senior Editor Sidney Olson, whose account of the Ninth Army's push to the Rhine you can read in TIME this week. And in the Pacific theater there is Teddy White, soon to take off again for the Burma front. There is Bill Gray in Manila and Robert Sherrod and Gene Smith on bloody Iwo Jima. From their reports and those of other TIME correspondents all over the world, TIME's editors write into TIME Magazine one clear, complete story of the week's news—a story that makes the war news really make sense. And that is just one of the reasons why more than a million busy, well-informed American families now turn to TIME—this week and every week.

VAN: War must always mean separation of fighting men from their loved ones. But one of the most tragic romances of this war concerns a young American officer in the Philippines and his sweetheart. It is the story, of Major Bernard "Andy"

Anderson, the greatest leader of Filipino Guerrillas, and it was cabled this week by TIME and LIFE correspondent Carl Mydans. A few days after U. S. troops had pushed into Manila into the American lines east of the Philippine Capital, came a man in a tattered and dusty uniform. He had lines on his face, and more years than his age. He was escorted to a nearby command post.

(SOUND: BATTLE EFFECTS IN B. G.)

ANDY: Major Anderson reporting, sir.

COLONEL: Not Andy Anderson!

ANDY: Yes, sir. United States Armed Forces in the Far East.

COLONEL: (BE SURE TO SMILE) Well, Major, if I wanted fifty thousand pesos, I could turn you over to the enemy.

ANDY: (SMILE) Yes, sir, I understand there is a price on my head. But all I care about right now is to get to Manila.

COLONEL: I'm sure we can arrange that, Major.

ANDY: You see, I'm going back to Betty Lou.

COLONEL: Betty Lou?

ANDY: My fiancee.

COLONEL: Oh!

ANDY: It's been a long time. It's been Betty Lou who kept me going when things got so tough in the hills I thought I was reaching the end. When the Japs were closing in and there was no food and you felt like this is it, I thought of Betty Lou and kept going.

COLONEL: (SOFTLY) We'll get you to Betty Lou, Major . . .

ANDY: I haven't seen her for more than three years, sir. It was New Year's day Nineteen Forty-two in Manila. I'll never forget it. It was early, very early in the morning. Her father, Captain Gewald, had already left for Bataan. (FADE) I was with her in her mother's apartment . . .

BETTY LOU Oh, darling, after you've gone, I'll think of so much we should have said.

ANDY: I know, Betty Lou, there's so much and so little to say. Here we were to have been married on January 10, but that will have to wait, now, until I come back.

(SOUND: KNOCK OFF)

ANDY: (UP) What is it? Oh, hello, Bert.

(SOUND: DOOR OPEN)

PETTIT   (OFF) Andy! Come on! We've got to go now. We're going to blow up the last bridge to Bataan.

ANDY: (UP) I'll be right with you, Bert. (LOW) Goodbye, Betty Lou. We'll be back as soon as possible.

BETTY LOU: Yes, darling, I'll be here. I'll be waiting for you.

(MUSIC: IN)

ANDY: Betty Lou and her mother stayed behind in Manila waiting for the Japanese. For them, it meant Santo Tomas internment camp. After the fall of Bataan and Corregidor, Bert Pettit and I managed to escape to the mountains. We planned to go on to Mindanao and Australia, but everywhere it was the same. Filipinos flocked around us.

(SOUND: SOME FILIPINO CROWD IN B.G., BRUSH EFFECTS)

FILIPINO I: You not going to leave us?

PETTIT: Yes, I'm sorry, but Lieutenant Anderson and I have to leave Luzon.

FILIPINO I: No, no!

ANDY: We'll come back with MacArthur!

FILIPINO II: You stay, please. You tell us what you want us to do.

FILIPINO I: We want to fight the Japans.

PETTIT   How about it, Andy?

ANDY: Bert, it looks like maybe we got a job to do here.

PETTIT: Yeah, it looks that way. All right, you guys, but understand this: There's no pay, no allowance. Any man who joins up does so for one reason and one reason only—love of his country. (APPROVALS) Okay.

ANDY: You know, Bert, I'm glad we're staying. I'll be closer to Betty Lou.

(MUSIC: IN)

ANDY: In three years, not one man backed out on us. It wasn't long before we had word from General MacArthur:

MACARTHUR: Hit the enemy wherever he can be hit. Destroy his communication lines, his dumps, harass him so he cannot move without protective strength!

(MUSIC: IN)

ANDY: Our problem was not in finding men. It was sorting the best out of the endless stream of volunteers. When our funds ran out, we were overwhelmed by offerings from Filipinos. They fed and clothed us. At first, I kept in regular touch with Betty Lou in Santo Tomas camp. And always, I could hear her say:

BETTY LOU   (FILTER) Yes, darling. I'll be here. I'll be waiting for you.

ANDY: Later, I had to stop writing for fear it might mean her life. Besides, we were always on the move. We now had hundreds of men and our chief shortage was arms. Two men, then three, were assigned to every pistol, every rifle, every machine gun, so that if one man was killed, another could carry on. Of news from outside, we heard nothing. The guerrillas would ask me:

FILIPINO I: When are the Americans coming back?

ANDY: I don't know, son. Honestly, I don't know.

FILIPINO II: When the Americans do come back, sir, will we be free?

ANDY: That will be up to you Filipinos. The problem now is to kill Japs.

(MUSIC: IN)

ANDY: Finally, in 1944, we made contact with guerrilla forces on Mindanao and Samar, and we became part of the United States Armed Forces in the Far East. Two Filipino radiomen arrived with full equipment. Supplies and men began to come in. Our orders were to avoid combat with the Japs that might endanger the safety of the people. But on January 6, three days before the Lingayen landings, a new order came through the island radio network:

VOICE: (FILTER) Now is the time for maximum violence against the enemy.

(SOUND: RUMBLE OF BLAST BUILDING TO)

(MUSIC: WIPE)

ANDY: For three years, my men had trained for this moment. Bridges
               were blown up. Railroads were cut. Jap units were cut off,
               annihilated. My job was done. Now I could look forward to
               Manila and to Betty Lou:

BETTY LOU   (FILTER) Yes, darling, I'll be here. I'll be waiting for you.

(MUSIC: STING AND OUT)

(SOUND: TRAFFIC IN B. G., JEEP TO HALT, STEPS OUT,
               CONTINUING UNDER)

COLONEL: This way, Major.

ANDY: Three years. I wonder how she'll look. It's been a long time.

COLONEL: Yes, and a horrible time for everybody in the prison. You'd
               best be prepared for . . . .

ANDY: I understand, Colonel.

(SOUND: DOOR OPEN AND SHUT)

VOICE: (FADING IN) Yes, Colonel?

COLONEL: This is Major Anderson. (AD LIBS) We're inquiring for a
               Miss—

ANDY: Betty Lou Gewald. Tell her Andy's back.

VOICE: I'm sorry, Major Anderson.

ANDY: Don't be sorry, fella. Just take me to her.

VOICE: Miss Gewald died two weeks ago.

(MUSIC: IN)

VAN: In Manila, Carl Mydans cabled, there are big pennants
               welcoming Major Anderson, greatest of guerrillas. As Andy
               walks down the streets Filipinos crowd about him, show off
               their babies named in his honor. But one welcoming face is
               missing, the thought of which sustained him for more than
               three years, brought him back to Manila.

               Betty Lou is not there.

(MUSIC: CURTAIN)

VAN: Here tonight at the March of Time's New York microphone
               is the first United States Marine to return home from Iwo
               Jima. His name: Marine Gunner Paul White. As combat
               photographic officer he has participated in D Day landings
               on three of the greatest Marine Corps amphibious operations

in the Pacific, and at Iwo Jima, working under Commander McLain, he was attached to the staff of Task Force Commander Vice Admiral Richmond Kelly Turner and Lieutenant General Holland M. Smith, tough, able commander of the Marines' toughest landings. Gunner Paul White!

WHITE: During D Day I spent most of the time in a small rocket-firing ship very close in shore, to coordinate the work of several teams of photographers. At dusk of D Day I saw one of the unforgettable sights of the war. The sun was setting on the other side of the island from us, which threw everything into sharp black relief. At our left was the volcano mountain Surabachi, which we knew was honeycombed with caves filled with Japs and guns. We went in at Iwo Jima with our eyes open. Every man who hit the beach knew as much of what to expect as our top commanding officers. We could see the black shapes of several of our tanks crawling up the slope of the mountain. In front of each one were the figures of four or five Marines, and in back of each, perhaps ten more. While they were advancing, our Navy ships were firing at the mouths of the caves, hoping to seal them up. But the Japs kept firing. Then I saw our first tank take a direct hit and burst into flame. We saw silhouetted figures hurled into the air by the explosion. Marines around the tank hit the dirt, then got up and moved ahead.

Then another tank was hit. I saw the silhouette of one man bend down to pick up a fallen comrade. But he couldn't pick him up alone. Another Marine came to help him. Then, very slowly, the three men came down the slope and disappeared into the darkness. That entire sight, in sharp black relief lit up only by gun flashes, hit me harder than anything I have ever seen. On shore for the next nine days the Marines fought slowly ahead through the toughest fighting they have ever faced. Iwo Jima is not like other islands we have taken, where we have been able to secure some territory and hold it safely after a few days. Iwo Jima is so small that even four days after D Day, every inch of the part we held was still under Japanese shell and mortar fire. The mortar fire especially inflicts horrible wounds. In spite of that, our wounded were evacuated with wonderful speed, by ambulance jeep from the fighting lines and by small boats out to the hospital ships. If civilian nurses could have been with me when I went alongside a navy hospital ship, and took a look at the hundreds of bleeding broken bodies waiting to be lifted aboard, the Navy wouldn't have to take our precious time and personnel to do recruiting. In battle when we are not doing our own jobs we pitch in on anything else we can find. We helped carry wounded, and I took messages back and forth between the fighting areas and the ships offshore. The worst of that was having to report the deaths of men who had been my friends. Compared to all the other shows I've seen, this one makes the others seem almost like rehearsals.

It is more intense, more explosive. In the eight or nine days I was there, there wasn't a letup. The whole thing is close-in, pointblank firing by heavy weapons. On an island only five miles long by two and a half miles wide, how could it be anything else? It is like getting caught inside an arsenal that's blowing up in every direction. On the night of D Day plus three, we heard a Japanese broadcast ordering the Japs on Iwo Jima to annihilate ten Marines each before they died. The score to date is the price of seven dead Japs for every one dead Marine.

VAN: Thank you, Gunner Paul White.

(MUSIC: HIT AND FADE)

VAN: This week, in Mexico City, the Inter American Conference is ending. Its prime accomplishment, the Declaration of Chapultepec, uniting twenty North, Central and South American republics against aggression from within and from without. One little noted meaning of this Declaration: It marks the failure of Fascist Spain under General Francisco Franco to win Latin American republics to a Spanish Fascist ideology. And, while Fascism fails in the west, in Europe, too, General Franco's friends are growing weaker. Spain, scene of the first military victory for Fascism in Europe, may soon be the last openly Fascist country in Europe. Therefore shrewd observers are asking these questions: Which will come first: peace in Europe or revolution in Spain? And will the overthrow of Franco really solve Spain's internal problems?

(MUSIC: BRIDGE)

VAN: Newest, most comprehensive report on Spain today appears in the current issue of TIME's sister magazine FORTUNE, based on first-hand material gathered by Gabriel Javsicas. Its title: "Spain—Unfinished Business." Its author: Henry Hart. Mr. Hart.

HART: Spain was the scene of the bloodiest civil war in modern history. It lasted from 1936 to 1939, cost a million lives, and incapacitated a million more, ended in victory for the Fascist rebels under Franco and a single Fascist political party, the Falange. Yet Franco is now certain of only one thing, that the people are waiting to get rid of him. On the surface Spain appears to have recovered somewhat from her civil war. There has been some revival of Spanish industry.

VOICE I: Most important cause of that revival: 160 million dollars poured into Spain by the American and British governments since 1941.

VOICE II: Its purpose: To buy up wolfram, the ore of tungsten, indispensable in war material, and prevent the Germans from getting it through conquered France.

HART: But the liberation of France last summer ended the Allied need for buying Spanish wolfram. Thus, Franco has lost his chief economic support. Now goods are getting scarcer. Prices are rising continuously. The masses of Spain wait grimly for the disintegration of the Falange, which has totally controlled Spain for six years.

VOICE I: There is no freedom of press, religion or public assembly. Four different kinds of secret police and armed guards spy on the populace.

VOICE II: All employment depends on the Falange, which supervises or manages all production and distribution.

VOICE III: The Falange rules by martial law!

(MUSIC: BRIDGE)

HART: Early in its regime the Falange tried to win the Spanish people over by a grandiose program of social and economic reform. [One of its main features—the export of Falange ideology to Spanish-speaking people elsewhere in the world—is a failure in Latin America. The workers, who were promised new rights, are instead kept in abysmal poverty by rigorous wage ceilings in the face of fantastically rising prices.] But the ten-year plan of industrialization is still only a blueprint. For example:

VOICE I: Out of four thousand kilometers of railroad scheduled to be electrified, only fourteen have been completed.

VOICE II: The new factories envisaged to make synthetic rubber, nitrates, gasoline and oil, do not exist.

VOICE III: The proposal to break up the great private estates has resulted in the resettlement of only six hundred families, at a cost of more than eighteen thousand dollars per family!

(MUSIC: BRIDGE)

HART: The real explanation of Spain's food shortage is the business activity of the Falange itself, which creates three different prices on food—all black market.

VOICE I: Farmers and land owners are compelled to sell their produce to government syndicates, at ceiling prices, but actually sell most on the black market.

VOICE II: The government syndicates in turn sell a great deal of produce on their own black market.

VOICE III: The *Army* contributes bread to still a third black market, because it sells its surplus at illegal prices.

HART: The result is that today the Spanish people get from one-fourth to one-half the minimum number of calories they need. As one Spaniard said:

SPANIARD I: They spilled so much blood to give us this!

(MUSIC: BRIDGE)

HART: Private business men are constantly protesting, with amazing frankness, against the arbitrary acts, regulations and corruption of Falange officials. For example: in the office of the transport ministry:

SHIPPER: Your new decree is graft! It is our ruin!

SECRETARY: But senor, you are free to join the new syndicate.

SHIPPER: Hombre! Much good that will do us! Our profits will go to the syndicate, to our competitors, and to the minister who signed this decree!

HART: In Spain such talk is a daily occurrence because so few of the people, even in the Falange itself, really believe in the Franco regime. One of the current jokes goes like this:

SPANIARD I: Hey, Gonzales, who is the greatest general in Spain today?

SPANIARD II: It is not General Franco. It is General Protest.

[(MUSIC: BRIDGE)

[HART: The top army officers have become hostile to the Falange. And finally, the Church has begun to oppose it. These are the facts about the Catholic Church in Spain:

[VOICE I: Before the civil war, only ten to fifteen per cent of the population were active Catholics.

[VOICE II: During the civil war, the Spanish Church supported Franco, which alienated many of those who had remained faithful.

[HART: Soon after coming to power, Franco helped the church by restoring property and schools to the religious orders. But he has now alienated the church by dissolving Catholic unions and, through Fascist youth organizations, loosened the hold of the church over the young.]

(MUSIC: BRIDGE)

HART: The present political situation was summed up for Fortune Magazine by Franco's hard-boiled, cynical Minister of Industry and Commerce, Demetrio Carceller:

CARCELLER: The monarchy gave us bad government and took recourse to dictatorship under Primo de Rivera. Then the Republic was rotten. We, of course, are no good, either. The fellows who come after us will be just as bad. Look at the Spaniards in exile. All of them are agreed only on the obvious: They don't like us. No one in Spain likes us, either. But no one can agree on what they want instead of us.

(MUSIC: BRIDGE)

HART: In spite of that cynical estimate all Spanish political leaders want to avoid another civil war. They want a parliamentary government free of the use of force. But whoever follows Franco will have to give land to the peasants in the South, and develop industry in the North. Until that happens, Spain will continue to be the most explosive element in Western Europe.

VAN: Thank you, Henry Hart, for that report on Franco Spain.

VAN: Time Marches On!

(MUSIC: IN)

VOICE: Over this same network every afternoon at 4 o'clock Eastern
             War Time, listen to TIME VIEWS THE NEWS, another
             program prepared by the editors and correspondents of TIME
             magazine. And next Thursday evening, at this same time,
             listen again to the MARCH OF TIME.

(MUSIC: UP AND DOWN FOR)
(MUSIC: CURTAIN)

— o —

A second news dramatization script—this one broadcast by WCCO-
Minneapolis on March 9, 1947, in the "Northwest News Parade"
series—makes some of the same points, and some different ones. Like
the "March of Time," the "Parade" series went on the air weekly.
Usually it included four episodes, the pattern changing according to
the news. It had two purposes: to "humanize" the news—that is, to
present human interest material—and to background the news.

The show given here* fulfills both purposes. The first story it tells,
heavy in human interest, also backgrounds a crime story so that the
listener unfamiliar with the situation will thoroughly understand its
curious aspects. The second, aimed primarily at explaining an involved,
difficult-to-understand matter, takes advantage of every opportunity for
human interest development.

Ralph Backlund, one of the script writers of the story of Ruben
Shetsky, has this to say of the script: "The Shetsky story was written
after midnight on Saturday (because the news had just broken) and
was substituted for two other pieces that had been incorporated into
the script earlier. When the cast arrived for rehearsal at 7 A. M. Sunday
(broadcast time was 10:05), they found it all waiting for them—but I
got only three hours of sleep that night. That, obviously, is the reason
we so seldom attempt to cover spot news in the 'Parade.' "

Like the "March of Time" script, the original script for the following
dramatization shows a number of deletions (they are not included
here). The "Parade" is a somewhat simpler script—using only organ
music, for instance, rather than orchestra—than the "March of Time."
The script:

* By written permission of WCCO, Minneapolis, September 17, 1947.

NARRATOR: It's deadline time again, and here is . . . .

ANNOUNCER: NORTHWEST NEWS PARADE!

MUSIC: THEME, FULL FOR TEN SECONDS, THEN DOWN TO BG

ANNOUNCER: Each Sunday morning at this time WCCO brings you the dramatized story of the top news of the week in the North-west. Every day the people of the Northwest make news. You hear those stories each day over your WCCO newscasts. And each Sunday morning the WCCO NEWS DEPART-MENT selects the best of those stories, and brings them to you in living drama . . . .

1ST MAN: Stories which make the headlines . . . .

2ND MAN: Stories from the backroads . . . .

3RD MAN: And the human side of the news . . . . the little-known, but fascinating sidelights discovered by WCCO's news reporters.

MUSIC: THEME UP FULL, THEN OUT

ANNOUNCER: And now, to report today's chapter of NORTHWEST NEWS PARADE, here is Paul Wann.

MUSIC: ESTABLISH DRAMATIC THEME AND DOWN TO BG

NARRATOR: Shortly before noon yesterday, a car pulled up before a modest house in Sunland, California. The address was 1-0 8-1-9 Woodward Avenue. Two men stepped out of the car, strode up the sidewalk, and rang the bell . . . .

SOUND: DOORBELL INSIDE HOUSE. DOOR OPENS

WOMAN: (VERY COMMON SORT) Yes? What do you want?

G-MAN: Is Lou Gimmel here?

WOMAN: Yes . . . no . . . I don't know. What do you want with him?

G-MAN: Take a look at this card, lady.

WOMAN: (SHORT YELP) Oh!

G-MAN: That's right—F. B. I. Now, call him. We know he's here.

WOMAN: (OBVIOUSLY SHAKEN) I'll . . . I'll go get him . . . .

G-MAN: No you won't. Stay where you are and call him from here.

WOMAN: (PROJECTING) Lou . . . Lou . . . come here a minute.

SHETSKY: (FROM INSIDE) What is it?

WOMAN: Come here . . . please.

SHETSKY: (ON MIKE) Yeah?

G-MAN: Are you Lou Gimmel?

SHETSKY: Yeh, that's me. Whadda ya want?

G-MAN: You are also Ruben Shetsky, aren't you—alias Wayne Saunders?

SHETSKY: Uh . . . oh . . . all right. I'm Shetsky.

G-MAN: Okay, come along. Your vacation is over, Mr. Shetsky.

MUSIC: UP DRAMATICALLY, THEN OUT

NARRATOR: And so the long-dormant story of Ruben Shetsky suddenly came to life once again. It is a strange, fantastic story . . . a sordid story. And it had its beginning on the night of July 27th, 1945, in a Minneapolis night club—the Casablanca cafe at 408 Hennepin Avenue.

MUSIC: SNEAK IN. SOMEBODY DOODLING ON PIANO. IF THIS DOESN'T WORK USE JUKE BOX. HOLD IN BG

NARRATOR: It was between two and two-thirty A.M., long after the closing hour. A few lights were still burning . . . and a group of people were seated around a table in an alcove, concealed from the street.

SOUND: STUDIO LAUGHTER AND GABBLE. SOME ARGU-ING. UP, THEN BACK TO BG

NARRATOR: Among those present was Ruben Shetsky, then known as Wayne—or "Big Waynie"—Saunders. Shetsky was part owner and operator of the Casablanca. His wife, Bernice, was there. So were two or three other women, including Ruth Hutchinson and Hilda Castle. So was Tommy Banks, reputed owner of several Minneapolis night spots. And so were two brothers—Al Schneider, organizer for General Drivers Union Number 544, and Fred Snyder. Exactly what led up to that brutal scene at the Casablanca is still a matter of doubt . . . but there is no doubt whatever about what happened next. Ruben Shetsky suddenly leaped at Al Schneider, and the two men started to scuffle.

SOUND: MEN SCUFFLING AND GRUNTING. CHAIRS AND TABLE OVERTURN. WOMEN SCREAM

SCHNEIDER: (GASPING) Listen, Shetsky, I don't care who you are or where you come from—you don't mean anything to me . . . .

SHETSKY: Okay, then . . . .

WOMAN: SHRIEK

SOUND: TWO SHOTS. CHAIR FALLS OVER. THREE MORE SHOTS

WOMAN: ANOTHER SHRIEK

SHETSKY: And now, Fred Snyder, I'll get you too . . . you . . . .

SOUND: QUICK SCUFFLE

BANKS: Leggo of me . . . .

SNYDER: If you shoot me, you'll shoot him too . . . .

SHETSKY: Get out of the way, so I can get the rat!

SOUND: MORE SCUFFLING AND YELLING

MUSIC: UP QUICKLY, THEN DOWN TO BG

SOUND: CARS PASSING IN STREET

WOMAN: (HYSTERICAL) Stop . . . stop, police . . . stop . . . .

POLICE: What's the matter, sister?

WOMAN: There's been a murder . . . inside. Somebody's shot . . . Al Schneider's been shot . . . go on in . . . (FACE) . . . it was a murder . . . .

POLICE: Hey, wait a minute, come back here!

MUSIC: UP AND OUT

NARRATOR: Ruben Shetsky was apprehended and charged with second degree murder. But before he came to trial, six affidavits were submitted in his behalf—one of them by Shetsky himself. It attempted to show that the shots had been fired in self-defense . . . .

LAWYER: (READING) The defendant was in deathly fear of both of these men, who were of exceptional strength and brutal force, with a temperament and desire to cause trouble. Thus he feels he was fully justified in protecting his life by shooting Schneider . . . It was a question of his life and his fear thereof, and his absolute belief in the fact that he knew he would have been beaten to a pulp and his bones broken, and killed if he had not acted in self-defense in the manner in which he did . . . .

NARRATOR: But County Attorney Michael Dillon shortly expressed his opinion of this fantastic document . . . .

DILLON: The proper place to try a lawsuit is in the courts and not by affidavits. It is a laughable matter to hear a man who is over 6 feet tall and who weighs over 220 pounds, and who is armed with a deadly weapon, say he was afraid of a man not quite so big, who had no gun or club, nor any defense of any kind except his fists. It is a cowardly thing to blacken the character of a man who is dead and unable to speak for himself . . . .

NARRATOR: And when the trial came up in district court, County Attorney Dillon said in his opening statement . . . .

DILLON: We will show you that while every one of the five shots from first to last was being fired, Schneider was in the corner of an alcove. He never moved from the time the first shot struck him. He was hit by a second and a third, and then he lay in that corner. There was blood in just one spot, and that was in the corner underneath the body.

NARRATOR: The testimony was long and often contradictory, but one fact was rather well established—just who fired the shots. It was brought out by Mrs. Ruth Hutchinson, who was one of the women present at the bloody scene . . . .

DILLON: Now, Ruth, as you were standing there, was your attention called to anything?

RUTH: Yes.

DILLON: By what?

RUTH: A shot.

DILLON: What did you do then?

RUTH: I turned quickly.

DILLON: In what direction did you look?

RUTH: South.

DILLON: What did you see?

RUTH: Mr. Saunders—Shetsky, that is—and Mr. Schneider were in a sort of a clinch.

DILLON: As you stood there, how many shots did you see fired?

RUTH: I counted five.

DILLON: How many did you actually see fired?

RUTH: Two.

DILLON: Who fired the shots?

RUTH: Mr. Saunders—Ruben Shetsky.

MUSIC: UP BRIEFLY AND OUT

NARRATOR: There was another witness who told almost the same story
             . . . Miss Hilda Castle, who was also present that night . . . .

DILLON: What was it, Miss Castle, that attracted your attention?

HILDA: A shot.

DILLON: What did you do then?

HILDA: I turned around. I saw Shetsky standing and firing two
             more . . . .

MUSIC: UP QUICKLY AND OUT

NARRATOR: But on Monday, September 24th, the trial took a sensational
             turn. Ruben Shetsky's two lawyers arrived at the courthouse a
             half hour early, and went to the office of County Attorney
             Dillon. The three of them then hurried into the offices of
             District Judge Paul S. Carroll. Police Chief Ed Ryan and
             Sheriff Earle Brown were called in. Clearly, something was
             up. Just what, was announced by Judge Carroll when he
             called in the reporters . . . .

CARROLL: Gentlemen, the defendant in this case has disappeared. He
             has been missing since yesterday morning. I have been told
             that he received a telephone call at his apartment . . . and
             went out. (FADE) He is said to have been expected back
             shortly . . . .

MUSIC: IN, UP BRIEFLY, AND OUT

NARRATOR: And that was the signal for one of the greatest manhunts
             Minnesota has ever seen . . . .

POLICE: (FILTER) This man, Ruben Shetsky, alias Wayne Saunders,
             is wanted by the Minneapolis Police Department. Age—38.
             Height—6 feet, 1 inch. Weight—210 pounds. Eyes—medi-
             um hazel. Hair—dark chestnut. (FADE) Complexion—
             medium dark. Build—stout . . . .

2ND POLICE: (NO FILTER) Every detective on our force has been as-
             signed to this case. The uniformed police, also, have been
             asked to be on the alert. In addition, the help of St. Paul

police, state highway patrol, and sheriffs throughout the state has been asked . . . .

NARRATOR: There were immediate reports that Shetsky had been the victim of foul play. As a matter of fact, that theory was advanced by his lawyer . . . .

MCMEEKIN: He was afraid of something. He was not the sort of man who would walk out on his friends. He appeared before the grand jury and he appeared for arraignment and for the trial. He has just disappeared. I think he'll be found in a ditch somewhere.

NARRATOR: But Ruben Shetsky was never found in a ditch. And as time went by, there were numerous—and completely unfounded—reports that he had been seen here . . . he had been seen there . . . in a St. Paul telephone booth . . . in Minneapolis . . . in Chicago . . . in Milwaukee. And then the case became unique in the history of Minnesota courts. The trial was resumed in his absence, and the jury brought in a verdict . . . .

SOUND: CROWD NOISES. THUMP OF GAVEL

JUDGE: Gentlemen of the jury, have you arrived at a verdict?

FOREMAN: We have, your honor. We find the defendant, Ruben Shetsky, guilty of murder in the second degree.

MUSIC: UP DRAMATICALLY AND OUT

NARRATOR: More than six months later—on June 6, 1946—Judge Carroll pronounced sentence on the still missing Shetsky . . . .

SOUND: GAVEL

CARROLL: The court hereby sentences Ruben Shetsky, in absentia, to serve the rest of his natural life in the Minnesota state penitentiary at Stillwater . . . .

MUSIC: UP AND OUT

NARRATOR: Thus Ruben Shetsky became the first man in the history of Minnesota to be tried, found guilty, and sentenced in absentia. A kind of raffish legend began to grow around the man; he was a riddle—was he dead, or alive? Today, we have the answer to that riddle. He is not only alive, but he will be returned to Minneapolis to pay his debt to society. And now, 18 months after his sensational disappearance, the final chapter in his career is about to be written. It is already being written by the people who were most deeply involved in the strange and lurid affair . . . by Mrs. Annabelle Schneider, widow of the man who was so brutally slain on the night of July 27th, 1945 . . . .

ANNABELLE: This whole thing upsets me very much . . . It brings it all back to me. I'd never like to hear about it again. Still, I'd like to talk to Shetsky, and find out what really happened . . . .

NARRATOR: It is being written by Shetsky's former attorney, Thomas McMeekin of St. Paul . . . .

MCMEEKIN: All I can say is that the case is over. He won't need me.

NARRATOR: And most of all, it is being written by Hennepin County Attorney Michael Dillon . . . .

DILLON: I am delighted to hear of Shetsky's capture. By absenting himself voluntarily, he has waived his rights to further trial, or even to be present at his sentencing. The mechanics of jailing him are all that remain to be done . . . .

MUSIC: DRAMATIC TAKEOUT

MUSIC: ESTABLISH. DOWN TO BG

NARRATOR: We Americans have an emotion, bordering almost on reverence, when we hear the word "Constitution." The feeling is the result of our acceptance of the Constitution of the United States as the cornerstone of all our rights and privileges, but that same respect has extended over into our attitude toward the constitutions of our respective states. For that reason, many of the people of Minnesota have been disturbed during recent days by a growing tide of criticism against their own state constitution.

MUSIC: OUT

MAN: (ORATING) And I say it's time we go to work and examine this horse-and-buggy constitution of ours. Gentlemen, we're using exactly the same document to govern us that we did ninety years ago. The struggling settlements of this great state were connected by ox-carts in those days. The oxen have been gone for generations, but we're still trying to get along with an ox-drawn constitution . . . .

NARRATOR: After hearing such statements, the people of the state are gradually becoming aware that a state constitution has nothing of the sacred quality of the document which governs our nation. They've been surprised to learn that many states have had half a dozen or more different constitutions. And now they're beginning to wonder about the document that governs Minnesota, and why there is a growing demand for a new one.

MUSIC: SNEAK UNDER AND HOLD TO BG

NARRATOR: Before we talk about the shortcomings of the Minnesota constitution, let's move back in history to the year 1856. A cluster of small villages had grown up on the St. Croix River and on the Mississippi across from Wisconsin. Everything else was unbroken prairie or forest belonging to the Indians. A territorial legislature sat in St. Paul and argued about statehood . . . .

MUSIC: OUT

DELEGATE I: Mister Speaker, I say it's time we think of taking our place among the great sisterhood of states. Think of the glorious prestige. But even more, think of the other advantages. A new state gets large grants of federal land. A state can borrow money. A state . . . .

DELEGATE II: And let me add that a state has to pay taxes. Why, our taxes are so light now we hardly think about them. Why not let well enough alone?

NARRATOR: And in the National Congress at Washington, there were also a good many who had no special desire to see Minnesota become a state, especially so the Senators from the South. Senator John B. Thompson of Kentucky was talking in the Senate . . . .

THOMPSON: . . . I am opposed to the admission of new states. I regret that Wisconsin and Iowa were ever admitted. For my part, I would rule the people of a territory as Great Britain rules Afghanistan, Hindustan and the Punjab, making them work for you as you would work a Negro on a cotton or sugar plantation. Territories should be governed by proconsuls, and should be made to know their place. I don't want Slavs, Germans and Swiss to swarm up in these northern latitudes and eventually come down upon the South. (FADE) I am not desirous of seeing Senators from a new state, arrogant, presuming, Free-Soilish . . . .

NARRATOR: But Congress, nevertheless, passed an enabling act, and Minnesota got ready to draw up a constitution as its blueprint for statehood. It was an unfortunate time to demand any action requiring sober judgment and cooperation. Democrats hated the new upstart Republican party with a bitter contempt . . . . and the Republicans responded in the same manner. The issue was largely the burning slavery question, and the newspapers of both sides rose to new heights of invective . . . .

MAN: The burning issue, as I see it, is between White Supremacy and Negro Equality. The Black Republicans are desirous of upsetting the laws of God and Nature. They wish to see the Negro in the jury box, on the witness stand, and even—and I shudder to write this—to see their daughters married to Negroes.

2ND MAN: The Democratic party represents the very dregs of all that is unholy. They are dough-faces and boot-licks; they are all that is looked down upon by us Republicans who represent the rights of man and the nobleness of human nature.

NARRATOR: These, then, were the two parties who were to take over the important job of writing a constitution for a new state. When the people of the territory elected their delegates to the constitutional convention, both sides claimed the victory. There were men from both parties who were elected by fair majorities. But in between was a large group of duplicate delegates, each claiming victory in his own district. And everyone of them came to St. Paul. On the July day set for the convening of the assembly, the Republicans were on hand early in the Capitol building, and sat apprehensively around . . . .

SOUND: STUDIO NOISES

MAN: Wonder when the Democrats are going to show up?

2ND MAN: Don't know, but I don't trust them. But I think we're all set for anything they might try. Right at noon John North is going to call the convention to order. If the Democrats aren't here by noon, that's just their misfortune.

MAN: Suppose they come early and try something.

2ND MAN: Then North will call the convention to order right away. (FADE) Don't worry—we have everything planned out . . . .

NARRATOR: And outside in the corridor the Democrats quietly collected.

SOUND: SUBDUED STUDIO NOISES

DEMOCRAT: (SOTTO VOCE) Now, you all know how this is going to be handled. The minute we open the doors we all rush in. Then Charlie Chase here takes over. You all set, Charlie?

CHASE: All ready. I'll rush right up front, and call the meeting to order. We'll be in charge before they know what's happened.

DEMOCRAT: And if they make any attempt to interfere, we'll adjourn the meeting right away. That still gives us control. All ready? Now, open the doors and let's go!

SOUND: GENERAL PANDEMONIUM. DOOR OPENING, FEET TRAMPING, AD LIB SHOUTS, ETC. GAVEL RAPPING

CHASE: (PROJECTING) The meeting is now called to order.

NORTH: Hey, just a minute. I'm in charge.

SOUND: GAVEL

NORTH: I am calling this meeting to order. Will the delegates please take their seats.

MAN: I move that the meeting be adjourned.

CHASE: (RAPIDLY) It has been moved that we adjourn. All in favor signify by the usual method.

CAST: SCATTERING OF "AYES" AND "NOES"

CHASE: The "ayes" have it. I now declare this meeting adjourned until noon tomorrow. That's all.

SOUND: GAVEL. ALL SOUND OUT

NARRATOR: The historians are still arguing over that incident. But the Democrats were gone as suddenly as they had erupted into the meeting. The Republicans stayed on, and went about the business of organization. The Democrats took over another hall, and proceeded to hold their own convention. And so instead of one, there were two separate constitutional conventions in the territory. Each one went about its business as though the other had never existed. And some of the matters debated sound strange to the people of the present state of Minnesota. For instance, there was a strong move to make the northern boundary of the new state a line running west through what is now the city of Little Falls, with the western boundary at the Missouri River.

MAN: (PROJECTING) . . . And let me say, gentlemen, the simplest kind of intelligence calls for the east-west boundary. Such a line would give this state the rich prairie lands lying between the Mississippi and the Missouri in the Far West. Common sense dictates that we forget about the northern part of this territory. After all, what does it consist of? An eternal wilderness, dark and impenetrable, which will never be inhabited by anyone save hunters, trappers, traders and Indians (FADE) from whom we would never collect a penny in taxes . . . .

NARRATOR: That argument sounds strange to us these days, when we contemplate the wealth of the northern part of the state which many of these constitution makers wanted to throw away. Today it includes the wealthy Mesabi iron range, the fertile farm lands of the Red River Valley, and the lumber and recreation facilities of the pine woods. It includes such thriving cities and villages as Duluth, Cloquet, Hibbing, Bemidji, and Crookston. Needless to say, that move failed. But as the two conventions continued, an uneasy feeling grew up on each side . . . .

MAN: We're getting to be the laughing stock of the whole nation. Maybe we should get both sides together.

2ND MAN: But wouldn't that look as though we were giving up the fight?

MAN: Somebody has got to compromise. Otherwise we'll never get anything done. I say we should appoint a committee. (FADE) Otherwise we never will be a state . . . .

NARRATOR: There were too many hot-headed younger men on both sides to prevent the two conventions from meeting together. But each one appointed a committee, and so the two groups got together. The meeting got along better than one might have expected, if you disregard such minor incidents as the time a Democratic delegate broke his cane over the head of a Republican. But they managed to compromise, and the constitution was drawn up. Two copies were made. One was ratified by the Republican convention; the other by the Democrats. And that fact has given the historians something else to argue about.

PROFESSOR: My studies have convinced me that the Congress of the United States received and approved the copy signed by the Democrats. However, there is a fair body of proof which indicates that it was the Republican version which was sent to Washington. (FADE) May I quote Peabody, Volume Two, Pages 98 and 99, in which he has this to say . . . .

NARRATOR: The constitution was accepted in Washington, and Minnesota became a state. But is there any wonder that a document drawn up in such a fashion should be full of weaknesses? The wonder is that it has lasted for ninety years. And what do the experts say about the constitution?

WOMAN: Pardon me, but may I be accepted as something of an expert? After all, I did my graduate work on the Minnesota constitution, and wrote a thesis about it. I don't think you could find a better example of the weaknesses of the constitution than by turning to Section Ten of Article Nine. Why, there's a whole

(OVERLAP)

tragedy tied up in that one section.	READER: Section ten: The credit of the state shall never be given or loaned in aid of any individual, association or corporation,
Listen carefully right here.	ual, association or corporation, except as hereinafter provided. Nor shall there be any further issue of bonds denominated "Minnesota State Railroad Bonds" under what purports to be an amendment to Section Ten of Article Nine of the Constitution which is hereby
Maybe you can sense the hard feeling in that talk about what purports to be an amendment. That all goes back to 1858, when there were a bunch of fly-by-night companies that	expunged from the Constitution (FADE DOWN) saving, excepting and reserving to the state, nevertheless, all rights, remedies and forfeitures accruing under said amendment.

promised to build railroads in Minnesota. The constitution forbade state loans to such companies, so it was amended. And, of course, the railroads went broke and the people lost their shirts. That section you just heard is a tombstone on a dream that died—and, incidentally, cost the people of Minnesota several million dollars. Why, if you want to look up the whole history of that episode, you'll find the reason why Minnesota came to be called the Gopher State.

NARRATOR: That sounds like a good story. How about telling it to us . . . .

WOMAN: I'm sorry, but I didn't put that in my thesis. But if you're really interested, I suggest you go to Folwell's History of Minnesota. (FADE) You'll find it in Volume Two, Pages 45 through 49 . . . .

NARRATOR: We can't forget that the Minnesota constitution changed through the years with all sorts of amendments. Some of them plugged up loopholes in the original constitution. Others just grew up to reflect the particular prejudices of the moment. By now it resembles a pair of work overalls, so thoroughly patched that there is very little of the original fabric visible. And what still remains is often disregarded. Ask any member of the state legislature . . . .

LEGISLATOR: I could give you a hundred examples. But just take, for instance, that bit about requiring that half the state Senators should be elected in alternate years. We've just ignored that in Minnesota. And in the legislature itself there's a constitutional provision that every bill should have three readings. We just forget about that over in the state Capitol. It just doesn't work out.

NARRATOR: But the greatest complaint is against the difficulty of amending the constitution. It takes a majority of all the people voting at an election to make a change, and most Minnesotans who go to the polls refuse to vote either way on an amendment. They just leave that square blank on their ballots, and so, by not even voting, they kill it.

MUSIC: SNEAK UNDER

NARRATOR: But this is the point where the people of the state take over. If they have any interest in their own government, they'll acquaint themselves with the issues. There's a movement in the state legislature to draw up an entirely new constitution and submit it to the people. If that fails, there's another campaign to make it easier to amend the document. We on NORTHWEST NEWS PARADE are taking no sides. But we do insist that it's the duty of the people of Minnesota to find out the issues at stake. Remember, without an enlightened public, there can be no democracy.

MUSIC: FULL AND OUT

MUSIC: THEME. FULL, THEN DOWN TO BG

NARRATOR: And so we end today's chapter of NORTHWEST NEWS PARADE, but already the Northwest is making the news stories you'll hear next week at deadline time on NORTHWEST NEWS PARADE. Be with us, then, as we open another chapter in the news of this great part of the United States.

MUSIC: UP FULL. THEN DOWN TO BG AGAIN

ANNOUNCER: NORTHWEST NEWS PARADE is a regular weekly presen-
(Optional   tation of Station WCCO. It brings you the drama behind the
if needed)   week's news events in the Northwest. Listen to your daily
                  WCCO news broadcasts for the news as it occurs, but be sure
                  to turn to NORTHWEST NEWS PARADE for the story
                  behind the news.

MUSIC: UP FULL. THEN DOWN TO BG AGAIN

NARRATOR: NORTHWEST NEWS PARADE was written and pro-
                  duced in the WCCO Department of News and Special
                  Events. Writers were Ralph Andrist and Ralph Backlund of
                  the news staff, with Bob Sutton directing today's chapter.

MUSIC: FULL AND CONTINUE TO END

8

Radio's Local News Service

Late in 1945, Illinois radio newsmen met at Springfield in a "radio news clinic" to discuss common problems. The clinic was the first of a series sponsored by the NAB News Committee; in the next eighteen months others met in some twenty other states. The program for each was arranged by a committee of station news editors from the region the meeting served. At each, one topic stole the show:

Local news: What are we doing with it? What can we do with it?

This was a surprise only to the benighted station operators for whom news had been no more than easy and inexpensive canned programming to fill spots between recorded shows. Everybody in the radio business who had given serious thought to radio's news service, either as programming in the public interest or as a highly salable commodity, had been predicting since before V-E Day that local news was destined to increase vastly in importance to the radio newsroom.

This prediction was coupled with a fear that, the war over and the flow of vital and dramatic news from abroad dwindling, listener-interest in news would go back to prewar levels. The fear turned out to be unjustified. Six months after the war ended, a CAB report showed that seventeen commercial network news programs had dropped less than one percentage point in average listener rating (eight of the shows increased their rating; two held it constant; seven declined). Two years after V-J Day (July 30, 1947), *Radio Daily* reported that a survey of 636 program directors' opinions showed news second only to music, "the perennial favorite," in audience pulling power. "This vote," said Frank Burke, editor of *Radio Daily*, "refutes the claim in some agency circles that interest in news broadcasts is falling off and that the quality of news programs fails to sustain interest among listeners." As further evidence, he pointed out that 398 of the 636 program directors expressed belief that news programs held as much audience interest as they had during the wartime period.

The prediction—that local news offerings must increase—had come from many quarters, and in many forms. Ralph W. Hardy of KSL-Salt Lake City, speaking before an NAB district meeting in February, 1945, had said, "Instead of trying to 'outnetwork' the networks, it would be wiser to augment the network services with features conceived and handled throughout from a local point of view and thus do a job the networks are not in a position to do." And a month later the NAB News Committee spoke more specifically. The closing paragraph of its lengthy set of recommendations for handling radio news said:

From the standpoint of local news reporting, it is recommended that stations study the possibility of their coverage in this field. Undoubtedly local material will form an ever-increasing part of news broadcasts after the war. Opportunities for added public service are manifold in this phase of news reporting.

Some newsmen had for years been cultivating—and reaping from—the rich local field. In 1930 KMPC-Beverly Hills had put ten reporters on the Los Angeles news runs. WFOY-St. Augustine started including local stories in newscasts in the early 1930's. WMBD-Peoria had offered ten minutes of local women's news daily since 1932. KYSM-Mankato, Minn., like a number of other stations in vigorous competition with local newspapers, had had local and regional coverage, with its own news staff, since 1937. Scores of stations—though certainly not a majority—had devoted some attention to local news.

Such stations had a generous lead over others when, with the end of the war, there came the inevitable re-evaluation of radio news service. The news clinics, enthusiastically supported by the radio stations (and credited by the radio editor of *Editor & Publisher* with contributing "to the general improvement of radio news which nearly everybody in the business recognizes"), were an evidence of the general interest in such re-examination. Another was the rash of pieces in print on successful local news operations; another the appearance of the National Association of Radio News Directors, led by John F. Hogan,

---

The first periodical solely for radio newsmen made its appearance just after the war. It was the *Newscaster*, a four-page monthly published by INS for free circulation "in the interest of radio men handling the news." Inevitably, its first few issues devoted a good deal of space to the selection of a Miss Radio News of 1946! Most of its material consisted of news of radio news personnel and of brief discussions of local radio news problems.

news editor of WCSH-Portland, Maine, and of a number of city, state, and regional associations. In May of 1946, the Institute for Education by Radio at Columbus, Ohio, offered two well-attended panels for discussion of radio news problems under the leadership of members of the Council on Radio Journalism; one was devoted entirely to local news handling, the other to radio news copy.

That news editors' re-evaluation of their craft was not confined to local news alone was suggested by Jack Shelley in the *Newscaster* (November, 1945). Shelley, director of the excellent newsroom at WHO-Des Moines, said in part:

The people who are going to get hurt most in this transition period are those who abused the "get-rich-quick" possibilities of the war boom in radio news.

They're the people who sold every newscast they could cram into the schedule, because any sponsor would buy news.

They're the people who filled their shows with nothing but war news, because it was so easy to use up ten or fifteen minutes with a couple of nice long round-ups off the wire.

They will find the adjustment to peacetime newscasts the hardest of all; but for all of us the signal is to swing more and more emphasis to regional and local coverage, plus good features.

There is, for example, no law which requires newscasts invariably to begin with overseas or Washington news. When you've got a good state or even local story, don't be afraid to lead with it.

Most of all, we are going to have to become reporters again. Now is the time to cover your police court and statehouse with your own men, if you've never done it before. With wire or film recorders, there are dozens of state and local stories which can be covered with on-the-spot material you didn't have room for during the war days.

In other words, Shelley urged that radio newsmen should think in terms not alone of finding substitute material for war news, but also of avoidance of stereotyped patterns; that they should provide news not only because of its salability, but because of its public service values.

Another shot in the arm came when the FCC, in March, 1946, made

---

In its December 2, 1946, number, *Broadcasting Magazine* published results of its second annual Broadcasting Trends survey. Among the findings:

Seventy-six per cent of American stations broadcast more local news in 1946 than in previous years.

Forty-one per cent either were broadcasting or planned to broadcast more news shows than formerly.

public its "Blue Book" called "Public Service Responsibility of Broadcast Licensees." Much of the report (reputedly written by the same
Charles A. Siepmann who criticized broadcasting severely in his *Radio's
Second Chance*) was devoted to the Commission's insistence that
the extent of a station's "live" local programs was an important factor
in FCC evaluation of the station's service, and that local news programs would receive high rating among local offerings. Though the
report rested on a firm base—the provision of the Federal Communications Act that the FCC would be responsible for holding stations to
operation in the public interest—it was received with anguished howls

---

The FCC Blue Book in its original form (dated March 7) defined as a
wire program (hence not a local live program) "any program the text of
which is distributed to a number of stations by telegraph, teletype, or similar
means, and read in whole or in part by a local announcer. Programs distributed by the wire news services are wire programs. A news program which
is part wire and in part of local non-syndicated origin is classified as wire if
more than half of the program is usually devoted to the reading verbatim of
the syndicated wire text, but is classified as live if more than half is usually
devoted to local news or comment."

Robert W. Brown, executive news editor of INS, protested to the FCC
that "it is arbitrary to force the licensee to devote more than half of all news
programs to local news to obtain a local live rather than wire program
classification," and that a licensee using a full news service, with editors
selecting news of interest to the area, is in reality performing a local live
function. Radio news editors were widely in agreement that arbitrary demand that more than 50 per cent of a news show be local was unreasonable
and unrealistic (though the FCC language was indefinite enough so that
nobody was entirely sure just what it meant). But they also pointed out
that the INS request for clarification might result in an interpretation favorable to INS over other news services. If the FCC should rule that a news
program *rewritten* in a station newsroom from a news service wire is a local
live program, they said, it would mean that stations using the INS wire
would be in safer position than those using AP, UP, or TP radio wires and
not rewriting them.

The FCC responded to INS that its language had been misconstrued and
misunderstood, but asked that INS suggest changed wording. Early in July
the FCC issued revised definitions; that of the wire program was altered
only by the insertion of the words "or virtually verbatim" after the word
"verbatim" in the last sentence.

On August 1 Brown asked for further clarification; on August 30 the
(*continued on next page*)

of "censorship! government control!" by a large portion of the broadcasting industry. Anguished or not, however, the industry was impressed; and one evidence was the fact that the rate of establishment of newsrooms in radio stations—a rate that had already spurted since the beginning of the year—was further stepped up.

FCC made response.. "It is not required," said the FCC letter, "that fifty per cent or more of a news program usually be devoted to 'purely local items' in order for such a program to be classified as local live. A news program based upon material received by wire, but more than half of which is very substantially edited and rewritten by a station staff member or by a writer employed by a sponsor and announced in its edited or rewritten form should not be classified as a wire program because of its being based upon material received by wire.

"The important factor in this regard is the treatment given locally to the news rather than its origin. For example, a program consisting of a verbatim reading by a station in New York of a wire news text about New York affairs would still be wire. On the other hand, a program of national and international news based entirely upon material furnished by the wire news services would be classified local live if more than half of it consists of material which has been very substantially edited and rewritten as indicated above."

This definition has been accepted by INS and by the radio newsrooms of the country. But it still leaves questions. What, precisely, is meant by "very substantially edited and rewritten"? Is it enough merely to clip 200 lines of copy from a printer, arrange them in some kind of order, and put them on the air? Is this "substantial"? If it isn't, the 25 per cent of 26,000 news scripts examined by Charter Heslep in the Office of Censorship during the war that, in Heslep's words, "hadn't had a pencil touched to them," would not qualify as local live. If it isn't, the relatively large number of stations that depend heavily or wholly on radio wires for their news shows, and that don't have genuine news editors to "edit and rewrite" them, must mend their ways if they wish to get local live credit. On the other hand, the stations with only newspaper wires, presumably facing a rewrite job in order to turn newspaper copy into radio style, would be in better position.

Those who believe that the public can best be served only by a writing newsroom would say that the definition, so interpreted, is desirable. Certainly it builds a fire under stations slow to establish their own newsrooms. But it also handicaps the small station that cannot afford a newsroom elaborate enough to do a thorough editing and writing job; and by the same token it favors the larger station which is already in better position than the little fellows to build up its hours of local live shows.

The FCC's interest in local news in station programming was under-scored in April, 1946, when it favored for a license in Orangeburg, S. C., the one of two applicants that showed both the intent and the facilities to place heavy emphasis on local news service. Of this situation the FCC said:

We believe that an essential function of a radio station's operations in the public interest should contemplate the gathering and broadcasting not only of national and state news received over one of the regular news wire services but also the gathering and broadcast of local news on a regularly scheduled news program. On the record, Edisto Broadcasting Company seems unwilling to assume that function. We do not believe that the business of dissemination of local news should be left solely to the local newspaper as proposed by Edisto, and we do not believe that the discharge of this function would prove unduly onerous to the owners of a radio station operating in Orangeburg.

Another stimulus to local news on the air came in the 1945-47 period from a series of newspaper strikes. When delivery services of most New York newspapers were tied up in mid-1945, radio stations in the area were bombarded by requests for news time (and for advertising time, by such advertisers as the movie houses). WABC canceled two regular shows to present news round-ups from the New York papers. WLIB, affiliated with the *Post*, broadcast three half-hour news shows for the duration. WJZ and WNEW doubled their news coverage. The *Times* station, WQXR, put on three emergency shows each morning. WEAF increased the percentage of local news in its regular shows. The *World-Telegram* and the *Journal-American* bought time for news offerings. WHOM mimeographed copies of AP reports and distributed them to hotels and restaurants. And Mayor LaGuardia acted out the adventures of Dick Tracy over WNYC, the municipal station.

KGVO-Missoula, Montana, found itself in a situation like WPAY's in October, when the Missoula papers suspended. But it took a different tack in meeting it. Analyzing its daily news output—network as well as local—KGVO discovered that it had 35,000 words of news on the air each week-day. This, it figured, was the equivalent of a sixteen-page paper. On this basis KGVO decided not to increase its news service. The analogy is not, however, entirely fair, since much news is repeated in a radio station's day.

In Portsmouth, Ohio, WPAY faced a similar situation. Pressmen on the local *Times* struck in November, 1945, and stayed out seven weeks. WPAY, a 250-watt station, serves almost precisely the same area as does the *Times*. The station at once arranged with the paper a cooperative news service. Four local news shows a day were provided by the paper's reporters; the paper's columnists and comics were read into WPAY mikes. In seven weeks WPAY became so convinced of the value of local news that it developed a local news-gathering staff, and after the *Times* resumed publication it continued a heavy and expanding program of local news.

That local audiences respond to local broadcasts was demonstrated in a survey of news listening in early 1948 conducted by the Bradley University Department of Journalism at Peoria, Illinois. Peoria audiences expressed a preference of more than three-to-one for a local newscaster, Brooks Watson of WMBD, over H. V. Kaltenborn and Edward R. Murrow, the next two on the list; and Kaltenborn and Murrow were only a shade ahead of two other local newscasters.

What Is "Local" Radio News?

To the newspaper man the term "local news" means just that: news of the area served in concentration by his paper, news of the town or city or county; news of city government, schools, sports, clubs, business, "society." In some newspaper shops with regional or state circulation, the term acquires a wider geographical meaning, but the news it describes changes little in kind.

To the radio newsman, it means many of these things—but with a number of differences.

A prime difference is that of the medium's coverage. Whatever a station's power, whatever its promotion literature describes as its primary area, its coverage is subject to considerable fluctuation. Atmospheric conditions, season of the year, time of day—all change the extent and power of its signal. Moreover, the extent of both primary and secondary areas is likely to be greater than that of the newspaper. The importance of this factor is greater for the clear channel station than for the local channel; Class I (50,000 watts) stations have listeners spread over tens of thousands of square miles. The man in Baton Rouge,

La., is little interested in the doings of the Knights of Pythias over in Shreveport; KWKH-Shreveport, with a primary area of forty-seven counties, can give little attention to what the Knights are doing. But KRMD-Shreveport, with 250 watts, covers a far smaller area, and can count on interest among a high proportion of its listeners in the intimate activities of Shreveport citizens.

A second difference is that of "space." This factor—the fact that newspaper stories can be, and usually are, longer than radio stories—has already been examined in this book. It is one that the local radio reporter must keep foremost in mind.

Also explored is the fact that radio news is informal in manner, that it can take advantage of color and human interest in news more effectively than can the printed word. This factor will be developed further in this chapter.

In brief, then: Local news for radio is the briefly and sharply told story of local events of fairly general interest to listeners within a station's primary area. For some stations, those with state or wide-area coverage, "regional" is a better adjective than "local"; but the term "local" is loosely used in this special meaning by radio newsmen, and it is so used here.

How Does Radio Cover Local News?

Nobody in radio or out of it has developed a method of news-coverage superior to that of the newspapers:—The use of reporters who cover major news sources regularly, and special occurrences—fires, accidents, conventions—as they come up. Radio has followed the essential pattern.

But with a number of significant departures.

A good many of the differences have been suggested or described, some at length, in this book. But it is worth while here to re-examine some of them in the light of the coverage problem.

Primarily, it must be remembered that radio—unlike the newspaper—is not fundamentally a news medium. The newsroom is the heart of the newspaper. News is the prime "programming" it has to offer. But the radio newsroom is only one of the sources of radio programming. The radio day emphasizes a variety of audience-attractions different from those of the newspaper; and, since a radio day normally includes more "editions" than does that of the largest newspaper, it demands more repetition of news and briefer development of most stories.

The effect of its shorter stories on radio's news coverage is, in a sense, to make it sketchier than that of the newspaper. The radio reporter, therefore, has to guard against interpreting brevity in terms of superficiality. He must know as much about the news he is covering as does his newspaper competitor; but he must be more selective in his fact-gathering, or he'll waste a lot of precious time in collecting material he can't possibly get on the air. For the newspaper man turning to radio, this means an adjustment of sights. His need for speed and accuracy remains; but he must learn to discard almost by instinct the nonessentials that he might weave into the later paragraphs of a newspaper story perhaps twice as long.

Partly because of this, the radio newsroom can usually do its job with a comparatively small staff. "Typical" staffs and their duties have been described in Chapter 4. Each situation has its own controlling factors—competition, management's attitude to the news function, area coverage, and so on—and no two are exactly alike. A 5,000-watt independent station with a relatively wide primary area, in a Rocky Mountain state where press service regional coverage is not complete, with a strong signal and with vigorous newspaper competition—an entirely hypothetical example—may well decide that it needs two news services and a six- or eight-man round-the-clock newsroom staff, augmented by correspondents. A clear channel station, on the other hand, may decide to let its network and a two-man force carry the load (though most radio newsmen would call it lunatic if it did).

Radio has not yet come forward with the station devoted to newscasting alone. Such a station may one day be projected. One can dream up a station, say, with contracts with two or more networks so as to have the advantage of big network names, and with a daily schedule made up entirely of straight news shows, commentaries, interviews, news dramatizations, specialized news of agriculture, sports, business, women's affairs, "cultural" matters and the like—*and* local news. What kind of audience such a station might build is a matter for speculation. One thing is certain: Its newsroom would be like none described in this book. And its reportorial operations would be far more extensive than anything here contemplated.

Best thinking in recent years is (as NAB has recommended) that, since news is of vital program importance, every station must have at least one competent, well-trained newsman to direct news operations. At a radio news conference in mid-1946, when one editor after another was detailing his station's experiences and practices, a representative of a Class IV station in a small city finally complained woefully that he did not see "how a 250-watter could afford a real news operation." His answer came from "Curly" Vadeboncoeur of WSYR-Syracuse, then chairman of the NAB News Committee.

"No station, no matter what its situation, can afford *not* to put in a news operation," Vadeboncoeur said. "From every point of view— all the way from the dollar angle to the public service problem—a competent newsroom is the soundest kind of investment."

The specific use a station makes of whatever news staff it maintains also depends on its special circumstances. Essential is the production of the copy in time for the ever-present deadlines, whether by typewriter or scissors-and-glue. The gathering of local news is worked out by the individual staff to fit its broadcast schedule—some of it by the standard legman technique of the newspaper, a great deal of it by telephone. Many radio newsmen with newspaper background find themselves making far more use of the telephone than they did as newspaper reporters, because of their more frequent "editions" and because they almost always can gather satisfactorily by 'phone the highlight material they need.

What About Recording Devices?

A brand new tool, the recording device, has become standard equipment in the enterprising radio newsroom, 250-watter or clear channel. Before the war radio had only the record-cutting machine, a clumsy and cumbersome instrument at best, for this purpose. The war saw development of portable magnetic-wire and magnetic-tape recorders (captured German tape recorders lent much to American development of this kind of machine). In the postwar years a number of these machines have become available; many newsrooms are finding tape recorders most useful because of the ease with which they can be "edited." It is certain that their efficiency and ease of use will increase in the hands of electronic technologists.

By the use of one or another of these machines, a newsroom man or crew can go to the mayor and get his own words, in his own voice, on the current city tax situation; or to a council meeting and record a hot debate; or to a fire and let witnesses, firemen, and those who inevitably fled into the icy night in scanty clothing describe the event; or to a speech and record it all; or to the gaffer who is celebrating his hundredth birthday anniversary and let him cackle his recipe for longevity into the mike. The recording can then be turned over to the newsroom, edited and cut to fit a newscast's pattern, and put on the air. (Such editing, as has been said, is easiest with the tape recorder because of the speed and accuracy with which the desired excerpts can be cut and spliced.)

One of the pioneers in use of the recorder on local news is William Ray, who holds the dual role of director of news and special events for the NBC Central Division in Chicago and news director of NBC's Chicago outlet, WMAQ. Ray's station uses the recorder not only to gather spots for insertion in regular news shows, but also for a daily ten-minute all-recorded local show, "News on the Spot." Ray, enthusiastic about the device, points out:

"The recorder lets radio take the listener where the news is. It has the vigor, realism and color of on-the-spot broadcasting, plus the advantage gained by careful editing, plus the important factor of being able to broadcast events not alone when they occur (as in genuine on-the-spot broadcasts) but at regular stated times, when listeners are in the habit of tuning in."

So WMAQ uses recorders all day long, and spices many news shows with their offerings. So do many other stations. But not all stations go all the way with Ray. George Lewin, former newsroom manager of KMPC-Los Angeles, had this to say:

We use our wire recorders to cover all local stories of special interest. We find that it is better to have a 2- or 3-minute insert in a regular show than to devote a 15-minute period to any one story unless it be of transcendent interest.

Occasionally, however, we take a full period for one story. When Douglas and the Navy unwrapped the new turbo-jet supersonic plane, we did a 15-

minute wire-recorded show at the scene, using description and interviews.
We put it on the air that afternoon in a sustaining period.

Our wire recorder goes to the state capitol periodically. We record interviews with the governor, other officials, and leading lawmakers on topics in the news, plus any good features kicking around. These are used in the 10 p. m. "Voices in the News" and on Clete Roberts' news commentary at 9:15 p. m.

Though the recorder broadens the base and scope of newsroom operations, its merits are subject to warm debate among radio newsmen. Most acknowledge readily that it is a valuable tool; but some say it should be used more sparingly than its more ardent partisans advise. Among the criticisms leveled at it:

1   The recorder is too often used "for its own sake"—for no profit beyond the unmeasured promotional advantage of boasting the recorded material in the show. One news editor who makes this criticism says that often the recorded quotation is less effective, and harder to knit into the show, than would be a quotation written into the body of the story.

2   The recorder sometimes closes the lips of news sources. Public figures who talk willingly to reporters often become close-mouthed when the recorder's mike is thrust before them. Herbert Hoover, holding a news conference for press and radio following his return from his postwar worldwide famine inspection tour, read a prepared statement to newsmen, but refused to permit its recording (on the ground that he was to make a full radio report a week later). General Omar Bradley talked freely to reporters on veterans' affairs, but denied KYA-San Francisco the right to put his statements on records. And many lesser figures get mike fright.

It has been cynically suggested that public figures who talk willingly to reporters but shy from recorders do so because they can always say of broadcast statements merely attributed to them that "I was misquoted," but that they cannot deny their own voices.

3   The necessity of editing recorded statements and tying them nicely into newscasts adds to the labor, time, and difficulty of producing news shows.

4   Some of the statements made on unrehearsed recordings—interviews, man-on-the-street shows, crowd scenes and the like—are nonbroadcastable, and editing recordings to remove such statements takes away from realism, color, and continuity.

5   Expense of using recorders in stations employing union labor is high, since union regulations demand three men to handle them (an announcer, a reporter, and an engineer). But one man can do the whole job with many recorders, and the nonunion shop does not face so heavy an expense.

6   Skill and experience are prerequisite for the man who is to handle the recorder—especially skill in ad libbing interviews and other nonscript shows. But no part of radio news work can be handled without skill and experience.

None of these objections is insurmountable. As experience in the use of recorders expands, more and more stations will use them, to greater and greater advantage.

The Public and Radio News

One distinctive radio news problem is that the public, longer accustomed to the press, thinks of the newspaper as the prime news medium. To whatever extent this attitude is justified, the distance between radio and press will be narrowed in the public mind as radio develops its local and regional coverage. One cause behind the attitude is the fact that radio offered relatively little local news in its first fifteen years as a news medium; because of this the man in the street who observes an auto accident, or the woman whose bridge club is going to entertain its husbands, thinks first of telling the newspaper about it. If radio were apparently as much interested in the local scene as it is in the national and international (affairs with which the average man has no personal contact), the man who knows some news would be far more likely to call the radio newsroom as well as the city desk.

In recent years a good many stations have taken active and effective steps to overcome this attitude. They have asked listeners to telephone news tips to the station; they have offered small cash fees for tips, put on contests, and used other devices. They have publicized their interest in news, their desire for tips, on the air and by mail.

Akin to public tardiness in recognizing radio's interest in local news is hesitation in many quarters to grant radio reporters the privileges

---

When CNKW-New Westminster, B. C., instituted a system of prizes for news tips—$1.00 for the best tip daily, $5.00 for the best of the week—it drew immediate results. On March 12, 1947, a male voice called the newsroom and announced that its owner had just robbed a Vancouver home of $230. CNKW broadcast the story and asked the caller to come to the station for his $1.00 award. The man telephoned the next day to reject the offer. But ten days later he called again to announce a second robbery, a $250 job! Neither CNKW nor the police caught up with him.

traditionally given to newspapermen. Fulton Lewis's fight to get radio newsmen into the Congressional press gallery, and the struggle to gain similar privilege for radio reporters in the Massachusetts legislature, have already been mentioned (Chapter 1). In 1942 Edward R. Murrow had to stage a minor rebellion in London to procure parity for radio war correspondents in the war and diplomatic news centers of the Western Front. The Association of Eastern Fire Chiefs resolved to limit radio coverage of fires to prevent hordes of radio-informed specta-tors from impeding fire-fighting (a genuine radio news problem); Dave Driscoll of WOR-New York won a promise of full cooperation with radio reporters from the New York fire commissioner by promis-ing to keep the problem foremost in mind in fire coverage. In Chicago, radio newsmen formed the Chicago Radio Correspondents' Associa-tion to stage a campaign against discrimination against radio reporters in court coverage. In 1946, the UN Security Council closed its doors to mike coverage but not to newspaper and periodical coverage; radio newsmen were not invited to a news conference at Alcatraz during a prisoners' riot.

But the attitude of news sources is slowly changing. In 1945 the Radio Correspondents' Association culminated three years of effort by opening a radio news gallery broadcast room in the Senate wing of the Capitol in Washington. The next year Harold Ickes not only invited radio men to his final news conference as a Cabinet member, but permitted WOL-Washington to record his red-hot remarks. And in 1947 live microphones were permitted for the first time at a Congres-sional committee hearing (the hearing on proposed aid to Greece and Turkey), and in June NBC was allowed to make special arrangements to present a vote-by-vote account of the Senate's action to override President Truman's veto of the Taft-Hartley Bill. In September, when the Daytona Beach, Florida, city authorities turned down the request of local WNDB for permission to broadcast a policeman's plea for reinstatement before the Civil Service Appeals Board, the *Daytona*

Radio itself has contributed to public failure to recognize its news rights by persistently referring to "press conferences." Radio news editors who see this problem urge their fellows to use the terms "news conference" or "press-radio conference."

Beach News-Journal attacked the refusal and upheld the station's—
and the public's—right to hear the proceedings.

Broadening the Coverage

Newsrooms that interpret "local" coverage as "regional" have taken
another leaf from the newspaper book: the practice of developing
strings of correspondents. This is an obvious and necessary step if the
station is to be on top of the news not alone in its own city but also
throughout the region it reaches. To depend entirely on news service
splits for regional coverage is to broadcast much of such news after
it has appeared in the newspapers in whose cities the stories originated,
for this kind of news usually comes to the services from "stringers" or
correspondents who depend heavily on local papers for their material
(often, as laudably loyal members of the local newspaper staffs, they
permit the papers first use of news).

So more and more stations have built up their own stringers. WRBL-
Columbus, Georgia, covers nine Georgia and Alabama counties
through correspondents in county seats and large towns—two weekly
newspaper editors, a drug store manager, a school teacher, a lawyer, a
filling station operator, an advertising man, and a clubwoman. It pays
half a cent a word for news for broadcast, double for especially fast
coverage, bonuses for scoops—of which it has had many. KYSM-
Mankato, Minnesota, uses high school journalism students in twenty
surrounding towns as stringers, and stimulates them by contests.
WMRN-Marion, Ohio, also uses high school students. WIGM-
Medford, Wisconsin, has correspondents throughout its coverage area.
WCCO-Minneapolis, with both AP and UP regional services, has
radio newsmen in Duluth and other stations as its correspondents.
And so on. Scores of stations now use the string system. The telephone
is the most common means of communication between correspondents and their newsrooms, though telegraph, mail, and even teletype
are also used.

A few examples of radio stations' cooperation in news-gathering
have appeared. A "co-op news bureau" set up in the Olympia, Washington, state capitol in 1946, under Carl Downing, former news editor
of KPQ-Wenatchee, prorated costs to seventeen member stations at

$4.50 to $26.50 weekly, and furnished spot service, response to queries, and transcriptions. In New York state nine upstate stations linked themselves together by telephone line to share stories originating in any of the nine localities; each station had the privilege of taking as many or as few stories as it wished, and shared costs accordingly.

In some situations radio newsrooms have cooperative agreements with local newspapers for interchange of news. This is a natural arrangement when radio station and newspaper are under the same ownership—as in Winona, Minnesota, where carbons of late stories are furnished by the *Republican-Herald* to KWNO. In St. Cloud, Minnesota, the *Daily Times* local staff gathers news both for the newspaper and for KFAM, and does much of the rewriting for radio.

KATE-Albert Lea, Minnesota, independent of the local newspaper, has a "swap deal" with the paper and with another in nearby Austin, whereby KATE is provided with the newspapers' local news half an hour after the papers' press time. This means that the papers and the station present the news at virtually the same time.

And in New York City WEAF (now WNBC) set up direct lines to newspapers in Newark, the Bronx, Brooklyn, Westchester, and suburban Long Island to increase its local coverage.

But there are many situations in which the local radio station, whether newspaper-owned or not, is in violent competition with the local paper.

WHAT Does the Newsroom Cover?

In the broad sense, news is news. Anything that the newspaper prints may be broadcast material; anything that the radio newsroom puts on the air is pretty sure to be newspaper material.

In a narrower sense, a sense already much discussed in this book, a lot of news given extensive space in the press gets little time, or no time at all, on the air. News that comes under the various taboos of "good taste" and undue emotional impact, or that is too detailed for broadcast purposes, or that is published in the press primarily in its function of daily historian (such as vital statistics), or that cannot be made anything but so dull or complex as to be unlistenable, is rarely broadcast. All these limitations, however, disqualify less news than might be expected; and the definitions of broadcastable news are broadening as radio newsmen learn to make more interesting, or less offensive, types of material they have shied away from.

In short, virtually all the local news to which the press gives more than routine play—virtually everything that makes front page or other main news columns, in contrast to compressed or departmentalized, standing-head coverage—is fodder for the radio mill. And even this generalization leaves loopholes.

For instance: A good many radio newsmen have worked on the principle that newscasting has no place for a counterpart of the newspaper "society" or "personal" columns, especially the detailed notes about the petty activities of the local citizenry: "Mrs. Abner Wilkins has gone to Emeryville to spend a week with her sick aunt." Yet a Peoria, Illinois, station, WMBD, has outstanding success with a ten-minute, six-day "Town Crier" program, one on which thirty-five to forty local items for women, gathered by one woman newsroom employe, are presented. WPAY-Portsmouth, Ohio, gives extensive time to "personals" and minor local items on its six local shows a day. WMAZ-Macon, Georgia, covers women's meetings and activities through its civic and education director. WHIZ-Zanesville, Ohio, broadcasts three local "calendars" each day: "Club Calendar" at 10:45 A.M., "Birthday Calendar" at 11, and "Obituary Calendar" (which has the highest audience-rating of the three) at 12:15 P.M.

Which is to say that the smaller station, aiming at developing its strictly local audience, can build better-than-respectable listenership for the precise kind of minor local news that is so important in every small city daily or weekly. Dozens of examples to buttress those just given might be cited.

KABR-Aberdeen, South Dakota, found that high school students were not always dependable news sources. KABR, like most stations, in winter storm periods broadcasts lists of schools which are to be closed because of impassable roads or severe cold. After it had several times been the victim of long-distance calls from students who, representing themselves as high school officials, announced the closing of their schools, KABR developed code words which had to be employed by principals in such telephoned announcements!

The clear channel station, or that selling essentially regional rather than strictly local coverage, approaches such news with a good deal more caution. But any newsroom maintaining a local operation must give time, attention, and manpower to such local sources as city and county offices, local businesses, and the like.

And even the clear channel, big city station knows that certain types of local news having to do with events other than governmental and political are always audience-pullers. Food news, for example. For years Don Goddard has had two successful fifteen-minute shows on WNBC-New York. Appealing to thousands of rural and small town housewives, Goddard invariably includes the latest market news on strawberries, cabbages, pork roasts, and so on—their availability, their prices. Rather than offer mere lists and prices, Goddard presents such material in chatty, friendly fashion, as though he were talking across the back fence with each listener.

This kind of news—news dealing with food, clothing, household necessities, the commodities about which every American is thinking every day—can always be handled effectively on the local level, more understandably and meaningfully than in regional or national round-up stories.

Regional or national stories on these and many other subjects, however, can almost always be turned into local stories. Suppose the wire brings a story saying that a government agency promises a sharp up-swing in the production of men's suits. The newsroom man hops on the telephone, calls three or four local clothiers, and comes up with a strong local story (but one with more than local implications) on what the increased production is going to mean in the retail stores—the listener's point of contact with the news development.

Another example: A Washington story forecasts vastly enlarged need for beef for export. The station in a cattle-raising area—Texas or North Dakota or Colorado—develops, through its local markets and perhaps the county agent or a livestock association, a local story that makes the national news intimately significant to the station's listeners.

Some stations apply the same technique to stories that break in the newspapers with which they compete. One Midwestern clear channel newsroom director explains it this way:

Though we maintain an elaborate news operation and write all our own shows, we can't hope to gather and broadcast all the local news the papers offer. We'd have to have a forty-man newsroom, instead of a seven-man, and practically twenty-four hours of air time to do it. Inevitably, we get beat on some local stories. But we can still capitalize on them. When a good story breaks in a local paper, we examine it carefully to see what it *doesn't* say— where it has failed to fill the gaps, where it needs explanation. Then we get busy, send a man out or put him on the telephone—and come up with a follow story that has all the virtues, for us and for our listeners, of an original news break.

Of necessity, whether the radio newsroom uses this technique or not, it must check its local competition, newspaper or radio, closely. What the other fellow is doing will always affect what it will decide to do.

"Backgrounding" the news, of which the technique just described is an example, is considered at greater length in Chapter 11. On-the-spot coverage, another phase of local activity, is given consideration in Chapter 9.

Two approaches to newspaper competition appear in the methods of two big newsrooms in one metropolitan center. The director of one says frankly: "Just before each news show we check the bannered or featured stories in the latest editions of our local papers. Then we make sure that we feature the same stories in our newscasts. Often our shows get to the public before the papers do. So we get credit for breaking the big news first."

The competing newsroom director speaking: "We decide in our own newsroom, before we see the papers, what are the feature stories, and play them regardless of what the papers do. In other words, we believe in our own news judgment. Often the papers' judgment and ours are the same; we think that when they differ we are at least as likely to be right as are the papers."

Most competent newsmen prefer the second approach.

Weather News

"The first training for a new man in our newsroom is learning to write the weather story."

That's the statement of the director of a clear channel station newsroom, made before radio newsmen at the Institute for Education by Radio at Columbus in 1946. It's one way of expressing a principle on which radio editors are unanimous: that weather news gets high priority on any kind of newscast.

The wire services pay their respects to the principle by providing frequent and full weather forecasts—they move on the wires several times a day, so that the predictions can be kept fully up to date—and by giving elaborate coverage to weather phenomena of any kind. Whenever there's a flood, a storm of more than local proportion, a blizzard, a twister, a Florida hurricane or a Los Angeles snowfall, a cold wave or a stretch of temperatures above ninety, the wires carry full reports both as separate stories—often headed UNDATED WEATHER if the story covers more than one locality—and in the round-ups and summaries.

A local newsroom can do fairly well in weather coverage by depending wholly on the wire. But only fairly well. Weather stories become more meaningful—and more interesting—if they're developed locally, following the method described above.

"We go direct to the United States Weather Bureau for our weather data, rather than rely on the printers," said the newsroom man at Columbus. "We use a full—and I mean full—analysis of weather conditions whenever it's justified; Temperatures, wind, barometric pressures, and so on. We don't hesitate to devote a full fifteen-minute show to weather alone, if in our judgment the story is really the headliner of the day.

"That means a lot more than bare statistics. When we're building a weather story, we get our men out into the weather, or on the 'phone if time presses, and find out what's happening to *people*. If it's a heat wave, we report on the swimming pools and the parks, the kids playing in sprinklers, the heat prostrations. In a blizzard, it's routine for us to give long lists of schools closed throughout our area—we have a

---

At KRKD-Los Angeles one morning, News Editor Doug Douglas was broadcasting a 5:45-to-6 show. At 5:50 he observed light fixtures swinging and the building shimmying. Without a pause, as Douglas finished a story, he ad libbed a Los Angeles date line and said, "There she goes, folks—it's a real earthquake. But don't let a little shake like this get you down. Just stay tuned to KRKD for all the latest earthquakes. Let's travel on now to Washington, D. C., for a few political shakes."

deal with county school authorities to keep us informed. And we get lots of information from the state highway department about the condition of the roads."

WDAY-Fargo reported, at a radio news short course at the University of Minnesota in 1947, that it had put on "a solid hour" of news during a recent storm, and that this kind of effort is not unusual in WDAY weather coverage.

In Iowa, the Highway Commission and the state's radio newsrooms have worked out a cooperative system whereby the state highway patrol makes immediately available to the newsrooms all information about highways. Individual stations in other areas have made similar arrangements. WHO-Des Moines has a fifteen-minute weather show daily at 8 A.M.—one that gives forecasts for eight states and abundant detail on Iowa temperatures, rain or snowfall, wind velocity and direction, and other such data.

The Feature Angle

The warmth and intimacy of the human voice and the informal manner of radio news give radio a notable advantage over the press in the presentation of feature or "color" stories. To emphasize such news is sometimes to limit further radio's already tightly-packed time for straight news detail; and it may be to run the risk of overplaying the feature angle. But feature material, used with caution, may do much to add to the effectiveness of radio news. Color is always more attractive to the consumer of news than the black-and-white of straight reporting. And, in the hands of skillful news editors and reporters, it often helps the listener to understand a news situation, to "get the feel of it," better than he could from less imaginative coverage.

Here is the area in which the local newsroom can do most to dress up its news presentation. In national and international news, the newsroom is at the mercy of its printers—if they don't bring color with their straight reporting, the newsroom can do little about it. But its

Once in a while a local newsroom can do something to add color even to international news. On D-Day in 1944, when its printer was grinding away factual detail on the start of the Normandy invasion, KUOM-Univer-
(*continued on next page*)

local news, gathered by its own men on the spot, can be plentifully spiced with feature material.

Suppose, for example, that an early morning fire occurs in an apartment building. The story could be presented factually and accurately something like this:

A two-alarm fire sent twenty-five Midtown apartment dwellers out into chilly fall weather about 3 this morning. The fire was in the Milmar apartments at the corner of Third and Main Streets. The building was entirely burned out before firemen managed to control the flames. Nobody was injured.

Fire Chief Maher says the fire started in a mattress in a first-floor apartment. The apartment was occupied by Miss Patricia Maloney, a stenographer. Miss Maloney spread the alarm, so that all residents of the building escaped.

And so on. The story tells the major news. It does not take the listeners to the fire.

Suppose, instead, a reporter goes to the scene, talks to spectators, interviews Miss Maloney and other residents of the building. His story may take a very different tack:

Miss Patricia Maloney, a Midtown stenographer, who lived in an apartment at Third and Main Streets, smoked a last-minute cigaret early this morning . . . and the result was that twenty-five occupants of the Milmar apartments had to rush from their beds into chilly fall weather.

Miss Maloney fell asleep before she finished her smoke—and her cigaret fell onto her mattress. She told about it as she stood shivering in a fur coat over her night clothes—all she saved from the fire.

"I don't know what woke me," she said. "The smoke, I guess." She went on to say, "Anyway, I realized my mattress was on fire. I just grabbed my coat and ran through the hall screaming."

Miss Maloney's warning roused all tenants of the building, and all

---

sity of Minnesota found on the university faculty a man who had spent many summers in the areas of France where Allied troops were landing. This man put on a fifteen-minute personal-experience account of the country—one in which he gave first-person knowledge of the terrain, the beaches, the railroads, the Norman towns and fields that lay in the path of the invasion. The result was a colorful and revealing picture that gave KUOM's listeners understanding they could not have got from the news service stories, packed as they were with detailed information.

escaped. But the fire was spreading fast by the time the firemen arrived—two alarms were turned in—and this morning the building is a total loss.

Edgar Upson was the last tenant to leave the building. He explains it this way: "I was halfway down the stairs when I remembered my new camera. I just got it yesterday, and I didn't want to lose it."

So Upson tore back to his apartment to grab his camera and two suits of clothes.

Upson was luckier than most tenants. Mrs. Walter Mandell told a KWWW reporter tearfully that she saved only the night clothes she wore.

She said she never saw anything burn so fast. And she continued, "I wanted to go back to bring some things out, but I didn't dare."

Spectators supported Mrs. Mandell's story. A motorist passing just as the alarm was spread says that he stopped his car half a block away—and that by the time he got back flames were shooting from half a dozen windows.

The story could go on for as long as the newsroom chose to extend it. And it would carry to the listener a much more colorful and interesting picture than the straight news account. It would also take more time—a factor the editor must consider.

Stories in this vein can, however, be employed more concisely than in the example, and in situations less dramatic than fires and catastrophes. The flavor of a taxpayers' protest before the city council can be better presented by a description of the council chamber scene, with some quotes, than by the unadorned report—and the *flavor* may be more meaningful than a factual, but colorless, report. A church picnic can be brought to life by telling of the mishaps in the three-legged race.

Siegfried Mickelson, newsroom director of WCCO-Minneapolis, who believes color reporting a prime factor in radio's local news coverage, has this to say: "I want my reporters to tell what they see, hear, smell. I want them always to get the major significant details, of course. But I want such details clothed in revealing human-interest color. Thus we show the audience that we are not merely reading from a newspaper, but that our men are on the scene. We gain not alone in interest but also in authoritative tone."

Newsroom men have experimented with first-person coverage in events they report—"I saw, I heard, I talked with . . . " Sometimes the technique is sharply effective. But some of those who have used it think the problems it raises discount its value. If the reporter is also the broadcaster, it is likely to work well. But if the announcer must introduce the reporter, a small production problem arises. Sometimes, indeed, the reporter cannot have returned to the studio in time for the program. Mickelson says on this point that "third-person writing, handled so as to show clearly that our reporters are on the job, has proved so effective that we rarely bother with first-person reporting."

The wire recorder is often a boon to reporting events of this nature. An account recorded by the shivering Miss Maloney of her experience at the apartment fire would lend greater vitality to the story than the announcer's quotation does.

Local News and Promotion

When the *Detroit News* started broadcasting in 1920, its purpose was promotional. At first by broadcasting news, later music, it thought (as its radio editor said in 1924) that "goodwill is about the only return we expect from our station."

Most of the other early broadcasters looked on radio in the same light. Of the 576 licenses in force on May 1, 1924, two-thirds were held by radio and electric companies and a few newspapers which thought of broadcasting not as a business for its own sake, but as a promotional adjunct of other businesses.

When broadcasting celebrated its twenty-fifth anniversary in 1945, it had become a billion-dollar business. And its thoughts of promotion were of self-promotion, not of building up other enterprises.

The relationship of the newsroom to this fact has two contrasting facets: A station's news programming may be used as one of its most vigorous avenues of promotion for the station as a whole; and the remainder of the station programming may be used to promote its news services.

The second half of this contrast is obvious. Throughout their broadcast days, many stations use station breaks to announce their next news shows; they call attention to newscasts, commentaries, special-event shows, and others emanating from the newsroom by familiar and simple devices.

The first facet is more complex. There are scores of methods by which a station may employ its news operations for station promotion.

Most common is the familiar advertisement of the extent or frequency of news programming. WMIN-Twin Cities, a 250-watt station, uses movie-screen and other announcements of its hourly on-the-hour news shows; WIND-Chicago, 5,000 watts, boasted more than fifty news programs daily in 1946 (twenty-four of them, five minutes each hour, sold to one sponsor). The "independent," non-network station is more likely to adopt and promote such a plan than the larger station; its time is freer, and with the limited programming facilities usually characteristic of the smaller station it may depend far more heavily on the relative ease of preparing news shows. When it does, it uses every kind of promotion to let its audience know that it is "the station with the news."

A number of stations, however, have developed more imaginative and probably more telling methods of using news in promotion. Some use specific news stories—especially local stories—for this purpose.

WFOY-St. Augustine, for example, which puts on the air each week more than 450 minutes of local news, issues the WFOY Daily News Sheet, on 8½- by 14-inch paper, with copies of local stories it has broadcast. Carrying the dates and times of broadcast, these News Sheets are mailed to local or primary-area citizens whose names have appeared in them. WKBH-La Crosse, Wisconsin, WILM-Wilmington, Delaware, and a number of other stations get out "news memos" of like nature.

Some stations believe that modesty about their news operations is not a virtue. John Verstraete, former news director of 50,000-watt KSTP-Twin Cities, considered it profitable to call unabashed attention to his newsroom's "scoops." "We always let the listener know when we have beaten the newspaper and radio competition," Ver-

---

The radio trade press—especially *Broadcasting*, *Radio Daily*, and *Radio Showmanship*—carry hundreds of stories detailing the promotional activities of American radio stations. Many such stories deal with the use of news in promotion, and the alert newsroom director has to keep abreast of them.

straete said, "not once but each time the story is used." KSTP closes most of its news shows with the reminder that its next newscast is to come at such-and-such an hour.

WRBL-Columbus, Georgia, prints its newsroom slogan—"Accuracy —Speed—Human Interest"—on cards and drops them on the desks of the sheriff, the city clerk, and other news sources. The practice, says WRBL, wins friends for the station and stories for the newsroom.

News shows may also be used to inform listeners of newsworthy events the station is to cover—political speeches, on-the-spot broadcasts, and the like. In these cases the newscast is providing news as well as promotion.

A Miscellany of Local News

WMAZ-Macon, Georgia (10,000 watts) puts a news editor and two reporters on duty early in the morning, and two more reporters on the afternoon and evening shift. They cover the city thoroughly, put on six newscasts with local and UP and INS news. The station also uses nine network news shows daily.

WINR-Binghamton, New York (250 watts) broadcasts seven straight news shows, two sports shows, and a local commentary daily. It carries local news on every show; believes that news shows should run to fifteen minutes because "five or ten minutes devoted to news is insufficient to present the complete news story." It has AP service.

WHIZ-Zanesville, Ohio (250 watts) found through a cross-section listener panel of fifty-eight listeners that they "got enough national and international news from network shows"; the station therefore concentrates on local and regional news in the newscasts it originates. One man gathers all local and regional news. The station has AP service.

WPAY-Portsmouth, Ohio (250 watts) sent several thousand postcards to "a selected list" of listeners telling them of the station's news department and soliciting news tips. One man gathers local news and edits shows, in direct competition with the newspaper which owns the station. It has AP and UP service.

WIZE-Springfield, Ohio (250 watts) has a "woman ace reporter from the newspaper" who gathers local news. She is "so well established" that local stories are often reported to her ahead of the newspapers. WIZE has three all-local five-minute news shows, at 7:55 and 10:25 A.M. and 4:25 P.M. It has UP service.

At WING-Dayton, Ohio (5,000 watts), one newsman gathers, writes, and broadcasts two fifteen-minute all-local newscasts at noon and 6 P.M., and a ten-minute all-local show at 3 P.M. These are "the station's major newscasts." WING has AP service.

WJTN-Jamestown, New York (250 watts) maintains a local news bureau of four full-time men because "our listeners want complete local coverage of news and sports." One of the men devotes his time to near-by Warren, Pennsylvania. WJTN has UP service.

WOW-Omaha (5,000 watts) has a staff of seventy-five correspondents. It picks them from names suggested by county sheriffs, pays them on "enterprise, initiative, quality, and quantity, with no set formula." It gives correspondents credit on the air for especially noteworthy work. It has AP and UP.

KNEL-Brady, Texas (250 watts) has no wire service, but operates its newsroom strictly on a local basis. Its listeners "have learned to depend on KNEL for news of their friends and neighbors." KPAB-Laredo, Texas (250 watts) also operates on this basis, without a wire service.

WBNY-Buffalo (250 watts) operates an aggressive newsroom with a five-man local staff, a full-time Washington correspondent, and three news services (AP, UP, and INS). A station without network affiliation, it makes extensive local and national news service its prime weapon to combat opposition. Roy L. Albertson, owner, advises straight-from-the-shoulder handling of local news, and has a number of successful "campaigns" against local abuses to his credit.

WSLB-Ogdensburg, New York (250 watts) has a sixty-man correspondent staff, puts on a daily "Rural Reporter" show at 10:30 A.M. It has UP service.

WLBR-Lebanon, Pennsylvania (1,000 watts) boasts three local and regional features: A ten-minute "Capital City Daily" show from Harrisburg, made up chiefly of Harrisburg local (as distinguished from state government) news; news of each of six primary-area communities, one a day, in a radio version of the community weekly newspaper; and a "Local News Review" at 7 P.M. daily, a rewrite of the day's local news for listeners who missed earlier programs. WLBR has AP service.

WLIB-New York (1,000 watts), the *New York Post* station, puts heavy emphasis on local news in its ten-minute hourly newscasts (which are broadcast by reporters rather than announcers). It maintains a full newsroom staff of reporters and editors, uses a wire recorder extensively, offers two periods of news devoted exclusively to Brooklyn and the Bronx. It seeks the local angle on national and international news, and sends special correspondents to cover important international events. It has AP and UP service.

WINR (see above) "never uses an individual story more than three times in a day." Each time a story is re-used, it must be rewritten.

WFBL-Syracuse (5,000 watts) has two daily regional news shows, at 9 A.M. and 5:45 P.M. Four correspondents in near-by primary-area cities report twice daily by teletype to the WFBL newsroom; eleven stringers at other points supplement these reports. WFBL has UP service.

KGKY-Scottsbluff, Nebraska (1,000 watts) has been offering a thorough local news service since 1938, with a small staff. Its "What-is-news?" policy is broad: "Drunkenness and drunken driver stories are never withheld—everything goes. That's what makes a newscast." KGKY has UP service.

KSTP-Twin Cities (50,000 watts) has activated its entire station personnel as a local news-gathering force by offering $5.00 for the first tip any employe turns in, $2.00 for each additional tip, and $10 for the best tip each month. The device has led to a good many scoops over radio and newspaper competition. KSTP has AP and UP service.

WIGM-Medford, Wisconsin (250 watts) broadcasts a fifteen-minute "Community News Show" daily. Four reporters—"all women with a nose for news"—cover not only major spot stories, but also personal news, births, deaths, "socials," and the like. The news editor spends five hours a day putting the show together. WIGM has UP service.

KELA-Centralia-Chehalis, Washington (1,000 watts), located two miles from the borders of the two cities, has twelve miles of leased wire linking the two communities to the station. It has forty-nine remote outlets along the system so that spot broadcasts may be made from almost any location in its area. One man does leg work, news writing, and broadcasting. KELA has UP service.

WIND-Chicago (5,000 watts), to meet a sponsor's need for a special-pattern show, developed "Today's News in Chicago," a seven-day fifteen-minute program of local and regional news. It has three sections: "Chicago News" (strictly local); "News of the Neighborhoods" (close-in suburban); and "Chicagoland News" (regional). Its materials are drawn from the regional splits of UP, AP, and INS.

KPO-San Francisco (50,000 watts) puts on at 1:30 P.M. each Saturday a fifteen-minute show called "News in Advertising." Ina Stephenson, assistant manager of KPO's news department, assembles for the show news culled from advertisements in magazines, newspapers, and radio—"ads telling the story of new developments in business and industry score the most often on the program, but also included are many institutional and educational advertisements."

At KVOO-Tulsa (50,000 watts), Ken Miller, news director, and his assistant— sometimes with added newsroom personnel participating— put on a half-hour show one night a week in which they quite frankly gossip about the news. As material for the program, Miller says, they save feature stories that don't rate time in regular newscasts, and instead of broadcasting them straight, present them in informal conversation. They throw in a few records, make and drink coffee during the show, and offer six to eight stories in this framework.

WKBH-La Crosse, Wisconsin (1,000 watts) and WLOW-Norfolk, Virginia (1,000 watts) both make broadcasting of city council proceedings regular features.

Bill Leonard puts on a forty-five-minute show called "This Is New York" at 9:15 each morning over WCBS-New York (50,000 watts)— nine minutes in commercials—which is "more like a magazine than a newspaper," according to Jerry Walker's excellent description of it in *Editor & Publisher* (January 31, 1948). Leonard stresses feature angles of the news and movie, book, theater, and radio criticism. "When Leo Durocher was having a press conference to talk about his return as the Dodgers' manager," says Walker, "Bill Leonard was telephoning Burt Shotton in Florida, asking him how it felt to be an ex-manager."

KATL-Houston (1,000 watts) has a "public service partnership" with the *Houston Press* whereby the newspaper provides full local news coverage to the station, as well as publicization of station activities, in return for standby announcement mentions of the partnership with the *Press* in five noncommercial news and feature broadcasts daily. KATL has the AP radio wire, the *Press* the UP news wire.

Harry Van Slycke of KSIW-Woodward, Oklahoma (250 watts) was in a Woodward cafe for a commercial broadcast when fire broke out in a shop across the street. Van Slycke, with his portable mike, gave seventeen minutes of live running commentary on the fire (until power was turned off as a precautionary measure), and summoned aid from fire departments in five near-by towns at firemen's request.

9

Special Events

Special events got regular broadcasting started, back in 1920.

8MK-Detroit and KDKA-Pittsburgh—to refer again to the pioneers—opened their regular schedules by telling their few thousand listeners about the outcome of elections. They chose these events because their audiences were ready-made, requiring no build-up; because, as matters of public concern, they provided excellent material for a bit of bragging.

There, in essence, are the characteristics of what radio today calls "special events." Events that have wide popular interest; events with a good deal of color, or drama, or warmth and human interest; events whose reporting may, one way or another, be considered "in the public interest."

As broadcasting developed after that flimsy start in 1920, it continued to make the special event its prime device for snaring public notice. The Dempsey-Carpentier fight at Boyle's Thirty Acres in 1921 . . . a Princeton-Chicago football game in 1922 . . . the opening of Congress in 1923 . . . the arrival of an unknown named Lindbergh in Paris in 1927 . . . the inaugural of Franklin Delano Roosevelt in 1933 (an event followed immediately by the first Fireside Chat) . . . the Munich conference . . . the outbreak of war in 1939 . . . Pearl Harbor . . . D Day, V-E Day, V-J Day . . . elections, coronations, Olympic games, atom bombings, conventions, funerals. The list is as long as the history of broadcasting.

Obviously, radio came early to realize that mere telling *about* such events wasn't enough. To describe them at second—or third, or tenth—hand failed to take advantage of one of radio's prime advantages over other means of mass communication: the advantage of taking the listener to the scene, of letting him hear the thud of the prize-fighter's glove, the cheers of the French mob at Le Bourget, the very voice of the most effective speaker radio has known. So—special events became part of the programming problem of every network and of every individual station.

For the problem is one for the station whose world is no larger than the boundaries of its own county as well as for the network. MBS may broadcast a national-championship football game; the 250-watter puts the local high school basketball games on the air. ABC tells the nation which of Hollywood's charmers gets the current Oscar; the station in Podunk broadcasts the county spelling bee. Opening of the United Nations Assembly or Midtown Fourth of July parade . . . Republican national convention or dedication of the new bridge across Swamp Creek: each is a subject of news interest to a particular audience; each has human interest; each is an activity whose broadcast in some degree serves the public interest.

Unfortunately, the harassed manager of a small station can't toss off a special event broadcast merely by writing a memo to his boys. Such a broadcast has to be thoroughly planned, sometimes long in advance—some stations and nets planned D Day and V-E Day broadcasts for years; it takes the efforts of many members of a station's or a network's staff. It demands imagination, time, and money. The small station has little time, and no huge reserve of money, to spare; and it usually takes both to put imagination to work.

Nevertheless, the small stations are more and more naming "special events directors" on their staffs—the big stations and the nets have had them for years. And in most cases the special events director is the news director. A special event is usually a news event; the link is a natural. Any news director who is more than a figure-head is constantly thinking up special broadcasts that conform to the type, whether or not he bears the title or uses the term.

A few notable broadcasting feats have taken on the flavor of special events although they were not planned in advance. Radio's observance of the death of President Roosevelt—of which more later—is one such feat; the reporting of Pearl Harbor is another. Broadcasting in connection with events like these, though it cannot be made ready beforehand, calls for the same kind of mobilization of radio facilities. Radio has met such emergencies with noteworthy success—perhaps in part because of its experience in preparing for the usual type of special event.

Arranging a Special Event

Here's station WWWW, in whose city the annual Fall Festival Parade is going to be the biggest ever. Two hours and scores of floats long, half a dozen bands complete with drum majorettes, a reviewing stand with the governor in it, and half the citizens of the county jamming Main Street sidewalks. WWWW's news editor thinks his station can carry the parade off Main Street to the stay-at-home half of the county. The job perhaps turns into something bigger than he bargained for, for these are some of the chores he has to do:

Get a map showing the parade's route; check it for desirable points from which to broadcast; arrange remote lines (doubtless WWWW has some remote lines in, but more may be needed); install microphones—especially one in the reviewing stand, so as to pick up the governor's bestowal of a medal on the most agile baton twirler.

Get a list of all participating organizations from the Fall Festival committee, complete with hundreds of names of marchers, float-riders, parade marshals, and the like; get a schedule of the order of their appearance in the parade. Prepare a card for each float, marching unit, or other element in the parade, giving pertinent names and other data.

Put a script-writer to work to prepare a hundred or more pieces of copy, thirty seconds to three minutes long—copy giving appropriate data on the history of the Festival, the overpowering size of the parade, the number of steps each marcher will take, the difficulty of making some of the floats, the donors of prizes, and so on. There must be, too, reminiscent bits on the time Joe Fobes' horse ran away back in the 1916 parade, and the fact that nine-year-old twins won the drum majorette award in 1945.

Assign announcers and engineers to each microphone; brief them thoroughly on their parts in the broadcast; give them batches of copy to use at appropriate times, including pieces for fill-in during the periods when the parade has been stalled by the breakdown of a truck. Warn them to be on the lookout for fox terriers that frighten parading horses or youngsters that wander into the line of march.

Arrange for interviews—perhaps set interviews with the parade chairman or other notables (the copy probably written in advance) and ad-lib interviews for which interviewers must be prepared.

Assign a man to do on-the-spot interviews among the crowd of spectators; arrange for his traveling mike or mobile broadcasting unit.

Plan and execute recorded features—interviews, brief speeches, band music, and so on. Arrange for their appropriate timing in the broadcast.

See that the station's regular schedule during the period is cleared for the special broadcast.

Finally, make sure that the station's studios are standing by to take over in case a cloudburst postpones the parade until Tuesday.

The success of such a broadcast will depend heavily on the amount of sleep the director misses during the preceding month. When the show goes on the air, it should have the effect of being spontaneous, unarranged; achievement of this effect is in direct ratio to the amount and skill of advance preparation—which is to say, to the degree to which it is carefully nonspontaneous.

The hypothetical special event here outlined is perhaps more elaborate than most. But it is also typical of special events. If a Fourth of July speech is to be broadcast, there are mikes and lines to set up, and announcers' scripts to get the main speaker on and off the air. When a football victory celebration seems to be coming up, man-on-the-street interviews and other events must be prearranged. When the local visit of a great symphony orchestra is to be broadcast, there are permissions to be gained as well as involved technical preparations to make.

— o —

Now an actual special event. This was a broadcast * by WCCO-Twin Cities on December 31, 1946. Siegfried Mickelson, news and special events director, started work on the show early in December, upon learning that the sixty-five-year-old Minneapolis Chamber of Commerce was to conduct special ceremonies to mark its relinquishment of its title to the Minneapolis Civic and Commerce Association. His first step was to confer with officials of the two associations and gain approval for the broadcast. Then he made preliminary arrange-

* By written permission of WCCO, Minneapolis, September 17, 1947.

ments with the WCCO program manager, and wrote the following memorandum:

FROM Sig Mickelson   December 6, 1946
TO

Joscelyn
Wilkey
Beloungy
Dawson
Ward
Lucas
Ziebarth
Woodbury
Haeg
Backlund
Newsroom
Master Control
E. C. Hillweg
Butler
Jim Hayes

We have scheduled a half-hour broadcast from the Minneapolis Chamber of Commerce on Fourth Street and Fourth Avenue for Tuesday, December 31. This show will be transcribed at approximately 11 A. M. and played back, subject to later confirmation from the program manager's office, from 5 to 5:30 P. M. the same day. The occasion is the yielding of the name "Chamber of Commerce" to the Minneapolis Civic and Commerce Association and the assumption of the name "Grain Exchange" by the present Chamber of Commerce.

Will the chief engineer's office please have lines installed to the floor of the Grain Exchange? The contact there is E. C. Hillweg, secretary. Our outlet should be at the pit end of the floor, just off the platform near a corridor on the side of the room closest to Third Street.

The lines should probably be available from approximately 10:30 A.M. until approximately 12:30 P.M.

We shall probably want to use four microphones on this operation. One would be on a stand for the speakers' platform, one on a stand for band music and crowd noises, one portable with sufficient cable to move around the room with some freedom, and one, either portable or on a stand, for the announcer handling the written copy on the show.

We do not as yet know the exact starting time for the broadcast, but assuming that the Grain Exchange on this day will close at 11 A.M. our schedule will follow roughly these timings:

10:55 to 11:00 A.M.   Color and background largely from prepared copy.

11:00 A.M.   The sound of the gong closing trading for the day.

11:00 to 11:08 A.M.   General celebration from the crowd with band music and spontaneous group singing.

11:08 to 11:20 A.M.   Ceremony in which the name "Chamber of Commerce" will be presented formally and officially to Emmett Salisbury of the Civic and Commerce Association and the assumption of the name "Grain

Exchange" by the present Chamber of Commerce.
There will be very brief talks by Mr. Tearse of the
Grain Exchange, Mr. Salisbury of the Civic and
Commerce, Mayor Humphrey and Governor-elect
Youngdahl.

Officials of the Grain Exchange are now developing
ideas for this ceremony. They will perhaps have some
sort of document which they will pass on to Salisbury, and there may also be some little ceremony
commemorating the assumption of the name "Grain
Exchange."

11:20 to 11:24.30   Group singing of "Auld Lang Syne" and general
crowd noises and celebration.

. This schedule is, of course, a very tentative one and is subject to constant
revision. It however will provide a working outline on which we can build
a show later. The exact timing will be dependent upon the scheduled time
for the closing of the grain exchange on that day. For example, if trading
should be closed at 12, our show will run from 11:55 to 12:25. It is also
quite probable that we shall wish to start a couple of minutes earlier than
five minutes before the hour for the end of trading. This will give us more
time to describe activities in the pit and also give us a chance to broadcast
the two-bell gong five minutes before closing time as well as the three-bell
gong at closing time.

At the moment, it is my assumption that no production man need be
assigned to this job, but I suggest that Mr. Wilkey assign an announcer as
soon as possible. It is my feeling that Larry Haeg, who is closely identified
with the grain business, handle the roving mike to describe the actual operation in the pit.

There then followed a series of conferences between Hillweg and
other officials of the two associations on the one hand, and Mickelson
and station officials on the other. It developed that trading would end
at 12:00, so the time of making the transcription was changed from
10:55 to 11:54. Frank Butler was assigned as announcer for the show.
Haeg, WCCO farm director, was briefed on his part in it.

Following these conferences, Hillweg presented to Mickelson, on
December 19, a revised tentative schedule. Starting at 11:54, it followed
Mickelson's original suggestion closely. It contained a good deal of
actual script—introductions of speakers and the like, and a resounding
pat on the back for the Pillsbury Mills band, which was to perform.

Mickelson responded with a second revision of the schedule—a simpli-fied version, omitting the script—and circulated it among station officials. In a letter to Hillweg with his revision, he commented in part:

12:00 NOON—I think we might allow a couple of extra minutes for a demonstration here. A band number alone should take a little more than two minutes and if we should get thirty or forty seconds applause, both be-fore and after the band selection, it should run our time out to a minimum of three minutes preceding the introduction of Mr. Tearse. I would like to see approximately three and a half minutes allowed here. . . .

12:08.30—There is a problem here as to whether, because of union regu-lations, we will be able to introduce the Pillsbury Band for a selection. It might be better if at the conclusion of Mr. Tearse's introduction of Judge Youngdahl the band automatically break into "Hail to the Chief" without any formal introduction. In that way we could carry the music as sound-effects and not as a definitely programmed band selection. I am checking now to determine whether the band is composed exclusively of union musi-cians. If it is, we can then disregard the union angle entirely. . . .

I am rather interested in having at least a five-minute pad at the end of the show. If the program runs at all behind schedule this will permit us to take up the slack at this point. If it runs directly on schedule this five minutes will permit us from three to four minutes of group singing and a minute or two of sign-off. . . .

There followed another conference—Hillweg, Mickelson, and Ralph Backlund, the writer assigned to the show—another minor revision of the schedule, and final instructions to performers and technicians. On December 27 Mickelson sent to all parties to the program a final version of the schedule. The day before the broadcast, he issued the following memorandum:

FROM Sig Mickelson   December 30, 1946
TO

Joscelyn	Haeg
Wilkey	Backlund
Beloungy	Newsroom
Ziebarth	Master Control
Dawson	Butler
Ward	Jim Hayes
Lucas	E. C. Hillweg
Woodbury	

Following is a relatively complete schedule for the grain exchange pick-up Tuesday morning, December 31, at 11:54 A.M. This show is being recorded for play-back at 5 P.M.

11:54 A.M.	Show opens cold from Grain Exchange by Butler doing voice. Butler reads two minutes copy prepared by news department.
11:56 A.M.	Butler cues in Larry Haeg in pit. Haeg describes pit operations, gets color and sound effects of Grain Exchange in motion.
11:58.30 A.M.	Haeg cues in Butler. Butler does more prepared copy up to 11:59.45, when he awaits sound of gong closing trading.
12:00 NOON	Gong—and we hope a demonstration from the brokers, traders, and guests on the floor. We will try to establish sufficient claque to make this demonstration work for at least ten or fifteen seconds. Following it the Pillsbury Band will play probably two selections. Butler can take the first selection straight and then ad lib about the second, describe the demonstration in the room and call attention to the program which is to follow immediately. He should also be able to describe the speakers' platform and the arrivals of the featured speakers.
12:06 P.M.	Butler calls attention to the fact that H. H. Tearse, president of the Minneapolis Chamber of Commerce, is to preside over the meeting and will start speaking at once.
12:06–12:09 P.M.	Tearse speaks and presents scroll to Emmett Salisbury.
12:09–12:12 P.M.	Salisbury responds.
12:12 P.M.	Band plays a few bars from "Hail to the Chief"—possibly about a minute.
12:13 P.M.	Tearse introduces Governor Youngdahl.
12:13½ P.M.	Youngdahl speaks.
12:16½ P.M.	Tearse introduces Haeg.
12:17 P.M.	Haeg speaks.
12:20 P.M.	Tearse announces group singing of "Auld Lang Syne."
12:23½ P.M.	Sign off.

NB If for any reason the program should run short, Butler will have adequate copy to fill the end. We could also use a minute preceding the show at 5 o'clock to introduce it if we need any further fill.

SPECIAL INSTRUCTIONS

1 Butler will be able to get copy from Ralph Backlund for his 11:54, 11:56, 11:58.30, 12:00 and closing pieces. He should note that there will be a gong at 11:55 signifying that only five minutes remain before the end of trading.

2 Haeg—It will help immensely if Larry will have his microphone as close as possible to the gong at 11:55, and then if he will have it back up there in a similar spot at 12:00; otherwise he can determine where he wants to work and where he can get the best sound effects and best description of the final moments of trading in the pit.

3 Engineering Department—Would it be possible to put earphones on both Haeg and Butler and feed them cue through ear phones? This would simplify the switching problem during the first six minutes of the show, when it may be a little difficult to throw cues because of the crowded platform.

4 Note to all hands—The program will carry itself from the point at 12:06 when Mr. Tearse takes over until approximately 12:22, when the band is playing and the crowd is singing "Auld Lang Syne."

Backlund, carrying out his part of the assignment, provided three pieces of copy. The first, of forty-four typewritten lines, covered the 11:54 and 11:56 items on the schedule; the second, of twenty-six lines, the 11:58.30 and 12:00 items; the third, of forty-five lines, the closing. Note that the third piece is divided into "takes," so that the announcer might cut it where necessary. The copy:

11:54 to 11:56

This is Frank Butler, speaking to you from the floor of the Minneapolis Chamber of Commerce. The sounds you hear in the background—the steady murmur of voices and the occasional sharp outcries—are those of one of the world's great grain exchanges in operation. For this spacious room, with its tall windows and slightly old-fashioned atmosphere, is the world's largest cash grain market, its second largest futures market. No other spot in the Twin Cities is so intimately tied up with the history of the Northwest. For sixty-five years, the men in this room have been keeping their fingers on the pulse of the Northwest's vast agricultural production. They have seen our good years and our bad years come and go, our bumper crops and our failures.

In a few seconds from now—at 11:55 A.M., on the last day of 1946—they, and you, will hear the sound of a gong striking twice. That will be a signal—a signal that only five minutes of trading are left under the historic name of the "Minneapolis Chamber of Commerce."

When trading is resumed here tomorrow, it will be under the somewhat more descriptive title of "The Minneapolis Grain Exchange."

(SOUND OF TWO BELLS)

Five minutes left—five minutes in which to recall some of the history of this famous institution. The Minneapolis Chamber of Commerce was officially incorporated on October 19th, 1881—and, if we want to be specific about the time—it was at 9:30 A.M. What was its purpose? Well, in highly untechnical language, it was to provide a market-place for all of the grain produced in Montana, North and South Dakota, Minnesota, Northern Nebraska and Iowa. Similar grain exchanges had been established elsewhere in the country, all of them operating under the name "Board of Trade." But that name already had been pre-empted in Minneapolis—by an organization equivalent to the present Civic and Commerce Association. And so the newly organized exchange became the "Minneapolis Chamber of Commerce."

During recent years, it has been the source of endless confusion. Every day the Chamber gets hundreds of letters from persons wanting to know about the business and recreational opportunities in Minneapolis.

And every day—exactly at noon—a messenger has carried a bag full of this mail over to the Minneapolis Civic and Commerce Association, where these questions are answered. Altogether, it amounts to about a ton of mail a year. That, in itself, has been reason enough to change the name. But the Chamber also has wanted a name more perfectly descriptive of its highly important function.

We've already told you what the function is. Part of it is to provide a place for trading in grain futures—the colorful "pit." Now, for a description of the last few minutes of trading in the pit, under the old name, we'll turn you over to WCCO's Farm Service Director, Larry Haeg.

11:58.30 to 11:59.45
That was Larry Haeg, describing the last few moments of trading in the pit of the "Minneapolis Chamber of Commerce." To the uninitiated, trading in grain futures sounds like the utmost in confusion. The air of excitement and the constant shouting make it seem like a very feverish business.

Actually, of course, it is just a highly-developed business routine. Much of the noise is explained by the fact that federal laws—and the rules of this grain exchange—require all bids and offers to be made by "open outcry." There's a very good reason for it—to assure that all offers are open to all buyers, and that buyers have access to all supplies of grain. In other words, it prevents "deals on the side"—and it assures the farmer of the best possible price for his crop in an open market.

Far less spectacular to watch, but equally important, is the cash grain market at the other end of this huge room. Here, clustered around high tables, are buyers and sellers with their samples of grain. They are all experts —men who can determine the exact value of a sample by its feel, looks and smell.

Because color is such an important factor with barley, the barley samples are displayed in the north windows—where the steady, cold daylight shows up the slightest variation in color.

But now, everyone is waiting for 12:00 NOON and the sound of the final gong. When you hear it, you will know that a kind of milestone has been passed—that 65 years of operation under the historic name of the "Minneapolis Chamber of Commerce" are over. The name will pass to the Civic and Commerce Association, and this great market henceforth will be known as the "Minneapolis Grain Exchange."

Closing

(FOLLOWS SINGING OF "AULD LANG SYNE"—CUT WHERE NECESSARY)

With the singing of "Auld Lang Syne," we have come to the close of an important day in the history of the Minneapolis Grain Exchange. But this is one place where "Old Acquaintance" certainly will not be forgotten. Under its new name, the Grain Exchange will continue to function just as it has for the past 65 years—during all the time it has been known as the Minneapolis Chamber of Commerce.

*   *   *

Those years have left few marks on this high, paneled room—with its pit, its blackboards, its balconies for the markers, its telephones, and its almost endless rows of buyers' tables.

*   *   *

But in 65 years, many things have happened. There have been tremendously dramatic moments on the floor of this grain exchange—moments that have been vital to the whole Northwest.

*   *   *

There have been days when word flashed round the room of a destructive wave of rust in the Northwest wheat fields, or of an expected crop failure—with its tremendous implications for our economy.

* * *

There have been moments of wild celebration, such as the time when wheat first reached the wonderful price of a dollar a bushel. That happened before the turn of the century, and was a fulfillment of every farmer's dream. Maybe you remember those popular old cigars—"P-V Cigars"—whose slogan was "As Good As Dollar Wheat."

* * *

But dollar wheat no longer has the same significance. Because wheat climbed to 2 dollars before the first World War, and up to 3 dollars before it was over.

* * *

The earliest days of the Grain Exchange are identified with some of the most famous names in the history of the Twin Cities and the Northwest—with the Washburns, the Crosbys, the Pillsburys, the Bells. H. G. Harrison was its first president, G. D. Rogers its first secretary. And among the original incorporators were A. C. Rand, C. M. Loring (for whom Loring Park is named), and D. C. Bell.

* * *

The early years were ones of struggle. But the Grain Exchange grew and expanded right along with the Northwest which it served.

* * *

The time of greatest expansion came during the Nineties—when the growers of the Dakotas and the Red River Valley started raising Northern Hard Red Spring Wheat. That was the finest wheat in the world—and the demand for flour made from it was tremendous.

* * *

Rail lines pushed out to the west and north. With them went the grain elevator builders—ready to buy the first crops almost as soon as the farmer had turned over his sod. Then came mechanization and diversification of crops—oats, rye, barley and flaxseed.

* * *

As the crops became bigger and more varied, the role played by the Grain Exchange in marketing them became greater and greater.

* * *

It is because the Exchange has been so closely identified with the growth of our region, that WCCO has been pleased to bring you this broadcast today. We have heard the formal ceremony in which the Minneapolis Chamber of Commerce relinquished that name—to be known henceforth, and more accurately, as the Minneapolis Grain Exchange.

— o —

The term "special event" usually is taken to mean a remote broadcast—one emanating from a scene outside the studio. But hundreds of studio broadcasts each year may properly be described by the term—anniversary programs, dramatizations to signalize important occasions, forums to discuss current problems of consequence. One series of programs that occupied a third of a station's time for six weeks may properly be described as special event: KUOM-University of Minnesota met a critical polio epidemic in 1946 by putting on the air some hundreds of programs whose purpose was to keep children occupied and entertained during a long quarantine period in Minneapolis—and, when the epidemic closed the schools, to get school work started at home.

The networks are in better position to stage long-planned special events than are individual stations. They have to their credit such notable programs as Norman Corwin's "On a Note of Triumph," an hour-long V-E Day dramatization, which CBS had commissioned Corwin to write six months in advance; the NBC series of United Nations programs in 1946 and 1947; the superb on-the-spot broadcast by ABC's George Hicks off the Norman coast on D Day; the coverage by all nets of the atomic bomb trials at Bikini; hundreds more.

Another type of special event of interest primarily to the local station is the big spot news-break. A three-alarm fire is an obvious example; or a flood, or a railroad wreck (or, indeed, a local epidemic). Usually such events cannot be predicted—their coverage is a challenge to the newsroom's energy, inventiveness, and split-second mobility. Broadcasting them is usually a matter of on-the-spot reporting, with no preparation.

Special-event broadcasting, whatever its type, is sure to become an increasingly important technique in the local station's operation. As competition grows, the distinction it lends to a station's programming will more and more demand its practice. It is one of the best means of making events intelligible as well as colorful. Moreover, it is always "local live" broadcasting; in view of FCC emphasis on locally originated programs as part of a station's public service, it can hardly be ignored.

"Man-on-the-Street" Broadcasts

Most radio stations now and again put traveling mikes on the streets, or into crowds at county fairs and the like, for on-the-spot ad lib broadcasts. These may be put on the air live, or recorded for broadcast later. Devoted to offering comments of average citizens on current topics, they are of several types:

The broadcast whose purpose is to bring to listeners the flavor of a particular situation or event: The New Year's Eve throng in Times Square, the crowd at a movie star's funeral, picnickers at the annual festival of the Polish-American Society.

The broadcast whose purpose is to discover typical attitudes toward current news: The cost of living, the latest decision by the United Nations Assembly, salaries for high school teachers (or taxes to pay them). Similar to this type is the feature broadcast, taking its cue from the familiar newspaper Inquiring Reporter column: Do you believe wives should work? Where do you intend to vacation this year? Do you think firecrackers should be permitted on the Fourth of July?

The commercial broadcast—one selling soap, bread, or sealing wax—in which the announcer takes a mike, for instance, into a grocery store and works in questions about the sponsor's product along with those on the topic chosen for the day. (This type is not ordinarily a newsroom project.)

The prerequisites for such broadcasting are evident. There has to be a certain amount of advance preparation—script, questions, and so on. The man on the mike has to be alert, and skillful at ad libbing; he has to be thoroughly versed in his subject if the broadcast is to deal with a topic in the news. Most such broadcasts are essentially for entertainment, even though their ostensible purpose may be to get serious

---

During the war, man-on-the-street broadcasts were outlawed by the broadcasting industry at the request of the Office of Censorship. Obviously it would have been possible for an agent of the enemy, knowing that such-and-such a broadcast went on the air regularly, to insinuate himself into a position to be interviewed, and to inject prearranged signals or code remarks among his responses.

answers to serious questions; this means that humor is important.

The dangers inherent in any unrehearsed show bulk large in man-on-the-street programs. The individuals interviewed—almost always picked at random—may be tongue-tied, or they may be given to tittering or telling all about Uncle Henry's operation. They may be annoyed at being questioned, or overcome at the fact that their voices are going on the air. They are sometimes given to profanity, occasionally to obscenity. Quick control of what goes into the microphone is a necessity.

A common objection among discerning listeners to shows of this type is the bad taste by which some of them are characterized. Some broadcasters have attempted to achieve the effect of humor by putting their victims on the spot, sometimes by being thoroughly insulting. That most giggling respondents don't appear to object makes this practice nonetheless offensive.

A Miscellany of Special Events

Two explosive-laden vessels in the Texas City, Texas, harbor blew up, and carried a good deal of the city with them. Communications, too—telephone, telegraph, railroad, radio. WOAI-San Antonio, a 50,000-watt station with a big news operation, sent a man 200 miles by police squad car to Texas City; he relayed messages to WOAI by police short wave. Jerry Lee, special events director, flew over the area and broadcast descriptions (some of which NBC picked up). Other members of the news staff worked on San Antonio angles. . . . Other radio stations in southeast Texas and adjoining states performed similar jobs. KCRC-Enid, Oklahoma (1,000 watts) was credited by the *Enid Morning News* with "an outstanding example of unusual and timely public service in a time of great tragedy."

Radio's coverage of the disaster was not without criticism, however. Pat Flaherty, news editor of KPRC-Houston, made these comments to a radio news conference at the University of Denver a few months after the disaster (July, 1947):

The most glaring fault among the many radio news crews working from the disaster area was the tendency to sensationalize a story which spoke of tragedy and pity from all angles of its presentation. The situation called for

a straightforward presentation of the facts and it was no place for radio
to become "newspaper-minded" and blare out with sensational headlines. . . .

Press services carried stories which were very much off base, and there
were times when our direct broadcast from Texas City contradicted network
newsroom reports on the same story.

In an effort to maintain a steady straight "filler" broadcast, some stations
brought unqualified persons to the microphone for their reports on a dangerous and threatening situation. I actually saw and heard people on the
microphone who were there just because they were dirty and ragged. . . .
It is safer to talk with these people first—to find out what their story is before they are given the liberty of an open microphone. That all goes back to
the fundamental that the spoken word is the most powerful. Therefore, it
must be right.

WJR-Detroit (50,000 watts), tying in with WFBG-Altoona (250
watts), put on two special pick-ups from the scene of the wreck of
the Pennsylvania Railroad's Red Arrow, near Altoona. Local tie-up:
The Red Arrow is a crack Detroit-New York passenger train.

WCPO-Cincinnati (250 watts) sent a newsman, Paul Dixon, crawling through a tunnel with a microphone to pick up calls for help from
six men trapped in the wreckage of a building that had collapsed. For
thirty hours WCPO and WKRC-Cincinnati (5,000 watts) continued
on-the-spot broadcasts describing the rescue work.

KILO-Grand Forks, North Dakota (1,000 watts) put on a two-hour
show in 1946 to find homes for veterans. It offered one pair of nylons
for a room and two for an apartment, and ended the two hours (originally scheduled as a one-hour show) by housing 150 veterans.

Both stations and networks regarded the United Nations organization conference in San Francisco as a special event. Networks sent
whole squads of newsmen and technicians to cover it, after weeks of
preparation; individual stations sent commentators and reporters.
Incidentally, both networks and stations came in for severe, and
deserved, criticism for "Hollywoodizing" the conference—devoting
too much time to feature broadcasts by Hollywood glamour girls.

The 1945 airwaves were laden with special-event programs commemorating broadcasting's twenty-fifth anniversary. Many stations

put on their own shows to celebrate a quarter of a century of operation. Many stations have arranged special broadcasts in the interests of traffic safety, prevention of juvenile delinquency, the fight against race and religious prejudice, and other matters of public interest.

KSD-St. Louis (5,000 watts) sent its news and special events director, Frank Eschen, to Rome to originate programs in connection with the formal election of thirty-two cardinals at the Vatican. All four major networks carried Vatican programs.

WTMJ-Milwaukee (5,000 watts) converted its entire programming, when an eighteen-inch snow fell on the city, to broadcasts on the crisis. Its staff, snowbound at the station, broadcast nearly a thousand announcements in twelve hours: messages from stranded victims, direction of volunteer services, lists of food distribution centers, postponements of meetings and other events, emergency instructions in case of fire or accidents, and so on.

ABC broadcast a special program in July of 1947 to present the ceremonies at the opening of the long-sealed documents of Abraham Lincoln. An ABC commentator was assigned to describe the scene and introduce the speakers.

KLZ-Denver (5,000 watts) broadcast an eye-witness account of "falling stars" as the earth passed through the tail of a comet. The program, originating on the hilltop location of the station transmitter, offered a description by a station announcer and technical comments by an astronomer.

Allen Stout, of WROL-Knoxville (1,000 watts) won the annual medal for "outstanding achievement in radio reporting" offered by Sigma Delta Chi, professional journalism society, for his 1946 on-the-spot broadcast of a gun battle between ex-GIs and politicians during an election campaign in Athens, Tennessee. The citation said in part:

Because he had to whisper in order not to reveal his position to participants in the gun battle near him, his voice was not always intelligible above the gun fire, but he was able to impart to the listener enough of the excitement, the danger, and the ebb or flow of the battle to permit the listener to see, feel, and hear the battle as it progressed. The broadcast undoubtedly ranks above most of the attempts of the armed service and radio correspondents to broadcast on-the-scene events as they took place in World War II.

WJR-Detroit (50,000 watts) and WCAR-Pontiac (1,000 watts) had remote mikes ready to broadcast news of the settlement of the General Motors strike in 1946 as the Federal mediator announced it.

The news editor of KXOK-St. Louis (5,000 watts) relayed on-the-spot reports of a million-dollar fire from an automobile with radio-telephone equipment.

Perhaps no event in American history has received the thoughtful, dignified, and appropriate radio treatment accorded the death of Franklin D. Roosevelt. The President's death was not a special event in the usual sense—it was not a foreseen piece of news, and not one which demanded speed in its handling. Rather it was a portentous occurrence whose every facet was of vast interest and importance to the American people and the world. Radio interrupted its programs to bring the shocking news to listeners, and canceled hundreds of programs as the story developed. It brought eulogies of FDR, testimonials of a nation's grief, from every corner of the land. Networks and many stations canceled commercial messages during the three-day mourning period after April 12, 1945. Radio's public service in broadcasting the full story to the people won accolades from the press and from public figures everywhere.

10

News of Special Fields

Broadcasting Yearbook for 1948 devotes some twelve pages to names of news, sports, farm, and home economics directors of American radio stations. About two-thirds of the stations are shown by this directory to have personnel specifically assigned to one or more of these special programming fields. The listing is not complete, for not all stations provided information to the editors of the *Yearbook*. On the other hand, it may be misleading, because some stations list individuals who give only a few hours a week to the specialties—part-time workers, or workers whose major operations are in other activities.

Nevertheless, the list establishes a fact: Radio stations are aware of the need for specialized treatment of material in certain fields.

Newspaper men have been aware of it for some years. One of the most recent of the textbooks on newspaper reporting is devoted to this thesis—that jack-of-all-trades reporters, though certainly not passé (particularly in the smaller newspaper shops), are being replaced or supplemented by specially-qualified men and women who can give to the intricacies of special fields the understanding and technical knowledge without which much news can no longer be made intelligible. The larger newspapers today boast specialists in fields ranging from business, agriculture, social service, politics, and science to stamps, chess and enameling of the finger nails.

Radio newsroom specialization has not gone so far largely because of the natural limitations of the medium. Radio, in the American broadcasting pattern, is not primarily a news and information medium, but an entertainment medium. Radio does not carry nearly as many words each day in any of the special news fields as do the newspapers. Radio does not present detailed box scores, or complete market reports. It offers less commentary, fewer individual stories (especially when repeats are omitted from the count), and, on the whole, narrower news coverage than do the papers.

Radio, in short, does not and is not likely to go all the way with the newspapers in specialization. The limitation on size of radio news staffs, which is an affecting factor, has been discussed in Chapter 8.

All of this to the contrary notwithstanding, radio is slowly building up its corps of specialists.

Let's examine that *Broadcasting Yearbook* listing a little further. It shows that sports directors, in numbers, top the roll (fewer than a fifth of the stations fail to list sports men). News directors come next. Perhaps three-fifths of the stations have "home economics" directors; a few less have farm directors.

Impressive figures. But not to be taken at face value. A lot of the stations show one man in two "directorships"; several show one man in three. Many of the listings describe part-time—which is likely to mean casual—operations. In one North Dakota station the farm director not only handles broadcasts beamed at farm listeners, but also sells time to agricultural industries. Few stations have full-time sports editors; it is not unheard of that the "sports director" is an announcer who used to play right field for his junior high school team.

And it must be observed that few radio stations boast business, or religious, or science, or political specialists—to suggest only a few neglected areas.

What is the relationship of the specialist to the newsroom?

One of the four categories shown by *Broadcasting* specifically represents the newsroom.

The sports director in almost all cases works closely with the newsroom.

The farm director usually depends heavily on news services, local and wire.

The "home economics" or women's director all too frequently operates without reference to the newsroom. Her area is commonly limited to "home economics"—recipes, child care, beauty hints—without reference to news. More of this later.

Let's look in more detail at these and other fields in which radio has done most to meet specialized news problems.

Agricultural News

"The farm director's job—the one we thought of a few years ago as a part-time one for an announcer—now requires a full-time man and a secretary, and a part-time announcer who can cover while the farm director is on the road. An ideal set-up would call for a full-time reporter in the field, acting as a teammate of the men in the offices and newsroom."

That's Earl Williams, manager of KFAB-Omaha, talking before a Nebraska radio news clinic. (His full talk, an excellent one, is reported in *Radio Showmanship* for August, 1946.) Williams has just finished pointing out that handling farm news—if it is to grow to full stature, and to deliver full value to station and listener alike—is no sinecure. "It's a job for a man with a nose for news, the ability to write, and, most of all, the natural feeling for the farm angle, which comes from background and constant association with the people involved, from those in government down to the smallest farmer in the area."

Specialization means specialization. The farm editor needs to be a man who *knows* the farm. He's a reporter, to be sure—one who can gather and write news. But he's a reporter who knows the difference between a barrow and a boar . . . who won't talk about sowing corn . . . who can make the term "parity" meaningful. He's one who will know what is important to farmers and, as well, to nonfarmers dwelling in an agricultural community; he's one who can talk about trends as well as about spot news.

It's obvious that stations in agricultural sections are those most interested in farm news service. Yet stations in Washington, Boston, New York, Philadelphia, Pittsburgh maintain farm directors. The reason is that the news of agriculture (as Williams of KFAB makes clear) can be reported and interpreted not alone to farmers, but also to city dwellers. Not in the same way for both audiences—not even always using the same news. But always recognizing that agriculture is, after all, one of the nation's top industries.

All of which is to say, first, that direction of a radio farm news service is a demanding job for a competent, well-qualified man; second, that such a service may be offered effectively by any station, anywhere.

How does a station located, say, in a city of a quarter million population in a predominantly agricultural area go about installing a farm news service?

First, it selects that competent, well-qualified man to direct it.

Then it examines its broadcast day to decide when to put on its programs for the farmers, and when to offer its agricultural news beamed to urbanites. The answers to these questions have been established by many surveys. The best time to reach farmers and farm families is at noon—12:00 to 1:00. Next best: early morning, 6:00 to 7:30. Third: supper time and early evening (rural listening drops off sharply after 8:30 or 9:00 P.M.). For the urbanites: any time when they are accustomed to listening to news programs—breakfast time, noon, late afternoon or dinner hour, the mid-evening hours. For this audience the farm news is knit into regular news shows, not segregated into specialized shows.

Now the station looks over the *kinds* of agricultural material it can offer to farm listeners. This depends to some extent on the station's purpose: Is the farm service being instituted chiefly as an audience builder, for promotional purpose? Then it is likely to concentrate on entertainment—familiar music, quiz and comedy programs—and news. Is it intended to buttress the public service record? Informational, religious, educational programs—and news. Is it to extend the station's news service as such? News programs of wide variety are the obvious means of achieving the third purpose. And since they also serve for purposes one and two, as shown by many competent studies, they are pretty sure to form the farm director's first concern.

What kinds of news?

Straightforward News of Community Agricultural Activities This includes 4-H Club meetings, gatherings of farm associations, county fairs and the like, soil conservation meetings, machinery demonstrations, farm sales, visits of county agents and home demonstration agents, and so on. Such news can be gathered only by vigorous reporting; it comes from a thousand sources. The farm director may need to develop his own string of correspondents.

News of Governmental or Other Broad-Scale Activities of Special Farm Interest   Such news embraces the doings of the Department of

Agriculture and its many branches, Congressional and legislative measures affecting the farmer, and so on. This news is likely to come from the news wire; often the farm director uses it as a springboard from which to jump into carefully-planned localized stories. How will the new plans for agricultural subsidies affect the farmers of the station's primary area? What are local plans for the forthcoming visit of the Rural Electrification administrator?

Weather News as It Affects the Farmer The range covers heat and drouth, frost and blizzard, flood and storm. What protective measures are suggested against a predicted late-spring freeze? Should farmers be warned to shelter livestock against a blizzard?

News of Individual Farmers' Activities Here are included feature stories on the new kind of incubator Farmer Brown has developed, the success of Farmer Smith with crop rotation, the fact that Farmer Jones is sending six sons and daughters to college. Opportunities for such stories are legion. Their development depends only on the amount of imagination and legwork the farm editor exerts.

News of Advances and Changes in Agricultural Techniques This news deals with stories that come from the county agent, from the special features carried by the wire services, from state and Federal agricultural bulletins, from the agricultural colleges and experiment stations (which furnish abundant news services, including radio scripts), from individual farmers.

News of the Economics of Agriculture Such information comes from many of the sources already mentioned, from local bankers, from farmers and farm marketing associations—stories of farm income, the

---

Listen to Larry Haeg, farm director of WCCO-Twin Cities and first president of the National Association of Radio Farm Directors:

"A distinction must be made, sharply and clearly, between farm NEWS which is urban as well as rural in interest, and farm INFORMATION—markets, weather news expanded for the farmer, technical stories, and the like. Every news show put on by a station in an agricultural area must carry current farm news; but only the shows directed specifically to farm homes should carry farm information.

"And of course it isn't enough for a station to carry just *any* farm news or information. I believe that every local station must do its own farm service job. There's no cotton in Minnesota!"

value of the farmer's dollar, the importance of adequate farm management practices.

Market and Crop Reports   This news is often carried in bulletin
form, as it comes from the wire services or from local agricultural
industries and organizations.

These categories, though they make no attempt to include all
possible varieties of agricultural news, suggest the wide possibilities
open to radio farm service; and they show why Earl Williams told his
audience that a farm director "must be willing to devote a tremendous
amount of time to the job, which will range from actual field work to
outside reading, from poring over the wire services to expanding wire
service stories into yarns of rare importance to the farm listener."

What about farm news for the city, or the general, listener?

It's similar news. In some newsrooms the farm editor, having completed his early morning farm news show beamed squarely at rural
areas, rewrites a selection of his stories for inclusion in the general
news show coming perhaps an hour later. A selection because the
general listener doesn't need—and won't take—as much detail as will
the farmer. And he isn't concerned in the technical aspects of farm
news that are of prime importance on the earlier show.

What about writing style in the two kinds of programs?

Again, within limits, it's the same. It's true that terminology may

---

The United States Department of Agriculture has issued an invaluable
little handbook—*Radio Handbook for Extension Workers*—which, though
it is intended for men and women seeking radio time, offers much that is
useful to the farm director and more to the small newsroom without a full-
time farm man. It is described as Miscellaneous Publication 592. Another
useful USDA publication, this one issued by the Bureau of Agricultural
Economics, is *Attitudes of Rural People Toward Radio Service* (January,
1946).

Also of value to the farm news broadcaster:

The People Look at Radio (cited in Chapter 2)

"Radio Comes to the Farmer" by William S. Robinson (Chapter VI in
  Radio Research, 1941, cited in Chapter 2)

Two articles in the August, 1942, issue of *Radio Showmanship*: "How to
  Reap Farm Dollars" by Harry Truax and "Farmer in the Dell" by Tod
  Williams.

be—indeed, sometimes has to be—somewhat more technical on the farm show. But ideal treatment means that both shows should be entirely understandable to any listener. A lot of farmers and farm families are tuned in on the general news shows. And at least a few city dwellers are listening to farm news programs. Robert White, ABC's agricultural director, recognizes this when he says that "what interests the farmer will interest the city man if it is properly presented."

The famous NBC farm show, "The Farm and Home Hour," and its ABC counterpart, "The American Farmer," both expect a minority of urban listeners, and they're edited with these listeners in mind.

It should be remembered that the farm news show is not limited to news of pigs, wheat, and the cost of tractors. Farm families are not insulated from contact with "the outside"; they want news of the world as well as specialized news. Herb Plambeck, farm director of WHO-Des Moines, always heeds this fact. During the war, his early morning farm program gave complete war coverage—the war news rewritten "not in the farm vernacular, but with a basic farm concept." All of Plambeck's shows are rewrite jobs—everything tailored tight to his purpose.

Ken Hutcheson, farm director of KGA-Spokane, is another of the many farm editors who tailor shows to fit. Hutcheson writes his daily "Farm News Reporter," 12:15 to 12:30 P.M., in "everyday, colloquialized American"—not in farm jargon, but in simple conversational form as understandable in the city restaurant as in the farm kitchen.

All of the special devices used by the newsroom in its general shows are of use to the farm editor. KLZ-Denver sends its Lowell Watts— KLZ calls him "farm consultant"—around Colorado with a recorder

---

KALE-Portland, Oregon, has developed two "farm emergency" services: The fire service and the farm labor service. Its agricultural area is one in which there are sometimes emergency demands for special types of farm labor, such as fruit-pickers; when such emergencies develop, KALE puts on repeated broadcasts to recruit labor and to direct it to the scenes where it's needed. As for fire service: "If people will provide authentic information on fires (farm or forest) in the Northwest," says Burton Hutton, head of the farm service department, "we will interrupt any program to call help instantly."

to talk to farmers, record interviews, and the like. Watts (who used to be a leader in 4-H Club work and studied agriculture at Colorado A. & M.) uses his gleanings on a special program, "The Farm Reporter," and on other news shows. Many stations are finding the recorder of special value in farm news work because it is not easy to bring farmers in to the studio.

KGLO-Mason City, Iowa, went the recorder one better in 1945 by sending a mobile broadcasting unit to every fair in twenty-four counties in its area.

Farm news programs may also use all of the program-patterns: straight news, interviews, dramatizations, special events of all kinds. Many farm shows originate at county and state fairs, livestock shows, farmers' meetings, and on agricultural campuses. Bill MacDonald, farm director of KFAB-Omaha, has covered for his station farm events in Columbus, Ohio, and Denver, and many points between.

Sports News

Sports fans like their news hot. They like it partisan. And they like plenty of it.

Radio has not been slow to take advantage of America's interest in sports—witness the fact that stations have more "experts" in sports than in any other field. Few stations are without their daily sports shows—everything from straightforward sports news roundups to features, interviews, on-the-spot coverage, and so on. Some stations, indeed, have made their sports service their prime promotional feature—KRSC-Seattle, for instance, known as a "sports station" because it plays up all sports, especially Seattle high school athletics; or WRRN-Warren, Ohio, with its daily fifteen-minute local sportscast and its on-the-spot coverage of Warren athletic events.

The straight news sports show follows a fairly standard pattern. It gives results of games, "dope stories" on forthcoming events, informative bits about athletes and coaches. The most common sports show is a five-minute roundup about 10 in the evening, scheduled across the board; it gives the day's baseball, football, basketball, and other scores, and perhaps saves thirty seconds or so—if there aren't too many scores —to tell fans that another big leaguer has been sold to the Boston

Braves. Many stations, during the baseball season, add another five-minute show in the late afternoon. Others save a few minutes at the end of regular news shows to cut in the baseball scores.

Sports news is usually handled by one man from start to finish—he gathers the news, gets it ready for broadcast, and puts it on the air. His sources: The wire services (including an A. T. & T. sports ticker in some stations) for major scores such as league baseball, college and professional football, most other college sports, hockey, and the like; local or regional sources for high school and other amateur sports which the wire services ordinarily are not equipped to handle. Building up these local sources is one of the prime jobs for the sports editor. Usually it isn't difficult—coaches, managers, or players are only too glad to telephone a station immediately after the last play and report the major facts. Sports directors build up lists of such sources by personal contact, or by the easy expedient of sending cards to all schools and other sports organizations in their areas. At the height of the basketball season a station's telephone switchboard is, on Friday nights, a madhouse of incoming calls, often with a corps of extra operators on duty.

Interviews with sports authorities or round-table discussions of current sports are common features in most stations' sportscast schedules. In the spirit of sports, such shows are most effective when they're breezy and informal. The sports editor interviewing the local coach is talking to a man he knows well, and it's more natural for the two of them to chat ad-lib, using first names or nicknames for each other, than to put on a formal prepared interview. The same thing is true of

---

Most sportscasters putting the scores-roundup kind of show on the air work not from a carefully-prepared script but from a mass of notes—strips of copy torn from the printers, scribbled messages from the telephone operators, and so on. Since one of the virtues of such shows is that their news is hot, sports editors rarely have time to work them into finished scripts. There's a lot of ad libbing in such shows: "The Red Birds down at Midvale won another basketball game tonight—their ninth in a row. They took Centerport, 51 to 39. The Midvale lightweights won from Centerport, too —squeaked out a 33 to 31 victory."

This method obviously won't work if the sports announcer isn't the sports editor—if he hasn't gathered and arranged his material himself.

the fourway discussion after a football game among the sports editor, the two coaches, and a visiting expert who saw the game.

"Dope stories"—predictions, analyses, commentaries—are also part of a sound radio sports schedule. But they're not to be indulged in unless the sports man is really a sports authority. It's dangerous business to let the high school senior or the part-time announcer go out on limbs —too often he gets the saw on the wrong side.

As in other kinds of radio news operations, the recorder is a useful instrument. It can bring statements by sports figures, perhaps a brief view of the players' bench, into shows. One of its best uses is to take the listener into the locker room after a game—a place he can't penetrate on his own.

Certainly the most spectacular kind of sportscasting is the on-the-spot coverage of a game itself. Like special events broadcasting of any kind, covering a game requires a lot of preparation, as well as a lot of knowledge, a gift for grasping the color and drama of an event, and high enthusiasm for what the boys are doing on the gridiron or the diamond.

The station staff and the sportscaster get busy days before the event— a football game, say. Likely the stadium is provided with broadcasting booth and remote pickups. Most such broadcasts require several microphone installations—two in the booth, one or more on the field.

The sportscaster equips himself with a sheaf of prepared material: Opening and closing announcements, histories of the teams and their current performances, elaborate data on every player, color and historical bits for fill-in purposes, credits, announcements, and so on. He has to train a "spotter" for each team—a man whose duties are to inform him who is carrying the ball, who makes the block, who the tackle. He needs a statistician to provide between-the-halves summary

---

"He Talks a Wonderful Touchdown" by Pete Martin in the *Saturday Evening Post* of October 12, 1946, gives an excellent picture of the trials and tribulations of a sportscaster. It tells how Byrum Saam, who puts 226 words a minute into the microphone during more than twenty football games a season—as well as during scores of other sports events through the remainder of the year—got that way. It's required reading for anybody interested in the art.

of downs, yardage, penalties. Perhaps he arranges one or two interviews to put on in the intermission. Likely he has a man to take over the between-the-halves commentary—and this man, in turn, must prepare himself with data on the band's gyrations on the field and other half-time ceremonies.

Finally, there are sports-feature shows. Many—perhaps most—such shows are based on the five- or fifteen-minute features provided by the AP, UP, or TP wire services. Several of these come over the wire each day, along with a number of weekly features. They have the disadvantage that they are almost never local, and not susceptible to local tie-ins. Some stations supplement them or straight sportscasts with local features—personality and success stories about local athletes, or, as at WMAQ-Chicago, interviews with local or visiting sports celebrities. (But the WMAQ pattern, easy to follow because of the wealth of celebrities always available, would be less effective in Midvale.)

A shortcoming of radio sports news is that (like newspaper sports news) it has become stereotyped—little inventiveness has appeared in sportscasting since its first days. Another, and more serious, defect is that many radio sports editors use neither their legs nor the telephone enough. Though there are distinguished exceptions, many titular sports directors let the wire services and mere box-score reporting do their jobs for them. They fail to vitalize their shows with thorough and imaginative reporting—and this in a field that yields hundreds of excellent stories to anybody who digs for them. Unquestionably some of the onus for this fact lies at the stations' doors—if the "sports director" is a mere teletype-tearing announcer, he won't be much of a news editor or

---

What about news of racing?

Some stations prohibit it as a matter of policy, just as do some newspapers. Others go all out, broadcasting on-the-spot descriptions from the track as well as elaborate stories on betting odds, racing personalities, and the like.

In 1947 the FCC was asked to decide whether racing news may not be illegal because bookmakers (illegal in all states but Nevada) use such broadcasts in their business. The 1948 decision: Such broadcasts are not illegal, since they are given in the ordinary course of news presentation, come from regular news services, do not go into undue detail, and are put on the air ten or fifteen minutes after the races are run.

reporter. And he certainly won't be up to "interpretative" news handling—a type of responsibility that finds its place in sports news as in
any other news field.

Women's News

Among radio's many hundreds of women's shows, few have been
news programs.

Critics of American broadcasting have been concerned because,
they say, the soap opera has been radio's prime contribution to the
happiness and advancement of the nation's womanhood. There have
been cooking and recipe programs, beauty hints, talks on child training
and care of the home, health programs (must interest in health be a
feminine monopoly?), educational and other shows—their subject
matter the kind you find on the women's pages of the newspapers.
Many of these have been excellent. But—to repeat—few of them have
been news shows.

Unquestionably this is partly due to the fact that there is no large
area of spot news development that is solely of interest to women.
Most of the news that appeals to women also appeals to their husbands
and brothers. Consequently any attempt to reach women with news of
interest to them alone is stymied at the start.

It is generally held—and supported by reader-interest surveys—that
personal news, society news, gossip are read more avidly by women than
by men. These are news categories in which radio has, until lately,
been little interested. Broadcasting has small place for gossip news as
such, thanks to the fact that most broadcasters consider this kind of
thing in bad taste; and small place for "society news" because the traditional interpretation of this news field restricts its subject matter to a
sharply limited audience. And personal news—the news of the minor
activities of average citizens—has been developed and used by few stations (Chapter 8, however, suggests that it is growing in importance in
the local news picture).

A type of women's program masked as news is the women's feature
show—the show built out of the women's feature material provided by
the wire services, or of like material. Once in a while such features are
genuinely newsy—when they develop meaningful discussions of new
theories of child care, for instance, or when they interpret current news

of the food markets (KLZ-Denver uses wire-recorded interviews with wholesale produce dealers during a regular newscast every Friday morning). More commonly they are devoted to personalities, to human interest tales—stories that have little real news in them.

There have been, also, interview and discussion programs carrying the "for women" catch line. Again, these have been more frequently feature than news shows.

Radio will undoubtedly provide special news service for women as newsrooms grow and as their directors provide more news-imagination. But they are not likely to carry this kind of news activity as far as they go in special fields such as farm or sports news.

Political News

News of the stratagems and tactics of American politics has not been developed as a separate news field. Political news is general news, and properly should be treated as such—given its place in the general news shows.

One influence that leads broadcasters to eye political news askance is the principle that radio must maintain an Olympian impartiality. If radio is not to take sides—since it must offer equal time and position to rival political views and candidates, and may be called to answer for failure to do so—it has felt that it must walk with extreme care at all times. In some cases caution has been translated into emptiness.

Radio's record in coverage of political news, nevertheless, is a good one. Though individual stations have developed few political specialists, they have covered most political events with straight news stories, they have provided plentiful network and some local commentary and analysis, and they have given excellent service on election returns.

WMAQ-Chicago met the problem of political impartiality in the 1946 elections (as described by News Director William Ray):

"On each 15-minute program during the campaign, we departmentalized the political news, lumping all Republican news and political statements together and making sure that an equal amount of copy on the Democratic side was used on each broadcast. We did not accept party handouts, but wrote our copy from candidates' statements and speeches. If we used ten lines of Democratic copy, we followed with ten lines of Republican. We

(*continued on next page*)

Radio reporters cover Congress and the legislatures—governmental bodies with sharp political implications. They often make national or local political conventions the occasions for special-events coverage.

Election returns provide a very special headache for radio newsrooms. The newsroom staff is never large enough to cover all the precincts to the fullest (indeed, the newspaper staff, much larger than its radio competitor, has to be augmented to do it). A common expedient to remedy this deficiency is a cooperative arrangement with the local newspaper—a deal whereby the newspaper is paid for service, or given air mention in return for its help. Newspapers were at one time generally chary of such an arrangement (see Chapter 1). But they have learned that broadcasts of election returns stimulate newspaper sales—the man who heard election returns in general terms last night wants them specifically, in black and white, this morning.

Most radio schedules—network or local—are shelved for election return service. Radio knows that its listeners are more eager on election nights for the news of the vote than for any of the regular shows, and it is more than ready to cancel programs—especially since this kind of service builds up the public service record.

News in Other Special Fields

If the newsrooms have done little to develop specialized services in the fields of politics and women's interests, they have done less in other fields. Further discussion is as much about what might be done as about what has been done.

---

did not attempt so strict a balancing of copy in programs shorter than 15 minutes."

WMAQ introduced such political material with a statement like this: "Now, here's the political news. In accordance with the policy of this station, equal representation is given each side."

In time and space, this is "fair" treatment. But what if the Democratic candidate made a hell-raising speech charging the Republican candidate with every crime in the book, and the Republican remained a clam?

In Texas in 1946, seventy newspapers and thirty radio stations banded together and spent $10,000 to cover election returns in the nation's largest state.

Take business news for example. Here is an area of news of the utmost importance—yet an area in which radio has done almost nothing in intensive or specialized treatment. Some stations—not all—use the stock market briefs carried by the wire services. Some put on the air the daily market or business features also provided by the radio wire. Many do good jobs in the development of spot business stories: the local angle on the story from Washington that real estate values are declining; or what local retailers have to say about a consumers' strike against rising butter prices.

But few stations put regular, carefully-planned, expert business news shows on the air.

One reason, of course, is the stereotype that business news is dull—that it is technical, limited in interest, hard to understand. This is a lame excuse. Business news is of interest and significance to everybody. It is available in abundance. The newspapers have shown that it can be presented simply and comprehensibly, and that there are business features inside every door in a downtown office building.

Radio newsrooms are missing an obvious bet when they fail to build regular daily business programs—not dry-as-dust listings of Wall Street transactions, but colorful and meaningful stories of what is going on in the local business community. What radio listener, man or woman, WCTU-er or alcoholic, would not listen with interest to a program telling what has happened to liquor sales as a result of the state tax imposed a couple of months ago? Or to one on the effect on local payrolls of the shortage in basic materials plaguing an important local industry? How about a success story on the local boy who is just opening the fifth in a prosperous chain of cut-rate drug stores? Is there any chance that the lack of millwork holding up new housing will be relieved? Should the Chamber of Commerce try to do something about diversifying the city's industry? And so on.

The opportunities slap the radio reporter in the face—if he is aggressive and imaginative, and if he's sensitive enough to the fundamentals of business to feel the slaps, and energetic enough to dig ably for their meaning. He doesn't need to be a Ph. D. in economics, but he shouldn't be the kind of cloistered intellectual who thinks business operations begin and end with the law of supply and demand.

Religious news is another neglected field. In this area, again, there are some effective attempts at coverage—"Tomorrow in Midvale Churches" is a Saturday show to be found here and there; Easter and Christmas church news sometimes gets adequate treatment. Most stations make feeble gestures by broadcasting Sunday services, network or local; these are not strictly news, and their use is usually perfunctory. Even the handful of stations operated by religious organizations and denominational colleges do little to make religious news as virile and meaningful as it ought to be.

There are few religious news editors in radio; and genuine effort and news-imagination devoted to religious activities—a field high in latent audience-interest—are notable only by their absence. Church conventions, Sunday school picnics, new pastorates, retirements, campaigns to raise funds for new churches, drives to combat juvenile misbehavior —these get passing notice. But the effort to develop significant "enterprise" stories, to cover adequately the religious holidays of the Jewish and other numerically smaller faiths, to provide illuminating interpretation of religious movements and trends, is lacking. This may be due in part to fear of showing partiality. It is an unnecessary fear. News is news, trends are trends; they can be handled fairly, revealingly, and interestingly. And there are millions of listeners to whom religious activity is a major passion.

What about news for children? Not news *of* children, but news *for* children? Is this a field for development? Can children be interested in news? Will the standard news program serve their needs? At what age do children develop interest in news?

Lazarsfeld and Stanton ("Radio and the Press Among Young People" by Frederick J. Meine, in *Radio Research, 1941*) have shown that radio listening is high among children from thirteen to eighteen; and, more significantly, that radio is the preferred news medium among them, especially the younger ones. They also show that, as children grow older, the extent of their radio news listening declines—they tend to turn to other news media.

Sound treatment of the problems and possibilities of radio news of religious activities appears in *Religious Radio*, a book by Everett C. Parker, Elinor Inman, and Ross Snyder (Harper, 1948).

The question arises, then: Should not radio newsrooms, in their own interest, make special effort to hold on to this audience that falls into their laps?

A few efforts at presenting news for children have been made—mostly by educational stations in the universities or public school systems. Here the purpose has been essentially to inform young listeners, to clarify the obscurities of the news for them, to cement and enlarge their basic news interest. That is to say, it has been an educational purpose rather than the commercial goal of building young audiences and holding them as they grow older. There appears to be no reason why commercial stations should not aim at, and achieve, both purposes.

Commercial stations might consider, too, the fact that the development of children's news programs—perhaps in five- or ten-minute spots —would be one way to meet the widespread criticism of cliff-hangers and thriller shows as radio's prime offering for younger listeners. Such shows, larded with human interest and audience-participation, with humor and perhaps with appropriate recordings, can certainly be made effective. They would never have quite the youngster-appeal of Jack Armstrong. But they could be built into attractive offerings, and they would serve excellently, for the station giving its news service big play,

---

An educational station which has for some years successfully broadcast a children's news show is KUOM, the University of Minnesota station in the Twin Cities. The show—fifteen minutes once a week—is part of KUOM's School of the Air schedule. The latest pattern for this show is: Four or five questions on important state, national, and international news, each followed by a fifteen-second pause during which children in school rooms answer orally or in writing; about ten minutes of elaboration on *one* of the topics suggested in the questions; finally, a record from one of the "Songs of Friendship" albums, selected to tie in with the major topic. Young listeners to the show suggested two changes: a minute or so of the week's sports news, and a brief quiz at the end of the major topic discussion.

Before arriving at this pattern, KUOM experimented with a standard newscast offering a fairly broad selection from major news stories of the week. The pattern was finally narrowed to the one major story, presented with background and explanation. The script writer says: "The show is not 'written down'; it is written simply, with unusual words eliminated, or explained by specific illustration. I use all the color I can, and as much humor as can legitimately be worked in. I make the script chatty and informal."

to establish early the habit of turning to it for news.

There are other areas of specialized news largely neglected to date but susceptible of development. Educational news is one such area. News of racial and religious minorities is another. Entertainment news —theater and movies, music, recreation of all kinds—suggests possibilities. And then there is cultural news, scientific news, social service news, veterans' news—the list can be refined indefinitely. Few of these areas deserve elaborate attention. All of them may be fields worth occasional specialized broadcasts.

11
Making the News Meaningful

The State Department's Board of Consultants on Atomic Energy issues a report proposing a "safe" method of control of the power of the atom.

Radio and the newspapers report the facts. They tell the public time and place of the report, personnel of the Board; they condense the proposals into language as concise and simple as they can manage. They report that "dangerous" aspects of atomic energy would be exclusively under the control of an international authority; that fissionable materials would be issued in "denatured" form for development of "non-dangerous" uses by individual nations and their citizens; and so on. They do a competent, thorough job of reporting what the recommendations say.

Have they finished their task?

Clearly they have not. For however sharply and precisely they tell *what has happened*, they have not helped their publics to an understanding of the event unless they find ways of telling *what it means*, what may be its impact on the life of a troubled world.

The atomic control story is a dramatic example of the need for more than mere factual reporting. But it is not in essence different from thousands of other stories. It is, rather, typical of thousands.

Newsmen of the last two decades have become deeply aware that the news methods of a simpler world will not meet the necessities of complex modern society. It is not enough merely to give listeners and readers the factual picture of the day's events, however complete and accurate it may be. The mass public is a lay public. It is inexpert in chemistry and physics, economics, politics, medicine, social welfare, psychology. It cannot understand the interrelations and impingements —*the meaning*—of news without more help than mere information gives it.

And so the newsmen have acknowledged that they must give the public material to help it understand as well as to help it know. When

301

workers in the gigantic steel industry strike, the public must not only be told when, where, why, how many, and the other basic facts; it must also be given a view of the effect of such a strike on other industries, a background to reveal the underlying causes, an insight into relationships with other current events and with the daily life of the common man. When a Central American republic overturns another government, the public must be offered historical and political and geographical background that will clarify the situation. When medical scientists produce a fantastic new drug under which infections dissolve, the layman has to be told how widely it can be used, how it will be made available, how its advent will affect medical practice.

Newspapers have developed a number of methods of meeting this new demand. Editorials have for many years been partly devoted to explanation, but they haven't been enough. Columnists have since 1930 become a standard phenomenon in daily papers, their function largely to explain and interpret the day's events. Supplement of straight news by background material has become common—Herbert Brucker's *The Changing American Newspaper* (Columbia University Press, 1937) and Sidney Kobre's *Backgrounding the News* (Twentieth Century Press, 1937) are among the soundest discussions of what the press can do in this direction.

The growth of *Time* and *Newsweek* stems in part from the need for backgrounding. Other magazines—*Nation* and *New Republic, Atlantic* and *Harper's, Free World* and *Christian Century*, a score of others—have lent their energies to meet the need.

Radio, of course, has envisioned the problem. The radio commentator is one of broadcasting's answers. Programs frankly called "Background of the News" are another. Inclusion of explanatory material in straight news shows is a third. Programs such as "Chicago Round

---

John Bartlow Martin, in the August, 1946, *Harper's*, quotes a typical whitecollar worker: "There are so many things in the background you don't know who to believe. Every newscaster that comes on says the UN did this, it did that, 'til it don't mean a damn thing and you shut it off. I get a bellyful. That may not be the right thing to do but I don't know what to do about it."

Table" and "America's Town Meeting of the Air" spring from the same impulse.

Most critics of radio news think, however, that radio has by no means done all it might. The commentator has done a part of the job; news dramatizations in some cases are helpful. But insertion of background in the ordinary news show is still rare enough that its absence gives point to the criticism.

Backgrounding the Straight News Show

Since there is never enough time on any news show for all the news its editor would like to include, the space available for explanatory material is limited. Every paragraph of background cuts out a paragraph of news. That underlines one of the problems in backgrounding—the need for simplicity and concision. If the background can be presented in one sentence, good.

And since the time for editing the show is also limited, an editor can devote to digging for background only a few minutes out of the two hours he ordinarily spends getting his copy ready—another reason that keeps the backgrounding brief.

A third reason is that the listener, though he may be subconsciously

---

Before World War II Elmer Davis's five minute evening news summary on CBS was one of the most highly-respected and most widely-heard newscasts. He gave it up to become director of OWI. The war over, he returned to broadcasting as a commentator on ABC. On December 3, 1945, he wrote these views of the meaning of the commentator's task:

"There never was a time when dependable analysis of the news, whether on the air or in print, was more important than today. . . . There are half a dozen lines of force in the world, and it is not yet by any means clear where some of them lead. The news is complex and confusing, and on the surface less interesting than the news of the war years; but it is just as important, and in the long run may be just as dangerous. How dangerous it will be, what will be the ultimate direction of some of the lines of force, what solutions may be found for our present problems—all that will depend in a large degree on what the American people decide to do about it; and the wisdom of their decision will depend on how well they understand what is going on. To analyze and explain that news to the utmost of his ability imposes a heavy responsibility on any commentator for the newspapers or the radio."

appreciative of background, tunes his news show in primarily to hear the latest developments on current stories.

To save time both in preparation and on the air, then, the editor needs a number of shortcutting aids.

The first of these is his own qualification for the job. This means that above all he has to be a thoroughly competent newsman. He has to be able instantly to evaluate the news as it comes to him, to decide whether it needs explanatory material to show its meaning or its relationship to other news. Ideally he will be able to supply the backgrounding for a good many stories without leaving his typewriter. In short, he must be a man with sound background himself—the kind of man suggested by the "Standards for Education for Radio Journalism" outlined by the Council on Radio Journalism (see Appendix B).

But no man can background every story that needs it merely by drawing on his own knowledge.

So the well-equipped newsroom supplies him with sturdy crutches. Many of these are suggested in Chapter 4—reference books, files of current newspapers, news magazines, and specialized periodicals, atlases, and the like. There should be also a "morgue," a carefully-built file of clippings, "obits," other material saved against just this need. Important in such a file will be background material furnished by the radio news wires—geographical and personality features, roundups of historical data, Washington columns, commentaries.

The editor writing his show from a newspaper wire will often find in the copy with which he works the background he needs. Newspaper stories, written more fully than those for radio, often contain explanatory material omitted from radio stories in the interest of brevity. The editor can often extract from such copy enough data to fill in the gap that mere factual presentation of the hot angle of the news might leave.

In short, the problem of material is not difficult when the radio newsroom has been properly set up—when it has competent newsmen and an adequate shelf of reference works.

Of course no such shelf, and no newsman's personal reservoir, will meet every situation. Occasions arise when the editor has to get on the telephone—call a local businessman, a chemist at the local college, a doctor, a city official. When he sees such a need arising in advance—

he'll see it often if he's on top of his job—he will make time to go out and interview some such expert, perhaps using a wire recorder, to fill out his program.

Writing background material offers no special problem. All the principles recited earlier in this book for simple, concise, conversational manner apply, just as they do to straight news presentation. Look at some examples.

A story comes over the wire—let us suppose—to the effect that Marshall Field has decided to establish a daily newspaper in San Francisco. The story:

> San Francisco is to have another daily newspaper. It will be called the *San Francisco Sun*, and its first issue will appear on July 1. Marshall Field, the Chicago multi-millionaire, is putting up the money.

The editor knows that most listeners, if they think anything about Marshall Field, think of a department store. He pulls some facts out of his head and writes:

> This will be Field's third venture in daily newspaper publishing. He established the *Chicago Sun* just before Pearl Harbor . . . and bought the New York "picture magazine" called *PM* just a month later. He has since sold *PM* . . . it's known as the *New York Star* . . . and combined the *Sun* with the *Chicago Times* . . . He's known as a political liberal.

Another story says that:

> From United Nations headquarters comes word that Belgium wants to put a territory in East Africa under UN trusteeship. The territory is called Ruanda Urundi. The Belgians have held it as a mandate since the Germans lost it at the end of World War I.

Here the editor is in luck. The name Ruanda Urundi rings a bell in his memory, and he digs into the morgue to find a UP radio wire feature, "Places in the News," moved a day or so earlier. From this five-minute feature he condenses an add to the original story:

> Ruanda Urundi is famous chiefly for having both the tallest and the shortest people in the world. It's pretty primitive—the Belgians have allowed its four million natives to govern themselves. The natives are grain and cattle growers—but the Belgians have successfully introduced coffee raising. And they have set up an enormous game reserve to keep the big game alive.

To a story reporting that a city in another section of the country has adopted the city manager form of government, the editor adds a sentence:

Three cities in this area—Midland and Central City in Pennsylvania, and Centerville in Ohio—will vote on the same proposal later this month.

A telephone call to the governor's office follows receipt of a story on Federal aid to would-be housebuilders. As a result of information the call develops, the editor completely rewrites the story, weaving the background material through the original rather than tacking it on at the end:

Congress plans to make liberal loans available to American home-builders. But a string attached to the plan will probably prevent citizens of this state from taking advantage of it.

Governor Blinkerton said today that the state doesn't have the necessary legislation to take part in the plan. And he says he has no intention of calling a special session of the legislature.

The Federal plan calls for loans from the national treasury for the actual home building. But it asks that state or municipality lend the money to purchase lots.

That's where, according to Blinkerton, this state can't go along. The governor says he doesn't think the Federal plan is sound—because, he goes on . . . .

In another case, the editor may put the additional explanatory material first, before giving the late news:

It looks as though Midland is going to go through another summer without a city swimming pool.

You'll remember that in four of the last five years groups of Midland residents have tried to get the city council to build a pool. Each time they've failed—due to lack of money, lack of agreement on a site, and other obstacles.

For the last few weeks it has seemed that this might be the year. The Midland Rotary Club had agreed to raise the money by popular subscription. And the Midland Golf Club had talked of deeding to the city three acres for a swimming pool and park.

But today the club voted against releasing the land—it's needed for expansion of the golf links. And the Rotary Club thereupon decided against a money-raising campaign. As President Wilmer Jones explained, "Money without a place to use it wouldn't do anybody any good."

So Midland's swimmers are high and very dry for another year.

Other methods of providing background for news presentation are described elsewhere—news dramatization, which is a most effective method of clarifying involved aspects of news situations; various multi-voice techniques, of which "Colorado Speaks," the KLZ-Denver show described in Chapter 7, is one (similar to this program is "Radio Edition of the Weekly Press," on which WHCU-Ithaca, New York, broadcasts news and comment from weekly papers in its area); the use of recordings with fact and comment from authorities; and so on.

Still another device is the show devoted entirely to backgrounding. Such shows, commonly under titles like "Behind the Headlines" or "Background of the News," are usually fifteen-minute programs; they are *not* commentaries, but are attempts to fill in the gaps left in the average listener's comprehension by mere factual recitations. Obviously they must hang directly on current news pegs. But they do no more than summarize the news pegs; they devote their time to what underlies the news.

Some such shows—important to a station because they build up its public service record—are handled in a pretty shoddy manner. One station each afternoon reads into its microphone articles from the *Nation*, the *New York Times*, and other sober periodicals as its contribution to understandability. The material is often excellent. The manner is not often good radio. Such material is likely to come out of the receiving set pretty formidable and stuffy.

Properly handled, each such show must be a rewrite job, just as newspaper news must be rewritten for the ear. There are no new rules—all the familiar ones apply. Aside from the problem of radio style, the important aspects are that the material these shows present be competent and authoritative; that it be nonpartisan, selected so as to offer conflicting views or explain contradictory influences on the news they discuss; and that the editor or writer who gets them up be himself a competent newsman, one well enough informed so that he can do an adequate job of selecting, compressing, evaluating, and interrelating his material.

What Is "Commentary"?

Commentary is something else again.

Commentary, in radio news usage, is generally taken to be explanation of a news event in the light of the speaker's personal knowledge *and judgment*. Its essential difference from backgrounding lies in this subjective element. Backgrounding, as has been made clear, is the presentation of factual material, offered without comment to build a framework into which the listener may fit the day's events. Commentary, seeking also to build a framework for understanding, is the expression of judgment. It is qualitative. The backgrounder tells his audience, after Colonel Lindbergh has made a speech on American foreign affairs and the speech has been reported, that Lindbergh was an avowed isolationist before World War II, that he withdrew from all political activity after Pearl Harbor, and so on. The commentator may say all this; but he adds that in his judgment Lindbergh's views are sound as a drum (or dangerously incompetent), that they will lead to peace (or war), that Lindbergh should stick to his own field (or that he should be made President). He seeks not merely to info m the audience, so that it can come to its own conclusions on the basis of the pertinent evidence; instead he tries to lead the audience's thinking in the direction in which he thinks it should go.

All of this may be very obvious. But it is obvious only to the student of radio news, to the man who has his thinking straight. Evidence of this is the general misuse of the term "radio commentator." To most radio listeners, anybody who talks into a microphone on anything having to do with news is a "commentator." Ask ten of your nonradio friends which commentator they prefer, and nine of them will name one or another newscaster—as often as not a man who knows nothing whatsoever about news beyond the fact that it is something that appears twenty-four hours a day on a convenient automatic typewriter in the radio station. These nine friends will lump Swing, Heatter, Sevareid, and the high school kid who reads the 7 A.M. news on the local 100-watter all into the same class. They're all—to these nine— "commentators."

It is equally obvious that the line between the newscaster and the commentator cannot always be sharply drawn. Winchell, almost always referred to as a "commentator," is primarily a newscaster. His broadcasts gain their character largely from the fact that he offers his particular brand of news—factual material. But as he has come more and more to view himself as a seer and a capital-letter Authority, he has larded his revelations with warnings, viewings-with-alarm, encomiums —in short, with comment. Drew Pearson is another who reports and gives views in consecutive breaths. Many of radio's top-slot correspondents, foreign and domestic, do both—often with extremely high competence.

On the other hand, Kaltenborn, Swing, Harsch, and Heatter are pretty definitely commentators. The character of their broadcasts derives not from the fact that current news forms the framework of what they have to say, but that the framework is clothed in their own subjective explanations.

"Commentary" or "Analysis"?

The American Broadcasting Company describes Elmer Davis, one of its most highly regarded newsmen, as "news analyst and commentator." CBS declares that it has no "commentators" on its payroll, but only "analysts." ABC says the two are one; CBS says they are sharply distinct.

The CBS view, announced as a company policy in September, 1943, immediately brewed a storm. Paul White, CBS news director at the time, had issued a memorandum "to CBS news analysts" on September 7, defining the distinction. CBS saw its news services, said the memo, as a public charge—a charge that, since the number of broadcasting channels is limited, CBS would violate should its "analysts" become special pleaders.

The analyst (said the memorandum in part) should attempt to clear up any contradictions within the known record, should fairly present both sides of controversial questions, and, in short, should give the best available information upon which listeners can make up their own minds. Ideally, in the case of controversial issues, the audience should be left with no impression as to which side the analyst himself actually favors. . . .

Actually freedom of speech on the radio would be menaced if a small group of men, some thirty or forty news analysts who have nation-wide audiences and have regular broadcasting periods in which to build up loyal listeners, take advantage of their "preferred position" and become pulpiteers. . . . Then freedom of the air, within the genuine spirit of democracy, would be merely a hollow phrase. . . .

The "analyst," in other words, explains, clarifies, elucidates, elaborates. He keeps clear of the presentation of personal opinion; he does not harangue, preach, nor tell the public how to think. If he does, he becomes a "commentator."

The CBS definition did not fall from a clear sky. The fundamental principle on which it was based—that the broadcasting channels are public property and that they must be used to further "the public interest, convenience, and necessity"—had been expressed in the Federal Radio Act of 1927 and the Federal Communications Act of 1934. It had been implemented by dicta of the FCC to the effect that holders of broadcasting licenses must not grant freedom of the air only to views they approved, but must treat all causes and all comers alike; by frequently-repeated suggestions from the NAB to its members that they not only avoid special pleading but also frown on broadcasts dealing with controversial issues; by codes of "ethics" or practice issued time and again by networks and by individual stations.

The "Mayflower decision" of the FCC was for years broadcasting's guide on the problem of editorializing. The decision was issued on January 16, 1941, as an incidental part of an FCC order granting license renewal to WAAB-Boston, whose channel had been asked for in an application from the Mayflower Broadcasting Corporation. After nearly two years of hesitation, the FCC decided in favor of WAAB; a factor in its hesitation, the FCC said, had been the fact that the station had for more than eighteen months "broadcast so-called editorials . . . urging the election of various candidates for political office or supporting one side or another of various questions in public controversy. In these editorials, which were delivered by the editor-in-chief of the station's news service, no pretense was made at objective, impartial reporting. It is clear—indeed, the station seems to have taken pride in the fact—that the purpose of these editorials was to win public support for some person or view favored by those in control of the station."

Nevertheless, the Commission concluded to renew the WAAB license, upon the station's promise to give up editorializing (it had in fact already done so, the FCC reported). But the formal statement of policy included

(continued on next page)

Nobody quarreled with the principle. There had been violations of it, real and imaginary; the FCC had before this time, and has since, called to account stations that failed to maintain scrupulous attention to presentation of differing or opposing points of view. There had been cases in which individual broadcasters had, according to public and private charges, failed to represent the public interest. Boake Carter, once the most popular, as he was the first, of the nationally broadcast commentators, had lost a sponsor, it was said, largely because of the extremity and virulence of the personal opinions he had expressed.

---

in the decision became a basic rule-of-thumb for broadcasters' guidance. It said, in part:

". . . Under the American system of broadcasting it is clear that responsibility for the conduct of a broadcast station must rest initially with the broadcaster. It is equally clear that with the limitations in frequencies inherent in the nature of radio, the public interest can never be served by a dedication of any broadcast facility to the support of partisan ends. Radio can serve as an instrument of democracy only when devoted to the communication of information and the exchange of ideas fairly and objectively presented. A truly free radio cannot be used to advocate the causes of the licensee. It cannot be used to support the candidacies of his friends. It cannot be devoted to the support of principles he happens to regard most favorably. In brief, the broadcaster cannot be an advocate.

"Freedom of speech on the radio must be broad enough to provide full and equal opportunity for the presentation to the public of all sides of public issues. Indeed, as one licensed to operate in a public domain the licensee has assumed the obligation of presenting all sides of important public questions, fairly, objectively and without bias. The public interest— not the private—is paramount. These requirements are inherent in the conception of public interest set up by the Communications Act as the criterion of regulation."

Through the war years the Mayflower decision stood apparently sacrosanct. But with the passing of war as the top news subject, and with the development of broadcasters' interest in local news and local topics, a few— and then many—radio men began to question it. Why, they asked, should not radio have the same editorial privileges of the newspapers? Why should not radio men, even under a system of private operation of public facilities, be permitted to take and express positions on public questions? Some broadcasters, it is true, commented cannily that the Mayflower decision removed from them the responsibility to stick their necks out. But in late 1947 a *Broadcasting Magazine* survey showed 88 per cent of managers of com-

(*continued on next page*)

Fulton Lewis had often been charged with representing essentially the
".NAM point of view"—a charge given color by the fact that he was at
one time in the employ of the National Association of Manufacturers.
Many other cases had arisen.

CBS's pronouncement, however, was the first broad-scale attempt to
draw a line between background and opinion in the offerings of the
men ordinarily called commentators. (CBS had announced a policy
based on the same principle in 1939, but it had not drawn much attention.) "Censorship!" shouted a number of such men. Cecil Brown,
burning under Paul White's sharp reproof for broadcasting, on August

mercial AM stations saying they thought stations should have the right to
editorialize, and 55 per cent that they would do so if they could; only 10
per cent said they would not. Most of the managers reported themselves
ready to face the new political, social, and other problems they thought the
privilege of editorializing would raise; two-thirds of them thought the
privilege should be limited to individual stations and not granted to networks.

Already—in September of 1947—the FCC had recognized the growth of
such attitudes by scheduling formal hearings on the problem to be held
early in 1948. Specifically, the Commission was responding to a petition of
WHCU-Cornell University for a flat statement as to whether a station
might broadcast its own views along with those of others on a subject of
local interest. Actually, it was influenced by statements of the NAB News
Committee, of many of the radio news clinics held in preceding months,
and of scores of individual broadcasters.

The hearings developed conflicting attitudes both within and without
the industry. Favoring abolition of the no-editorials ruling were the NAB,
which stood consistently against any kind of programming control by the
FCC, a number of stations which held that broadcasters should have the
same right to expression of opinion as have the newspapers, and others who
expressed the view that the Mayflower doctrine is an abridgment of Constitutional freedom. CBS, incidentally, asked abolition of the doctrine—departing from its 1943 position—largely on the ground that the "theory of
scarcity" of broadcasting channels is no longer valid. Many of those desiring the *right* to editorialize, however, said they had no intention to put it
immediately to use. Opposed to change in the doctrine was an array of witnesses who held that the public interest demands that the "privileged
group" holding broadcasting licenses should not be given the right to express opinion.

The decision of the FCC had not been rendered up to late 1948.

25, "what Cecil Brown thinks" (White's words) rather than, as White saw it, facts to enable the listener to decide what to think, resigned from the CBS roll. H. V. Kaltenborn, perhaps CBS's top man in the public mind, resigned some time later to join NBC. The small but impressive Association of Radio News Analysts, of which Kaltenborn was a leader, objected vigorously. Essentially, the objections asserted that CBS was denying its men the right of free expression.

This, of course, White denied. He declared that what the ARNA asked—freedom for qualified men to express their views freely—was inconsistent with public responsibility. He quoted Kaltenborn to show that what Kaltenborn and ARNA wanted was substantially what CBS wanted:

> The radio news analyst (Kaltenborn had said in a recent speech) cannot and should not function night after night as preacher and soap box orator. He cannot constantly make himself the medium for passionate expression of personal or minority opinions.

Kaltenborn had gone on to say that "no news analyst worth his salt could or would be completely neutral or objective"—that news evaluation, selection or rejection of material, exercise of editorial judgment all must be subjective. To which White replied that "complete journalistic objectivity is probably only an ideal, but the fact that it is difficult if not impossible to attain does not impair the ideal itself, nor excuse the broadcaster from a constant and vigilant effort to attain it."

The views of Edward R. Murrow CBS are pertinent. When Murrow opened a series of newscasts over CBS in October, 1947, he explained his conception of his job:

> News periods should be devoted to giving the facts emanating from an established newsgathering source, to giving all the color in the proper sense of the word, without intruding the views of the analyst.
> The news analyst further can and very often should give as much light as possible on the meaning of events. In other words: The news analyst should not say that they're good or bad in his opinion, but should analyze their significance in the light of known facts, the results of similar occurrences, and so on.
> And in this he should always be fair. He is fully entitled to give and should give the opinions of various persons, groups, or political parties when these are known, leaving the listener to draw his own conclusions. . . .

We shall do our best to identify sources and to resist the temptation to use this microphone as a privileged platform. . . . And we shall try to remember that the mechanics of radio which make it possible for an individual to be heard throughout the land don't confer great wisdom or infallibility on that individual.

Most newsmen have appeared to feel that the dispute is somewhat academic. "Analysts" and "commentators" alike have said that the CBS definition would make little difference in their work. They agree with Kaltenborn that the self-respecting and competent analyst-commentator has no right to mount a soap box. They agree with White that the ideal of objectivity in the approach to facts is a goal to shoot at. They present their broadcasts, they say—under whatever descriptive title—with the aim of helping listeners to understand the news as they think it ought to be understood, always as soundly as their knowledge, judgment, and experience let them.

The difficulty of hitting on an acceptable definition of the term "analyst" is aptly illustrated by an article in the April, 1946, *Free World* by Cesar Saerchinger. Saerchinger, for years an NBC commentator, defines the news analyst as "the man who not only selects his news but analyzes or interprets it, either with or without personal or political bias." In Saerchinger's dictionary, "analyst" means precisely what CBS says it doesn't.

Evidence mounts, in any case, that the CBS policy has not hampered its news service. A Peabody Award for "outstanding reporting of the news" went in 1946 to CBS, with a special orchid to Paul White. The

---

In the *Atlantic Monthly* for November, 1943, appeared a discussion of the problem of control of radio commentary, "Policing the Commentator," by Quincy Howe. It elaborates some of the points discussed in this chapter.

An excellent longer dissertation on radio commentary and commentators also appeared in the *Atlantic:* "Hearing Is Believing," a series of three articles by Dixon Wecter (June, July, and August, 1945). Mr. Wecter devotes most of his space to comment on individual radio news figures— Swing, Harsch, Kaltenborn, Thomas, George Fielding Eliot, Dorothy Thompson, Pearson, Winchell, Heatter, Lewis, and Upton Close.

Further development of the subject will be found in *The American Radio*, by Llewellyn White (University of Chicago Press, 1947), one of the series of reports of the Commission on Freedom of the Press.

CIO-PAC, making a study of thirty-three daily news programs on the four major networks during seven weeks of the 1944 Presidential campaign, concluded that CBS alone maintained a balance between pro and con in "moral judgment" in matters related to the PAC. And more than one critic has declared CBS news service to be the soundest of its kind.

Commentary and the Station

Radio listeners are aware that commentators and analysts are usually employees of networks rather than of individual stations. Upwards of a hundred men (and a few women) go on the chains, daily or weekly, with analyses of the news; the total number of such broadcasters in the employ of individual stations is probably no larger, though there are more than a thousand stations and only a handful of networks of all kinds.

The prime reasons are easy to define: cost and fear of charges of partisanship.

Cost of putting a commentator on the air is relatively high because the commentator is ordinarily a select kind of performer. Dixon Wecter, in the *Atlantic* articles just cited, presents a glib account of "the typical evolution of a commentator" in which he declares that commentators are usually golden-voiced boys who grow up from jobs as news announcers to find themselves suddenly become authorities. This is a little too glib. Most commentators are individuals who, before they turn oracles, have attained a degree of public acceptance in the news or public affairs fields. They are foreign or Washington correspondents, social scientists, or authorities of other kinds whose special distinction gives their comment on current affairs public standing. Because they have such standing, they can command bigger figures on their salary checks (as is indicated in Chapter 4) than most stations care to pay for talent for only one or two shows a day.

The second reason derives from the thinking that has led much of radio to avoid controversy. The local station, particularly the small local station, knows that it must make its facilities available equally to all parties to contested issues. Commentators—even "analysts"—no matter how objective and fair and conscientious they try to make their broadcasts, can at times hardly avoid taking, or seeming to take, sides. From the point of view of the public interest, this is not necessarily objectionable; but it can become troublesome. Most stations choose the course of avoiding trouble rather than seeking it. Ergo, few commentators.

There are other reasons why many stations do not employ commentators. Even though a small station might be willing to stand the cost and face the charge of taking sides, it is not likely that it would find a competent commentator easy to come by. And even though it should overcome this obstacle, it could hardly hope that his offerings would do much to raise its Hooper ratings. Comment on public affairs does not draw big audiences.

All of this to the contrary, some stations have made significant efforts in this field. KDAL-Duluth puts a daily three- or four-minute commentary on a local subject into the middle of its major local news show. WINR-Binghamton, New York, schedules local commentary regularly at 7:45 P.M. each day. A. D. Willard, NAB executive vice-president, told an Ohio news clinic in 1946 that "soon radio will accept the same responsibility" assumed by newspapers in presenting views on local issues. "NAB will do everything to hasten the day," he said, "when every radio station will build for itself the same position newspapers have built for themselves in their editorial policies, and in standing up for what they believe is right." The NAB radio news committee, in 1947, went on record in favor of radio "editorializing" as a function of the competent radio newsroom.

Closely related to controversial commentary is the matter of vigorous championing of causes in the public interest on which there is no controversy. Nobody denies the desirability of attacking municipal corruption, juvenile delinquency, unsanitary restaurants, and the like; what is needed here is not the willingness to engage in controversy so much as the energy to dig into hidden situations and the courage to say what needs to be said about them. Radio stations offer many examples of this

---

C. A. Siepmann, in *Radio's Second Chance* (Rinehart, 1946), writes stimulatingly about the questions of partisanship, discrimination, and other matters of radio's public policy. The book is worth every broadcasting worker's time.

kind of thing. WBNY-Buffalo, by hard-hitting, insistent reporting, caused a clean-up in a local police problem that had been given scant attention by other local communication agencies. WSB-Atlanta and WCCO-Twin Cities won widespread praise by their repeated shafts at racial and religious intolerance—WSB in its series of dramatized "The Harbor We Seek" programs and WCCO in a special series of six documentary shows, "Neither Free Nor Equal," which has not often been equaled in calling spades spades. Harry M. Cochran of WSTV-Steubenville, Ohio, won a 1946 Sigma Delta Chi medal for documented reporting of the criminal background of one of the operators of local gambling dens. WCAU-Philadelphia put on a campaign to aid the "Philadelphia Plan" of reducing food costs. Radio stations throughout the land put on all kinds of programs, in 1947, to combat the juvenile delinquency problem. KRNT-Des Moines aided its community in an impressive reduction in the number of traffic fatalities. And so on.

In any case, commentary is an integral and a vital part of the radio news profession (or business). That it is difficult, that it is seeded with booby traps, that it is costly—all such facts do not justify radio's avoiding it. American broadcasting will not, indeed, be fully accepting its responsibility until it shoulders the burden of leadership implied by its position as trustee of a vastly important means of mass communication. The FCC appears to feel that it is a necessity, and so does the public. Radio—as shown by the demand for modification of the Mayflower

Evidence of public interest in what a station does with its commentators came dramatically in Los Angeles in the spring of 1945. Station KFI announced in February that all news analyses would be restricted to employees of the station. In the following months the California legislature denounced the action by resolution, and a citizens' "Emergency Committee on KFI" was formed to protest—on the ground that such action removed from the air competent commentators whose broadcasts were of value to the public, and that limiting comment to KFI employees *might* mean that only the views of the station's owners would be broadcast. KFI countered later, after formal protest to the FCC had been made, that it had no intention of taking off its schedule its NBC network commentators. The FCC promised to watch "developments" in the case. The important point is not the merit of the specific problem, but the fact that a portion of the public was aroused to action against what it thought might be a threat to freedom of expression, and to radio service in the public interest.

principle—seems ready to devote more and more time to this kind of leadership, in its own interests as in the interests of its clientele.

How the Commentary Grows

Most commentators "write their own stuff." They choose their subjects, decide on their attitudes, write their copy, and broadcast it themselves. Cases crop up in which commentators have ghosts who do their real work, leaving to them the glory of microphone appearance, but they are rare.

This is as it should be. Commentary is nothing if not personal, and the "commentator" who does no more than parrot analyses prepared for him by a hack—no matter how competent a hack—not only is a parasite and a fake, but is also pretty sure to lack conviction in presentation. In a day when the trend is toward making newscasters their own writers and research men, it is doubly important that commentators be the real thing.

Commentary—to repeat—is a highly personalized business. No two commentators approach problems in just the same way, nor work in the same mental or physical environment, nor turn out the same kind of copy. Each man, if he is to maintain the individual flavor that is so important a factor in his effectiveness, must write copy that is distinctly *his* copy—copy that would be less effective (and perhaps nothing but hash) in any mouth other than his. For this reason, precise and absolute rules for the writing of commentary copy cannot be laid down.

Here, then, are general suggestions rather than specific precepts. Though Raymond Swing and Gabriel Heatter produce widely differing broadcasts, they have some of the same starting points. What is said here is not intended to shape the individual commentary, but rather to

---

The copy of a commentator who here shall be nameless has for years been the despair of other writers in his newsroom. Sample sentences from one of his wartime broadcasts: "We have been subjected to a series of rude shocks, militarily, and, as a result, on the homefront. Now, increasingly disturbed, the American people are buckling down, but, even so, are starting to inquire the reasons for mounting casualties, and a situation that presages a war barely begun." Nobody but the man who wrote them could put such rhetorical monstrosities over. But this man somehow made them both meaningful and forceful.

present the broad, common aspects of the commentator's task.

What are the common starting points?

First, long and thorough grounding in public affairs. Most commonly such grounding is that of the newspaper man. Most of the commentators who were big names during the war were former newspaper men —Godwin, Sevareid, Lewis, Pearson, Swing, Kaltenborn, and a host of others. These are men who have for years been deeply concerned with the understanding and evaluation of news; men, too, who approach news with respect for it and with a passion for making it meaningful to a public that hasn't their background.

Work directly with news, however, is not the only avenue. George Fielding Eliot was a professional soldier and a pulp-magazine writer before he became a military commentator. Edward Murrow was an educator and a youth worker; Upton Close was a world traveler and student of Far Eastern affairs. Many commentators, especially those allied with individual stations, are university professors or specialists in social science fields. After V-J Day there was a swing toward the employment of prominent political and governmental figures: Sumner Welles, Harold Ickes, and Fiorello LaGuardia are examples.

A second starting point is constant access to latest news reports. Most commentators work in intimate contact with network or big-station newsrooms, where printers chatter twenty-four hours a day. Heatter has printers installed in his Long Island home, his Connecticut farm, and his New York apartment. Many commentators, in addition, have their own personal news channels. The modern commentator is a "big name," and he can usually gain access to important news sources by picking up a telephone. Some, like Pearson and Winchell, capitalize on what they say are private sources—"men in high position," "authoritative voices on Capitol Hill" who, they would have their listeners believe, open their hearts to Pearson or Winchell alone. It goes without saying that every commentator draws heavily on his own experience and knowledge, and that he has at his right hand many shelves of reference material.

Finally, the commentator must have certain special skills. He needs to be able to turn out effective radio copy—effective either in the sober, orderly manner of a Swing or the flashy, sentimental style of a Heatter.

He must have a presentable radio personality—not necessarily one characterized by golden voice and broadcast glamour, but at least one that carries conviction and has the ring of authority.

And it doesn't hurt if he has a touch of the crusader, and at least a modicum of showmanship. Commentators who draw largest audiences are those who can, on occasion, get excited. Though commentary is a serious business, it can be made more effective by the impassioned voice (if it isn't worked to death) and by the use of the showman's devices of suspense and color.

All of this suggests that the commentator works hard at his job. He does. Most commentators do no more than one show a day, and no more than five a week. They ordinarily put in a full day's work at each show. Typically, a commentator rises in the morning along with the rest of the world, has breakfast by 8 o'clock, and starts his day's routine. This means reading a variety of newspapers (the *New York Times* is a "must" for most commentators) and news and discussion periodicals, perhaps "catching" several news broadcasts, checking the printers for late news developments. It also involves going through a mass of "handouts," bulletins, special pleas, and other such material which comes by the mailbagful—some bidden and welcome, some routed direct to the fireplace. By noon (supposing that his show goes on the air in the evening), a commentator will usually have decided what subject or subjects he is to treat.

After lunch the commentator may start to work on his copy; or he may need to do some reporting, some additional fact-finding and research and opinion-sampling. At any rate, he will need to have put himself before his typewriter four or five hours in advance of broadcast time. No two men work at the same speed. One political scientist who has a three-times-a-week evening commentary of ten minutes clears all the time after noon on broadcast days for his job. Another who writes his copy longhand allows five hours for the actual writing.

This discussion deals with the commentator whose work is essentially confined to news in the term's broad sense—current social, political, and economic developments. There are also specialized commentators: Men like George Fielding Eliot and Hanson Baldwin in military matters, Clifton Fadiman on books, Jimmy Fidler on movies.

In any case, the commentator must make sure that he has ample time for final polishing, and for checking again the latest news developments before he goes on the air. Once in a while he may find such developments completely altering a situation, so that he will have a thorough revamping job to do. If he's a Kaltenborn, perfectly at ease in an ad-lib broadcast, his problem may be simple. If he isn't, there may be a hectic hour just before air time.

Organization of the commentary is, and should be, simple. Ordinarily a five- or ten-minute show deals with only one or two major subjects, and a fifteen-minute with no more than three. The commentator chooses topics of wide interest, or importance, or—preferably—both. Since his job is to illuminate, to explain, to show values, rather than merely to report (though at times he may choose to do nothing beyond report relevant facts bearing on a subject in the news), he needs at least several minutes for each topic. Consequently his main organization problem is to decide which topic will make his opening most effective, and perhaps how to move smoothly from one topic to another. If his show carries a mid-commercial, he needs to devise a convenient break —either a pause in the discussion of a single topic, or a shift to another subject.

Most of what there is to say about the actual writing, the rhetorical form, has already been said. Though the commentary is a special type of news broadcast, it is still a news broadcast. Therefore it needs to have the qualities of informality, of directness, of simplicity, and of color that characterize any effective news show. Within this generalization, however, there are several specific requirements:

1. The news peg—the current news on which the comment is to hang—must appear early in the script. Unless the news is of transcendent importance and interest—the death of a President or of a price control system, for example—the commentator must write on the principle that many among his audience will not be intimately conversant with it. He must therefore show in his opening remarks precisely the occasion for his choice of topic, and present enough of the current factual news so that no single listener will be puzzled.

2. The commentary must get a running start. Commentary audiences are never large—most radio listeners vastly prefer a Jack Benny

to a Joseph Harsch. The commentator has to take hold of the dial-twisters in his first sentence, or forever lose them. Use of a vital news peg in the opening sentence is often effective. Posing a question to which thousands want to know the answer—"How high are food prices going to go?"—is another. An anecdote may do the job: "Here's a story that will interest you. . . ." Or a personal experience: "I heard two housewives in the corner grocery talking about the price of butter to-day. . . ." Promise of something striking may do it: "What happened to the price of butter in a little Southern town today, thanks to short-ages, scares the life out of me. . . ." These and other devices have a number of common characteristics: they talk in listener-terms; they show immediately that the subject is of current and broad interest; they promise something to come.

3. Most scripts should be plentifully larded with specific facts. The listener can tie his imagination and his attention to specific facts; but he is puzzled and often bored by generalization or by philosophical rumination. The use of incident, anecdote, concrete example or illus-tration, moreover, is one of the sure methods of putting life and color into a broadcast. Finally, much of any commentary normally consists of the presentation of factual background behind the news of the day. Though the commentator is picked for his job because his opinions are competent and trustworthy, he is expected not merely to offer think-pieces to his audience but rather to show that the facts add up to what he considers a logical over-all view of a news situation.

4. The commentator has responsibility like that of the newscaster to avoid sensationalizing, sentimentality, and overemotionalism. Not that all do: Pearson and Winchell glory in sensationalizing, and Heatter gives sentimentality and emotionalism (as much in his fervent, dedi-cated voice as in his words) high standing among his wares. On the other hand, Swing with his Olympic calm seems to make a fetish of avoiding any suggestion of excitement about the news or what it means. The ideal, doubtless, is somewhere between the extremes. The point is that a commentator who depends on overcoloration, either in voice or words, is gaining audience but rendering it a disservice and, in some cases, doing it positive injury; one who consistently understates, orally or verbally, loses audience and may also be guilty of disservice.

5. The commentary must "come out right." The newscaster, with an eye on the clock, can pick and choose among short news stories as he nears the end of his air time so as to bring his show to a close within a few seconds of his allotted period. The commentator usually has no such handy adjusting device. Since his comment on a subject is in the nature of a brief essay, its organization demands that the conclusion— often the most important part of what he has to say—be timed down to the last period. ABC boasts that Swing, working with a stopwatch in his hand and the knowledge that thirteen lines on his typewriter account for a minute on the air, invariably comes to the end of his last paragraph on the nose. Most commentators have not figured it so fine; but all must give serious attention to timing.

Radio commentators have come in for a lot of attention from American magazine and book publishers in recent years. Two books dealing with them are *The Columnists* by Charles Fisher (Howell, Soskin, 1944) and *Molders of Opinion*, edited by David Bulman (Bruce, 1945). Fisher's book, though it is concerned with newspaper as well as radio commentators (many men are both), is the more complete and revealing.

Among magazine articles on commentators (in addition to those cited earlier in this chapter):

"Edward R. Murrow" by Robert J. Landry, *Scribner's*, December, 1938

"Fadiman for the Millions" by John Chamberlain, *Saturday Evening Post*, January 11, 1941

"The Crier" by Philip Hamburger, a Profile on Gabriel Heatter, *New Yorker*, January 20, 1945

"Radio's Public Opinionators" by Jessyca Russell, *Magazine Digest*, July, 1945

"You're on the Air" by Cesar Saerchinger, *Free World*, April, 1946

"The Role of the Radio Commentator" by Hadley Cantril, *Public Opinion Quarterly*, October, 1939

"The Voice" by R. O. Boyer, a Profile on Raymond Swing, *New Yorker*, November 14-21 (two parts), 1942

"Pugnacious Pearson" by Jack Alexander, *Saturday Evening Post*, January 6, 1945

"Kaltenborn Edits the News" by Giraud Chester, *American Mercury*, October, 1947

"The Shortage of News Analysts" by Charles A. Siepmann, *Nation*, January 24, 1948

6. The commentator who likes his job must avoid becoming a special pleader.

7. The commentator ought to try to avoid confusing himself with God.

The Professionals at Work

Through the good nature and courtesy of H. R. Baukhage, Gabriel Heatter, Eric Sevareid, and Raymond Swing, readers of this book are here given an opportunity for line-by-line examination of several of their actual scripts.

First, there are two by Baukhage, for years a member of the ABC Washington news staff. Baukhage works from a triple-spaced script which he types himself. He is an inexpert typist, and there are many errors with penciled corrections. Since he reads his own copy, he permits some errors that won't mislead him to go uncorrected, and he pays no attention to the standard rule that sentences or words must not break from one page of copy to another—he is so familiar with what he has written that he can deliver it smoothly. To the script that follows, broadcast from Washington on September 9, 1946, he has appended his own comments. His preface:

Many people express surprise at the answer to one of the most frequently-asked questions about broadcasting: "How long does it take you to prepare your script?"

It takes as long to prepare most good broadcasts as it does to prepare for the painting of a good picture. Whistler said *that* took *him* a lifetime.

Working on a single script, if you simply count the time which has elapsed on the day you do the writing, would be from about 7 A.M., when I reach my office, to 1:15 P.M., when I leave the microphone. However, all my working day except the time devoted to the preparation of a weekly column and the writing of a few articles and lectures is spent on the broadcasts.

Now the script,* with Baukhage's comments where they apply:

"The script starts with a description of the weather, which required a perusal of the weather map. Frequently I call up the Weather Bureau and consult them when there

Baukhage talking.

If I had my way this morning I'd be talking about the weather and nothing else. It isn't unusual or un-

* By written permission of H. R. Baukhage, September 17, 1946.

is some unusual meteorological phe- expected—it is just Washington
nomenon worthy of comment." showing us what I told you it would
—that these delightful pre-fall days
didn't mean we weren't going to have a post-summer. 90 is predicted for
this afternoon. Yesterday it was hotter here than it was in Miami or New
Orleans. Somewhere in between those two cities a lot of hot air pushed
north out of the Gulf of Mexico, and I understand that it pushed clear up
into the Susquehanna Valley. It looks as if the chilly spot was Reno, which
is more or less advantageous to the city's leading industry.

"The second paragraph takes up the question of strikes and, while it is more or less factual reporting, it reflects a long interview I had the previous day with a member of the Labor Department, dealing with the machinery of conciliation, and also opinions garnered from various officials on the current situation—perhaps two or three separate conversaations."

Strikes are the chief topic of the day again, and the pessimists who warned us to look for another round seem to have been right. As far as I have been able to learn at this hour, it looks as if the Maritime people had the government where they wanted it, right out on a limb, and the prediction is that they'll have to saw themselves off. And when the stabilization bough breaks, up will go wages and prices and all.

I suppose there will be more than the 30 lines which the Russian papers gave to the Byrnes speech in Germany, devoted to our internal troubles.

I'm sure most of you blame the governmental labor machinery for the present dilemma. What would you have done? The CIO maritime workers on the west coast struck and the government stabilization board okeh'ed a minimum wage raise. Meanwhile the AF of L was negotiating on its end. The ship owners granted a higher rate to them than CIO won.
The government had named its limit and so the workers struck against the board's decision. That is one of the disadvantages of having two rival union organizations which have to hold their membership by competing. Today there is less chance of amalgamation than ever, if we can judge from some of the choice remarks CIO head Murray made about AF of L head Green.

"I mention 'the disadvantages of having two rival union organizations.' Views stated there are based partly on an interview I had with Secretary of Labor Perkins when she was in office and also on a telephone call confirming the fact that the breach between the two organizations is as wide as or wider than ever."

That isn't the only obstacle in the government's path when it comes to labor disputes. There is a breach between the White House and the labor department. It is no secret to Secretary of Labor Schwellenbach that President Truman has been valiantly seeking some other nice job for him. Schwellenbach is not one to quit if he is under fire, but the way the President answered a question at his conference last week made it plain that the Maritime strike was entirely the Labor Secretary's hot potato. Some people said it wasn't a potato —it was just a straw—but one that was intended to break the camel's back. Others said it would merely make Schwellenbach hump himself and keep on going.

"This paragraph mentions the differences between Schwellenbach and the President. My comment on this situation is the result of at least half a dozen recent interviews with people who reflect the attitude of the White House, the Labor Department, Schwellenbach and his friends. Among the interviews is one I had earlier with Schwellenbach, two long conversations with one of his intimate friends, the report of a very reliable source concerning the advice given him by another of his counsellors. On that is predicated my view of the policy he may pursue."

The strike is no joke. If it starts a chain reaction, Paul Porter won't have to resign as OPA head—as Broadcasting Magazine said he was going to and the President said he wasn't. There won't be any price control. And the stabilization board will find it's no use to try to lock the stable after wages have stolen another upward march.

As John Steelman, chief stabilizer, says in the current American Magazine (I'm quoting it and him), "Before winter sets in it will be apparent whether those old forces—supply and demand—can operate quickly enough to stabilize our economy with the controls which we now have available. If we are to avoid a riotous price and wage chase ending in a crash, we must cooperate with the government agencies . . . Business and industry must police themselves and refrain from seeking bigger mark-ups and high-priced lines. Labor must seek higher wages only in cases of obvious hardship. . . ."

"Two articles are quoted—one from *Fortune* and another from the *American*. I read both at home, outside of office hours."

There is more advice to bankers and farmers and buyers. But the boom is on, and the consumers are the craziest of all. As Fortune Magazine remarks, there seems no bottom to the American purse. Mink coats at fifteen thousand and men's wrist watches at a thousand dollars all sell just about as fast as egg beaters, table radios and pork chops. They're off, and you might as well try to stop a bandersnatch.

As Fortune comments, there are more people in insane asylums than ever before. Maybe, what with the housing system, THEY are just crazy like Reynard—R-E-Y-N-A-R-D (the class can look up the allusion for tomorrow).

The latest embroidery to the labor situation is the assumption of the duties of the State Department by the International Longshoreman's union. They have decided to amend our foreign policy toward Jugoslavia. Joseph Ryan, president of the organization, says no more ships carrying supplies to Jugoslavia will be loaded. La Guardia says there are 37 UNRRA ships now unloaded—how many are bound for Jugoslavia he didn't say. While many people will think it's at least rough justice to amend the ancient saying and cease feeding the mouth that is biting you, after all, it would seem proper to let Mr. Byrnes do his job until we decide to make Mr. Ryan secretary of state.

One thing it is well to remember. UNRRA is not an American organization. It is an international organization. All of its employees, regardless of nationality, are working for it, not for the country of which they are citizens. The United States has made certain pledges to deliver certain supplies. If we don't want to live up to our pledges we can get out of the organization, I suppose. But we can't change the rules arbitrarily. In any case, we won't spite Tito or his bosses.

"On the question of UNRRA and America's relation to it, no authorities are mentioned. But the opinions expressed are based on three long and intimate talks with one of my friends who at the time held a position in UNRRA very close to the Director General."

We'll just starve some poor Slav who doesn't even know we had a plane shot down—and who perhaps has been kind to his mother.

With the speech of Secretary Byrnes still echoing over Europe, some saying it is a challenge, others saying it's an invitation to Russia, the Peace Conference pursues its weary way. And may still pursue to the point of postponing the meeting of the assembly of the United Nations in New York set for the twenty-third. Molotov managed to get through a resolution to poll the UN members as to whether they would be willing to wait a month. The United States didn't vote. Some of the delegates are said to be already en route.

Criticism of the Peace Conference swells into a bitter chorus. Even the more conservative observers are beginning to grow a little bit cynical. I note the magazine Corps Diplomatic quotes an Austrian journalist to this effect:

"Most of the rest of the broadcast is purely factual. Reference is made to a third article on the peace conference, late news developments on which I got from the Associated Press."

"This is the 123rd international conference which I have covered," he says, "and it's always the same; the debate is only for the gallery. There are only two worlds, a capitalist and a non-capitalist one, which are trying to make a temporary truce." Well, I'm glad our Austrian friend feels it's a TRUCE. But from where I sit, it's a truce stranger than fiction.

I am afraid that there isn't much more unanimity on the question of foreign affairs in the peace conference than there is here at home. Unless you whole-heartedly approve of a sentiment you are a fanatic. I was highly amused by two letters that arrived at the same time, one from Ohio, one from New York. The Ohio lady accused me (I'm quoting) of "red-baiting, labor-hating and being a Roosevelt-smearer." She explains that fairness and justness have colored all of her living.

Which reminds me of the swain's lament: "If you be not fair to me, what care I how fair you be?" That goes both ways.

However, this is mild compared to the New Yorker, who signs his card with a not-too-modest pseudonym. He calls me a New Deal pundit and accuses me and my horrendous ilk of the following: 1) Unleasing the atomic bomb in spite of the fact Japan had made peace moves; 2) selling out Poland, Finland, China, Korea and Mihailovitch—et cetera ad nauseam ad insomniam.

As I have remarked, I have long since learned that good and evil, black and white, are to a large extent in the ear of the listener.

There was good and bad in the Byrnes speech according to the private interests of the listeners, too. France was frightened at the thought of a stronger Germany; Poland sent angry crowds screaming at the American Embassy in Warsaw.

A rumor immediately spread that Russia, in order to outbid Byrnes for German cooperation, was about to offer her Silesia, a part of the now-occupied Russian zone lying between the present Polish border and Germany.

What the Russians seemed to consider the important thing in the Byrnes speech—and it WAS the important thing—was that he made clear that any power, including Germany, that thought we were going to fold our tents like the Arabs and silently steal away from Europe had better revise its plans.

The Soviet-controlled Berlin radio announced that with half the precincts heard from, the communist unity party was running ahead of its two conservative opponents in the communal election of yesterday. That was for Thuringia only. Yesterday it looked, in Saxony at least (from which there is no report today), as if the anti-communist votes were higher.

As Greece welcomes back her king, Bulgaria ousts hers. The Bulgarian plebiscite established what they call a Republic, and little nine-year-old Simeon the Second will go into exile. He helped his mother pack, and expressed his formerly royal pleasure that he was going to see his grand-daddy, ex-King Victor Emmanuel, and all the other exiled Italian royalty. He is interested in botany. He was popular, personally, with his former subjects, but his best friends probably feel that it will be better for him to study his daisies and other flowers from the top, looking down, than to run the chance of difficulties that might enforce a root's eye view of them. His head will doubtless rest much easier than the crowned one of his neighbor, King George. Already there is thunder on the left in Greece. The initials of FDR, in sky-writing half a mile long over Athens, okey'ed the Greek verdict, but they have gone with the winds and the Aircraft Carrier Franklin Roosevelt, out at sea, has long since beheld dock-lights die.

The British cabinet discusses the Palestine problem preparatory to the forthcoming conference, which dispatches say may have to include the Jewish Agency on its own terms—those terms are statehood for the Jewish state and adequate territory.

It was learned today that under Chiang Kai-shek's orders a translation of the New Testament had been completed last February, but kept secret. The translator, Dr. WU, noted Chinese jurist, worked closely with the Generalissimo on the translation. The other news from China said government troops were fighting through the defenses of Tsining.

Now Baukhage adds general comments on his news sources and his characteristic methods of operation:

News sources are broadly divided into three classifications: 1—White House press-radio conference, which I never miss; others held by government officials which I attend if possible; and those held by private persons of importance or representatives of non-governmental organizations. 2—

The hand-out or mimeographed statement written by the publicity staffs of agencies in and out of government. I read many of these personally, and have others digested by my assistants. 3—Perhaps the most important, the personal interview. Many such interviews dealing with late news are conducted over the telephone, and they are quite as satisfactory as personal visits if one has sufficiently intimate acquaintance with the individuals interviewed.

Comment, interpretation, explanation, and background in a single broadcast might call upon data assembled years before. For instance, material which I gathered while covering the Versailles Peace Conference after World War I is of value in reporting similar international gatherings today.

As to use of the script, once it is prepared, I might say that I believe the commentator must look upon radio as a medium requiring a style of writing and delivery of its own. To attempt to apply the technique of the printed word or the platform is wrong. The style must be informal and conversational, for the listener is in an informal atmosphere. The speaker is a visitor in a home, not a lecturer on a rostrum. You can't *talk* the way you talk, either, unless your script is *written* the way you talk.

Another factor: The listener is blind. Therefore, the speaker must substitute for gestures and facial expression, special phrasing and inflection which convey the desired impressions without distracting the thought.

A broadcast can, of course, be too informal. Personally, except when I am describing some event happening before my eyes, or one so recent there is not time to prepare a text but whose scene or facts are deeply etched on my brain, I want a script in front of me. But in reading (I use the word as it is used on the stage) the art must, as in the theater, conceal the art. There is nothing so "spontaneous" as the speech that has been carefully prepared. Commentators can't and shouldn't memorize, but I want to be familiar enough with what I am going to say so that I know exactly how a sentence is going to end when I start it.

Examination of Baukhage's script reveals a number of characteristics. It opens "soft," with a weather story of wide interest; it closes with several short stories so that Baukhage can adjust his closing to the clock. It discusses only three main topics: the current economic situation, the meaning of the Byrnes speech, and an aspect of the Balkan situation. But it embroiders each of these with what Baukhage views as their important ramifications. It strives throughout for a light, informal tone—

both in the language employed and through the use of frequent quips and puns.

In his general comments above, Baukhage speaks of the situation in which he may broadcast ad-lib. The script * that follows is of this nature. It won a Headliners' Award for 1945, and was given an accolade in the *Congressional Record*, where it was reprinted, as "one of the classics of the several programs" describing its subject—President Roosevelt's funeral ceremonies. Of the script, Baukhage says: "It was taken from notes I put down while the Roosevelt funeral services at Hyde Park were going on, using the fender of a Signal Corps truck parked in the rose garden for a desk. There was no time between the end of the ceremonies and the broadcast itself to prepare a script. The transcript was taken down in shorthand from the broadcast as recorded."

Baukhage talking from a little house down the Boston Post Road—a bit from Hyde Park where I've come, following the President's funeral. A little way from the rolling farmland, the woodland and hedgerows, and stone fences, and plowed fields, the old home behind the trees where Franklin Roosevelt first saw the light over the hills of the Hudson, and where I've just left him in the midst of his own acres, taking his last long rest.

I'm not going to talk about the death of the President today because I'm thinking of something else. I'm thinking about an American—like others who fell at Lexington, Appomattox, at San Juan Hills, and Chateau Thierry, on the Normandy beaches, on Guadalcanal, at Aachen, and now at the very gates of Berlin. I am thinking of Franklin Roosevelt that way because of the last broadcast I made from Hyde Park on September 8, four years ago on a mellow autumn day. On that day thousands in America were not thinking of the most thought-about man in the country then in terms of politics or policies or rank or title or achievements or failures. But they were thinking of him humanly, and vainly trying to share the grief that a son alone must bear when he repays with the anguish of parting, the debt for the travail of her who bore him. That was the day when Sara Delano Roosevelt passed away. And that is what I said then—then, not a President but a man mourning for his mother.

And today a Nation mourns not for a President but for a loss made the more poignant by the sorrow of the mothers all over the Nation whose sons

* By written permission of H. R. Baukhage, September 17, 1946.

have been lost on the wide battlefields of the world. To me there is no question whatever but that Franklin Roosevelt died in the service of his country, a service grown too great for any single man to bear, just as other mothers' sons have died for their country, the ones who gave their lives in action. To me, this ceremony that I have just witnessed is part of the great panoply of sacrifice that men since time began have made, giving their life to preserve an ideal which lived on because they were willing to exchange their own lives for it. A part of the eternal miracle of nature when earth takes back her seed only to return it in the rich harvest, in flower and stalk, to be the nourishment of others that mourn.

I have come, as I say, from Hyde Park where in an ancient old-fashioned garden, protected by the high walls of a hemlock hedge, another American has gone to rest on the acres where he was born, the acres he loved. He chose this spot among the old-fashioned blooms, now only brown shoots I noticed before me, brown and unobtrusive compared to the mountain of riotous color heaped above the grave. But those were plucked flowers—they will fade. The others, they will bloom again in this eternal miracle of spring. Over the boxwood hedge the old red barn looks down. Thousands of those red barns are on America's farms. Beyond and hidden by the great trees is the old home; and beyond—the Hudson River is flowing gently to the sea.

And now, as I have taken the notes down, I'll give them to you:

First there was the roar of planes overhead and then the sharp order "Attention," the salute, and then echoing over those deep hills of the Hudson, like Hendrick Hudson's bowling balls, came the salute of 48 guns. And between those shots all was so silent that you could hear bird songs everywhere. And then "Present arms," and then the planes coming back. And then last in the distance, the low tap of the muffled drums from the West Point band and then the sound of the slow rhythm of the dead march which grew louder and louder as they entered the grounds. And now they come in before us, and the West Pointers follow at that strange slow march, and finally the caisson is outside the hedge—you can hear it. It halts just beyond the little entrance where I am standing. The bombers soar over and now the colors are advanced—the Stars and Stripes, the gold of the Presidential flag. And now "Order arms," "Present arms," and the bugles sound off, the Star Spangled Banner, and at that moment the cool wind from the Hudson River blew and whipped out the flags. "Order arms," "Parade rest," and now softly the band began "Lead, Kindly Light." And now a choir boy with the crucifix comes in, behind, in white surplice, the white-haired minister, and then the coffin with the pall bearers, soldiers and sailors and marines, and next the wife and the daughter and the son,

Elliott, and then President Truman. The coffin rests, a flag upon it—the flag is raised and held above it. And now, the minister speaks, there comes a prayer, and then the poem that he reads with this refrain: "Father in Thy gracious keeping leave we now Thy servant sleeping." And then, after the silence, bird songs again. And then the sharp order to the firing party: "Fire three volleys," "Ready," "Aim," "Fire." The shots ring out—three times the volleys are shot over the grave—and after each the bark of a little lonely dog. And then that sweetest and saddest of all music—the bugle sounds "Taps." There is a pause as the echoes die and the coffin is lowered into the earth. The sergeant, with military precision, marches over and lays the flag that decked the coffin in the hands of Mrs. Roosevelt. And so, an American has gone to rest in the green of the garden, in the shadow of the old red barn, and his spirit, like that of all his fallen comrades on the battlefields, rolls on like the eternal river flowing softly to the sea.

— o —

The following broadcast—a wartime Sunday afternoon program (January 7, 1945) by Eric Sevareid of CBS in London—may be examined in light of the CBS distinction between "analyst" and "commentator." In the script Sevareid reports late news; he offers related facts, or background, to give the listener points of reference for the news. All of this comes within the frame of the CBS definition of analysis. But few would argue that Sevareid does not also present his own personal views of the meaning of the news. Note, for instance, the two paragraphs at the middle of the script beginning "Mr. Archibald MacLeish. . . ." "A beginning [of freer flow of news]," says Sevareid, "will have to be made in some high places . . . it is not so much because information was *stopped*, as because *bad* information has been issued . . . apparently our aviation experts have been the worst offenders." Sevareid is considered one of radio's most careful and thorough reporters, a man scrupulously careful of his facts; when he makes statements like those just quoted, he usually presents dependable facts to back them up. But he does not *merely* present the facts and leave all conclusions to the reader; he suggests or states flatly the conclusions he has reached. Is this analysis? or is it commentary?

And what about the remarkable essay to which Sevareid devotes the second half of his broadcast? It is well documented, with specific factual examples and with generalizations for which it would be easy to produce factual basis (for instance, "generals—and journalists—use big, standard words like 'teamwork' or 'soldierly behavior' "). But is it not essentially the speaker's attempt to aid the listener to see what war means as he, from his vantage point, sees it? Whole paragraphs are strictly, and peculiarly, personal.

Analysis or commentary?

Aside from this question, other points in the script may be noted. Its opening paragraphs offer the latest news, not in the detail that a straight newscast would present, but packed into a few sentences (note the eleven-word paragraph on a bombing attack—the straight newscast might devote a paragraph to this). As it moves through the following paragraphs, each new subject is introduced by brief reference to current news, and each is developed with material to show how it looks in London.

Note, also, certain mechanical peculiarities. In the first half of the script, Sevareid uses semicolons to separate closely related sentences, suspension points (. . .) to separate closely related subjects, paragraphing for sharper breaks.

The script *:

This is Eric Sevareid in London.

The news reaching London from the Western Front this afternoon shows no decisive *change* in any sector, though there have been local *gains*. The most important, in the German salient, has been the cutting of the road between Saint Vith and Laroche, accomplished by our Third Armored Division; this is important, because the whole struggle in this area is basically a battle for the network of roadways; and now Von Rundstedt is reported to be left with only *two* minor routes with which to supply the central and western part of the salient; the Saint Vith road was cut yesterday; details of the fighting since are sparse but the First Army offensive was still moving on, however slowly and painfully, at last report this afternoon . . . all that one can say is that the battle of the Salient has not yet been won or lost; it just goes on and it is very hard; there are no authoritative reports of any big scale German evacuation of the salient—indeed one story today puts the German strength there at a new total of thirty divisions. . . . The big German attack in the Saar, which appeared dangerous at first, has apparently made little general progress in the last day, but more Germans have crossed the Rhine.

* By written permission of Eric Sevareid, August 1, 1946.

From England, hundreds of bombers went to west Germany this morning.

Today, millions of British people were reading the President's speech to Congress; in its confident tone, there was tonic for all those depressed about the turn of battle; in his plea for unity there was relief, to all those who are tired of Transatlantic bickering; his generalities about American foreign policy were at least the right kind of generalities and a sedative, to all those upset about isolationism in America.

More and more British people understand that the President can accept the political responsibilities which follow in the wake of battle, only in the measure the *Congress* allows; they do not understand that when a Congressman makes a reckless attack upon an ally at a critical moment in the war, he may be just acting a part for a home town audience and the headlines; here, voters are accustomed to a legislative system which permits lawmakers to think of national duties first and local obligations second; the American Congress bewilders them. . . .

And so this country waits to see how far America will follow the President's lead; people wait for the Big Three meeting, which may include General DeGaulle before it is ended; there were hints here today that the meeting will occur early in February, that none of the three leaders will be host at home, but that all will have to travel. . . . In Britain, the public attitude has changed about these conferences; the mere fact of meeting will no longer satisfy people; general declarations at adjournment that all sides agree upon all matters will not be enough this time. Upon all but the most secret military plans, people here will insist upon knowing what the principles of agreement actually are. . . . Too many people agree with the British Journal, which writes of Teheran, Quebec and their aftermath: "The fruits of secret diplomacy are gathered even before they have ripened, and the taste is already bitter in the mouth."

Most of those here who write and speak are convinced the Big Three must make at least two major decisions. One is purely military—how to find and send the tremendous reinforcements now obviously required in Western Europe; military commentators here claim the German offensive and our reactions to it show clearly that we had *no* strategic reserve behind the line; that those reserves are in the Far East, committed there by the Quebec assumption that we could go at full steam against *both* Germany and Japan at the same time; the other necessity is military *and* political:—Solid agreement upon a truly *allied* policy for Germany; men still talk of unconditional surrender of Germany when Germany already knows some of the conditions—uprooting of millions in East Prussia; loss of the Rhineland and

Silesia; these at least are the conditions being announced—by the French, Russians, British—unilaterally and piece-meal.

Mr. Archibald MacLeish calls for a freer flow of news among the Allies. A beginning will have to be made in some high places. Interlocking agreements among governments for political censorship have developed all over the world. The Chinese, with the concurrence of the American War and State Departments, stopped nearly every attempt to tell the truth about internal China—and so the public was surprised and shocked by the Stilwell affair; from New Delhi it was impossible to tell the whole truth about India; in Cairo, by connivance of various authorities, Americans included, no reporter could tell the political truth about Egypt, Syria, Greece or Yugoslavia for a long time; and so people were shocked to find liberated Greece actually in a state of civil war, and puzzled over the disappearance of Mihailovitch. There was, and is, political censorship in Italy and Belgium; it is called military censorship and the stock excuse in all these places is that military and political affairs are so intermingled that news about politics *has* to be bluepenciled. . . .

If people are also shocked by present *military* events, it is not so much because information was *stopped*, as because *bad* information has been issued; nearly every important general and admiral has been seriously and publicly wrong in his estimate of enemy resistance; which means that our intelligence, about German morale, manpower, oil reserves, aircraft production, has simply been bad intelligence; apparently our aviation experts have been the worst offenders; and perhaps there is some explanation in this fact: that the people whose mission it is to smash German plane production are the very same people who estimate the results, for government and public; there is no independent judge in the picture. . . .

A great many people here have a maddening sense of having been led up the garden path; and at least one paper calls for a purge among the experts. . . .

*   *   *

We began this broadcast by describing what the war is like, this Sunday afternoon.

That's what *all* those called correspondents or commentators, analysts or observers will be saying it's like; they believe it, the listeners and readers understand it and what we say *is* true enough—but only within *our* terms of reference; in the unreal language of standard signs and symbols that you and I must use. To the *soldier*, in the line, that isn't what the war is like, at all. He *knows* the real story, he *feels* it sharply, but he couldn't tell it to you, himself. If I plucked one from his foxhole now and put this microphone before him, he would only stammer and say something like this: "Well, uh, I was lying there, and uh, I saw this Jerry coming at me with a bayonet, and uh, well . . ."—That's how most of them would talk. I know because I've tried them. If the soldier can't tell you what happened to his stomach at that moment, what went on in his beating heart, why the German's belt buckle looked as big as a shining shield—if he can't tell you, no onlooker ever can.

The *army* treats all men alike, but the *war* does not. Not this war. It's too big and far flung. It has a thousand faces and a hundred climates. It has a fantastic variety of devilish means for testing a boy's brain, for stretching his nerves, for making him ashamed or making him proud; for exposing his heart, or for burying his heart. It treats no two exactly alike; and so, even two soldiers from the same front sometimes don't understand what the other is talking about.

Generals—and journalists—use big, standard words like "teamwork" or "soldierly behavior," which are like interchangeable parts and can be fitted into the machine without thinking. But the soldier's handbook gives little guidance on such matters as how to learn the patience of a saint, how to quench bitterness when your officers make a costly mistake, or how to master the homesickness that comes at Sunset.

Who is to relate these things, which make up the real but secret story of the war? Who is to reconstruct, in scenes and acts, the drama of that American on the desolate airfield in the gulf of Aden? The one who sat three hours, unmindful of the crashing heat, his eyes fixed upon a stone. He had been at that airfield eighteen months, and he didn't talk to his comrades any more.

What about the soldier with the child's face, who stumbled from the exploding wheatfield near Anzio, with not a mark on his body, but his eyes too big, his hands senselessly twisting a towel, and his tongue darting in and out between his teeth?

What was it had expanded in the soul of a young man I first knew when he was a press agent lieutenant three years ago; then, he was rather silly and talked too much and his men smiled behind his back. I met him next in a French forest; he had learned control and dignity; he was a Major commanding a fighting battalion, and the *General* was silent while he spoke.

There was a regimental Colonel at Anzio who received notice one night that he could go home next day to Des Moines, where his business was prosperous and his family large. His division had been decimated, but this man's life was now assured. Why, at dawn, at his regular hour, did he risk the mortar shells, and crawl on hands and knees from foxhole to foxhole, not missing one, just to speak a confident word to his men?

Who could *really* explain about that young Corporal with the radio post deep in the Burma jungle; the one who rose suddenly from his bunk in the night and walked straight into the woods—walking westward?

Only the soldier really *lives* the war; the journalist does not. He may share the soldier's outward life and dangers, but he cannot share his inner life, because the same moral compulsion does not bear upon him. The observer knows he has alternatives of action; the soldier knows *he* has none. Their worlds are very far apart, for one is free—the other, a slave.

This war must be *seen* to be believed; but it must be *lived* to be understood. *We* can tell you only of events, of what men *do*. We cannot really tell you how, or why, they do it. We can see, and tell you, that this war is brutalizing some among your sons, and yet ennobling others. We can tell you very little more.

War happens *inside* a man. It happens to *one* man alone. It can never be communicated. That is the tragedy—and, perhaps, the blessing. A thousand ghastly wounds are really only one. A million martyred lives leave an empty place at only one family table.

That is why, at bottom, people can let wars happen, and that is why nations survive them and carry on. . . . And, I am sorry to say, that is also why, in a certain sense, you and your sons from the war will be forever strangers.

If, by the miracles of art and genius, in later years, two or three among them can open their hearts and the right words come, then perhaps we shall all know a little of what it was like. And we will know, then, that all the present speakers and writers hardly touched the story.

— o —

No two commentators could be much farther apart than Gabriel Heatter (MBS) and Raymond Swing (ABC). The two scripts that follow, broadcast two days apart and dealing with some of the same news configurations, show the contrasts. (The contrasts in the attitudes, methods, and personalities of the two men are vividly portrayed in the two *New Yorker* Profiles cited earlier in this chapter.)

Heatter thinks of himself as a kind of people's evangelist. He is ready to comment on virtually everything. Not that he talks about everything —what he calls "Heatter stories" are those high in human interest, in opportunity for sentimentalization. Note in his script that every news subject to which he gives more than a line or so is treated emotionally; that his comments are largely emotional and opinionated rather than the outgrowth of careful logic (and that they frequently raise the specter of impending doom). He uses a baseball story as an avenue to annoyed ruminations on the lack of "a reasonable and decent civilized old age pension payment" (his audience of somewhere near fifteen million each night is heavily rural, and a high percentage of it is of an age to which the Townsend movement appeals); after mentioning the desire of small nations for majority rule in the peace conference, he does not analyze the meaning or effect of the movement, but expresses his opinion with a hearty "more power to them." Note the ominous admonitions of his closing passage on the atom bomb—effective soap-box oratory but hardly factually supported reasoning. Note the characteristic "good news" passage just before the mid-commercial, one predicting nirvana largely because Heatter foresees it; and the copybook transition to the commercial itself (included in the script because Heatter writes and delivers it himself).

Note all these things. But don't miss the simplicity, informality, and directness of Heatter's style, the homely and effective figures of speech, the easy popular diction. Whether or not one likes what Heatter says, his skill and craftsmanship cannot be denied.

The script * (opening and closing commercials, voiced by an announcer, omitted):

Good evening, everyone. Here's an echo of last week's underwater atom bomb explosion at Bikini. The Japanese battleship Nagato has gone down. It went to the bottom in Bikini Lagoon five days after the underwater atom bomb went off. The Nagato weighed 32-thousand tons, one of the heaviest armored ships in the whole world and the third largest capital ship sent to Davey Jones' Locker by that one underwater explosion.

Here's a prediction. The cost of nearly everything men and boys wear is going up . . . way up.

* By written permission of Gabriel Heatter, March 18, 1948.

And here's another. The war profits investigation has only begun. President Truman tonight gave full authority for the inspection of all tax returns, income and excess profits filed by war contractors.

A third prediction. If and when war comes again, cost plus on war contracts will be a thing of the past. Washington is shocked tonight to hear that government officials and Army officers were fraternizing with war contractors. That many who handled settlements of war contracts running into untold millions of dollars later went to work for the same companies covered by those settlements . . . shocked to hear that cost plus made it possible to tack on entertainment bills which will cost John Q. Taxpayer plenty. All this while GI Joe was sweating it out in foxholes.

Well, the new decontrol board is in—OPA—the new board approved tonight by the Senate. Perhaps you've wondered how high can prices go. Here's one—a watermelon brought $2.25 recently. The man must have had a tremendous yen for watermelon.

We're waiting for new prices on new cars. Tonight's indications are about $85 more on the popular priced models.

The Big 4 domination of international affairs may be over. Dr. Herbert Evatt, representing Australia, opened a real fight in Paris today to give smaller nations a real voice in the Peace Conference. I once heard a diplomat say that when you come out of a conference with Mr. Molotov you get more perspiration than you get negotiation. Well, now 17 smaller nations have determined to make Mr. Molotov experience perspiration. They want majority rule. More power to them.

One thing is plain tonight. The French are going to lose again. Great Britain is going along with the United States to merge both their zones in Germany into one economic unit. France has been holding out for internationalizing the Ruhr where the coal, iron and blood make wars. You remember France fought for that in 1919 and lost. She'll lose again. And so we get the amazing paradox—Trieste internationalized—but the Ruhr where war is born—the Ruhr remains intact.

Another paradox. Finland, Rumania, Hungary, Bulgaria are probably done for. They're completely behind the Russian iron curtain. That's where they're likely to remain. And Germany is to come out strong and intact.

Well, they're hunting for Martin Bormann tonight. Bormann, Hitler's party leader. Munich is alive with rumors saying Bormann was seen a few days ago. Put me down as saying if they find Martin Bormann alive, they may find Hitler too.

Well, here's some good old fashioned figures. 10-thousand head of cattle delivered to mid-west markets today. You can have meat for breakfast, meat for lunch and meat for dinner now.

Here's some figures of another kind. Farm land up 65% in cost over pre-war figures in Illinois. 55 in Iowa. And a late report reveals farm land generally over the entire country is now selling at 60% over the figure of 7 years ago.

For any man who wants a brand new field with a future, here are some figures. Total sales of frozen foods are now nearly 10% of all the grocery volume business in the entire country, and they're going up every day. Frozen food—there may be a real future in that for a man who wants a new deal.

The men who want a new deal in baseball may get it. The conversations began today. 26 men representing 480 players began their talks with the management. What do they ask for? A minimum salary somewhere between $5000 and $7500 a year. 10% of whatever money they bring when they're traded. 50% of all money brought in by exhibition games. And most important of all—they want old age pensions. Yes, a few men who made big money were in good financial shape when their playing days were over. A few could move into other good paying jobs. For the most part ball players are old at 40. For the most part it isn't easy after that. We'll hear more about that phrase old age pensions in a good many other fields. We're a hundred years behind on that matter. We look upon old age pensions as charity or a crackpot scheme. We forget how many millions of elderly persons whose toil and whose very lives are poured into a given industry are forced to depend on their children when they want and need and deserve the dignity of independence which old age has certainly earned. They put billions of dollars into appropriations of all kinds and never worry about the cost. Mention a reasonable and decent civilized old age pension payment and we look upon anything over a pittance as a crackpot idea.

Now here's some really good news. I want to emphasize it—good news! We've made the turn and here it is. For the first time since VJ-Day we're turning out as many tons in steel, we're loading as many freight cars, we're using as much electric power—and this may be the most important of all— we are finally building as many new cars as we did in a really good week at any time before the war. We're on our way at last. If we can avoid rocking the boat now, if we'll just be good to ourselves long enough to let the tide roll along for, well, a year or even half a year, we'll fool everyone who is waiting for the next American depression. You know we've been fooling people that way for a long time. In '76 we put out a new trade mark—and called it Liberty! They'll never make a go of it, said the broken down royalty in Europe. Well, you know what we did. In '64 we had a war at home. There they go, breaking up, said the tumbled down chancellories of Europe. We came out united and fooled them again. In '39 Hitler said the war would be over before America could deliver a plane. Did we fool Hitler? Now the gentlemen in dark glasses say we can't make it without another depression. We've made the turn—the biggest and most important turn of all. We're back to prewar figures in production for the first time! Let no man rock the boat now and we're away. Figures never lie and they tell an eloquent and heart-warming truth tonight. Department store volume up again for another week, up again for the entire month of July when it generally falls off. The profits [sic] of gloom point to disaster—the figures point to better business, more jobs and an amazingly healthy national economy and better living for millions of American homes. . . .

. . . . There's bound to be more room now for the men who are determined to plug and get ahead.   •

You know the right appearance helps a good deal. And Kreml on your hair is a good password to better hair grooming. No, water don't [sic] do it, can't do it. Kreml Hair Tonic will. Kreml to help keep your hair soft and smooth in appearance. Keep it well groomed for every occasion. Thousands upon thousands of men everywhere know it and rely on it, and use Kreml every day. They know there's a treat to look forward to every day and they feel all that quiet inner confidence a man feels when he knows his hair is well groomed . . . looks his best and he feels it and knows it. I know you'll like Kreml. I'm sure you'll look forward to it every day. Will you begin tomorrow? Thank you very much.

Well, Congress is preparing to go home, possibly by Friday. . . .

. . . . And tens of thousands of men who fought the war can't find a home. The Housing Bill seems to be dead for this session. Divorce is setting all time records. One reason—they are forced to drift apart—they can't live together—they can't find a home. Children are in trouble. We've never had so many children in trouble before. They're without the great American influence—a home. Congress is going home. There are millions of homes where they've been waiting two and three years for the 65¢ an hour minimum in pay, where they can't live on less. Congress is going home and the bill remains pigeon-holed. Yes, Congress is going home and blind children are waiting for the appropriation which makes life bearable and the everlasting dark in which so many are compelled to live.

Old friends of Hitler, now masquerading as friends of America, they have their hands out. We don't seem to have the money for our own people.

Hitler's old friends, they have their hands out. I know what I'd like to put in those hands and you would too, I'm sure.

Ladies and gentlemen—the greatest race in all history is on tonight. A race between man and the atom bomb. For the first time in thousands of years man has finally built a weapon which makes mass suicide possible for the entire human race. Will it be suicide or will it be the end of war? The end of fear, the end of violence, and that dream—that golden dream of peace on earth. The race is on to a finish. There can be no halfway victories in this race. Man or the bomb will win. You know other forms of life have lived on this earth and vanished completely. Is it man's turn to blow himself out of existence now? Are we going back to the cave, to the deepest, darkest kind of cave to live in fear and trembling—fear of atom bombs? Or will man live with the dignity with which God has endowed him? This is it—last call. This conference in Paris and the others to come. Let the little men all over the world who think this is the time to say my way or else think well and think hard. We are racing against time and we're late. The odds are on the bomb. In the past four thousand years man had only 265 years without war. The drunk who could barely stand but had to have just one more—the one that finally finished him off—he would fit the role of any man who was mad enough to think we can handle just one more war. The dead move in their sleep tonight. They move silently and come together and ask each other—will the living keep faith? The mothers of all the dead have taken up their vigil and they wait, and the mothers of all living children pray and wait. Watch out for the man who would tell everybody where they get off now . . . whatever his nationality . . . watch out for him. Watch out for the man who can't speak with the humility we all need in this fateful hour for he's like a man reeling and yet demanding just one more. Well, which will it be, the atom bomb or peace? It can't be both. This is last call . . . the very last.

Half a minute, please, your good friend and mine, Frank Waldecker. . . .

Now contrast to this the Raymond Swing commentary of two days later (July 31, 1946). Swing's script is more nearly "pure commentary" than any of the others reprinted here. He gives no news as news—he uses news pegs, such as the Paris conference and Secretary Byrnes' comments, but he appears to assume that his listeners already know the news-facts involved (not often a valid assumption, especially when the news is "difficult"; it may account in part for the fact that Swing's audiences have never been large). He makes no concession to anecdote, wisecracks, homely allusions, sentimentalization, or folksy language.

Instead, he subjects the news to calm and almost cold analysis, marshaling his comments into a carefully unified construction—really a single essay on intimately related subjects. Note the painstaking transitions from paragraph to paragraph. Note, too, that when he talks of the desire of the smaller nations for more voice in international affairs, he does not stop, like Heatter, with a mere expression of approval (though he does express approval), but rather shows exactly what he believes the desire means and what its chances of achievement are. This is commentary at its most meaningful.

Swing's script *:

Two observations need to be made about the Paris peace conference. One is that it is not really a peace conference at all. The most accurate name for it is a peace discussion. It is not writing the treaties, it cannot change the drafts already written. It cannot prevent the treaties as written from being adopted. It is a debating club. It will debate the treaties as already drafted, and it will make recommendations on these and on the portions of the treaties not yet agreed to by the Big Four. In the course of its deliberations it will come to vote on what it recommends. But that vote is not binding on the Big Four, who are pledged only to give the recommendations of the Paris conference their consideration.

Never before has such a conference of nations been held. It is unprecedented that many nations, members of the coalition which won a world war should have so little authority. But *they* did not win the war, it was won *for* the coalition by the great powers. And the peace will be made by those who won the war. Therefore, the peace conference, socalled, is not the proper address for the prayers which a hopeful world is sending up for the writing of a real peace. This is not a second Versailles which might learn from the mistakes of the first Versailles. This is a second-class conference, with considerably less than second-class authority.

One must go on from there to say that it also is making recommendations on what are in fact no better than second-class peace treaties. And that is the other observation that needs to be made.

An editorial in the current issue of the Free World pleads eloquently for a peace treaty that will establish true peace. It must, it says, "put an end to the tragic cycle of history: war, defeat, agitation against conditions of previous peace treaties, and again war; must break up the endless chain

* By written permission of Raymond Swing, August 2, 1946.

of elements of hatred which have brought so much sorrow on humanity, and must open up new vistas. In other words it must not be like the Versailles Treaty or like the other treaties of the past, all of which were fifty years or more behind the times—it must be a truly twentieth century treaty."

But the draft treaties laid before the twenty-one nations do not come within hail of the world as it is, as is shown by the single fact that they do not even mention atomic energy. The defeated powers, so far as the drafts cover the problem, are quite free to make atomic bombs. They are not listed among the banned weapons, though there is a loophole which permits the addition of other banned weapons at a later date.

But mention of atomic energy is not what distinguishes the atomic era. That can be done only by making peace that leaves no chance whatever of war. The Paris treaties have no such objective. They have arisen from a war and are drawn up with the possibility of another war in view. The treaties are punitive, the territorial changes are strategic or mainly represent conquest. In a world of war, a peace treaty is bound to express the terms of victorious power. And the terms of victory have never yet been the terms of permanent peace, nor are they this time. Such a peace will not be under discussion by the twenty-one nations at Paris. Indeed the conference is dealing with only one nation, Italy, which fought against the Western powers, and with four which fought only against Russia. So most of the treaties are drawn up in the interest of Russia, and nothing said or done at the Paris conference is likely to change that aspect of them.

Moveover, the Paris conference does not deal with the central peace problem, Germany, or with the Austrian treaty, on which an end of military occupation in that country, and in Hungary and Roumania, depends. What is done with Germany will set the pattern for the Europe of the next decade or more, not what is done with Germany's satellites. Hence the conference in Paris is not only limited in scope and without any authority, it cannot be expected to lay foundations for a world of law and justice, which alone can sustain the world of peace.

Seen in this perspective, the doings of the conference are hardly of remarkable importance. And the mere fact that holding this conference was counted a great victory for American diplomacy should not lead us to attribute undue significance to anything taking place there. It is, of course, good that the small nations should be meeting and lifting their voices. But that they are doing so does not make their meeting a peace conference, and it is inaccurate, if not dishonest, to call it one. Everything happening in Paris has to be understood in these terms. Thus it is not a revolution in diplomacy that all sessions of the conference are to be open to the press, not only the plenary sessions but commission meetings as well. If that happened at a real peace conference, it would be realizing the Wilson aspiration of "open covenants openly arrived at". But at Paris, no covenants are being arrived at. What is to be open will be discussion, recommendations and voting. The treaties then go back to the Big Four, who are utterly free to reject any and all recommendations.

Nor is it of great promise that Mr. Molotov for the Soviet Union today bespoke equal treatment at Paris for all nations, great and small. That sounded almost like Mr. Evatt, the Australian delegate, with his resumed campaign to break the dictatorship of the Big Four. But equality of all the nations at Paris means only equality in discussion and recommendation.

An issue has arisen over how the conference should vote—whether by a two-thirds majority or a simple majority. If a two-thirds vote is required, eight states can defeat a decision by the conference. If a majority vote is enough, it will take eleven states to defeat a decision.

The two-thirds rule was recommended by the Big Four, and Secretary Byrnes has duly backed it, as he was bound to do as one of the authors of the recommendation. A two-thirds vote was more liberal than Versailles, where there was unanimity on substantive matters. Mr. Byrnes seemed to be modifying the Big Four unanimity by a promise he made in his speech before the conference yesterday. In this he said that he would undertake to back any recommendation made by two-thirds of the conference powers. That looks like taking the small powers into peace treaty making so far as the United States is concerned. But closer examination gives Mr. Byrnes' promise a much narrower effect. Since it takes only eight votes to prevent a two-thirds majority from forming, four of these eight can be supplied by the Big Four themselves, and the other four could easily come from the Soviet bloc, consisting of Poland, Czechoslovakia, White Russia, the Ukraine and Jugoslavia. The Big Four are pledged to stand by the parts of the treaties they themselves have accepted. And Russia can be counted on delivering all her satellites on demand. So the Byrnes promise cannot change what already has been agreed, unless he and the British or French change their minds about standing by the decisions already reached, which would be a breach of faith.

As to the parts of the treaty on which agreement has not yet been reached, the Soviet Union still can muster six of the eight votes needed to prevent a two-thirds majority going against Soviet interests, and it is quite possible that Russia in many cases will be able to pick up two more votes. So it is no foregone conclusion that Mr. Byrnes has pledged himself to back up much in offering to support all decisions by a two-thirds vote.

Most Americans probably have sympathy with the determined fight of Mr. Evatt of Australia to whittle away from the power of the Big Four and get more power for the smaller allies. But it is one thing to have sympathy for what appears to be a move toward greater democracy, and quite another to believe that what Mr. Evatt wants is practicable or even desirable. It is to be doubted that Americans as a whole would approve of settling questions affecting their own rights by a majority of sovereign nations. They would hardly give the final say over United States rights to a majority or even a two-thirds vote of sovereign nations. There would be no freedom in that for us. Just now it is popular to wish to see Russia outvoted, but to this the Russians object, as should we if we found ourselves outvoted in vital matters.

If there are to be unlimited sovereignties, there can be no hope for international agreement by which a great power is overruled in what it considers vital matters. Moreover, the basis on which the Russians were brought into the United Nations was the maintenance of sovereignty with a veto in all matters of vital importance to the great powers. So the small powers are trying to talk their way into sharing power which is not theirs and will not be given to them, since power is not something that nations can be talked into giving away.

The one way to obtain a really democratic rule of international affairs is the subordination of national sovereignty to a world sovereignty. In this naturally there could be no veto. But in this, decisions would not be reached by diplomacy and conferences but by the enactment of laws, which would be enforced. But until there is a system of enforced law, the veto is the only final assurance of the freedom of the states which might otherwise be outvoted.

Even if there were a world parliament to enact world law, that could not function by the formula of a simple majority vote of nations for that would permit the small nations to dominate the big ones. Such a parliament would have to be chosen, too, by some other criterion than the democratic basis of population. Otherwise, the countries with the most people would become the strongest lands politically, which in fact they are not. India and China, with more than 800 million inhabitants, would never be permitted to outvote the United States and the Soviet Union with fewer than half that many. That is just as obvious as that the United States and the Soviet Union would not permit any three small nations to outvote them.

So what the small powers propose would not work in the world as it exists, nor would it in the world one must hope is going to exist. And the small powers are not greatly serving the cause of the peace in asking for more power for themselves, even though the diffusion of power is something devoutly to be desired. For the present, the one thing that keeps the peace is good relations between the United States and the Soviet Union. So long as they agree there can be no world war. The longer they disagree, the more probable world war becomes. Nothing the small powers can offer will change that truth. No majority of nations conceivable can enforce its will on either us or the Russians.

The Discussion Program

The discussion program—the show in which a group of "experts" talks and argues about a topic current in the news—is ordinarily not a concern of the newsroom. Radio's two top discussion shows, the "Chicago Round Table" and "America's Town Meeting," are both produced independent of newsrooms. Nevertheless, this kind of program has as its main function the topic of this chapter: the backgrounding and illumination of significant current subjects. As such a program, it may well become a newsroom function, especially since the FCC dictum of early 1946 increasing its emphasis on public service programming.

Consider the structure of the "Round Table" and the "Town Meeting."

"The Chicago Round Table"—described as "a cooperative enterprise of the University of Chicago and NBC," though NBC's share consists only in providing broadcast time—is strictly an ad-lib program. But this fact does not mean lack of preparation. Advance work before the show takes the air at midday Sundays is arduous and lengthy. Here is the procedure:

Some ten days in advance of the date of broadcast the staff of the University of Chicago radio department selects a topic for discussion— one that will remain newsy and, preferably, controversial ten days later —and chooses three experts to discuss it. Men or women with differing points of view are picked when possible. If the topic involves labor and management, participants are likely to be a CIO official, a United States Chamber of Commerce representative and, perhaps, a professor of economics who may be expected to be "disinterested."

The radio department's research staff goes to work, assembling data on the topic, making bibliographies, briefing and digesting pertinent material. The result of this work is provided to each participant, three or four days before the broadcast.

Saturday evening the participants meet at dinner in the University's Quadrangle Club. There they sit from 6 o'clock often until midnight, arguing, planning, discussing many phases of the subject. The director of the radio department makes notes; then he prepares a detailed outline, showing major topics on which the participants have put their fingers and offering an orderly plan for the program.

At 10 Sunday morning the three meet around the triangular "round table"—there is no moderator for this program—and, using their outlines, proceed to go through a half-hour discussion. A transcription is made, and immediately played back. From it the participants discover their errors—in manner, in under- or overemphasis, and so on—and make plans for the final presentation. At length, after all this preparation, they go on the air.

It has been argued that a show with such elaborate rehearsal and planning cannot be spontaneous. Perhaps. But it has the *effect* of spontaneity; and it is unquestionably a sounder and more effective discussion than it would be were any of the preparatory steps omitted.

Few radio station newsrooms are equipped to undertake anything so elaborate as the "Chicago Round Table" plan, though simpler modifications of it are part of the broadcast schedules of many stations. "America's Town Meeting," of different format, is also a model on which stations may base presentations.

The "Town Meeting," though younger than the "Round Table" (it started in 1935, the "Round Table" in 1931), is better known. This is largely because more ballyhoo and showmanship have been exerted on the show—it tours the country, uses New York's well-known Town

---

On occasion, careful advance plans may be discarded to permit the "Round Table" to take up a "hot" subject. When Germany invaded Czecho-Slovakia, ten days of preparation were thrown out the window and, on twenty-four hours' notice, Dr. Edouard Beneš, former Czecho-slovak president, was substituted.

Hall as its base of operations, is an audience-participation show. It is broadcast at an evening hour, and it has at times been sponsored.

Unlike the "Round Table," it is only in part an ad-lib program. Its format employs from two to four authoritative speakers, representing opposing views of the topic under discussion; George V. Denny, Jr., owner and director of the show, serves as moderator. The program opens in a large theater or auditorium about half an hour before broadcast time. Mr. Denny explains to the audience the plan of the show, gives essential background on the topic, starts discussion. When broadcast time arrives, he introduces the speakers, each of whom has been admonished to use his few minutes and no more. After their formal speeches, which may be from script, Mr. Denny propels them into informal debate and discussion—the more spirited the better. Before the hour closes, a number of questions from the audience are read and answered by members of the discussion panel. After the show goes off the air, the discussion continues for fifteen minutes or half an hour— this to carry out the structure of the program as a version of the old New England town meeting.

Sponsorship of the "Town Meeting" by *Reader's Digest*, in 1944, aroused anxiety among a good many listeners that the nature of the program would change—that it would suffer from dictation, censorship, and "packing" on the part of the sponsor. Vigorous among such worriers was George Seldes, whose concern stemmed from his opinion that *Reader's Digest* was a "native fascist" organ. Mr. Denny has just as vigorously denied that any such influence existed. The sponsorship increased the show's broadcasters from 120 to 181 stations, he says, and gave it additional income that enabled it to set up a research department to provide factual material to speakers in advance of programs. But it gave the sponsor, he says, no control of any sort over selections

---

Transcripts of the "Chicago Round Table" programs, with bibliographies and discussion questions, are offered at low price by the University of Chicago radio department. Transcripts of the "Town Meeting" programs appear in the *Town Meeting Bulletin*, published by the American Education Press, Inc., Columbus, Ohio. Both enterprises provide manuals for speakers—manuals jammed with useful hints for planners of discussion programs.

of topics or speakers, and in no way affected the conduct of the program.

Mr. Seldes was also concerned about the fact that Mr. Denny, before each broadcast, "plants" a number of questions in the audience. Mr. Denny, however, explains that this is not an ideological but a showmanship device—that its purpose is to make certain that there will be questions at the proper time. Unplanted as well as prearranged questions are always included in the programs, he says.

Directors of both programs offer suggestions as to qualities vital in such shows. Sherman H. Dryer, for a number of years director of the "Round Table," says that "in the long run, the audience of any (discussion) program will grow in size and loyalty in proportion to the efforts of the program to provide three things, in this order—information, clarification, stimulation." Mr. Denny, speaking of techniques of interesting audiences, says in his *Discussion Leader's Handbook* that vital qualities are conflict (divergent views as to methods of meeting common problems), suspense ("anything may happen at these meetings"), and fair play ("questions must relate definitely to the subject, and no personal or libelous attacks may be made").

How these elaborate and costly network discussion programs may be scaled down to fit the limited budgets, production and research facilities, and time of the individual station is a problem for each individual station to solve. It is not always easy. But it is being done, and effectively, by an increasing number of local broadcasters.

12

The Law Says . . . .

Most of the books that would fill a long shelf titled Radio Law are yet unwritten. When they get into print, a heavy majority of them will concern license applications, frequency allocations, and similar complex subjects—subjects that gray the hair of station managers and owners, but that trouble the boys in the newsrooms little.

Radio law as it affects the newsroom is no more formally codified than are its other aspects. An NAB Radio News Clinic in Minneapolis in mid-1946 petitioned the NAB to prepare a "workable treatise" on libel and slander in broadcasting, but to date no such compilation has appeared. Let's look first at this matter of defamation on the air—the area of law that harasses newsmen more than any other.

Libel—or Slander?

No one, be he a Supreme Court judge, a justice of the peace, a corporation counsel, or an LL. D., can tell you whether defamation by air is clearly libel or slander. Indeed, it has been declared libel in some situations, slander in others. Libel is defined as defamation in writing or print; slander, defamation by word of mouth. But defamation in a radio script is written, and when it's broadcast it is oral. Which does that make it? Or is it both?

No, because each is a separate category of law, and you can't be put in jeopardy twice for the same offense. It has to be one or the other. Which?

The safest approach to this ticklish question is to consider it libel. Here's the reason: The law considers libel the more serious offense

---

A discussion of "Defamation by Air: Libel or Slander?" appears in the *Quill* for May-June, 1946. Its author, Norris G. Davis, presents a number of relevant opinions and decisions—some pointing one way, some the other—and arrives at the conclusion that radio defamation ought to be made a "new and separate class of offense with its own penalties."

(since published defamation is judged more permanent and more damaging than oral defamation) and it carries heavier penalties. Radio defamation is of course oral, but court opinions and decisions have pretty well established the legal fact that to broadcast is, in effect, to publish. Consequently, to guard against committing libels is the smart thing to do. By guarding against the greater danger, you're helping to protect yourself against the smaller.

To establish a statement as actionable under the libel law, three elements are necessary:

1. That the statement is published.
2. That it is defamatory.
3. That it refers to an identifiable person.

If you broadcast it, you publish it. No proof is required.

What makes it defamatory?

Defamation, says the law, is holding a man up to "contempt, obloquy, scorn, hatred, or ridicule." Some defamatory statements accomplish this *per se*—on the face of it; others *per quod*—by insinuation or "extrinsic circumstance." In the first category are words like "burglar," "corrupt," "drunken," "prostitute"—words or phrases that impute characteristics that are socially or professionally unacceptable. In the second category are such statements as one that such-and-such a man is "not qualified to hold a teaching position" (if the man is a teacher) or that he "has been known to participate in business deals with the convicted embezzler." These references to the man are not defamatory in their actual words; the question—one for the jury to answer—is, are

---

By Illinois law, radio defamation in the state is definitely libel rather than slander. A New York state court decision in 1947 supports this view. But the California Civil Code makes such defamation slander rather than libel.

The courts have held that to call a man "Communist" is to libel him *per se*.

And they also are inclined to the opinion that a kind of "statute of limitations" sometimes operates on certain truthful libels. They won't let you speak of a man as a Communist or an ex-convict, for example, if the truth is that the man *was* a Communist some years back, or if his conviction dates back some years, but that he has in more recent years lived a life to which such terms do not apply.

they accepted by a reader (or listener) in a defamatory sense?

The third element, identification, means this: Is a specific person called to mind by the defamatory statement? When a name, or name and address, or other such specific information is presented, there is no question about identification. When no such highly identifying information is given, however, identification may still be present. Suppose a broadcast says, "A well-known local lawyer was seen among the mob of drunks." This doesn't name the lawyer, and there may be any number of lawyers who are well-known locally. But if one of them can produce evidence that, rightly or wrongly, he was believed by some of the listeners to the broadcast (or even by one listener) to be the man so indicated, identification is established.

What does all this mean?

That any broadcast of a defamatory story applying by any stretch of the imagination to a specific person may be actionable.

But *not* that any such broadcast will necessarily open the broadcaster to payment of damages.

For there are a number of defenses for the publication of libelous material. Some of them are absolute; others serve only to "mitigate damages."

The absolute defenses, in most cases, are:

1. Truth of the libel.
2. The doctrine of qualified privilege.
3. The laws permitting "fair comment and criticism."

The first defense, truth, means that whenever the accuracy of the defamatory statement can be established, the defamed individual cannot be successful in a suit for damages. A man may safely be called a

---

Since many libelous statements may safely be broadcast, the news editor needs to be doubly on his guard. He becomes so accustomed to handling *safe* libel that he is likely in a moment of relaxation to let dynamite slip through—something that is indefensible, and that may cost his station money (and, perhaps, deprive him of gainful employment). The best rule for any news editor or reporter is this:

Look on anything defamatory as potentially actionable libel.

If he thus schools himself to see every red flag, then examines the flags to see whether they are in the safe or the unsafe category, he's fairly sure to avoid trouble.

burglar if proof is available that he is a burglar. You can call a woman
unchaste if you can show a court without cavil that she is unchaste.

But don't take a chance if you can't prove what you say. There may
be a lot of reason to believe that Joe Doe is the guy who poisoned seven
pet dogs; but don't put mere belief on the air unless you can produce
the evidence. Don't broadcast news telephoned by volunteer informers
unless you have checked it.

"Qualified privilege" is the legal doctrine that gives anybody the
privilege of reporting *fairly and accurately* the proceedings of judicial
and legislative bodies, without liability for any libel such reporting may
contain. This means that anything that is an official part of the proceeding in a courtroom of any kind, or in Congress, a state legislature, or the
city council, may safely be broadcast, as long as the broadcast remains
factual and strictly accurate and fair reporting. But everything in it
must be relevant to the proceedings; it must contain nothing that has
been officially erased from the record or that has been officially ordered
nonpublishable; it is not "fair" if it reports, however accurately, only
enough of the proceeding to give a one-sided picture. Moreover, comment, insinuation, or deduction is likely to destroy the privilege; and
inaccuracy destroys it—as, for example, describing a criminal charge
by anything but its formal title (if the formal charge is "breaking and
entering in the night-time," call it that—not burglary, or robbery, or
anything else). In Atlanta, substitution of the word "Academy" for
"College" in a damage suit story got a wire service into trouble.

Under this doctrine, you may safely report a trial in which some of
the statements turn out to be untrue. If a man charged with drunkenness is found by judge or jury to be innocent, you may report the charge
and the trial without fear of liability, even though the charge is later dis-
proved. You may also report that one city councilman, without proof,
calls another a liar, if he does it in the course of regular council proceedings. But beware of putting it on the air if he makes the charge while
talking with you in the washroom. Beware, also, of reporting a libelous
outbreak by a spectator in a courtroom—it isn't part of the proceeding,
and it isn't privileged. Beware especially of such an outbreak if your
mike is in the courtroom; you're responsible if it goes on the air.

Remember that in most states privilege does not apply to court proceedings until they have somewhere been acted upon by a judge. That is to say, preliminary papers filed with a clerk of court are usually not privileged merely because they have been filed; they do not become a formal part of judicial record until a judge enters the case. Grand jury reports similarly are usually not privileged until they have been returned in court.

Another caution: Don't assume that because a policeman makes a statement to you, you have privileged material. A cop, even if he's a captain, is neither a judicial nor a legislative officer. A few states have statutes making police statements and police records, such as the police blotter, privileged; most don't. The best rule is something like this: Use what a policeman says if you are convinced that its truth can be proved. Otherwise, watch your step.

Most states do not have specific laws relating to defamation by radio. Where laws or judicial interpretations and decisions exist, they vary from state to state, and from state to Federal jurisdictions. The description of laws, practices, and precautions given in Chapter 12 is generalized for general use. But every radio newsman needs to check the laws under which he practices to ascertain the areas in which they are the usual ones, and the areas in which they depart from the usual.

The NAB in 1947 proposed a standard radio defamation law (calling it libel) in an effort to strengthen and make uniform the state laws in this field. This law—providing protection to stations which exercise due care— has been adopted by *Colorado* and *Wyoming*, and a similar one by *Virginia*.

A *Utah* law limits liability where malice is absent, and offers certain other protections. A *Florida* law eliminates liability unless lack of due care can be proved. In *Illinois* stations are relieved of liability when neither station nor employes have advance knowledge of broadcast defamation, or opportunity to prevent it; defamatory statements by candidates for public office are not liable. *Indiana* and *North Carolina* laws eliminate punitive damages if retractions are made. *Iowa* has a law similar to the NAB standard law, as has *Oregon*. *Montana* law says that recovery can be had only when actual malice is proved. An absolute defense is provided in *Washington* if a retraction is broadcast promptly upon written request and if the station can show that the defamation was made without its knowledge and "against (his) wishes by one without authority" to broadcast it. *California* provides that recovery may cover only damages to property, business, or occupation if a retraction has been properly broadcast. Other states appear not to have special protective laws for radio.

Moreover: Don't make the mistake of thinking that you're freed from responsibility because you attribute a libelous statement to its source, or because you call a man "the *alleged* burglar." Such devices may serve to show that your motives are good, and so to reduce penalties. They won't do more than that, if the libel is false. You're still liable.

The doctrine of qualified privilege has been extended to the proceedings of "quasi-judicial" and "quasi-legislative" bodies such as committees, standing or special, of legislative bodies, as well as to administrative bodies like the Federal Trade Commission. But, again, be sure the proceedings you report are official and open, if you need to rest your security on the doctrine.

"Fair comment and criticism," the third absolute defense, is absolute only under carefully restricted circumstances. It means that anybody who is offering himself or his performances or creations for public approval may be criticized. An author's writing, an actor's acting, a radio commentator's speaking and opinions may all be criticized, however scathingly. But criticisms must be directed strictly to the public performances. You can't criticize an actor by saying that he beats his mother-in-law (unless you stand ready to prove that he *does* beat his mother-in-law). You'd be safest not to take a raucous middleaged movie comedienne to task on the ground that you think she would act Ophelia badly. If she does act Ophelia, and you think she has done it badly, you can say so.

Allied to the principles of fair comment and criticism are those of comment and criticism on public officers and candidates for public office. Your latitude for adverse comment on such individuals is wide. Again some cautions, however: Be certain that the *facts* on which you base your criticisms are true—and that your criticisms are reasonable deductions from the facts. Be sure that there is no ground for accusing you of malice—of having reason other than the public benefit for making the criticisms. If it can be shown that you once threatened "to get

---

The remarks in this chapter refer to actions in civil libel—the type in which an individual who considers himself damaged seeks redress from the libeler in a civil suit. The provisions of criminal libel laws, except in a few states with special statutes, do not apply to radio.

the so-and-so because his son hit my son with a shillelagh," and this appears to be the prime reason behind your criticism, you're in trouble.

The principles of fair comment and criticism apply not alone to individuals but also to businesses seeking public patronage or enterprises desiring public support.

A measure of protection to radio stations broadcasting political speeches is suggested by an FCC report of mid-1948. "It would appear," says the FCC, "that a station is not liable under Federal law for libel in such broadcasts." This interpretation grows out of the controversial case of WHLS-Port Huron, Michigan, charged with libel after a 1945 speech by a supporter of a candidate for city office. Because of the libel charge, WHLS withdrew permission for further speeches for the same and opposing candidates. The FCC found WHLS guilty of violating Section 315 of the Communications Act, which forbids station censorship of political speeches: "The most effective means of censorship is complete suppression. . . . Licensees . . . having once exercised their discretion to carry such programs, may not censor."

In other words, if a station grants a request for time for a political speech, it may not retract the grant; it may not censor the speech; and it must grant time for broadcast of opposition views. Since the station may not censor, it cannot ask for deletion of libelous material, and this might put it in unreasonable jeopardy. Therefore, says the FCC, "it

---

It is impossible, within the limits of this chapter, to present all the shadings of the laws of libel and slander. To the newsroom man who wants more detail, the following sources are recommended:

W. R. Arthur and R. L. Crosman, *The Law of Newspapers* (McGraw-Hill, 1940)

Paul P. Ashley, *Essentials of Libel* (University of Washington Press, 1948)

R. W. Jones, *The Law of Journalism* (Washington Law Book Company, 1940)

J. G. Moser and R. A. Lavine, *Radio and the Law* (Parker & Company, 1947)

F. S. Siebert, *The Rights and Privileges of the Press* (Appleton-Century, 1934)

Warner, Harry P., *Radio and Television Law* (Matthew Bender & Co., 1948)

would appear that the station is relieved by operation of Federal law from any responsibility for libelous material."

But there have been court decisions—one upheld by the United States Supreme Court—that question this interpretation. The state of Texas, through its attorney general, has served notice on the FCC that it will continue to hold stations liable, under state law, for libel in political broadcasts. Other states may do likewise. So the FCC interpretation is not a foolproof safeguard. Newsrooms should note particularly that in any case it applies not to all political broadcasts (such as political news), but only to material originating outside the station.

Liability

Who is "liable" in cases of indefensible libel—who foots the bill when an actionable libel leads to assessment of damages? The answer in broad terms is that anybody who may be considered responsible for the libelous material may be called upon to pay. This means the ownership of the station; the station manager; the newsroom director; any newsroom employe who has worked on the material (as reporter or editor); and, possibly, the announcer. The source of the information, too, if he has knowingly given false libelous information for broadcast.

Not that all these *must* be named defendants in the suit. When a playwright felt himself defamed in a 1947 "America's Town Meeting of the Air" program, he asked damages from Town Hall, Inc., the program's "packager"; from the speaker who had called him "Communist" during debate; and from six individuals described in the suit as having aided the speaker in the preparation of the offending script. The 226 network affiliates and the cooperative sponsors were not named in the action (a California slander rather than libel case).

But in a New York libel suit at about the same time, an account executive of a New York advertising firm asked damages from a network, from an advertising agency, and from a radio producing firm that had prepared the show for broadcast. The suit charged that the plaintiff had been libeled in the course of his impersonation by an actor in a dramatization of certain North African operations in World War II.

The knottiest problem of liability in broadcasting arises in the case of the libelous ad-lib statement thrown in by a performer in spite of a carefully prepared, pre-read, nonlibelous script. Al Jolson, in a 1939 network program, threw in an ad-lib remark that such-and-such a hotel was "rotten." The hotel sued; a lower court awarded $15,000 damages, but the Pennsylvania Supreme Court reversed the decision on the ground that the network had exercised due care in preparing a libel-free script, and that it could not be held for Jolson's unrehearsed and unforeseen remark. The difference in opinion of the two courts illustrates the fluid state of the law on this point; there seems to be a tendency to hold as did the Pennsylvania Supreme Court. Davis, in his *Quill* article cited earlier in this chapter, elaborates on this subject.

Watch Out for Lotteries

When Congress passed the Communications Act in 1934, it told broadcasters, "Keep anything about lotteries off the air." That's a flat and all-inclusive mandate. You'll be violating the law if you tell your listeners that a lottery is to occur, or that it did occur with such-and-such results. Avoiding the word "lottery" won't help. You may offend if you so much as mention, for example, an Irish Sweepstakes winner. (This doesn't alter the fact that many radio newscasts *do* mention lottery news; but it's risky.)

What is a lottery?

The law says that, to constitute itself a lottery, an event must present three elements: prize, chance, and consideration.

For many years the Post Office Department has had a regulation forbidding newspapers their customary mailing privileges if they contain news of lotteries. Until 1947 this regulation was interpreted strictly—in the same terms as Section 316 of the Communications Act, forbidding broadcast of lottery news. When a news story involving a lottery in a subordinate relationship became of national interest, however (the story of a Negro in North Carolina denied a prize he had won in a lottery), the *St. Louis Star-Times* won a fight to liberalize the regulation. According to the 1947 Post Office ruling, stories containing "incidental" mention of lotteries will not bar newspapers from the mails.

The Communications Act provision has not yet been so liberalized. Action to bring it into line with the Post Office attitude, however, may be anticipated.

The meaning of "prize" is easy. If somebody gets out of the event something he didn't buy—a Cadillac or a penny pencil, a movie pass or a trip to Calcutta—the element of prize is present.

"Chance" is also simple to define. "Chance" means that the prize went to its winner in a manner completely outside his control—in a manner that he had no power to affect. If there is competition present, or if the element of skill enters, you may be fairly sure there's no legal chance. If the prize goes to somebody who throws a beanbag farther than other competitors, or who writes a better last line to a limerick, or who stands on his head longest, there's no "chance"—it's skill. But if his name is drawn at random from a hat, or by random choice from the city directory, or if his winning ticket is designated by a whirling spindle on a movie stage, chance is present.

"Consideration" is a little more difficult to pin down. It means some kind of effort on the part of an individual to make himself eligible for the prize: the payment of money, the purchase of a ticket or filling out of an entry blank, the rendition of a service. If his name is drawn at random from the city directory, and he can do nothing to aid such drawing, there's no consideration. But if he buys the raffle ticket that goes into the hat, there is.

Some examples:

A woman attending a movie fills out a card and puts it into a box along with others like it. Her card is drawn, and she gets the turkey. Verdict: a lottery, because prize (the turkey), chance (random drawing), and consideration (buying the movie ticket and filling out the card) are involved.

A man walking down a street strictly on his own business is pointed out at random and given a $5.00 bill. Verdict: no lottery, because there's no consideration (the man had made no effort to make himself eligible), though there are prize and chance.

A child at a church supper has his name read off as the first drawn from a box containing names of all those present, but receives no other

In response to inquiries from its members, the NAB in 1947 issued a "General Guide on Lottery Law in Day-to-Day Station Operation." The "Guide" appears in *NAB Reports* for June 9, 1947, page 459.

reward. Verdict: no lottery, because chance and consideration (the child's presence) aren't supplemented by prize.

A man is given a pair of boxing gloves for having named more dead prize-fighters than anybody else in the room. Verdict: no lottery, for there's prize and possibly consideration, but no element of chance.

In 1948 the FCC proposed tightened regulations to drive from the air the fabulous "giveaway programs" that had become so popular. The proposal had hardly been made public when it was discovered that Congress had removed from the Communications Act the sections covering lotteries, and transferred them to the Criminal Code. The FCC, undismayed, announced promptly that it intended to see that the law was respected, whether it lay in one statute or another. It held firmly that most "giveaway" shows are lotteries.

As for Censorship . . . .

Radio is protected against governmental censorship by the First Amendment to the Constitution, and the Fourteenth, just as are all other avenues of communication. And the Communications Act says that the FCC shall exercise no censorship over what is broadcast by the stations it licenses. As has just been pointed out, the Act forbids lottery news; it also denies the right to broadcast obscenity, indecency, and profanity. This is censorship of a sort. But it is a sort that fits with American mores, and laws of this kind are not disqualified by American judicial practice or opinion.

The radio industry has more than once leveled the "censorship!" charge at the FCC. It did so in 1946 when the Blue Book was issued, and again when the FCC held extensive hearings on an application for a license by the *New York Daily News* to listen to allegations that some of the *News's* editorial opinions rendered it unfit to broadcast. Every time the FCC examines a station's or an applicant's program content the cry is raised. The FCC has, however, stayed pretty clear of dictation of content. It has insisted that a broadcaster devote a portion of his time to programs "in the public interest," and it has emphasized balanced programming—programming consistent with the Communications Act provision that no station may be a special pleader, that balancing time must be provided for divergent controversial views.

But this provision does not restrict views or statements—it says only that if Jones gets time to say black is black, Brown must be given equal opportunity to say it is white.

The Communications Act also provides specifically that stations may exert no political censorship on scripts. The FCC interpretation of this provision is discussed earlier in this chapter.

Radio is about as subject to internal and external, but *unofficial, nongovernmental, extralegal* censorships, as other communication agencies. The officials of a network, the manager of a station, may and do set up restrictions on the types of matter that may be broadcast. They may, if they are unwise, even lay down dicta as to what views and opinions may go on the air. Sponsors are entirely free to put into their programs commentators who espouse their attitudes, and to remove, or keep off, those who see things differently. (But the station over whose channel a sponsored commentator presents one-sided views may have to provide equal time for opponents to have their say.) Women's clubs, churches, political parties, fellow-travelers may bring all the pressure they can command to persuade radio to say this and not to say that.

But don't confuse this kind of censorship with that contemplated, and guarded against, by the First Amendment. They are cats of quite different breeds.

A word about "indecency." Indecency (blasphemy and obscenity, too) is what each day makes it. Values on which judgments are based change constantly. The Communications Act does not say that specific words or ideas may not be broadcast, but merely that obscene words or ideas are barred. But to the Victorians no one had "legs"; today they're practically universal. As broadcasting has grown a bit beyond adolescence, and as its listeners have altered attitudes, a great many ideas and words once spoken only in Pullman smokers have been accepted as socially permissible. This subject has already been treated in Chapter 3.

So the rule is, simply, that of good taste—good taste that takes into account the particular mores of the listeners to be served and the social values of the news. Often it's more desirable to omit entirely news that may be offensive—if it's not of real importance—than to present it with verbal disguise that enhances rather than covers its saltiness.

What Is "Privacy"?

The man who comes up with a thoroughly workable definition of the "right of privacy" and a suggestion as to how, in a democratic society, to enforce it will have the blessing of the law book writers. Most such writers agree that whatever the "right" may be, it's difficult to make it meaningful. Some fifty years ago the chief justice of the New York Court of Appeals said that "the so-called right of privacy is . . . founded upon the claim that a man has the right to pass through this world, if he wills, without having his picture published, his business enterprises discussed, . . . or his eccentricities commented upon whether in hand bills, circulars, catalogs, periodicals, or newspapers." But ten years later a court in Seattle said that "unless controlled by some independent consideration, it has been generally held that there is no such right. Not so much because a primary right may not exist, but because, in the absence of a statute, no fixed line between public and private character can be drawn."

Boiled down, this means that every citizen has the inherent right to live his private life as he wants to, without finding himself in a fish bowl. The apparently insoluble problems are: Exactly how, except in the broadest of general terms, can the right be defined? Where does a man step from the private to the public? Where can the line be drawn? What is the damage when an indubitably private act or situation is laid before the public?

Many of the relatively few suits that have been brought for compensation for invasion of the right of privacy have yielded verdicts of "no recovery." Courts have more than once declared sympathy for the offended plaintiffs, but have pointed out, in effect, that definition of the tenuous line might result in as much injustice to individuals, or as much infringement on society's right to know what is going on, as does the shadowy *status quo*.

Broadcasters have not often been charged with overstepping the line. In one California case, involving a radio dramatization of an auto accident seventeen months after its occurrence, a chauffeur characterized in the play sued and was awarded damages. Most cases in this field, however, have grown out of newspaper publications—a high percentage of them involving photographs of individuals only secondarily connected with news events.

In short, invasion of the right of privacy is not a common radio newsroom headache. This is partly due to the fact that radio has not gone in elaborately for sensational news, or for personal news; and to the additional fact that it has stuck fairly close to the major facts of the news, and has not embroidered them with peripheral "angles."

Good taste, again, is a first-rate bulwark against offense. News that is properly news—accounts of events the knowledge of which keeps the public informed—rarely invades privacy. For both law and common sense hold that a man who by will or accident becomes involved in an event of interest to a considerable number of listeners has lost his inherent privacy insofar as the ramifications of the event are concerned. One caution: You're safe and justified in reporting that a man has been charged with drunken driving, or that he has been struck by a street car. But neither fact gives you the right, moral or legal, to inform the public that he hasn't kissed his wife in ten years.

The Right to Report

Public business is public business. Most facts that are a matter of public record are open to the public; and courts have held that newspapers have a special pecuniary and social interest in access to public records. (This question has not arisen specifically with regard to radio; but there is no doubt that the same principle would hold.) This means that almost all activities of government are legitimate news for radio's reporters: court proceedings, legislative action, official city actions, and so on. It means not only that the records are open to inspection, but that the proceedings themselves are ordinarily open to attendance and coverage.

The rule is not absolute. Any judge may close his court and seal records. Most legislative bodies may go into executive session. Grand jury proceedings are held in private. Quasi-legislative and quasi-judicial bodies such as the FCC or the National Labor Relations Board, as well as Congressional and similar committees, usually hold hearings in public, but conduct deliberations behind closed doors. Executive records are not open to inspection except by executive order. Records of such public agencies as mental hospitals and the state fire marshal's office are ordinarily closed, in the public interest. Reporters may not hamper the activities of peace officers by reporting news of prospective arrests, unless the officers themselves release the information.

But all these exceptions constitute only a small percentage of the sources of public news. The general rule holds in a vast majority of cases: Public business is properly the business of the public, and the accepted agencies of news dissemination have a special right, in the public interest, to report it.

As for unofficial news—that coming from private sources rather than public—radio's right of coverage is precisely that of any other news service. The president of General Motors doesn't *have* to tell anybody that his corporation is going to increase wages; but the radio reporter is prevented by no law or principle from trying to get him to talk. It's the right of a Kansas farmer whose hog was sweepstakes winner at the International Livestock Show to keep to himself the secret of his success—and equally the right of WWWW's farm editor to attempt to persuade him to change his mind.

The obverse of the right to report, of course, is the right not to report. No radio station is obligated to broadcast any news it doesn't want to. Neither the mayor, the local utilities magnate, nor the press agent for an aldermanic candidate may direct a radio newsroom how, when, or whether to use a story. (But when a station permits broadcast of views on one side of a controversial issue, it must grant equal time to the other side.)

Who Owns the News?

Anybody may "own" all the news he wants to.

Anybody has the right to gather whatever news his energy, facilities, and desire make available to him, and to publish it by whatever medium he chooses. There is no legal or moral monopoly on the news business.

Radio reporters have not always been given an even break with newspapermen in access to public information, as has been shown earlier in this book. But the difficulty here is not one of law, but rather one of convincing those who make news, official or unofficial, that radio should receive the same treatment as the other news agencies.

But does he own it after he gets it?

The answer is "yes," but in a qualified sense. The fact that he has gathered the facts of an event but has not yet published them does not hinder anybody else from getting them and beating him to publication. But no one may take from him the facts he has gathered and publish them without his permission. The law of ownership is one of fair competition: He has the right to whatever profit may accrue from his own efforts, and the right to control the use of the product of his own efforts.

The radio news law, in general, is exactly that applied to newspaper ownership of news. No afternoon newspaper may "lift" a story from a competing afternoon newspaper and publish it immediately. The courts have held that such news is the property of the original paper during the period of its commercial value—usually considered the period from the paper's publication time to the appearance of the next succeeding morning paper. Under the same principle, a radio station may not record a competitor's news show and rebroadcast it; the first station owns "quasi-property" rights as long as the news is fresh. And a radio station may not lift news from a newspaper, nor a newspaper from a radio newscast, under comparable circumstances.

The idea for a story—the tip on which it is based—is another matter. A radio station may—and most alert newsrooms do—take a tip for a story it has missed from a competitor's newscast, or from a competing newspaper, send its own man out on it, develop its own story, and broadcast it. In this case it has expended its own time and effort, and has full rights in its own story.

Note this point: Ownership of a story lies not in the reporter who has gathered it for his station, but in the station. News is the property of the ownership of the organization which develops it, not of the employes who do the actual work.

The fact that radio "may not" lift newspaper news does not always prevent it from doing so. In one American metropolitan center a newscaster made a practice of taking a handful of clippings from the latest edition of the city paper to the mike with him—until the newspaper called the station on the practice and let it be known that ownership rights would be legally protected. Most radio newsrooms, however, stand on their own feet—both as a matter of legality and as a matter of pride.

What about copyright and the ownership of "literary style"—the precise rhetorical form in which news goes on the air?

Copyright laws, designed to protect writers against plagiarism, protect literary style. When a script has been properly copyrighted, it may not be published or broadcast in its copyrighted form except by permission of the copyright owner. This prevents any except brief verbatim quotations from it. But copyright does not protect the subject, facts, ideas, or substance in the script. These may form the basis for any number of other broadcasts, provided they are rewritten or paraphrased so as not to follow the original literary pattern.

Radio scripts are given broader protection in one direction than newspaper material. Uncopyrighted material published in a newspaper becomes public property after its commercial or news value has vanished. It may be republished in its original form without penalty. But uncopyrighted radio material, even after broadcast, is not "in the public domain"—its literary form remains the property of its owner. Therefore the rule that a newscast may not be recorded and rebroadcast without proper authorization applies not only during the life of its news value, but also to any later period.

NAB Reports for May 19, 1947 (page 406) offers a general statement on the copyright law as it affects radio broadcasters.

The Last Word

Radio law as summarized in Chapter 12 is a societal development—a two-way bulwark built up for the protection of society and the protection of the broadcaster in his service to society. The radio newsman who observes its suggestions and precautions, and who fortifies himself with knowledge of the peculiarities of the laws of his state, is likely to be able to steer clear of legal involvements. He may add to its protective value by adopting the precept, "When in doubt, move slowly and talk to a lawyer."

But no radio newsman worth the name will be as much concerned about the letter of the law as about the fulfillment of the high responsi-

---

Copyright on a radio script is obtained by filing a complete copy with the Register of Copyrights, Library of Congress, Washington, together with copyright application Form D-2 and a money order for $1.00.

bility he has assumed. The law's protection implies the newsman's obligation: to inform the public as fully, as lucidly, and as promptly as his facilities and his judgment permit; to look on broadcasting not as a private perquisite but as a social instrument; to make accuracy and impartiality the touchstones of his profession; to clarify where the stream of the news runs muddy; to accept the social responsibilities of radio news service as a privilege supported by courage as well as competence; to make the public interest his necessity.

Appendices

A

Codes for Self-Regulation
by News Broadcasters

A Codes of the National Association of Broadcasters

1. The NAB adopted a "standards of practice" code in 1939 containing the following paragraphs relating to news broadcasting:

News shall be presented with fairness and accuracy and the broadcasting station or network shall satisfy itself that the arrangements made for obtaining news insure this result. Since the number of broadcasting channels is limited, news broadcasts shall not be editorial. This means that news shall not be selected for the purpose of furthering or hindering either side of any controversial public issue, nor shall it be colored by the opinions or desires of the station or network management, the editor or others engaged in its preparation or the person actually delivering it over the air, or, in the case of sponsored news broadcasts, the advertiser.

The fundamental purpose of news dissemination in a democracy is to enable people to know what is happening and to understand the meaning of events so that they may form their own conclusions, and therefore, nothing in the foregoing shall be understood as preventing news broadcasters from analyzing and elucidating news so long as such analysis and elucidation are free of bias.

News commentators as well as all other newscasters shall be governed by these provisions.

2. In 1948 the NAB adopted a revised statement of standards of practice. The passages of the statement dealing with news broadcasting are as follows:

NEWS

News reporting should be factual, fair, and without bias. Commentary and analysis should be clearly identified as such.

Good taste should prevail in the selection and handling of news. Morbid, sensational, or alarming details not essential to the factual report, especially in connection with stories of crime or sex, should be avoided. News should be broadcast in such a manner as to avoid panic and unnecessary alarm.

Broadcasters should exercise due care in their supervision of content, format, and presentation of news broadcasts originated by them; and in their selection of newscasters, commentators, and analysts.

Broadcasters should exercise particular discrimination in the acceptance and placement of advertising in news programs. Such advertising should be appropriate to the program, both as to content and presentation, and should be distinctly set apart from the news content.

In programs of news, news commentary, and news analysis which are less than ten minutes in length, no more than two commercial announcements should be used, and they should be given at or near the beginning and end of the program.

Agricultural and market newscasts should be governed by the same general standards applicable to news broadcasts.

POLITICAL BROADCASTS

Political broadcasts, or the dramatization of political issues designed to influence an election, should, if accepted, be properly identified as such. (Because of the present confusion concerning the laws with respect to political broadcasts, broadcasters are advised to consult their lawyers in all cases where they have the least doubt as to the proper method of handling.)

PUBLIC AFFAIRS AND ISSUES

A broadcaster, in allotting time for the presentation of public questions, including those of a controversial nature, should use his best efforts to insure fair presentation. Such time should be allotted with due regard to all other elements of balanced program schedules, and to the degree of interest on the part of the public in the questions to be presented.

Discussions of controversial public issues should be presented on programs specifically intended for that purpose, and they should be clearly identified as such.

The presentation of controversial public issues should be made by properly identified persons or groups.

Freedom of expression of opinion in broadcasts of controversial public issues should be carefully maintained, but the right should be reserved to refuse them for non-compliance with laws such as those prohibiting defamation and sedition.

GENERAL

Sound effects and expressions characteristically associated with news broadcasts (such as "bulletin," "flash," etc.) should be reserved for announcements of news, and the use of any deceptive techniques in connection with fictional events and non-news programs should be unacceptable.

The regular and recurrent broadcasting, in advance of sports events, of information relating to prevailing odds, the effect of which could be expected to encourage gambling, should not be permitted.

Simulation of court atmosphere or use of the term "court" in a program should be done only in such a manner as to eliminate the possibility of creating the false impression that the proceedings broadcast are vested with judicial or official authority.

TIME STANDARDS FOR ADVERTISING COPY

The maximum time to be used for advertising, allowable to any single sponsor, regardless of type of program, should be:

Program Length	Between 6:00 and 11:00 P.M.	All Other Hours
Five-minute	1:00	1:15
Ten-minute	2:00	2:10
Fifteen-minute	2:30	3:00
Twenty-five-minute	2:50	4:00
Thirty-minute	3:00	4:15

B   Codes Adopted by Associations of Radio News Men

A number of associations of radio news editors—at national, state, and local levels—have adopted codes of practice for their members' guidance. Following are three such codes:

"STANDARDS FOR RADIO NEWS" ADOPTED

BY THE NATIONAL ASSOCIATION OF RADIO NEWS DIRECTORS, 1947

1   The basic function of radio news presentation is in the public interest and, therefore, the news director's first responsibility is to the people.

2   The news director should be responsible (within the station organization) only to the station manager, as recommended by NARND and NAB.

3   The news director should be consulted in all station programming pertaining to news and special events for the purpose of attaining sound news program balance.

4 Only the news director should be granted authority by the manager to accept or reject news.

5 Adequate coverage of his own area is the primary obligation of every news director.

6 The minimum essential for every station is one trained news man.

7 Commercials should be separated definitely from the news content, and NARND recommends that a different voice be used.

8 Selection and presentation of news should be unbiased, accurate, factual, impartial and in good taste.

"A CODE OF STANDARDS" ADOPTED

BY THE OHIO ASSOCIATION OF RADIO NEWS EDITORS, 1947

Radio news broadcasting is a particular type of journalism. Therefore, the basic principles of journalism shall apply to the operation of a radio news department. Because of its nature, certain other principles also should apply to radio news broadcasting.

The standards which shall govern the members of the Ohio Association of Radio News Editors are:

1 Radio news must always consist of material of good taste, inasmuch as the radio enters the family circle in the home. Material on the borderline of good taste shall not be broadcast except in cases in which the material is of such nature that honest journalism requires its use. In such cases, lurid details which in themselves add nothing basic to the report shall be omitted.

2 Material for news broadcasting shall be judged for its newsworthiness alone and shall not be reported for the special benefit of any private group or individual.

3 All news reports from private sources shall be broadcast only after they have been confirmed as to source, accuracy and truthfulness.

4 Radio news reports shall be honest, sincere, accurate, truthful and unbiased, and none of these attributes should be sacrificed for brevity.

5 Freedom of speech as guaranteed by the First Amendment to the Constitution means freedom to speak the truth. The freedom to speak the truth implies the freedom of the listener to hear the truth. The responsibility for safeguarding these two freedoms is primarily the responsibility of the executive head of a radio news department, subject only to the authority of the licensee and/or his representatives in management. The news executive should be endowed by management with the authority to determine content of news programs in line with station policy. Editorializing should be clearly labeled in context as such. Commentators and news analysts should be identified and labeled in context to distinguish them from the straight news reporter.

6 News broadcasts must not violate the rights of privacy unless such an invasion is of definite public interest and not merely public curiosity, and is otherwise legally permissible.

7 A news editor should make every effort to be fair, to present equally both sides of a controversy and to give each individual an opportunity to reply to any news story which represents him to the public unfavorably.

8 Every radio station should have the services of at least one full-time news editor.

9 Radio news reporters are entitled to equal access to news sources, and shall be recognized as having the same privileges, legally and otherwise, as representatives of other news media. Radio equipment necessary to broadcasting shall be given equal consideration to equipment used in reporting by other news media.

"STATEMENT OF STANDARDS" ADOPTED

BY THE HOLLYWOOD (CALIFORNIA) RADIO NEWS CLUB, 1947

A well-informed public—in our own country and in all parts of the world—is the greatest single hope for peace in an atomic world. Presentation of the news and of other matters of public interest is the greatest contribution in the interest of the public performed within radio broadcasting schedules. As such, it is also the most forceful single answer the broadcasting industry has to its critics who proclaim that radio has been subverted into the sole function of a merchandising mart. Since presentation of the news occupies this position of importance in radio broadcasting, it logically follows that the means of presenting the news is a matter of primary concern to ownership, management and sponsorship, as well as to those in the profession. Therefore, those of us engaged in the profession submit the following recommendations as goals to which radio broadcasters should aspire in the interest of further improving this vital means of public information.

1 Newscasts, special events, news commentaries, and news analyses should be plainly labeled as such.

2 Programs of a feature type based on events in the news involving such production devices as dramatization or impersonations are logical adjuncts to news programming, but should be clearly disassociated from newscasts, special events, commentaries, and analyses by being labeled for what they are.

3 Each story should be presented in proportion to its total significance in the news, and never for the purpose of advancing a special selfish interest. The implementation of this objective will depend on the measure of responsibility and integrity of the news man or news staff.

4 It should be borne in mind that the news editor's job does not end

with the teletype. It is his responsibility, whenever possible, particularly on regional or local stories of a controversial nature, to secure first hand facts.

5 The line of demarcation between commercial copy and the news content should always be clearly defined. An ultimate goal in this respect would be that the newscaster, analyst, or commentator not read the commercial message. Lead ins to commercials should include no reference to subsequent news.

6 Joint air credits in the case of news broadcasts prepared and delivered by different persons are a desirable professional standard.

7 News is a special medium and as such demands specially trained personnel. In staffing radio newsrooms close attention should be given to the news background and training of news writers, editors and broadcasters. In order to insure an accurate and impartial presentation of news, station management must exercise unusual care in the selection of a radio news editor. He must be competent and capable of accepting full responsibility for the content of all news programs and such content must continue to be based entirely on his judgment, without interference by sponsor or any outside agent. Continued vigilance against any relaxation of this policy is urged.

8 The radio audience is more diverse than the press audience and hence more rigid standards of good taste should apply in the case of crimes of sex, violence, and the coverage of accidents of a gruesome nature.

9 Those who prepare and voice the news should constantly bear in mind the power for "slanting" material which rests even in the tonal inflection employed in delivery. Objectivity in material and voicing should be at all times the goal of good radio news presentation.

10 Minimum news staff standards for all stations should be established. It is recommended that at least one experienced news man be on duty at all times during the hours of broadcasting operation.

C "Radio News Recommendations" by the NAB Radio News Committee, February 28, 1945

News is the industry's No. 1 public service obligation. It commands the eager interest of all ages, all classes.

News broadcasts have come to be a "must" in 33,100,000 homes with their 120,000,000 listeners.

Since each news program must be acceptable to all groups and all ages, broadcasters are obligated to exercise meticulous care in the handling of all matters concerned with their commercial sponsorship.

It is the hope of the NAB Radio News Committee that recommendations which follow will prove helpful to those engaged in the specialized field of radio news.

PART I   HANDLING SPONSORED RADIO NEWS PROGRAMS

Acceptable Sponsorship of News Programs   In the light of the industry's obligation to the public, *is* every type of business acceptable for sponsoring the news?

It is the belief of the Radio News Committee that to a greater extent than is the case with any other type of radio program, the type of sponsorship must be given careful consideration. What might be acceptable sponsorship for one type of program might very well be questionable sponsorship for a news program.

It is suggested in all sincerity that the type of sponsorship of radio news programs be determined with the same judgment of good taste and seriousness which governs the preparation and presentation of the news itself.

Commercial Copy and Length of Commercials   It is felt that better over-all service would result if commercial copy used in radio news programs were prepared in a simple, clear, concise, and straightforward manner to match good news writing. The commercial message should be live copy; the use of the transcribed musical jingle and other novelty types should be discouraged with the idea of ultimate elimination.

Length of the commercial in news programs should be severely limited, with particular attention given to shortening the opening. After specifying limitations in the NAB Code, the Code Committee recommended "further restrictions by individual stations" so far as 5-minute news programs were concerned. This policy is endorsed by the Radio News Committee with "further restrictions, etc." applying to news programs of 5, 10, and 15 minutes in length. Short commercials build good will for both sponsor and station.

Simply as a guide it is suggested that stations think in terms of 150 and 250 words of commercial, respectively, for 5- and 10-minute news programs, these figures to include open and close.

Stations which may sell three 1-minute commercials to three different sponsors, in one "unsponsored" 5-minute news program, are violating the NAB Code as amended April 28, 1943. Such practice is also inconsistent with Radio News Committee recommendations. On 5-minute shows a short open and close is an ideal arrangement.

Identification of Sponsor's Message   Commercial sponsor identification and the commercial message should in no way be made an integral part of the news. Sponsor message should not employ tie-ins with news copy nor other artificial devices to attract listeners' attention.

The use of a separate announcer is helpful when commercials are given.

This is not considered mandatory as long as a clear-cut identification of the commercial segment of the broadcast is given.

Placement of Commercials in News Programs In common practice there are variations, predicated on local conditions, as to whether news commercials are given before, after, or within newscasts. The *manner* in which the commercial is placed is more important than mere mechanical arrangement. The position of a commercial with respect to its proximity to certain subject matter of the news is of *utmost importance*, particularly in wartime.

When placed within the newscast, the commercial may be delivered at the conclusion of any news item, but there should always be a clean-cut line of demarcation between the news and commercial copy. An individual news story should never be interrupted for the sponsor's message. It is equally important to guard against improper placement from the standpoint of the nature of the news immediately preceding the commercial. For example: the commercial should not immediately follow reports of casualties, ship sinkings, domestic disasters, etc.

The number of stations reporting elimination of middle commercials is increasing. A station which embarked on such a policy reports that its news sponsors are now adhering to this plan and are finding it completely successful.

PART II   PROPER IDENTIFICATION OF MEN AND NEWS SOURCES

Commentators and News Analysts Describing staff announcers and other personnel as "commentators" or "news analysts," unless such announcers or other personnel are, in fact, qualified to write and deliver legitimate news commentaries or analyses, should be eliminated. Long continued, such practice would tend to break down the public's confidence in the integrity of news broadcasts.

It is urged that all prepared commentaries, analyses, or other news features, furnished by news wires or other sources, be unmistakably identified as to source, as a simple matter of honesty and information. For example: "Here is John Smith with a news commentary by Global News." The Radio News Committee urges credits so full and frank that there can be no doubt as to whether a commentary or analysis is actually written by the speaker, or whether it is prepared by some other plainly identified source and merely *delivered* by him.

Identification of Radio News Sources In peace or war it is indispensable to accuracy and clarity to identify fully the source of all news (particularly unconfirmed reports) even at the expense of a few extra words. For example: "The Russian armies today reached a point 150 miles from Berlin, the Berlin Radio announced this afternoon in a broadcast which has not been confirmed by Moscow." Identification should always be specific and complete since this very identification of the source may be a major factor in evaluating the news it gives out. (Although most stations and the networks already follow the above principles, there are some stations which in the past have not exercised care in these respects, and it is to them that these recommendations are directed.)

PART III   RADIO NEWS EDITOR MUST BE SOLE JUDGE OF CONTENT

The NAB Radio News Committee re-affirms the principle of presenting as completely as possible, within the time limitations of news broadcasts, an unbiased and factual account of events as they occur in the world, in the nation, and in the locality of the station originating the news program. In order to insure an accurate and impartial presentation of news, station management must exercise unusual care in the selection of a radio news editor. He must be competent and capable of accepting full responsibility for the content of all news programs and such content must continue to be based entirely on his judgment, without interference by sponsor or any outside agent.

Continued vigilance against any relaxation of this policy is urged.

In a restatement of "Radio News Recommendations" on September 17, 1948, the NAB Radio News Committee repeated its 1945 suggestions, with alterations to conform to the 1948 NAB Code (see A, 2 above), and added two paragraphs: One urging the expansion of local news operations in all radio stations; the other supporting the NAB position in the Mayflower case—that stations should be permitted to editorialize.

D   Codes of Individual Stations

Most broadcasting stations that operate newsrooms guide their practices by codes—more often informal than formal, sometimes written and sometimes tacit. Such statements of standards, when they are codified, vary little in general form or in detail from those presented earlier in Appendix A. Their principal variations lie in adaptation of broad principles to specific applications—to the specific conditions their stations must meet.

An example of the precepts set up to govern individual station practice is shown below—excerpts from the mimeographed statement provided by William R. McAndrew, director of news and special events of WRC-Washington. WRC is the NBC outlet in Washington, and originates many network shows; as such, it is not "typical." But its statement of standards is typical in two directions: It uses carefully-worked-out network standards as a starting point, and it incorporates some of its general standards of practice in its style book (presented in Appendix C).

Its broad policies are described in the following paragraphs:

News Policy of WRC The station news policy is governed by the "NBC Program Policies and Working Manual," regardless of whether the show is sponsored or is sustaining. Here are the introductory guiding principles from the Manual:

"Those who exercise a stewardship over the broadcast facilities of this nation have, the duty to bring to radio listeners a full and impartial presentation of news and public affairs, and of men and events important to public understanding. The fundamental purpose of news and opinion in a democracy is to enable the people to know what is happening and to understand events.

"The editorial responsibility of the National Broadcasting Company in its service of news, commentary, and public discussion is to maintain freedom of expression, but to guard against inaccuracy, unfairness, and partiality; to see that all important phases of opinion are reflected in its broadcasting services; to cooperate in every way with public authority and government in the interests of national defense and civilian morale; and, finally, to eliminate from the current day-by-day news and commentary, the slanderous or the malicious."

Policy on Rewriting News The general policy provides that the news editor writing a show shall read the various wire service stories, together with what information may be provided by special NBC coverage, and then evaluate this information. Tack-ups [paste-ups direct from a radio wire] are permitted on certain daily 5-minute newscasts because the sponsor has a contract with United Press Radio to provide news for these shows. UPR runs a special report of date-lined one-paragraph items which are used for this purpose. On other news shows, tack-ups are not used unless the news editor is so pressed for time that he does not have room to rewrite last-minute items.

Policies on Special Events The policy of WRC is to carry as many worthwhile public events as possible, subject to schedule limitations. WRC carries all the President's radio addresses and also devotes much time to carrying talks by cabinet members, other government officials, and nationally known leaders.

The general policy on this is governed by the NBC Manual, which has the following to say about "Discussion of Public Issues":

"The requests of all individuals, groups, or organizations for time to discuss public issues of a controversial nature shall be considered in the light of the contribution which their use of time would make to the public interest and toward a well-balanced program structure. Each such request will be considered solely on its individual merits without discrimination and without prejudice because of the identity of the individual, group, or organization desiring such time.

"The policy of the NBC on public issues of a controversial nature is one of open-mindedness and impartiality. In connection with its own sustaining programs, the Company attempts at all times to give fair representation to opposing sides of every controversial question which materially affects the life or welfare of any substantial group. The NBC does not censor the opinions of speakers who have been given time on the air. It must, however, check for violations of the law and for inaccurate, defamatory, and seditious statements, as the courts have held broadcasters responsible for damaging statements over their facilities."

In addition to carrying such talks of national and international interest, WRC makes every effort to present purely local District of Columbia issues to the public.

Special Rules for Handling Important Bulletins　Each news break or bulletin is judged on its own merits. If the bulletin is of sufficient importance, WRC notifies the NBC newsroom in New York and arrangements may be made to interrupt a program in progress in order to announce the news. If the news is of lesser importance, the network may delay the start of the next following program to read the bulletin. Or if the bulletin is only of local interest or is minor in nature, it will be read at the next available "break" between programs, either at the quarter-hour, half-hour, or hour. There is a standard NBC introduction and close for these bulletins. Special arrangements are provided for announcing tragedies and the deaths of prominent persons, so that the next thing heard by listeners will not be considered frivolous or otherwise be offensive to good taste.

B

Standards for Education
for Radio Journalism

The Council on Radio Journalism was established in January, 1945, by joint action of the National Association of Broadcasters and the American Association of Schools and Departments of Journalism. Its purposes, as defined by its constitution:

1   To coordinate education for all fields of radio journalism with the expanding requirements of this rapidly-developing industry for trained personnel.

2   To bring together for counsel and advice representatives of the educational institutions and the industry to the end that the educational programs of the institutions shall result in the adequate preparation of personnel for radio journalism.

3   To study and investigate such problems in the field of education for radio journalism as may be referred to it by the educational institutions or by the industry, or as may be proposed by the Council or its individual members.

4   To define and, insofar as possible, gain acceptance for minimum standards for education for radio journalism.

5   To establish itself eventually as the voluntary accrediting agency for education programs in the field of radio journalism.

Council membership consists of five members appointed by NAB and five elected by the AASDJ.

In its first several years, the Council prepared the statement of standards for education for radio journalism given below; it prepared and published two bibliographies on radio journalism; it established a continuing program of "internships" for teachers of radio news, whereby journalism teachers might serve in carefully-selected radio newsrooms and gain the experience necessary for effective teaching in the field; it provided material for a "radio news number" of the *Journalism Quarterly* (June, 1946); it made a national survey of the nomen-

384

clature and content of college and university courses in radio journalism, and made recommendations for their strengthening. Headquarters of the Council are in the office of Arthur Stringer, secretary-treasurer, at NAB, 1771 N Street N.W., Washington 6, D.C.

The statement that follows comes from a booklet issued by the Council in October, 1945.

This statement of minimum standards for education for radio journalism is intended as a guide to colleges and universities offering curricula to prepare young men and women for employment in radio newsrooms and in other forms of radio journalism. It is not the purpose of the Council on Radio Journalism to lay down detailed requirements for individual courses, nor for departmental jurisdiction. The Council contends, however, that any program of education for radio journalism should be designed to conform effectively to the general principles and specific goals here presented.

I   The basis of all education for radio journalism is sound general education that will provide a foundation for an understanding of the modern world in which radio is a vitally important means of communication.

Preparation for radio journalism should be offered as part of a curriculum of not less than four academic years, leading at least to a bachelor's degree.

At the completion of such a curriculum, the student should have gained a comprehensive background in the social studies—government and political science, economics, history, geography and sociology; a grounding in natural science and in psychology; a reading (and, when possible, a speaking) knowledge of at least one modern foreign language; and a broad knowledge of English and American literature and composition. It is urged that this background of general education constitute the major portion of his academic work.

II Students should be provided opportunity to acquire an understanding of the importance of radio as a social instrument and of its relationship to government, industry and the public.

The student should be thoroughly grounded in the broad field of communications, especially radio and the press. Such grounding should include the history of communications; government regulation and the relationship of radio communication to government in the United States and in the major foreign countries; radio's social and legal responsibilities, its influence in the formation of public opinion, its position as an implement of business and as an advertising medium;

standards of practice in broadcasting; and the attitudes of the public toward broadcasting, together with an introduction to the techniques of radio audience measurement and other pertinent survey methods.

III   Students should be provided training of professional quality in the skills and techniques of radio journalism, together with an adequate understanding of other aspects of broadcasting.

Essential among these skills and techniques are:

The handling of news (news sources; news gathering and news writing; news editing); the structure and operation of the news services; the operation and use of newspaper and radio wires.

Handling news for radio; radio news style; news broadcast patterns; gathering and writing local news for radio; special events and on-the-spot coverage; the commentary; the interview; news dramatization.

Microphone technique—fundamentals of the actual broadcasting of news.

The student should also have the opportunity to obtain basic knowledge and training in other aspects of radio broadcasting. These include:

Radio production, radio programming and allied subjects.

Radio advertising—its economics, script forms, merchandising, marketing, servicing and sales.

Station operation, management, public relations, and promotion.

Elementary electronics; control room and studio operation; the development of television, frequency modulation and facsimile.

IV   Teachers of radio journalism should be soundly equipped, by practical experience, by education and by broad understanding of radio's special values and implications.

Members of faculties engaged to teach courses in radio journalism must have had adequate professional experience to enable them to present courses at the professional level. They should be fully qualified by college or university training and professional experience to deal competently and understandingly with their subjects. Those responsible for instruction in graduate courses should have had sufficient advanced academic training or professional experience to equip them to teach such courses on the level of competency existing in other disciplines.

V   A college or university, to offer acceptable preparation for radio journalism, should possess or have access to adequate laboratory equipment and library and other facilities.

Courses in radio journalism can be effectively offered only where adequate laboratory facilities provide opportunity for realistic practice and experiment. Such facilities should include standard radio studios, record libraries, sound equipment, record-cutting and playback equipment, etc. Arrangements for students to broadcast their work, and to hear it broadcast, are recommended. For students of radio news, a regular wire news service is considered minimum equipment. Arrangements with radio stations for "internships" are strongly recommended.

There should also be available library facilities with radio materials comparable to those available in other disciplines. These should include an extensive collection of the books on radio journalism, the press and communications; a collection of radio scripts; files of the principal trade and technical publications dealing with broadcasting; files of governmental and radio industry reports, brochures and like material in the field; and readily-available reference and background material necessary to provide practical experience in radio news work.

C

A Radio News Style Book

The WRC-Washington "Style Book," a seven-page mimeographed statement, was prepared in 1945, and contains a number of suggestions for handling war news. These have not been deleted because, though they are specifically out-of-date, they suggest rules or policies for editing other types of news.

WRC Style Book

This is a list of do's and don't's in the writing of WRC newscasts. It's impossible to lay down a set style for radio news writing, because that would defeat our primary purpose: to write shows that sound as naturally conversational as possible. That word "sound" is the most important thing to remember. Good radio writing may read poorly, but if it sounds the way people talk, then you've done your job well. You don't even have to use full sentences. You can disobey many of the rules of grammar and still do a good job.

Keep it simple Forget the obscure language and the technical data. If you can't explain it in everyday language, you're in the wrong business. Don't use too many large figures. Make them round wherever possible. You can say "about four hundred B-29s" rather than "four hundred and 32 B-29s."

Watch those subordinate clauses Take them out of the middle of sentences and make them separate ones. Never begin a sentence with a subordinate clause. You can't lead a listener's attention in through the back door.

Avoid people and places which are not an integral part of the story Say "the Paducah police chief" rather than "Police Chief Amos J. Winterbottom of Paducah." Say "a suburb of Tokyo" rather than "Mitsubishihansan." But once a place becomes vital to the day's news, so important that it cannot be ignored, start using its name, so that the public can become familiar with it.

WRITE a show! Any Vassar girl can process a news wire. Don't take the wire services' literary style as gospel. Make your copy alive. Write the way people talk. Write for the ear instead of the eye. And be accurate. Remember—here in Washington a lot of the people who are in the news

388

listen to your shows. Get their names correct. And their titles. But you can abbreviate a few of their jobs: Make cabinet members the War Secretary, Labor Secretary, etc., but it's always the Secretary of State. The Chief is always President Truman, Mr. Truman, or the President. He's seldom the Chief Executive. Only his wife calls him Harry.

Cut out first names of persons, if they're famous enough. But some celebrities' names sound better with first and last, as Clement Attlee, Anthony Eden or Cordell Hull. Only if they wear five or four stars are officers called simply "General" or "Admiral."

When speaking collectively of members of Congress, you may call them Congressmen. Individually, members of the House are Representatives; members of the Senate are Senators.

Don't say Senator O'Mahoney, Democrat of Wyoming. Say "Democratic Senator O'Mahoney of Wyoming" or "Senator O'Mahoney, the Montana Democrat." Watch the cliches, the slang and the gobbledy-gook. It's better to say "order" than "directive" and "infantryman" than "doughboy." Occasionally use "just about" instead of "virtually." And they're always Russians, Soviet forces or officials or Reds. They're never Soviets. A Soviet is a collective village.

There's no such abbreviation as "there're."

Keep your copy clean. In this job you're combining the duties of a writer, editor and printer. The final draft of your show has to be read by somebody else. Don't forget to copyread your shows.

As an editor, sift out the trash from among the day's news. Qualify a story if it doesn't look too reliable. NEVER, NEVER put a flash of major importance on the air, until a bulletin has moved to back it up.

Here are the opening and closing times of all our wires: AP is a 24-hour service, on both duplicate printers. UP wires also run 24 hours. INS day wire opens at 2:00 a.m. and closes at 6:00 p.m. Before the night man leaves, he should strip all printers, turn off the INS night wire and turn on the INS day wire.

UPR is a 24-hour service. We use the latest World in Brief for a 5-minute tack-up, but sometimes these are poorly written, so supplement the World in Brief items with other UPR copy.

Five-minute tack-ups run 55 lines including local and weather. This is the proper length for announcers' ease. Local usually is one story, but that's not the limit. Use more if they're good. Remember that you can't judge local news on the same bases as national or international items and that our criteria for a good local story differ from a newspaper's.

Always check the Washington City News Service local copy carefully and look over the late *Star*.

Try not to use more than two similar datelines in a row, but if this interferes with orderly presentation of the news, forget it. Keep datelines as short as possible. UPR has a habit of running datelines almost as bad as "Aboard Admiral Turner's fast carrier task force off Honshu." That's a story in itself. The dateline is for quick mental identification by the listener.

Dateline Radio Tokyo items "San Francisco." Dateline European radio stories "London" or the city in which the station is situated. If it's been heard by NBC, make it New York.

Keep 5-minute show stories short. A six-line item is the maximum. Two sentences is enough to get the idea across.

Keep the weather concise. Delete "the weatherman." He doesn't exist. It's a bureau, like everything else in Washington these days.

The midnight news runs approximately sixty lines locally and seventy lines on network. The network announcer gets the top copy; the local man the carbon. Don't cut the ten lines piecemeal out of the entire show. Usually there will be one domestic item running ten lines.

The proper introduction for network news shows is "From the NBC Newsroom in Washington." The sign-off is "That's the news from the NBC newsroom in Washington. This is the National Broadcasting Company."

It's important to put a new top on the midnight show. Most of the day's news will have been wrung dry by the evening commentators. Don't blow up some insignificant item just to get a new lead. Hit one story hard. If it's a few hours old, but important enough, start it with a new slant.

Since the midnight show is a Washington origination, national news should get a slightly heavier play. Try to make your second lead story a big domestic piece. Give it the works for about twenty or so lines. Then a few short domestic items. Then, if possible, a cutie.

The big morning show goes on at 7:00 a.m. weekdays and Saturdays. It's a 15-minute shot and runs about 180 lines. It opens and closes with a headline summary of the late news, but not one written in the headlines of a newspaper. If you like to leave out articles, get a job on *Variety*! About 50 lines of each show are foreign; 125 domestic. Washington isn't the only domestic news source. There are a lot of good stories breaking all over the country these days. Don't let the second half of the fifteen minutes sag. Get some color into it. Make 'em laugh and cry.

The domestic portion of the 7:00 a.m. show is written by the night desk. The overnights can't be stale. They, too, must cover all national news, not only Washington. Get that "today" angle into your overnights, but don't fake it. A story about the House passing a tax bill should read: "The Senate takes up the tax bill today, now that it's been passed by the House." *Not,* "The House passed the tax bill yesterday. It goes to the Senate today."

Occasionally you can use a very good foreign feature on the overnights, if you're certain it won't be duplicated in the morning in the show's first section.

The purpose of the 8:30 a.m. show, like all 5-minute shots, is to sock one hot story hard and brush off the rest of the news briefly. The 8:30 is a feature writer's dream. You're surrounded by morning music and the audience wants the lighter stuff. Don't ignore big news, just because it's serious, but if there is none, here's the place for those domestic stories, features and an extra helping of local news. The 8:30 runs about 50 lines.

One danger in working with more than one news wire is that they sometimes are contradictory. Make sure all your stories agree, and come in sequences on different shows.

If you have to begin with "It is rumored in authoritative circles that the Ankara radio has a report from Berne that . . .," call it an "unconfirmed report from Berne" or else be smart and throw it out.

Don't put a bulletin into a network show until you've checked with New York by phone. When you put a bulletin into a local show, hand it to the announcer on duty, not the talent. If it's a bulletin about a tragedy, a serious one, tell the producer about it in advance and he'll order up some music. A bulletin should be slugged locally "A bulletin from the WRC newsroom in Washington." The word "flash" is never used on the air.

Don't use "hell" and "damn" unless they're in a quote by some appropriate authority or unless it's some usage like "the Second Armored 'Hell on Wheels' Division."

Never call the Japanese "Sons of Heaven," "The Mikado's men," "Nips," "Nipponese" or "yellow." Call them Japs, the Japanese or the enemy.

Watch the army slang. Beware of snafu, SOP and Sad Sack. CI is OK. If you say General Vandegrift went to his CP, the average person will think he went to the john.

Frequently our own correspondents in Washington and abroad have good stories. Use them with name credit and an NBC plug.

Slug each page of your copy this way:

| wrc | the date | your initials | the time |

Don't slug each page with a description of the story. Save that information for the show itself. Keep your copy concise. It's what it says that counts, not the number of pages.

Be polite on the telephone. The guy on the other end may be an NBC vice president. When something big breaks, call McAndrew. When some news regarding the FCC or the radio industry breaks, call McAndrew or Mrs. Borras.

Change the teletype paper and ribbons occasionally. Don't get dignified just because you're now a member of the Congressional Radio Galleries.

Keep the schedule board up to date. Get your shows out fifteen minutes before air-time.

Once again: Write the way people talk, if not your kind of people, then those with education. Keep it simple. Keep it concise. Keep it accurate. Keep it clean.

D

A Check List
for Radio Newsroom Self-Analysis

This check list is designed as a guide by which most newsrooms may analyze the adequacy of their news handling and presentation. Positive answers to the questions posed by the list count in the newsroom's favor.

1 PERSONNEL

a Is the newsroom director qualified, by training, experience, and judgment, to meet the responsibilities of his position?
b Are his staff members qualified to carry out their assignments in news evaluation, news gathering, and news writing and editing?
c Are there enough members of the newsroom staff to meet all ordinary demands? Is there "personnel-leeway" for emergency situations?
d Is the personnel varied enough in abilities to meet differing types of demands (editing and writing straight news, news gathering, dramatization and other special script work, on-the-spot coverage, etc.)?
e Are members of the staff qualified to broadcast news?

2 NEWSROOM FACILITIES

a Is the newsroom provided with wire service adequate for all needs?
b Is the newsroom provided with adequate library and reference materials?
c Is the newsroom provided with adequate working facilities (typewriters, desk space, broadcasting equipment, monitoring equipment, recording devices, remote lines, etc.)?
d Is the newsroom budget adequate?

3 RELATIONSHIP TO MANAGEMENT

a Is full authority for newsroom operation vested in the news director?
b Has the news operation the full and sympathetic support of station management?
c Do other departments of the station (production, programming, engineering, promotion, sales, special services, etc.) understand the newsroom's necessities and cooperate in meeting them?
d Does the newsroom offer full cooperation to the station's other departments?

4 NEWS COVERAGE

a Are significant local and regional news sources covered fully and regularly?

b Is the regional coverage system (correspondents, etc.) adequately developed?

c Does the newsroom pay proper attention to special events, on-the-spot coverage, special occasions, etc.?

d Does the newsroom, either with its own staff and facilities or in cooperation with other station departments, give adequate coverage to news of special fields such as agriculture, sports, etc.?

e Are recording devices, remote lines, and like facilities used to advantage?

f Is full use made of the wire news available, especially in localizing wire stories?

g Does the newsroom pay adequate attention to nonroutine coverage, "enterprisers," background of the news, etc.?

h Does the newsroom or the station conduct audience surveys to provide reliable, adequate audience information?

5 NEWS WRITING AND EDITING

a Is wire news edited, or rewritten if necessary, to achieve concision, smoothness, balance, and full comprehensibility?

b Is copy handled in the newsroom made to conform to accepted principles of effective radio news presentation?

c Is newscast copy written and edited to suit the individual needs and characteristics of the announcers who present it?

d Is the newsroom deadline schedule such that newscasts go to the microphone only after adequate opportunity for final editing and checking?

e Are precautions taken to insure that sources of information are adequately described and that rumors and unauthenticated reports are adequately labeled?

f Is editorial opinion kept scrupulously out of newscast copy?

g Are both sides of controversial questions fairly and accurately presented?

h Do news scripts avoid sensationalism and undue emphasis on minor news?

i Do news scripts observe accepted canons of "good radio taste"?

j Are the laws governing libel, slander, and other matters affecting news practice kept in mind in writing and editing newscast copy?

6 NEWSCAST PATTERNS

a Are newscast scripts logically constructed?
b Is there sufficient variation in newscast pattern and content from show to show through the day to provide variety?
c Is due attention paid to patterns of competing newscasts?
d Are newscasts, of whatever pattern, smoothly knit together, with adequate (but not too much) attention to transitions?
e Are "commercials" used with newscasts placed with due regard for established principles of good taste and effective practice?

7 NEWS PROGRAMMING

a Are newscasts scheduled in number and length to meet both the interests of the audience and the program needs of the station?
b Are newscasts scheduled at hours to take advantage of the periods when news audiences are largest?
c Are newscasts for audiences with special interests (such as agriculture and sports) scheduled at most effective hours?
d Does the newscast schedule pay adequate attention to differing needs and interests of local and regional audiences?
e Are commentary and analysis shows given due attention in news programming?
f Does the schedule of newscasts of local origin take into account network news programs?
g Does the schedule of newscasts take into account the news offerings of competitive stations?
h Does the news schedule include a wide enough variety of shows of differing nature—straight newscast, commentary, dramatization, interview, background, etc.?

8 NEWS PROMOTION

a Does the newsroom give adequate attention to legitimate methods of calling audience attention to its news services?
b Does the newsroom give adequate attention to informing news sources of the services it offers?
c Does the station's promotion department aid in publicizing news services?

9 NEWS BROADCASTING

a Are announcers who broadcast news qualified to present it understandingly and effectively?

Radio Station Index

Subject Index